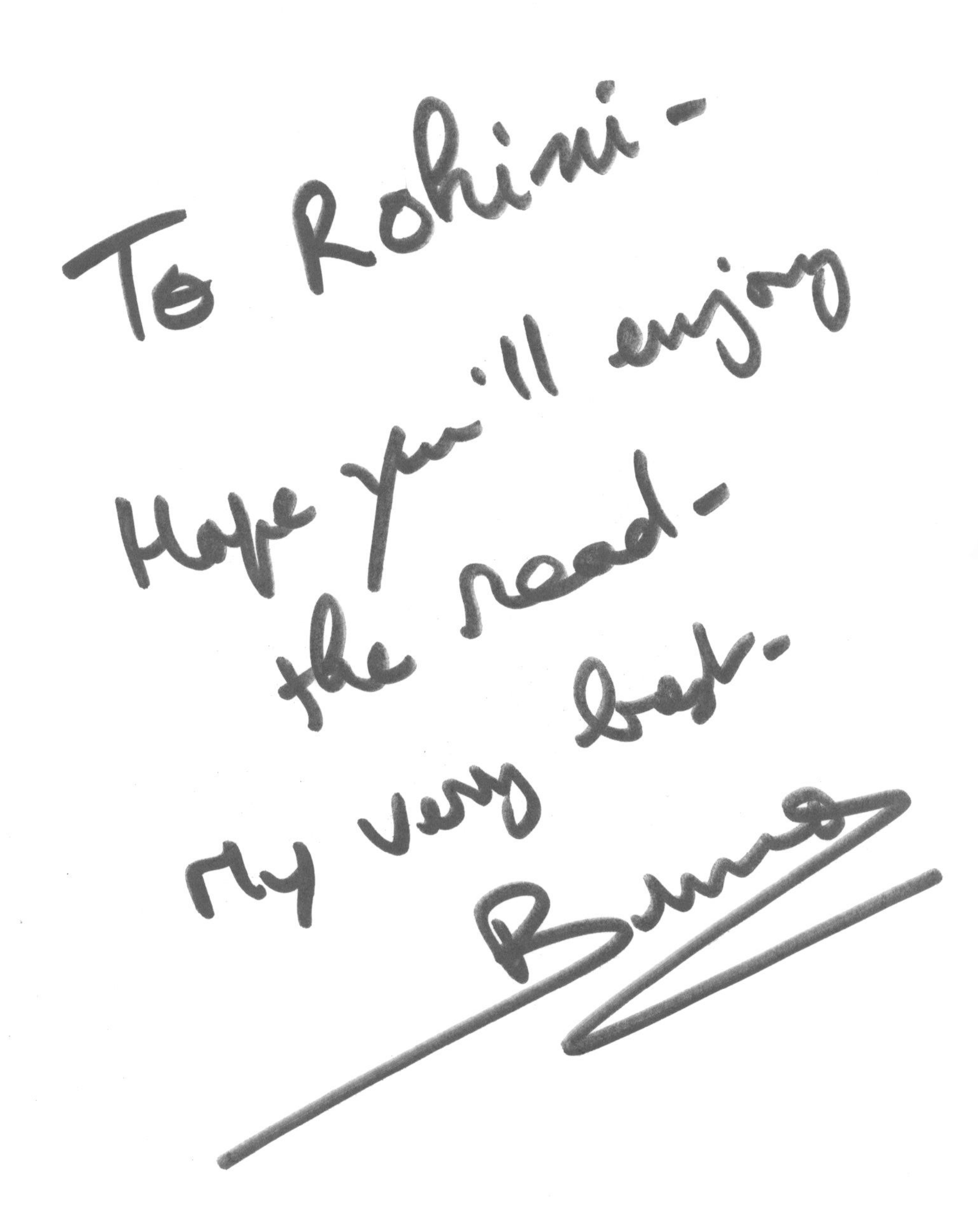

To Rohini -
Hope you'll enjoy
the read -
My very best.
Bruno

BRUNO GRALPOIS

SelectBooks, Inc.
New York

This edition published by SelectBooks, Inc.
For information address SelectBooks, Inc., New York, New York.

First Edition

ISBN 978-1-59079-205-6

Library of Congress Cataloging-in-Publication Data

Gralpois, Bruno.
Agency mania : harnessing the madness of client/agency relationships for high-impact results / Bruno Gralpois. -- 1st ed.
p. cm.
Includes index.
Summary: "A seasoned and well-respected marketing professional advises advertising, marketing, and communication agency managers and their clients about how to get the most from their client/agency partnership. He guides readers to adopt the industry's best practices and to avoid the common pitfalls"--Provided by publisher.
ISBN 978-1-59079-205-6 (hbk. : alk. paper)
1. Marketing--Management. 2. Strategic alliances (Business) 3. Customer relations--Management. I. Title.
HF5415.13.G69 2010
658.8'04--dc22
2010014510

Interior book design by Janice Benight

Manufactured in the United States of America

10 9 8 7 6 5 4 3 2 1

I want to thank my wonderful family, especially Tiphani,
for their remarkable love, patience, and support throughout this journey.
Tiphani, Anaïs, Max, Lauren and Carter, this book would not have
been possible without you. You are my everyday inspiration.
And finally, a big "Merci" to my parents Yves and Josette,
for giving me the opportunity to explore the world
and its many treasures.

CONTENTS

FOREWORD

"Agency Mania"

What a fresh title—and what a fresh perspective! This book presents wonderful insights that will undoubtedly guide the marketing industry to pursue the next generation of client–agency relationships. We should all be grateful that Mr. Gralpois has brought the full extent of his experience to bear on this remarkably engaging and important subject.

Working with and managing agencies is, for marketers, one of the great pleasures and challenges of their jobs. It's a subject I love to discuss and debate because I think agencies are terrific and provide enormous value. They provide the strategic pathways and creative inspiration that enable marketers to continuously pursue effective brand development.

Unfortunately, over the past decade, agency management has become increasingly difficult and, in some ways, destructive. "Managing the agency" often consumes such an extraordinary amount of time and energy that marketers begin wondering why they hired these firms in the first place. Before marketers can begin addressing the challenges of creating great work for their brands, they must wrestle with issues like:

- What is fair agency compensation?
- How will the agency be evaluated?
- What agency talent will support the brand?
- What will the ongoing role of procurement be?
- Who will coordinate the efforts of multiple agencies to ensure that strategies and messages are fully integrated and supportive of the over all brand positioning?

Managing agencies should not be so difficult! Agency personnel should function as a seamless part of the brand or corporate management team, bringing their objectivity, strategy, creativity, media savvy, and experience grounded in the case histories of all of their past relationships. Most importantly, client/agency relationships should be uncomplicated so that agencies can freely provide the valued skills that many marketers don't possess—skills that are crucial to building brands and building businesses.

Frustratingly, over the past decade, the business system for managing agencies in a way that affords marketers the full array of needed resources has become maddeningly complex. Just think about the array of agencies that populate some brand teams:

- General agencies
- Digital agencies
- Multicultural agencies
- Media agencies
- Sponsorship and event marketing agencies
- Social media agencies
- Customer relationship management agencies
- Public relations agencies

While each of these agencies makes an important contribution, it's ridiculously exhausting to organize this vast pool of talent and get everyone on the same page. And what does that "page" look like? Again, not an easy subject. At the Association of National Advertisers (ANA), we've developed a "blueprint" that outlines ten "marketing musts" for long-term marketing effectiveness. We call this document "The Marketers' Constitution." Here are the first seven of its ten articles, which provide a sound framework to guide effective client-agency relationships:

1. Marketing must become increasingly targeted, focused and personal.
2. Marketing must build real, tangible and enduring brand value.
3. Marketing must become more effective--more creative, insightful and accountable.
4. Marketing must become more integrated and proficient in managing expanding media platforms.
5. The marketing supply chain must become more efficient and productive.
6. The marketing ecosystem—including agencies, media and suppliers—must become increasingly capable.
7. Marketing professionals must become better, highly skilled, diverse leaders.

Can agencies and marketers fully embrace these principles and get to the finish line? Well, *Agency Mania* is the "kick in the pants" needed to make it happen! *Agency Mania* is a brilliant, insightful digest of how marketers and agencies can successfully navigate today's immense challenges and opportunities. It insightfully analyzes the current state of marketing and suggests ways the business system should transform to adapt to the dynamic marketing ecosystem of tomorrow.

Mr. Gralpois has a unique vantage point. With experience on both the agency and client sides, his personal history provides him the latitude to explore the entire landscape and devise new, sensible business practices that cut through the issues that handicap client/agency partnerships.

Our increasingly complex, technologically enabled world has many wonderful advantages and possibilities. However, it provides us with no footprints to the future. Mr. Gralpois suggests what the new footprints should look like. In doing so, he greatly helps us learn how to lead our respective organizations more confidently and more capably in the future.

I applaud this book—and recommend it to the entire marketing community. It will help you understand what's working and what's not within your organization. It will help you move to a better plane with your operations, strategy, creativity, and partnership. I am delighted Mr. Gralpois has given me this opportunity to share my perspectives and to express my wholehearted encouragement for his superb work!

Bob Liodice
President and CEO
Association of National Advertisers

ACKNOWLEDGMENTS

The source of my knowledge and inspiration over the course of a career spent on both the client and on the agency side includes a vast amount of anecdotal stories, learning experiences, and vivid conversations with colleagues, partners, and friends—a group of brilliant professionals and subject-matter experts at world-class client organizations, agencies and trade associations who shared many success stories and failures that ought to be told and are now included in this book.

I want to acknowledge the incredibly generous and talented contributors to this project who are (or were) working for the most prestigious, respected brands in the world. In no particular order: Richard C. DelCore at P&G, Kevin Parham at Campbell Soup, Jeff Devon at HP, James R. Zambito at Johnson & Johnson, Martine Reardon at Macy's, Susan Markowicz at Ford Motor Company, Michael Fitzgerald at AT&T, Tim Whiting at Motorola, Mariann Coleman at Intel, Brett Colbert at Anheuser Busch InBev, Delmar Wyatt at Qwest Communications, Carla Dodds at Walmart U.S. , Julie Gibbs at Adobe, Mollie Weston at Best Buy, Sherry Ulsh and Claudia Lezcano at Burger King, Michael E. Thyen at Eli Lilly and Company, Amy Fuller and Charlie Silvestro at MasterCard Worldwide, Jennifer Berger at Starbucks, Mike Delman at Microsoft, Tom Chetrick at Bristol-Myers Squibb, and others who chose to remain anonymous.

All of them are highly successful executives who share a common passion for "Harnessing the Madness of Client/Agency Relationships for High-Impact Results." The marketing and business world is benefiting from their well-scribed wisdom. They all contributed significantly by sharing their opinions, best practices, and experiences (the good, the bad, and even the ugly). I want to thank them for their time and for giving me the opportunity to share some of their ideas and words of wisdom throughout this book.

I also want to acknowledge another group of tremendously talented individuals who provided a unique and complementary perspective to the client views expressed in this book: Jeff Goodby at Goodby, Silverstein & Partners, David Kenny at Vivaki, Lynne Seid at Heidrick & Struggles, Patricia Berns at MRM Worldwide, Tim Williams at Ignition Consulting Group, Marc A. Brownstein at Brownstein Group, Eric Samuelson at Jack Morton Worldwide, and Sarah Rush at In-House Agency Forum. Other contributors and supporters include Casey Jones at Brief Logic, Randy Wise at WiseInsights, Brian Hunt at Hunt Marketing Group, and Bill Fritsch at Anthology Marketing Group. Thank you for your support and valuable point of view.

I would like to express much gratitude to Bob Liodice, President and CEO of the Association of National Advertisers and his A-team (Bill Duggan, Shepard Kramer, Tracy Owens and many others) for their unwavering commitment to marketing excellence and successful client/agency relations. I also want to thank Skip Walter, Founding CEO and CTO of Attenex Corporation, for his fresh and unique outlook at the end of this book.

I've been privileged to meet leaders in many aspects of the business and marketing world, and in agencies and client companies of all sizes. The business world and marketing community is a better and a more fulfilling, purposeful place because of their generous investment in time, creativity, and efforts.

I want to seize this opportunity to acknowledge my brilliant colleagues of many years on the client and the agency side, and more recently at Microsoft, for their inspiring devotion to pushing the agenda of marketing excellence through strong client/agency partnerships and for giving me the opportunity to pursue my passion at one of the most respected companies in the world.

I want to especially acknowledge my colleague Katherine James Schuitemaker for her continued partnership and collaboration over the years. Her remarkable business acumen and intellectual curiosity have led to continued advancement in the field of agency relationship management.

I also want to acknowledge the hundreds of talented, large and small advertising and marketing communication agencies I've had the pleasure to get to know and work with over the years, including Wunderman, Publicis, McCann Erickson, AvenueA/Razorfish, Universal McCann, JWT, Digitas, Crispin Porter + Bogusky, Hunt Marketing Group, GroupM, Cole&Weber, MRM Worldwide, Zaaz, The Brownstein Group, AKQA, Ascentium, Young & Rubicam, DDB Seattle, Dentsu, Jack Morton Woldwide, and Goodby, Silverstein & Partners, just to name a few.

I would like to also express gratitude to my book agent, Bill Gladstone for his faith, guidance and professional wisdom. I want to acknowledge the team at SelectBooks for their remarkable efforts throughout this project as well as Christopher Mosio at Mosio Media and Laura Carriker at French Dog Films for their support. Finally, I want to thank my friends Frederic Vimeux and Jean-Francois Heitz for their valuable counsel.

INTRODUCTION

Drawing Greater Value from Client/Agency Relationships

In a world saturated with eye-catching advertisements targeted at fragmented in-control audiences, and delivered on a multiplying number of media channels, companies around the globe are investing billions of dollars to address the ultimate challenge: how to drive demand, build brand loyalty and in the end, grow market share and profitability.

Chief Executive Officers (CEOs) are answering that challenge by turning to their busy marketing departments to break through the media clutter and help consumers cope with information overload. CEOs count on their Chief Marketing Officers (CMOs) and marketing leaders to come up with ideas that engage, educate, or entertain consumers and create differentiated and sustainable brand value. They, in turn to come up with ideas that engage, educate, or entertain consumers and create differentiated and sustainable brand value. They, in turn, rely on the vast expertise of talented advertising and marketing communication agencies and their wide range of powerful creative, media, analytical, and specialized communication skills to connect brands and consumers.

An estimated one trillion dollars[1] is funneled through these agencies, which in turn stimulates a large portion of our global economy. Companies of all sizes, in all industries, are eagerly partnering with skilled professionals who understand their business, and have mastered the art of creating magical moments for their brands. They can deliver a wide range of communication solutions to produce outstanding results. A well-managed relationship between a client and its agency has been shown to multiply brand equity and the company's bottom-line profits, exponentially driving value from their partnership. Conversely, a poorly-managed relationship is incredibly wasteful and seriously undermines a company's ability to compete effectively.

Why a Book on Agency Management? And Why Now?

Everyone gets one of these pivotal moments in his or her career, the type of epiphany that makes you do something out of the ordinary: finding a new vocation, joining a new cause, or perhaps writing a book about something you are deeply passionate about. I had mine on multiple occasions throughout my career on both the client and the agency side. I became an avid student of the agency and client business, learning from my experience and those from my peers what makes two companies click and do wonders together. Or makes them fail miserably.

Companies often wonder: What constitutes a strong client/agency relationship? What do we absolutely need to know about agencies to get better work from them? How do we get greater value from this partnership? Over the years, I realized the frequent and rising gap in a company's knowledge and skills, despite the best intentions in the world, prevented them from turning advertising and marketing communication agencies into powerful competitive assets. Starting in the 90s the world was profoundly changing, as well as the marketing discipline and the client/agency dynamic. Today, change is still the flavor "du jour." The marketing discipline is still going through a profound paradigm shift fueled by the spectacular explosion and fragmentation of media channels.

Radical changes in consumer preferences with the emergence of new digital technologies, social media, user-generated content, and consumer-driven communities enable converged brand experiences and conversations that redefine the essence of the connection among agencies, media, and clients. Gone are the old ways of doing business. Technology is drastically transforming business, media, consumer habits and, therefore, the way companies market to consumers. The relationship between brands and consumers is being redefined. Content creation and distribution are coming together to enable rich customer scenarios and draw in audiences. In the process marketing is becoming increasingly more measurable and therefore accountable. Marketers are getting increasingly more sophisticated, more demanding, and are expecting to do more with less. Will they still need agencies? What type of agency will they rely on to compete and grow their business?

As working with agencies becomes more complex, the quality of the partnership is also more than ever critical to a company's success, requiring client/agency relationships to reinvent themselves. Understanding what they need or expect from each other, and how they can work together isn't an insurmountable challenge. But even the most sophisticated companies are ill-prepared to make the best use of these valuable partnerships. This universal problem is about to get worse before it gets better. There isn't any blueprint. No roadmap. No guideposts for clients or agencies to follow. How will companies harness the madness to drive high impact results?

Today, small, medium-size, and large multinational companies face a similar challenge. They want to get the most from their agencies in this increasingly more intricate digital age. The rate of change is unprecedented in the history of advertising and marketing communications. These industry trends have brought a new level of intricacy for clients attempting to adapt and take advantage of these new opportunities. More than ever, clients need to partner with agencies that can help them make sense of this cacophony, invest their limited resources into more impactful, measurable content and activities, solve brand connection issues, break down barriers, and come up with new ways to strengthen conversations with consumers to show them the way to success.

How can you tell whether your company's marketing budget is working as hard as you are? Or even harder? This is a question every budget owner and every business executive, whether in marketing, finance or procurement, must answer.

Extremely large portions of company operating budgets are poured into advertising and marketing by every size of company. Budgets end up in the hands of agency executives given the task of turning them into gold. And they often do. Yet perhaps no other relationship in the corporate world today has received so little oversight or historically has been so poorly managed. Yet it flies in the face of decades of undeniable proof that successful brand advertisers have successful agency partnerships.

Savvy companies, versed in the art of nurturing productive agency relationships, know how to take full advantage of their agency skills and resources to fulfill their vision. By efficiently leveraging such a valuable asset, savvy marketers are able to drive greater return on investment (ROI) out of their campaigns to create optimal business impact in the marketplace. The less skilled will unavoidably be unsuccessful.

Over the years, I've seen client/agency relationships fail or succeed based on whether or not they've engaged a set of universal principles and best practices that can apply to virtually a company of any size. This is what *Agency Mania* is all about. It's about viewing the partnership with agencies as vital corporate assets, and nurturing and managing them as such. And I mean relentlessly, rigorously, and enthusiastically. The word "mania" comes from the μανια, "*to rage, to be furious.*" In the Greek Mythology, a "mania" was the personification of insanity.

In this sense, it's absolutely insane to see clients painfully fail over and over to fully leverage their agencies to further advance their marketing efforts and grow their business. It's heartbreaking to see the many opportunities lost on increasing the client's bottom lines. It's distressing to see agencies failing to do for themselves what they preach to clients: Create differentiated value for their offering while under the pressure of disintermediation and the growing involvement of procurement.

It's upsetting to see sophisticated clients and their brilliant agencies go through trials and errors, unable to work effectively together and as a result, lose themselves in today's "Wild Wild Waste." It's truly enraging to see the incredible missed opportunities that result from swiftly declining levels of satisfaction and trust between clients and agencies.

It's absolutely insane that while an agency is often a company's single largest marketing expense and one of the most powerful competitive weapons at a company's disposal, there are no formal rulebooks or guidelines on how to effectively make the best out of this unique type of partnership.

Agency Mania is such a guide. It's an invitation for clients and agencies to explore new ways to draw even greater value from their partnership in today's new world order. It guides companies on how to achieve the multiplier effect of successful client/agency relationships in business performance and their mutual obsessive pursuit of marketing effectiveness. It advocates for a renewed interest on both sides to unleash this untapped force multiplier.

In this business environment where consumers are more empowered than ever before, and harder to engage and motivate, clients are now demanding more from their agencies. They are pushing the envelope and driving aggressively their agenda of effectiveness and efficiency through new forms of compensation, solid contract arrangements, and greater expectations. They want more rigor in the way creative and digital communications are produced and media channels are leveraged.

Conversely, agencies are challenging the status quo to build new competencies and business models. They are embracing new opportunities and pushing clients to be innovative and to think outside the box to deliver compelling stories and consumer experiences.

Many books have been published over the years about the agency business or how agencies work. Although they offer different and valuable opinions on the subject, they don't provide a client's unique perspective. These books are often written by high-profile and iconic agency executives, but are written from an agency's viewpoint. *Agency Mania* gives companies the opportunity to be agency-savvy, to know how to get the best from an agency without necessarily having worked inside an agency. It also provides the agency profession a perspective rarely voiced about client challenges and expectations.

Business executives and marketing and procurement professionals are looking for ways to answer everyday questions about their agency relationships: How do we find the best agency for our business? Is our approach to working with agencies effectively supporting our organizational needs? How do we set up a contract that is a win-win for everyone? How do we know we are not overpaying for their services? How do we motivate our agencies to assign their best talent to our account? Are we unwillingly behaving in a way that is sub-optimizing our relationship? What common mistakes or roadblocks should we avoid? What should we do to improve the quality and outcome of our partnership? Where should we invest our time and efforts to get the most value?

There is limited professional development training available to clients on this subject. There is little or no curriculum on the discipline of successful agency management at business schools. There are limited reference materials available to business executives, procurement, finance professionals, or marketers on how to build and sustain successful relationships with agencies that are so vital to their companies' success. Yet everyone seems to unanimously agree that without successful relationships, a company's marketing investment and long-term brand assets are at risk or can be seriously under-optimized.

After years on both the client and agency side, I have experienced firsthand the tremendous challenges and opportunities associated with both well- or poorly-managed client/agency relationships and their profound impact on business performance. Later in my career, I have been privileged to establish and lead the thoughtful discipline of Agency Management for one of world's largest brands and a leading marketing powerhouse. There is no doubt that companies like AT&T, Wal-Mart Stores, and Johnson & Johnson would not be the successful companies they are today without the contribution of their agencies.

However, you don't need to be an Intel, P&G, Coca Cola, or Macy's to reap the benefits of a well-managed strategic partnership with an agency. Every company, regardless of the size of its marketing department or budget, can adopt best practices in working with agencies and apply those to its business with varying degrees of depth and breadth.

But if you simply don't know where to start, or are unclear about how to work with your existing agency, you are not alone. This book will answer some of the questions that perhaps you were afraid to ask. It may challenge pre-conceived notions and will give you some ideas eminently worth considering. It will raise a number of issues surrounding the need for change and innovation in client/agency relations, presenting viewpoints that will hopefully stir readers to take action. *Agency Mania* advocates for stronger, more effective and efficient client/agency partnerships that generate outstanding results. These valuable partnerships must be based on understanding, trust, active collaboration, and mutual respect and accountability. I hope you will realize those benefits after reading this book and improve your own company efforts. It's about survival, after all. Consider yourself now one step closer.

How Should You Read This Book?

The book is organized in simple, intuitive, successive chapters, guiding the reader from the initial process of selecting an agency to optimizing long standing relationships. In the first part of the book, I describe the unique value advertising and marketing communication agencies bring to their clients. I also provide some insight into the often multifaceted and confusing world of agencies. I give an overview of managing agencies as a professional discipline and much-needed skill set in today's corporate world.

In subsequent chapters, I walk the reader through common-sense best practices on how to build a sound agency strategy, conduct an agency search, set up a solid contract, negotiate fair compensation, brief agencies to set realistic expectations, and how to then measure and improve performance to get most value from the partnership.

Along the way, I share the insight and experiences of my peers, friends, and industry experts, some of the most brilliant minds and world renowned leaders in the field. Their vast professional expertise and their opinions on the client or on the agency side provide a unique perspective that strengthens our understanding of the agency management discipline. At the end of each chapter, a short list of best practices is provided to conclude the discussion and provide actionable ideas that can be applied immediately. The last chapter will attempt to describe where the industry is heading and what that means for clients and agencies.

But although the book offers answers to common challenges faced by companies, like so many other things in life, knowledge alone isn't the answer. It's ultimately what we do with it that matters. As you implement what you learn through these chapters, face new challenges and celebrate successes, I encourage you to share your experience, voice your opinion and contribute to harnessing the madness of client/agency relationships at www.agencymania.com. This is a journey and you are not traveling alone.

* * *

The industry is at a crossroad. Clients are experiencing a new array of business and marketing challenges, originating from greater global competition, changing consumer habits, a more complex set of digital options, and tougher economic circumstances. The intricate nature of the consumer/advertiser/agency/media confederation is being re-examined as we see the power shifting to media channels and consumers. Similarly, the agency business is in rapid transformation, with new competencies and operating models emerging every day in a desperate attempt to adapt to new demands, avoid being commoditized and to ultimately survive in these changing market conditions.

The ecosystem of partners is more diverse and intricate than ever before. The approach to working with agencies from the past few decades is now almost completely obsolete. Clients must find new, more effective ways to manage and partner with a multitude of agencies. In a world in which the old ways no longer seem to produce results, clients and agencies must move toward a new level of strengthened partnership through mutual accountability and greater risk-taking.

Fasten your seat belt and prepare yourself for a wild ride. *Agency Mania* will show you the path to the client/agency relationships of the 21st century and how to get unprecedented value from the strategic partnership with your advertising and marketing communication agency. These best practices are not meant to be applied rigidly and blindly.

If the title of the book implies that a healthy level of obsession is necessary to turn agencies into powerful strategic marketing assets, it's to underscore how little attention the critical partnership between client and agency has received over the years. It calls out some of the most common mistakes clients and agencies make. It sets the record straight on a number of topics where clients and agencies have allowed themselves to damage previously productive relationships and handicapped their chances for success in the process.

If you feel pressured by your competition to turn your agencies into powerful partnerships that grow revenue and build brands, if you face tough market conditions, or if you feel unprepared to ignite your agency to address those challenges, this book is for you. Companies need help in both turbulent and prosperous economic climates. *Agency Mania* will help you draw the line between weak supplier relationships and energized agency partnerships, between sterile and breakthrough marketing, between the mediocre and the best in the business. And between your success as a company or crushing failure.

*aut vincere aut mori**

*Either to conquer or to die, in Latin

1 THE MULTIPLIER EFFECT

Why we need agencies

"The work of an advertising agency is warmly and immediately human. It deals with human needs, wants, dreams and hopes. Its 'product' cannot be turned out on an assembly line."

—Leo Burnett
Adman Extraordinaire

Have you ever wondered what a world would be without advertising? No commercials during the Superbowl. No catchy billboards on your commute to work. No colorful ads in magazines. No window displays downtown. No swirling banners on Web sites. No clever ads on Facebook. No reason to "go Google" or to "Bing" something. No advertising-supported free anything, for that matter. Well, don't hold your breath. While I doubt if there were "Flintstones' Dinosaur Meat" signs carved into prehistoric cave entrances, advertising probably goes back to whenever people first attempted to change perception and influence human behavior.

Advertising remains an integral part and a deep fabric of our culture and society. Advertising is also a synonym for FREE. Free makes advertising tolerable, even enjoyable. In this Free Economy caricaturized by people like Chris Anderson, editor for *Wired* magazine, more and more consumers across all generations are refusing to pay for content or information—on podcasts, newspapers, and magazines. They are refusing to pay for entertainment—videos, music, games, applications, and services of all types—when they can find them for free, whether online or in the physical world. Free everything. Advertising will continue to increase in importance in a world where free is its new currency. And as long as modern enterprises need to find ways to reach, engage, and sell to existing and new customers, advertising and marketing communications agencies will continue to flourish. Advertising and marketing communication disciplines are vital growth engines for companies that drive intrinsic value and fuel innovation.

For years, basic wisdom or simple survival instincts have led companies around the globe to use big agency networks and indie shops to help them address their marketing and communication challenges, come up with ways to get customers to buy from them, seize new market opportunities, rethink their business, and improve their bottom line. It would be insane not to. At the core of agencies' fundamental purpose lies the simple, perhaps existential question: *Why do we need agencies in the first place?*

A Deeply Rooted Sense of Purpose

At the core of an agency's raison d'être lies the promise of an energetic group of business professionals with common values and beliefs, who combine their tremendous creative and intellectual brainpower to form an agency. They matter greatly to their clients. They typically possess deep subject-matter expertise in various disciplines, unique knowledge of audiences and proprietary methods, and their own philosophies that set them apart from the rest. But more importantly, they are agents of change or renewal. They share a burning desire to take on new challenges, tell stories that boost brands, and express vibrant ideas that resonate deeply with audiences to capture consumer devotion. They are committed to driving high-impact business results for their clients. They influence their clients' marketing budgets and priorities. They are a transformational business partner. For that reason, the agency world has been considered a greatly desired environment to start a career in marketing, learn a trade, and gain exposure to a multitude of clients.

Client Viewpoint

"Clients do not want agencies; they want strategic partners that are looking out for the best interest of their company. I've seen agencies over the years that conduct themselves as vendors, not strategic partners. Strategic partners know your business inside out, the internal workings of your organization and know how to sell ideas."

MICHAEL FITZGERALD
Associate Director, Business Advertising, AT&T Inc.

For decades the world of advertising and marketing communications has attracted talent from a wide array of professions with diverse, rich, and often complementary personal and professional backgrounds. In perhaps no other profession can you find a more eclectic group of gifted right- and left-brained individuals meshed together from the various social and cultural segments of our modern society. They are visionaries, entrepreneurs, intellectuals, developers, writers, musicians, technologists, artists, producers, philosophers, innovators, brand builders, humanists, 3D animators, instigators, strategists, filmmakers, psychologists, researchers, activists, statisticians, thought-leaders, illustrators, linguists, anthropologists, planners, photographers, designers, data analysts, engineers, programmers, and digital czars, media mavens and zealots, geniuses and wizards, and gurus of all kinds—representing only a fraction of the many audiences they reach on their client's behalf.

Don't be fooled by their job titles. They have worked in many types of businesses and industries. They have dealt with every possible marketing or communication challenge that clients have thrown at them. They are likely to be some of the most perceptive business people you might ever encounter. Of course, all that talent vanishes on paper to more sterile, pragmatic job titles on business cards. They go by titles of account executives, creative directors, planners, copy writers, media directors, Web designers.

But no matter their title, these individuals all share a common desire to create magic, to tell a story that deeply moves people and to build experiences that create brand affinities. They are relentless and resourceful innovators. They are passionate advisers. They use our billboards, television and computer screens of all sizes and shapes, radio waves, cell phones, video games, magazines, newspapers, Web portals, social networks and other effective media vehicles as destinations and communication channels that tell a compelling story to those exposed to it and prompt them to take action.

Client Viewpoint

"We expect our agencies to bring holistic thinking to our business, a depth of business understanding coupled with superior strategic thinking, proactively coming up with ideas, competitive intelligence, and depth of expertise across multiple categories beyond ours."

KEVIN PARHAM, **Director Global Advertising, Campbell Soup**

There are many different types of advertising and marketing communications agencies, fulfilling complementary roles and tasks. The creative agency has historically played the role of middle man between the client and a wide number of specialty agencies in media, PR, events, retail, branding, and many other communication disciplines. The agency creative staff has previously defined the culture of a particular agency by the imaginative and ingenious ways of expressing their ideas, coupled with their unconventional personal style, ponytails, and fashionable attire. Creative minds like Alex Bogusky, Jeff Goodby, and Bob Scarpelli, among many others, have demonstrated the impact of their creative powerhouse to help top advertisers introduce breakthrough work that sticks in the marketplace.

In a world where customers are increasingly multi-tasking and over-stimulated, with access to significantly more information that they can possibly assimilate, creative plays an important role in engaging them in exciting, fresh, and compelling ways. Even in the digital world where data tsars and technologists now have a predominant seat at the agency table, a powerful idea well executed and filled with "oohs and aahs" is what prevails and wins consumers. The essentials of storytelling in the digital age have profoundly changed. The media agency, historically associated with big budgets, is producing rich insight about evolving media consumptions and consumer behavior. The PR firm is now associated with earned media, influence, and social marketing. The digital agency is creating platforms, and even product experiences for real-time brand and customer exchanges.

This is a unique business. Perhaps in no other industry can you attend an "Idea Conference" in which creative geniuses gather to discuss the genesis of creativity and idea-making. What clients truly want is ideas that persuade and engage people. Whether you consider it art or science, persuasion and engagement are difficult to create.

This is why these story tellers love to energize brands, and to come up with big, lasting ideas that speak to people with a distinct emotional voice. They have found a creative outlet in their professional life to express it and make a difference. They want to be highly regarded and effective change-agents. They partner with other specialists in research, media, technology, and analytics to channel their creativity and turn ideas into powerful, viral consumer experiences such as Ogilvy & Mather's "Evolution" for Unilever/Dove (as part of Dove's "Campaign for Real Beauty," a Web film directly attacking the artifice of beauty in advertising), Fallon's BMW "The Hire" (Hollywood-quality online shorts starring Clive Owen as the driver in action-packed scenes available at BWM's Website) and Crispin Porter + Bogusky's "Subservient Chicken" Burger King video (an online experience inviting customers to give commands to a chicken-suited actor). Grateful and opportunistic business leaders grab this superb agency talent to unleash the potential of their company brands.

Agency Viewpoint

"Clients should expect agencies to reformulate people's most basic perceptions about the world, and a product or service in that world. To do that, the client must simply expect brilliance. Sometimes that brilliance comes from objectivity and fresh eyes, which is why outside agencies can be useful. But ideas can, theoretically, come from anywhere."

JEFF GOODBY
Co-Chairman and Creative Director, Goody, Silverstein & Partners

How Do Clients Benefit from Agencies?

Agencies in the advertising, media, public relations, digital, direct marketing, branding, promotions, and merchandising disciplines (to name just a few) are so prevalent in the business world that perhaps we take for granted what they do. To brand advertisers who have reaped the benefits of working with agencies, the question seems silly and grossly irrelevant. If you are using an agency today, you might even be tempted to skip this chapter. Yet the question seems to boil down to this: Are agencies a luxury or a necessity? Stated differently: What do agencies offer that is so unique that their clients cannot achieve on their own and replicate internally? It would be crazy paying for something you can do in-house. So what makes them so valuable to their clients?

Agencies, often considered a mere extension of their clients' marketing teams, fulfill many critical and diverse functions on a client's behalf. They help publicize products and services. They choose media channels that maximize target audiences. They compose persuasive copy and press releases, produce elegant ads and memorable radio jingles, sharp and witty 30-second commercials. They tap into their knowledge of a category (like Health Care), or a demographic segment (like Youth or Women for example) to come up with messages that truly resonate with an audience. They leverage technology to build tools and applications, and produce highly interactive experiences and conversations.

Agency Viewpoint

"Agencies must develop points of views and build products and services that support them. They must be brave enough sometimes to have less clients but do more for them."

DAVID KENNY
Managing Partner, Vivaki

They persuade loyal customers to become brand advocates. They take an active part in the successful launch of new product lines and major events. They attend key client planning discussions and invite them to think "outside the box." Occasionally, they challenge the status quo, provoking clients out of complacent attitudes. They collaborate. They consult. They guide. They develop innovative concepts on what seems to be an unlimited number of media channels. They create games, online and mobile services, and software programs. They come up with new business models, new distribution channels, new means to facilitate conversations between brands and audiences. They conceive breakthrough ideas. They bring them to life, using talent, tools, processes, or even approaches that are distinct to their agency.

Client Viewpoint

"Agencies can make themselves more valuable to their clients by constantly seeking out new opportunities and ideas, keeping freshness and innovation constant."

CARLA DODDS, Director, Multicultural Marketing and Marketing Vendor Management, Walmart U.S.

The value proposition of agencies has historically been anchored into the right side of the brain where creativity, subjectivity, and emotional connections converge. As the world becomes digital in all aspects of our society and communication infrastructure, agencies' value proposition is increasingly more about the left side of the brain where the power of measurement, analytics, and the science of marketing come together to provide brand advertisers with more targeted, more scalable, and more accountable capabilities.

In short, agencies can be a valuable think tank, and the amplified voice of you, the client. They bring together a mix of talent and experience of skilled practitioners in the specialized field of advertising and marketing communications. Because of experience no company can match, they do it better, more efficiently, more quickly, with greater depth and deeper insight than you, the clients, can. This is value that can be best realized over time.

While the average tenure of a client with an agency is estimated to be between four and seven years, and is shrinking rapidly along with CMO tenures that are insanely short, some of these client/agency relationships exceed 50 years. In the case of GE, their relationship with Omnicom goes back to the beginning of the 20th century, when BBDO became the agency for GE's lighting division in 1920. L'Oreal's relationship with Publicis Groupe goes back to the early 1930s with the company founders, Eugène Schueller and Marcel Bleustein-Blanchet.

On the opposite end of the spectrum, sadly enough, we've all witnessed relationships that don't survive long enough to celebrate their first year anniversary or their first project. Longevity of an account is often the sign of a strong relationship. Isn't this true in any business—including yours? Clients gain more value from their agencies over time as the agency resources assigned to the account develop a deeper understanding of their business and ways of getting things done. They also build personal ties and friendships that they can rely on during difficult times. Business is personal, especially in the business of agencies. But to fully benefit from the role agencies play, clients must acknowledge what their unique competencies are.

Want to Do It Yourself?

Fundamental questions about the value that agencies deliver to clients have been the source of heated discussions and industry debate for years. One of these highly debated topics is: What do agencies do that clients can't truly do themselves? There isn't a client in the world that hasn't at least once had this thought: *Why don't I do this myself and save all those agency fees? Why don't I do it in-house, and have more control over deadlines and deliverables? Should I create an internal team to deal with collateral and other basic creative services?*

And yes, this idea extends across industries and the general population as well. Companies consider doing the same in IT, legal, and many other departments as people in their non-working roles try to sell their houses themselves, do their own taxes, fix their own plumbing, or defend themselves in court.

Sarah Rush, Associate Director at the In-House Agency Forum, has seen successful in-house agency models among member companies: "Our member companies are reporting greater benefits from having dedicated resources on site, better internal collaboration, lower costs, and unmatched knowledge of the brand. Once established, most companies will definitely benefit from having an in-house advertising team. This doesn't mean the external agency would disappear. It depends on the company and their advertising needs."

Forming an in-house department for handling all or some creative or marketing communication duties is an important consideration for any company. An in-house agency model might make sense for some activities but clients must objectively evaluate their options and decide whether building an in-house agency or hiring an external one is the way to best support their business needs. Occasionally, you will encounter large companies such as CVS Pharmacy, Bank of America, Disney, and Yahoo! Inc. that have built a creative services operation internally, as a service organization to the rest of the company. They have done so to reduce costs, build a permanent skill set, or meet particularly unique needs that might be challenging to secure externally due to the specialized nature of the company's business (for example, highly technical fields or regulated industries).

The in-house agency doesn't have to compete with external agency resources, which they can often complement. It is structured similarly to any other creative service agency but handled by accounting as a cross-charge from another department to the in-house team. In-house agency departments do not need to be limited to creative services. The in-house department might also be set up as an internal media buying team, instead of relying on the services of a media company.

But most internal agencies have limited scope and fulfill a very specific purpose. Although there might be some benefits in having internal creative services, in the long run advertisers are getting greater value from a talent base that is constantly sourced, upgraded, and trained to far exceed what a client could do on its own. Why is that? The answer is threefold: (1) we're not an expert in everything (no matter what we think); (2) it would be too costly to set up an in-house agency (some might disagree); and (3) we miss out on a lot of experiential advice.

Client Viewpoint

"We've changed our approach over the years. We used to manage a fair amount of work internally. We now rely on agency partners to help us successfully engage with customers, bring new big strategic ideas and co-innovate"

MOLLIE WESTON
Director Agency Management Operations, Best Buy

First, the media and technology landscape has grown in diversity and complexity, making it virtually impracticable to have expertise on staff in every facet of advertising and marketing communications, especially in digital services where innovation and cross-polarization of talent is critical to keep up with industry demands. It's way too difficult to keep up with these advancements internally.

Second, the overhead of having a fully dedicated copywriter, art director, media director, planner, strategist, and a host of other talents would probably be highly cost-prohibitive at first and most certainly cost-ineffective in the long run. You may not need all of these resources at all times. Why keep them on payroll? Agencies can spread these expenses across multiple clients.

And third, agencies service a range of unique, value-add competencies that make them a valuable and irreplaceable resource. The last point is perhaps the most cogent. Rigid client methodologies and internal procedures often minimize creativity and therefore are not ground for innovation or freedom of creative expression. This is why the most common scenario still involves the use of an external creative service agency or even multiples ones based on the type and scale of services needed.

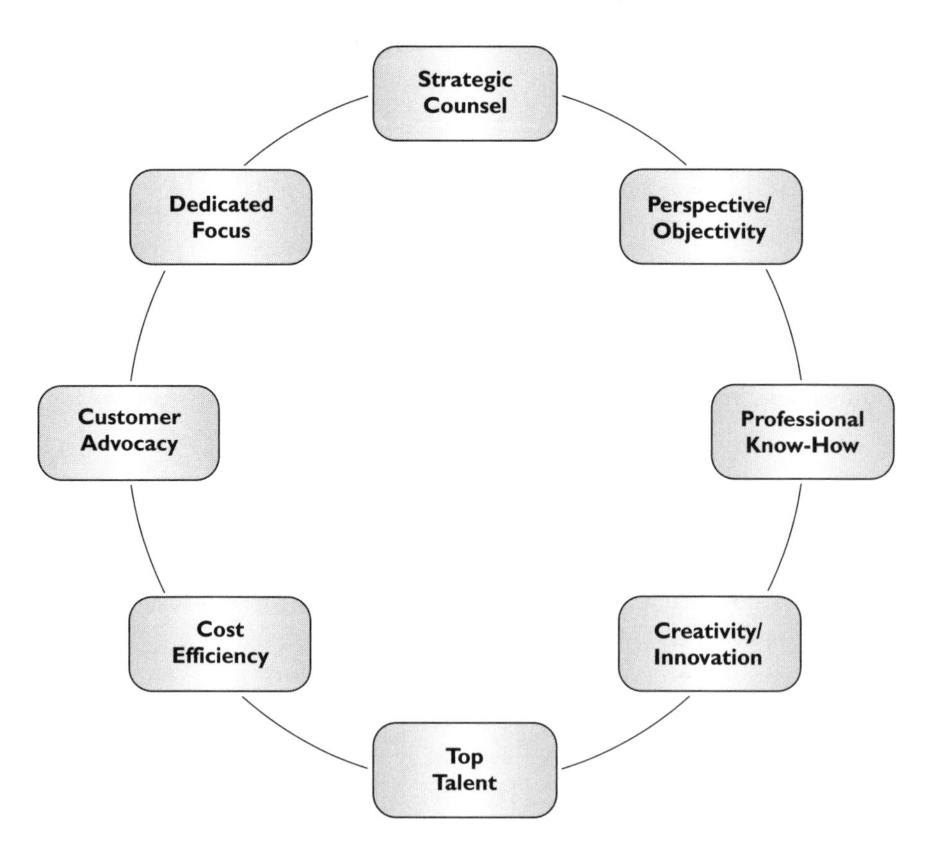

Summary of Key Agency Benefits

Strategic Counsel Advertisers get the most value from their agencies when those act as strategic consultants and trusted advisors to their business. The essence of the agency business is to deliver strategically-grounded ideas based on consumer insight and forward-looking perspectives. Agencies employ talented resources such as strategists and account planners to confront and conquer challenging client situations. They take into consideration how consumers interact with brands. Consumer insight is vital to understand and enhance the relationship between consumers and brands. Agencies can be powerful think tanks that turn information into insight, insight into strategies, strategies into action plans, action plans into measurable business results. As trusted advisors, agencies share their professional opinions, suggest alternative courses of action, and come up with creative ideas for clients in need of answers.

Client Viewpoint

"Agencies are instrumental to our marketing success. The value our agencies deliver to our business is a function of the services they deliver. We look to creative agencies to deliver innovation and strong ideas that resonate with our audiences. We look to our media agency to deliver creative media plans and efficiencies"

MARIANN COLEMAN
Director, Global Media Relations and Performance, Intel

But this role can only be played successfully by agencies that have earned the trust of their clients and have been invited to actively contribute to strategic agendas. That is, once you've learned to trust your agency, its members are invited to attend events like company sales meetings, product planning sessions, and marketing seminars. They must be given the opportunity to come up with sound recommendations backed up by credible research and years of solid, relevant experience in their field of expertise. Agencies make a significant contribution by leading, guiding, or simply enabling better strategic client decisions.

Perspective/Objectivity Not unlike business consultants before them, agencies bring a vast amount of collective experience from current and past clients. Obviously experience comes in many different flavors. If an agency specializes in a particular industry, audience, or business category, it can significantly profit clients with similar interests. Agencies look for synergies in current and past client engagements. The larger the client portfolio, the richer and the more relevant are the agency offerings. The agency knows what works, what doesn't, and learns from past successes and failures, so clients don't have to at their own expense. Agencies may hire externally when they need deep knowledge of a particular industry or consumer audience.

By sharing their diverse portfolio of local or international clients over the years, agencies can deliver unique perspectives based on the wealth of knowledge accumulated, one client at a time. To have ground for innovation or even experimentation, they can apply what they have learned to solutions for specific business challenges with new and existing clients. They eliminate wasteful redundancies and potential inefficiencies, and increase chances of success for their clients.

Too close to the trees, clients do not always see the forest and do not always know how to dialog with customers objectively. It can be quite difficult to remain truly objective when balancing priorities and facing business pressure. Agencies can demonstrate their impartiality by speaking up on issues that might not be possible for an employee to raise for a number of political or organizational reasons. As a neutral agent, agencies cam provide an independent view that would otherwise be challenging to bring to the surface at critical times in the process. Acting as a third party resource, agencies are more likely to be unbiased when confronted with difficult business decisions.

Client Viewpoint

"Agencies must invest the time to understand their client's business and industry. When your agency is sending you something they've seen in the news that is industry specific, you know you have more than an agency partner, you have a trusted advisor."

TIM WHITING, Senior Director Global Marketing, Motorola

Professional Know-How

Years of hands-on expertise in a particular discipline or skill set translates into procedural knowledge, distinct philosophies, and approaches that are worth gold to clients. To create compelling messages and experiences on a wide of media channels, agencies must employ talented individuals with highly specialized skills and the operational know-how that comes from years of practice possibly unique to that agency.

Whether an agency is tasked to evaluate the strength of a particular brand asset, shoot a TV commercial, or send rich media emails, it relies on well-defined processes and the working knowledge of experienced practitioners that would not otherwise be available to clients.

Client Viewpoint

"The industry is changing so rapidly. Agencies must stay ahead of the curve. I look to our agencies to come up with new, breakthrough ideas. What's the next big thing is in digital for example? The agencies must the ones telling us what we should be doing In the next few years."

MARTINE REARDON VP of Marketing, Macy's

To create sustainable value that increases the client stickiness factor and monetizes their intellectual property, agencies develop innovative proprietary tools, unique approaches, structured processes, and measurement systems based on proven best practices that enhance the quality of client planning and in-market delivery.

Examples of this success are OMD's *OMDCheckmate*™ and Saatchi & Saatchi's *Dreamstate*™ to redesign the shopping environment around the consumer, and Lovemarks' approach that focused on unleashing emotional connections between brand and consumers.

Other proprietary solutions include Mediaedge:cia's *MEC Navigator*, ZenithOptimedia's *The ROI Blueprint®*, McCann Worldgroup's *Demand Chain*™, Grey's *Brand Acceleration* global strategic planning model, Y&R's brand management tool, *BrandAsset Valuator®*, Ogilvy & Mather's *360 Degree Brand Stewardship®*, and Neo@Ogilvy's *Personal Circuits*. The list goes on. They also leverage sophisticated solutions such as Microsoft's *Atlas Advertiser Suite*, *adCenter*, and *Atlas Search*, to name a few, or DoubleClick's *Dart* to automate, scale, and focus more energy on value-added services that are distinct and unique to their agency. In the end, it doesn't matter how good or fast the car is if the driver is grossly inexperienced. Agencies use their professional know-how to build differentiated value for their offering.

Creativity/Innovation What agencies commonly offer is innovative, culturally-relevant ideas and creativity. Although this may vary slightly based on the discipline they specialize in, there is always some element of creativity, whether in PR, retail, or media. Agencies are story-tellers by trade. They have the unusual ability to distill the essence of an idea, blending their passion for solving business issues with a strong instinctive creative panache that leaves audiences begging for more, as evidenced by hyped campaigns like DDB's Budweiser's "Whassup," TBWA/Media Arts Lab's Apple's "Get a Mac," and McCann Erickson's MasterCard's "Priceless."

Client Viewpoint

"In a world of transcreation and adaption, what do we need from the creative lead agency? The big idea."

JEFF DEVON, Director Global Marketing, HP

They tell stories that move, connect, and captivate people. They create rich, memorable communications and environments for clients and their audiences to dialog and exchange. Agencies must have the creative expertise to get communications planned and executed, even in the most complex digital environments.

But what differentiates them from their competition and makes them lasting partners, is their ability to demonstrate their ingenuity at solving marketing problems with breakthrough ideas and innovative thinking. High-tech giant Intel hired independent agency Mother New York, to do just that. Mother recruited up and coming artists as well as the agency's own designers to create beautifully designed laptops called Dell Design Studio, pushing creativity from messaging to the product itself.

In a world where digital video recorders enable audiences to fast-forward or, worse, skip commercials, advertisers are paying attention. Innovation has become a critical proficiency, and an intimate part of the creative process.

Agencies must find new, innovative ways to communicate and engage with their audience. They hire a Creative Technology Officer and armies of technologists to re-engineer the creative process, with technology-enabled scenarios as the center of gravity. They come up with fresh, inspiring ideas that survive the remote control or the click of a mouse. It's rarely just about the ability to get work out-the-door, although clearly this is important to clients.

Client Viewpoint

"The value agencies bring to clients is their perspective, fresh ideas, benchmarking and best practices. If they are constrained by their clients, as clients sometimes do, then they will not achieve the full value of the relationship."

MICHAEL E. THYEN
Director, Marketing and Sales Global Procurement, Eli Lilly and Company

Accomplishing this through unconventional means is where their greatest value lies. After all, this is why they are treasured by clients and often recognized at major industry events like Clio Awards or Cannes Lions Awards. Clients want to encourage them to bring out their very best during the ideation process. The alchemy of creativity and innovation is a fundamental agency competency.

Client Viewpoint

"An agency's core value proposition is the fresh perspective they bring to a client. They bring talent to help market products and services in a way that might not have been considered internally. Agencies partner with clients specifically to help grow their business."

DELMAR WYATT
Director Advertising Operations, Qwest Communications

Talent The agency business, arguably like any other service industry, is a business of people. A strong talent base will determine the fate of an agency and its ability to attract clients. If you have been working with agencies for a while, you've noticed that the agency ecosystem, for the most part, is well contained. People tend to know each other. Big agencies can afford to hire big names in account planning and strategy, account management or creative talent that then attract key clients.

Talented agency staff blossom professionally when they are hired, trained, and managed by individuals with similar backgrounds. They benefit hugely from ongoing direct exposure to peers with similar skills and interests from which they can learn and improve their trade. They are given outlets to grow and enrich their skills.

It's very difficult, if not impossible, for creative talent and agency specialists of all kinds to thrive within the confines of a small company selling only one category of products such as package goods, automobiles, or financial services. In such an environment, creative people would lack the constant exposure or insight that only a diversified client portfolio can provide to them. It's not that these less diversified companies do not attract top talent, but they simply do not have the type of agency talent resources that can be found mainly in major cosmopolitan and cultural epicenters like New York, San Francisco, London or Paris, among other cities, where agencies with a large and diverse client base prosper.

The rich cultural diversity that the top talent is exposed to every day leads to a better agency product in the end. Agencies in major cosmopolitan areas are able to attract people of similar passion, professional interests, and career inspirations. The clients' access to this talent is an important part of what agencies offer.

Agency Viewpoint

"Agility. Accountability. And a commitment to evolve to meet the clients' needs before the clients asks the agency to meet them. External agencies will remain relevant because they bring perspective, and better talent than in-house agencies can attract."

MARC A. BROWNSTEIN
President and CEO, Brownstein Group

Cost Efficiency The economic value of agencies is well understood but not always easy to articulate. There are real and often substantial cost benefits by engaging with a certain type of agency rather than hiring resources internally, especially when dealing with media agencies. Media agencies can buy media in large volume, offering economies of scale that no client could replicate on his or her own. That benefit is passed on to the client and clients gladly pay for that service. Cost efficiency can also be realized when sharing resources, getting things done in less time and with fewer resources.

The flexibility that comes along with hiring external resources must be highlighted as well. Clients can hire a portion of agency resources they couldn't afford otherwise. When advertising or marketing budgets fluctuate as they often do, agencies can spread the impact of these fluctuations on multiple clients by adjusting staffing plans and managing the workload. Clients can more easily adjust the number and type of resources utilized, whether dedicated, partially dedicated, or freelance, leaving that responsibility and headache to their agencies. Global agencies can provide access to international markets that would otherwise be cost-prohibitive for an advertiser to enter. Typically, clients call on their agencies because they are expected to do more with less than they would do on their own.

Customer Advocacy Influencing marketing decisions by using customer research, applying rigorous scientific methods, relying less on creative intuition and putting the customer at the center of the creative development process from the start, has been possible with the creation of the Account Planning function by J. Walter Thompson in 1968.[2] By establishing a department that brings the consumer into the process, clients and agencies can develop relevant and effective communication based on a clear customer value proposition and sound customer insight.

Many agencies now have an Account Planning Department, providing a must-have capability for clients keen to be more customer-centric in their advertising approach. Closeness to customers is a powerful necessity for any successful company. But it's important how the client and agency approach this. It's important to understand how agencies can learn to think holistically about the customer experience and challenge the silo, discipline-based approach that advertisers might otherwise follow.

Agencies represent the interests and needs of the end-customer, the client's customers, and put them at the center of everything they do. That means being customer-centric and therefore, media-agnostic. Having deep insight into the audience is critically important to clients. To influence human behavior, agencies must have empathy for and understanding of their audiences if they are to strike a human note in their communications. Agencies know how to connect emotionally with audiences. They don't want customers to feel like they are being advertised to. By taking this "customer first" approach, they advocate not just for the buying of more products and services, but for solutions to customers' needs. Clients want to reach out to consumers in a way that generates value beyond the transactional nature of that exchange.

Client Viewpoint

"The agency value proposition is to provide capabilities that are outside of a client's core business, and to deliver those effectively, efficiently and do it at a lower cost. It hasn't really changed."

JULIE GIBBS, Director, Corporate Brand Marketing, Campaign Management, Adobe

Agencies are well known for their ability to read and interpret the attitudes, behaviors, and preferences of customer audiences. They are valued for their aptitude to find ways to catch the customers' attention, build a positive connection to the brand, influence their perceptions, and persuade them to take action. Agencies do this in a way that is both relevant and mutually satisfying to the clients and customers, building good will for the brand, and fostering customer intimacy, loyalty, and advocacy.

Dedicated Focus In the end, clients have their own business to worry about. It takes unique dedication, undivided focus, and long hours to compete successfully in any industry. The company pours all it has into being the best at what it does. Similarly, agencies are laser-focused on developing their core expertise. Companies subcontract to third party experts in a number of business expense categories, and advertising and marketing communications services are no different.

Advertisers want to work with agencies that have built deep expertise in areas that they don't master and probably never will.

And with focus, comes speed, which is increasingly critical to companies that must respond in real time and on a constant basis to competitive situations or rapidly changing market conditions. Some agencies have built specialized skills and rich capabilities, such as Public Relations, Search Engine Marketing (SEM,) or Hispanic Marketing, just to name a few; others offer "full-service" to provide one-stop shopping and integrated offerings on the client's behalf. But in either case, their dedicated focus to build deep professional skills and deliver best-in-class capabilities is paying off and clients are hugely benefiting from their dedicated efforts.

Client Viewpoint

"To deliver optimal value to their clients, agencies must refuse to be order takers or simply presenting what the client wants. They must take a seat at the table, being the eyes and ears of what's happening externally and advocate for work that is effective in the marketplace."

MARIANN COLEMAN
Director, Global Agency Relations and Performance, Intel

One client may value one agency benefit more than another, of course. When asking clients what they want and expect from agencies, answers may look slightly different for each client. Agency needs varied by relationship length, and client size and industries, but a few needs consistently ranked high among clients: campaign effectiveness in meeting client goals, provision of strategic counsel and insights, implementation of outstanding ideas, understanding of the client's business, and delivering outstanding services. In the end, clients want well-balanced agencies that produce high impact results for their business.

Agency Viewpoint

"In an increasingly fragmented media world, it's not viable to buy reach, the role of the agency is to help their clients win reach!"

PATRICIA BERNS, EVP,
Worldwide Account Director, Verizon, MRM Worldwide

The Multiplier Effect

What's keeping most CEOs and their CMOs up at night? Is it the struggling economy and shrinking budgets? Is it a constantly changing business environment? Is it the socio-demographic and psychographic profile of customers constantly shifting? Is it the uncertainty of how to sail through a storm of technology innovations and new media? Or is it the unexpected marketing strike by a key competitor launching a new product?

Perhaps all of this and more. Companies are facing an insane number of business challenges and more intense competition. Executives at every level understand well that the key to business longevity for their company is not to sell commodities and compete on price, but rather to sell innovative products that can be differentiated and sold at a premium. This is what companies with strong brands do. Most CMOs and their marketing staff wake up in a cold sweat at night worrying about the company's brand equity, which falls on their shoulders. They may occasionally surrender to the box of Ambien sitting on their nightstand.

Client Viewpoint

"At Burger King Corporation, we value our agency partners and look to them for their subject matter expertise, their knowledge base, and their ability to keep us on the cutting edge of marketing and communication."

SHERRY ULSH, Director Global Marketing Finance and Procurement, Burger King Corp.

Savvy leaders worry about their ability to build sustainable brand value that differentiate them and give them a competitive edge. They are anxious about keeping up with changing consumer habits, media preferences, emerging channels and new marketing techniques that the competition might already be tapping into. They are concerned about finding the right mix for their marketing investment. They agonize about over-investing in some areas and under-investing in others. They wonder about a world where consumers are in control and the brand is harder to manage.

Mostly, they worry about retaining existing customers and finding new ones. CMOs are under tremendous pressure by CEOs and CFOs alike, preoccupied with meeting short-term business goals while building for the long term. Balancing the need for short-term performance such as revenue and share growth without sacrificing future market opportunities, long-term brand equity, and customer satisfaction, can be a delicate balancing act.

This is where the agency comes in. CMOs need the professional expertise and know-how of an experienced advertising and marketing communications agency that will help them to tackle these burdensome questions. I like to think about it as the "multiplier effect" of agencies on a client's business. In the military world, they refer to it as "force multiplier," a factor that dramatically increases the combat effectiveness of a given military force.[3] In the field of economics, it's described as the effect that occurs when a change in spending causes a disproportionate change in aggregate demand. Whether you apply this concept to the military, engineering, macroeconomics, or mathematics, you get the idea.

In the world of business, it's about multiplying media exposures, marketing opportunities, innovation, customer experiences, and brand value, to ultimately cause a disproportionate impact on business results. Building a brand, protecting it, and ultimately strengthening it so it favorably differentiates a company's offering and decisively influences consumer preferences at those moments of "truth," requires the type of expertise and services that only top-notch agencies offer.

Therefore, a company's potential to successfully tackle its challenges and win in the marketplace is directly correlated with its ability to partner with the right agency. Carefully executed integrated campaigns have propelled savvy brand advertisers to the front of the race, giving them a lasting competitive edge. Agencies offer creativity, strategic insight and guidance, know-how, and access to best-in-class skills that make them priceless resources to their clients. Agencies are not all consistently strong in all service categories. The optimal agency/client relationship will be based on a sound assessment of what's needed by the client and matching those explicit needs to the skills offered by one or multiple agencies.

Client Viewpoint

"Because of our size and scale, many firms will view Walmart as a vehicle for margin growth. However, we look for agencies willing to join in our mission to save people money so they can live better. We also believe in being a growth partner; and in turn seek to expose our partners to other parts of our business to increase their opportunities."

CARLA DODDS, Director, Multicultural Marketing and Marketing Vendor Management, Walmart U.S.

Ultimately, advertisers need access to agencies because they provide something that is exceptional or unique, distinct and critical to their marketing success: They know what consumers like. They know where and when to reach them. They know how to approach them, talk to them in their own language in a compelling voice. They help create and sustain growth. They provide strategy, based on experience, customer insights, and research findings. They know how to engage them, to interact with them in a relevant way that ties the experience to the brand, the need to the product, the company to the customer.

They understand the media landscape and how to navigate its rich landforms and living elements. They have access to powerful tools to deliver flawless campaigns to market that are then optimized to improve ROI. It would be absolutely insane not to consider using an external agency to strength your marketing muscle. An agency's dedicated focus on delivering best-in-class advertising and marketing communications competencies can pay off big time on your company's own bottom line.

2 GOLDEN EGGS

Understanding the mysterious world of Madison Avenue

> "There are very few men of genius in advertising. But we need all we can find. Almost without exception they are disagreeable. Don't destroy them. They lay golden eggs."
>
> —DAVID MACKENZIE OGILVY
> *Adman Legend*

For most people, Madison Avenue is a north-south avenue in busy Manhattan, characteristic of a crowded and noisy New York City neighborhood with tall, grey, imposing buildings. In the world of advertising and marketing communications, Madison Avenue has a much different connotation. For years, it symbolized the explosive growth of the advertising industry of the 20th century as it saw famous agencies like BBDO open shop there and grow insanely rapidly. Madison Avenue became the gold rush of advertising as companies poured substantial budgets into the capable hands of agencies to build iconic brands, to gain market share, and lay their client's golden eggs.

Although Madison Avenue saw its fair share of agency success stories and rising stars, more than anything it represented the birth of a respectable profession and, in many ways, institutionalized it. Madison Avenue became synonymous with an entire profession.

At the heart of the relationship between agencies and clients is the marriage of innovation and creativity. The advertising industry has always been grounded in the business of generating compelling ideas and engaging consumer experiences from the relentless creative minds that walk the halls of agencies. Despite its glorious past, the agency industry has not always benefited from a solid reputation. Madison Avenue has also often been stereotyped as a business that is more reckless and more ruthless, arrogant, egocentric, and competitive than other professions. Because the benefits agencies provide to clients have historically been difficult to demonstrate with quantifiable precision, it often led to high profile agency reviews as incumbent agencies attempted to defend themselves.

To add shame to injury, the industry's image has been often tarnished by scandals and lawsuits due to improper billings, accounting irregularities, claims of fraud such as kickbacks, and other types of illegal practices. The reputation of globe-trotting agency executives with larger-than-life personalities with lavish, glamorous lifestyles, has fueled growing concerns among clients and forced them to scrutinize agency billings and conduct regular audits. Thankfully, legislations such as Sarbanes-Oxley significantly improved client confidence as a result of greater transparency in agency financial and accounting practices.

Recent AMC Originals' hit television show *Mad Men* exemplifies the fact that agencies have been for decades synonymous with sexy 30-second TV commercials, interruptive one-way communications, clever taglines, and three-martini lunches with glamorous women. The Golden Globe-winning TV drama series plays on stereotypes and truthfully captures the lives of ruthlessly competitive men and women of Madison Avenue in the ego-driven 1960s' world of advertising. After all, unflattering events such as the Julie Roehm-Wal-Mart Stores, Inc.-Draftfcb saga, the Shona Seifert ONDCP conviction, and the Dentsu sexual-harassment and discrimination scandal[4] have given prosecutors and the public something to chew on, blurring the line between 1960s' fiction and 21st century reality.

These scandals that involved massive timesheet inflation schemes, accounting fraud woes, and lawsuits involving brothels and bathhouses in Asia, have given a black eye to the whole industry. But the insular Madison Avenue following World War II and today's communication industry has, arguably, less and less in common. The principles of how agencies produce their art form might not have changed much perhaps, but the acceleration of technology and changes in consumer behavior and media outlets have changed the game.

Client Viewpoint

"The agency business is reinventing itself and we're a part of that transformation."

JAMES R. ZAMBITO, Global Marketing Group Controller, Johnson & Johnson

The industry has grown up, and it made changes of cataclysmic nature to deeply alter its course, from Madison Avenue to its new centers of gravity in Paris, Tokyo, London, and soon New Deli and Beijing. Yet New York Mayor Michael R. Bloomberg still referred lovingly to his city as the "international creative capital and a global hub for the advertising industry, with nine out of the ten largest firms based in our City."[5]

Today, despite the few hiccups of the past, the agency world still enjoys the solid reputation established by industry pioneers and legends such as Marcel Bleustein, David Ogilvy, Leo Burnett, Bill Bernbach, Lester Wunderman, and Jay Chiat. Most of these charismatic founders proudly named their agencies after themselves, extending their creative vision, business philosophy, and wisdom for many years to come. These respectable business leaders also helped put the business of marketing and communication services on the map, bringing together marketers, agencies, and media companies. More importantly, they built a reputation for hard work, breakthrough ideas, and an undivided passion for their profession. They were and remain the soul, the spiritual stone, on which this industry has been built and the source of its ethic code and its integrity.

Their footsteps have been followed by a new era of talented agency entrepreneurs in creative, media, and digital, such as Alex Bogusky, David Kenny, Jeff Goodbye, Irwin Gotlieb, Dan Wieden, Daniel Morel, Laura Desmond, and Bob Greenberg, to name a few, as well as the infamous financial moguls and industry captains Sir Martin Sorrell (WPP), John Wrench (Omnicom), Maurice Lévy (Publicis), and Michael Roth (IPG). This industry has profoundly reinvented itself over the years, adapting to rapidly changing market conditions, a transformed media landscape, evolving consumer habits, and high client demands. If there is one thing constant in the agency business, it's change itself.

Overcoming the "We do it too" Syndrome

Although slogans like Nike's "Just Do It," Avis's "We Try Harder" or De Beers's "A Diamond Is Forever" are memorable, and icons like The Marlboro Man, The Energizer Bunny, and Ronald McDonald stick with us as avid consumers, they are the tip of the iceberg and a gross under-estimation of what agencies do today for their clients. Agencies now go much further and deeper in their client's marketing communications layer than clever messaging: They now tell compelling stories, create brand experiences while educating and entertaining, and eventually turn customers into fervent brand advocates. Agencies are no longer in the business of disrupting, but are instead adding value to the brand through relevant storytelling and consumer conversations.

Consumer consumption of media has evolved significantly in the past two decades. The number of channels on broadcast or network TV, magazines, newspapers, and radios has never been greater, leaving consumers with more options to choose from but with the same amount of time to make choices.

Inevitably, each of these channels is getting less reach and media fragmentation and is forcing advertisers to rethink their marketing investments. Emerging technologies have opened the door for ongoing media innovations (on-demand, data visualization, social networks, PVRs, and others) while creating new challenges. Today you can't leave an agency meeting without hearing about the next big thing—new media opportunities and new exciting consumer applications that, yet unproven, have great upside potential.

Are agencies prepared for this unprecedented demand for innovation? Did agencies overestimate their importance to advertisers? Do they have the skills to tap into these opportunities? Clients want to shift their spending to reach consumers where they are and that means while playing games, or on their smartphone, iPad, in their instant messengers, their Xbox game console, their blogs or Facebook accounts, so be it. They want to speak to the diversity in their customer audiences (Hispanic, Asian, Gay/Lesbian, and other consumer segments).

Media fragmentation is not likely to slow down. Advertisers will need to weigh the benefits of having increasingly fewer mainstream, large-scale media options, or the highly targeted, small-reach, innovative, but more expensive channels that are offered to them.

Agency Viewpoint

"The agency landscape has been profoundly impacted by the migration from mass to 1:1 media. We are going from mass persuasion to mass customization and most agencies are not ready. They are still reluctant to embrace data and analytics. Years ago, you went to work for an agency because you didn't like math. Things have changed."

TIM WILLIAMS, President, Ignition Consulting Group

Clients continue to hire top talent in this area to identify and harness new opportunities. This is changing the balance of power and agencies are challenged to deliver incremental value from client engagements. Companies are putting a premium on understanding customer behavior and how they respond to various media exposures. These new communication and distribution channels inevitably demand specialized skills. Thankfully, agencies have responded to the demand by introducing a wide array of specialized offerings that take full advantage of these new consumer trends. They have built in-house specialty departments or forged relationships with technology players. They want to remain clients' trusted advertisers beyond the traditional world that Madison Avenue has been known for. They are also eager to cash in on faster-growing, higher-margin opportunities. For clients, relying on one agency to cover such a wide spectrum of media and audience segments is more difficult than ever and few agencies are in a position to do so seamlessly for their clients. The need for specialization, segmentation, and innovation often requires them to hire specialized firms to access resources that wouldn't otherwise be available to them.

The agency business is no longer what it used to be. The landscape is changing so quickly, it's hard to keep track of who's who, between the new guys on the block and this year's top players. There is always a new competency being developed, a new branded offering being introduced, a major shape-up on the way, another game-changing merger or acquisition. It's quite easy to get lost these days in the maze of the complicated world of Madison Avenue. However, to make informed decisions, clients must fully understand its dynamic and complex nature.

Unfortunately, there are no definite ways to organize the vast, rapidly changing, and unpredictable world of advertising and marketing communications services. I wish there were, for the marketer's sake. Anyone looking up the extensive and diverse list of services provided by agencies on their Website can testify to that fact. *"What is it that they do again?"* Agencies certainly know how to spin, sometimes promising capabilities they are unable to truly deliver. And no agency wants to be put in a box.

Agencies have mastered the art of talking about themselves in ways that make you wonder what they actually "don't" do (what I like to fondly call the "we do it too" syndrome). It's apparent that no agency wants to miss the phone call from a prospective client simply because the agency didn't list everything they "could do" in their presentation materials.

Over the years, I've met with all kind of agencies all praising their unique proposition, from the boutique shop, proudly raving about its independent spirit, speed, and low overhead, to the proud network-affiliated agencies singing the praises of end-to-end integrated offerings and the benefits of economies of scale and global reach. For most of them, having a value proposition that was truly authentic and differentiated was half the battle. The other half was convincing clients that they were uniquely qualified to do the job.

Types of Advertising and Marketing Communication Agencies

Although there are no industry standards per say, there are some fundamental principles on how to logically group agencies that haven't changed much over the years. First, agencies range in size and scope. From the large full service agencies headquartered in major cosmopolitan cities with satellite offices in every corner of the continent, to the small agencies operated out of a single office space using Web conferencing, there is an agency offering for every client. Small indie shops have a few clients, less than ten employees, and billings ranging from six figures to millions of dollars. Large agency networks have big clients, domestically and internationally, with thousands of employees and billings in the billions of dollars. Their organizational structure, whether small or large, is for the large part identical with functions like

Client Viewpoint

"I am always amazed by the stamina and energy of agencies. It is truly a unique business."

DELMAR WYATT
Director Advertising Operations, Qwest Communications

account management, creative, production, and media. It's likely to vary slightly based on scale and specialized areas.

Second, the agency industry has been mainly composed of two primary types of services: advertising or marketing services. Advertising services (also historically known as "above the line" agencies) usually involved the creation of broad-reach messages delivered on traditional media—television, radio, magazines and newspapers, cinema, outdoor. Marketing services (also commonly referred to as "below the line") usually included Direct/Relationship Marketing, Public Relations, Branding and Identity, Market Research, Retail and Packaging, and other forms of marketing consultancy. Marketing services are growing in popularity as advertisers diversify their investment and explore alternative marketing disciplines to reach their goal.

Agency Viewpoint

"What's next? A big move to non-paid media. Like PR, which includes fast-growing disciplines like social media. Implications are exciting, as PR promises to grow rapidly, as well as all things digital. Brand strategy continues to grow, because clients need to differentiate their brands in an ever-changing and competitive marketplace. Media planning and placement shops will be challenged, as clients will resort to non-paid forms of promotion, such as social media."

MARC A. BROWNSTEIN
President and CEO, Brownstein Group

The proliferation of digital that can now be found in most marketing disciplines has blurred the line, making the distinction between above and below the line now virtually obsolete. Who does what is much harder to tell. "How" the work is produced or distributed is no longer a meaningful way to distinguish advertising and marketing communications disciplines. It's rather the "role" they serve in the marketing funnel that is most helpful to understand how they contribute to the mix (such as awareness building, perception change, engagement, lead conversion, loyalty building).

No discipline can operate in a silo today; it requires partnerships and alliances among independent agencies, integrated or combined offerings by large agencies, or internal client coordination to turn these aggregate resources into more effectively channeled and unified efforts. Social media, for example, have profoundly changed how we define the PR discipline today. PR is now increasingly about engaging and monitoring influential audiences through social networks and earned media. Although most agencies would rightfully argue that being labeled as either a "creative" or a "PR" firm in a multifaceted marketing world is no longer that distinctive, it still remains a practical way of categorizing agency services and making sense out of today's cacophony.

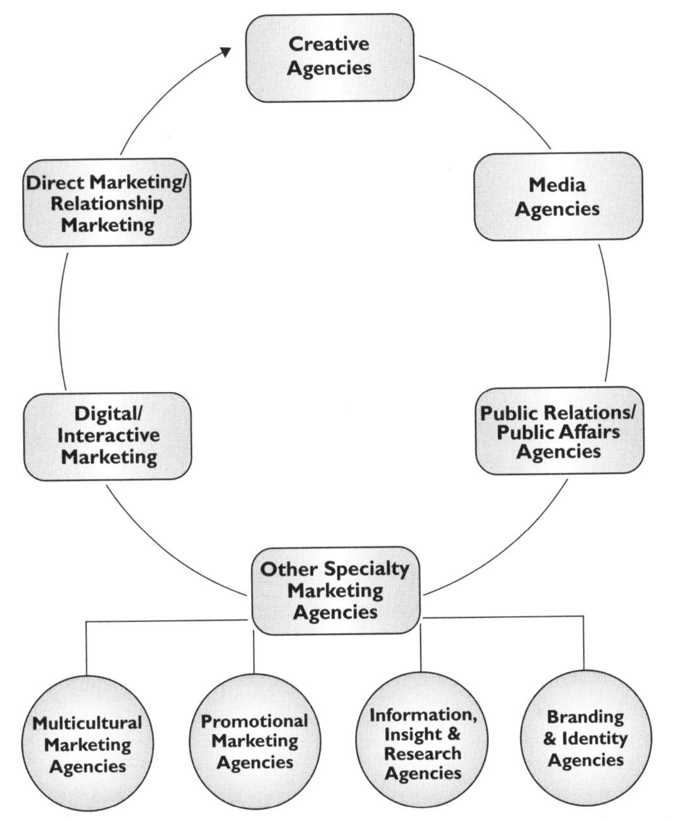

Categories of Advertising and Marketing Communications Agencies

Creative Agencies These agencies are primarily focused on traditional advertising services (creative, media, research) with creativity, branded content, and entertainment at their core. They range in size, from small independent creative boutiques (that offer limited services) to large prestigious full-service creative agencies associated with publicly-traded network holding companies. They are known to offer great creative thinking and breakthrough ideas that go beyond advertising and messaging. This type of agency is particularly tailored to clients exclusively looking for creative services, perhaps to complement a roster of specialized agencies or for clients looking for highly creative work. Examples of creative agencies include Fallon Worldwide, Campbell-Ewald, The Martin Agency, Goodby, Silverstein & Partners, and Crispin Porter + Bogusky.

Media Agencies These agencies handle full service media planning and media buying on their clients' behalf. Decoupled from advertising services as the media landscape became more complex to maneuver, media planning and buying across media channels requires economies of scale to secure competitive buys and deep subject-matter expertise to provide insightful planning recommendations. Some of these media companies have built specialties, such as print advertising, insert media, outdoor advertising, paid and organic search, branded entertainment, asset barter, and so forth. Others combine multiple media agencies to form powerful and diverse media agency networks. Examples of media agencies include ZenithOptimedia, Starcom MediaVest Group, Initiative, Universal McCann, OMD Worldwide, PHD Network, Prometheus, GroupM (MediaCom, Mediaedge:cia, MindShare).

Direct Marketing (DM)/Relationship Marketing (RM) Agencies These agencies provide direct response, direct mail, database marketing, and customer relationship services. Unlike advertising and media services that have historically been focused on driving awareness and perception change, direct marketing/relationship marketing aims at triggering a response that can be acted upon. These services are typically used by clients looking to build relationship programs, increase customer loyalty and advocacy, run direct sales and demand generation, and lead qualification/maturation campaigns in traditional media, and increasingly more in digital media. Examples of DM and RM agencies include Wunderman, Rapp Collins Worldwide, DDB Direct, Grey Worldwide, OgilvyOne Worldwide, KnowledgeBase Marketing, Targetbase.

Public Relations (PR)/Public Affairs (PA) Agencies These agencies help clients handle their PR and PA activities and tend to focus on traditional activities such as corporate image, media relations, media training/events, press releases and media materials, issues management, speech writing and speaker placement, as well as innovative PR competencies such as blogging, social media, reputation, and sentiment tracking. Some agencies have built specialties such as Crisis Management or Reputation Management. Examples of PR and PA agencies include Edelman, Weber Shandwick, Hill & Knowlton, Burson-Marsteller, Ogilvy Public Relations Worldwide, and Cohn & Wolfe.

Digital/Interactive Agencies These agencies focus solely on digital, offering a wide range of services, from online advertising to Website design, e-commerce, search (paid or organic search), email, mobile, online video and podcasting, in-game advertising, community building, and social media. Typically technology or datadriven, these agencies are usually born digital and do not venture into traditional media. This is by far the fastest growing category, the marriage of Madison Avenue and Silicon Valley with further segmentation in specialized digital services as niche capabilities are rapidly emerging. Although highly capable as creative resources, some of these agencies are hired by clients as full-service agencies with digital at the core. Examples of Digital/Interactive agencies include R/GA, Razorfish, Tribal DDB, Digitas, AKQA, Schematic.

Other Specialty Marketing Agencies Equally important to both clients with specific, specialized needs and those with generally smaller overall marketing expenditures, these marketing agencies can add to advertisers' marketing arsenal. These specialty marketing agencies include:

- ***Branding and Identify Agencies:*** These agencies help clients with their brand strategy and provide services that include brand assessment and audits, brand portfolio strategy, value proposition development, brand architecture and positioning, brand valuations, naming and messaging, graphics, and identity and packaging design, just to name a few. Examples of Branding and Identify agencies include FutureBrand, Landor Associates, Fitch, Hall & Partners, and Interbrand.

- ***Information, Insight and Research Agencies:*** These agencies offer a wide array of research services such as customer research, usage and attitudinal studies, product testing, marketing segmentation, customer satisfaction, panel research, and much more. Examples of information, insight and research agencies include The Kantar Group, Research International, and M/A/R/C Research.

- ***Promotional Marketing Agencies:*** These agencies provide clients with promotional services that range from marketing incentives, sales promotions, product sampling, promotional events, consumer promotions, fulfillment services such as sweepstakes, contests, and games, sponsorship activities, and more. Examples of promotional marketing agencies include Alcone Marketing Group, and TIC TOC.

- ***Multicultural Marketing Agencies:*** Agencies focusing on speaking to minorities understand their purchasing patterns and media preferences, whether ethnic or cultural. Agencies can be specialized in one or multiple specialties such as Hispanic/Latin American, African-American, Native American, and Gay/Lesbian. Examples of multicultural marketing agencies include The Bravo Group, Cultura, Footsteps, and LatinWorks.

Other Types of Specialized or Industry-specific Agency Services

Some agencies have developed deep subject matter expertise in various specialized forms of marketing or communication, such as Entertainment/Event Marketing, Field/Channel Marketing, Data Management and Data Mining, Retail Marketing /Point of Sales/Merchandising, Employer Branding/Recruitment Communications, Media and Film Production Services, Custom Media/Publishing, Experiential Marketing, and Digital Directory Advertising/Yellow Pages. New emerging digital capabilities such as viral marketing and social media can be found here as well as in end-to-end integrated digital agencies.

Agency Viewpoint

"Creative agencies have often been named after their founders for a reason. It's about great talent. But longevity comes with intellectual property, insights, and tools that make the talent more effective and the outcomes more reliable."

DAVID KENNY
Managing Partner, Vivaki

This category of agencies also includes firms with deep segment-specific expertise like Industrial Advertising or Healthcare Communication agencies (for example, Ogilvy Healthworld, Grey Healthcare Group) that focus on health care and pharmaceutical and have a very intimate knowledge of advertising and marketing communication practices in this highly regulated industry sector. Other agency vertical segments besides Healthcare Communications include (but are not limited to) Technology Marketing, Urban Marketing, Youth Marketing (kids, tweens and teens), Real Estate Marketing, Nonprofit Marketing, Foodservice Marketing, Sports Marketing, Financial/Corporate BtoB. The list goes on.

Client Viewpoint

"In a world increasingly more digital, one may wonder what place traditional media holds. At what point does the media landscape get so saturated that it becomes wallpaper? How do companies break-through? This is where partnering with the right agency can make a difference."

JEFF DEVON, Director Global Marketing, HP

When it's all said and done, because there is no right or wrong way to cluster agencies, don't expect all your agencies to naturally fall into these categories. Some standards have emerged as agencies establish new capabilities like search engine marketing or mobile advertising once backed up by fast growing client billings. We should expect to see changes in the way the agency industry organizes itself over time.

Certainly, there are a number of other ways, besides core competencies, to divide up agencies: revenue ranking (from top to bottom), agency affiliations (e.g., BBDO Worldwide Network); public vs.

independent; geographic location (international versus domestic, by city); specialized (media, healthcare, multicultural such as Hispanic, African-American, Asian-American) versus non-specialized. These criteria can prove to be most helpful for clients seeking to filter down the list of agencies. If a client needs to focus its marketing efforts on the Asian-American audience, they should consider agencies such as PanCom International or Kang & Lee. If they are in the pharmaceutical business, they should consider health care and medical advertising and marketing divisions of Omnicom Group, WPP Group, and Interpublic Group, or independent agencies like GSW Worldwide or Abelson-Taylor.

The agency supply chain is often richer than what meets the eye. Agencies typically subcontract with other specialty vendors for skills that they do not have readily in-house such as printing, production, material fulfillment, premiums, studios, and many others in various complementary industries and professions. They do so to provide clients with a one-stop solution for all their needs. These vendors tend to be either highly specialized or too infrequently used by advertisers to economically justify the agency having these services available in-house.

The Epochal Battle of Four Titans

Perhaps one of the greatest challenges faced by any company is to understand the complex and evolving nature of an industry consistently innovating and reinventing itself. We've all heard of the glamorous agency names like BBDO, Young & Rubicam, Ogilvy, and JWT that made Madison Avenue a name for itself. How about all the others? Unless you do this for a living or for some circumstantial reasons, it's unlikely that you have much visibility of the intricate makeup of large agencies or to the number of boutique agencies with catchy names like Mother, Anomaly, Ascentium, Rockfish, Firstborn, Barbarian Group, Switzerland, Naked, 72andSunny, Big Spaceship, Strawberry Frog, or Wexley School for Girls. You are not to blame. And you are not alone.

Agency Viewpoint

"Agencies preach to their clients on how to create sustained value but sadly enough, they have not applied these principles to their own brands."

TIM WILLIAMS, President, Ignition Consulting Group

No offense to those great outfits, many of which are now working with marquee clients and have been widely acknowledged by industry peers. Mother, for example, was named agency of the decade by *AdAge* in late 2009, along with more established agencies like Crispin Porter + Bogusky, RG/A, AKQA and TBWA, among others. So why is it so hard to keep a pulse on newcomers and the industry at large? Well, because there are so many of them with various skills and credentials. This is a highly fragmented industry with agencies renaming themselves regularly, being acquired, being merged, or, for the few unfortunate, going out of business. So fragmented in fact, it is estimated to include over 100,000 advertising and marketing agencies in the United States alone.[6]

Without industry resources such as the Association of American Advertising Agencies (4As), *AdWeek* and *Advertising Age*'s infamous annual list of top agencies, we would be hard pressed to keep a tally. Now it's time we put some of these agencies under microscope. So what do we know about them?

As in any other industry, the advertising and marketing communications agency business has a few big dominant players, and a small number of holding, parent companies, which are all publicly traded and account for a disproportionate share of the advertising and marketing communications business worldwide. The holding companies represent a federation of companies, together yet independent, giving them the flexibility to adapt to diverse and ever-changing client scenarios, and the ability to come as one to meet the requirements of global Fortune 100 companies. These holding companies were initially formed by a few large agencies merging to create greater economies of scale, and stronger, more complete offerings and synergies while working around client conflicts. The four largest holding companies are WPP Group, Omnicom Group, Publicis Groupe, and Interpublic Group of Cos (IPG).

Holding companies provide professional services to clients in all industry segments through multiple agencies around the world, on a global, pan-regional, and local basis, across multiple communication disciplines comprising advertising, marketing services, specialty communications, interactive/digital, and media buying and planning services. They promote the value of independence to better foster agility, creativity, and innovation among its members. Holding companies were created in response to the globalization of the marketplace as well as to resolve client conflicts that previously prevented them from taking on many clients in the same business category. They responded to the need of brand advertisers like Procter & Gamble, Johnson & Johnson, General Motors Corp, Unilever, and many others looking to build global brands and speak as one voice. This was a need that could only be met by coordinating resources across geography and offering an integrated offering so clients would be able to work with "one stop-shop" for all their needs in order to ultimately gain greater efficiency and effectiveness.

In return, holding companies were now able to take on competitive clients by aligning them to different in-network agencies, therefore avoiding loss of new business opportunities. This is how WPP was able to take on Microsoft Corp. as a new Young & Rubicam Brands/Wunderman client in 2003 while continuing to serve IBM Corp., one of its largest clients.[7]

This is how IPG was able to maintain the lion's share of MasterCard's digital business in 2009 by handing off duties from sibling MRM, the digital unit of McCann, to R/GA.[8]

The Genetic Makeup of Holding Companies

Although all holding companies share common characteristics, they are often run very differently. The operating units under each network collaborate in a formal or informal virtual network, aligned around unique client marketing needs, in modular fashion. IPG pioneered the concept of the holding company approach, following rapidly by the other now large players, WPP Group and Omnicom Group. They act as a "virtual network" giving them the ability to integrate services across all disciplines and delivering those across networks and geographic regions simultaneously. Their network strategy is believed to facilitate better integration of services to meet the demands of the marketplace by pulling the resources best suited to meet the needs of a client. A holding company allows local markets to take advantage of the strong creativity, strategic resources, know-how, tools, and new technologies that they might not otherwise be able to do. They can deliver integrated services via a web of interconnected yet autonomous companies, balancing global and local client needs.

Client Viewpoint

"The advertising industry is highly fragmented. Now we have experts in media, CRM, etc. Everyone is struggling on how to make agencies work together. But we clients want integrated solutions. I don't want my agencies to compete for land grab. Give me an agency with a 360 degree solution on how to best reach my customer. Clients are looking for agencies with these capabilities, so they don't have 10 agencies calling them to get an assignment. I want one agency which has full accountability."

SUSAN MARKOWICZ, Global Advertising Agency Manager, Ford Motor Company

On principle, the critical mass generated by the holding company model allows them to focus their efforts on attracting, retaining, and developing the best talent pool possible. Their operating units may be asked at times to come together and partner to serve a particular client. Or they may end up competing with each other. They can play on the strengths of the network and minimize its potential weaknesses. Clients and employees, for example, can be moved from one agency to another that might be a better fit. The holding company sets company-wide financial targets and defines corporate strategy, directs collaborative inter-agency programs, establishes common financial management and operational controls, guides personal and compensation policies, handles investor relations and manages and approves mergers and acquisitions.

In addition, it lessens the administrative burden of operating agencies by centralizing basic functional services such as real estate, legal, accounting and finance, travel, recruitment, compensation, investor relations, procurement, insurance, tax and legal affairs, information systems and technology, and financial support. Those benefits come at a cost as some overhead is charged back to the operating units, a cost ultimately paid by clients.

Client Viewpoint

"In my opinion, the optimum organizations (on the holding company side) that support client desires for truly blended media channels are completely unresolved."

AMY FULLER, Group Executive Worldwide Consumer Marketing, MasterCard Worldwide)

It wouldn't be fair to assume that all holding companies are structured the same or pursue similar goals. For example, WPP Group has clearly shown its commitment to the parent company approach, beyond the financial purpose served by holding companies. WPP Group acts as a sort of central nervous system, a single point of accountability to leverage all group assets as any other holding company, but does so in the pursuit of new business. An approach it took with HSBC, Intel, Samsung and Nestlé.[9] WPP Group is not singular.

Omnicom Group has been involved in a few holding company pitches for large clients such as Bank of America. At the core of company holding pitches is the client's desire to reduce the conflicts and territorial issues that prevent them from pursuing media-neutral approaches with multiple agencies when those services are not available from a single full service integrated agency. The concept is not new, of course.

Agency networks fulfill a similar role on a smaller scale. Getting better coordination from multiple agencies with individual P&L is not always easy, but it certainly hasn't stopped the proliferation of combined entities hoping to appeal to clients looking for integrated offerings. Look at Publicis. In late 2007 Publicis USA decided to bring together multiple entities into a single one branded as Publicis Modem & Dialog, a combination of Publicis Dialog and Publicis Modem. It did it again under the brand name Insight Factory, combining creative services from Leo Burnett, media agency Starcom MediaVest and interactive shop Digitas.[10]

The four giant holding companies are responsible for a disproportionate share of the business of marketing and communications, working for a much diversified client portfolio, both in size and industry type. The holding companies play a large influential role in the combined successes of all of their operating units. They each employ thousands of employees working all around the world, in hundreds of individual companies in various disciplines. Let's take a closer look at the top four holding companies.

WPP Group[11]

Wire and Plastic Products was originally a U.K. manufacturer of wire bakets, an investment through which Sir Martin Sorrell started to build his worldwide marketing services company through massive and highly publicized acquisitions such as JWT Group, Ogilvy Group, Young & Rubicam, Grey Global Group, 24/7 Real Media and Taylor Nelson Sofres, and many others. Renamed WPP Group in 1987 and headquartered in London, its mission is to "develop and manage talent; to apply that talent throughout the world for the benefits of clients; to do so in partnership; to do so with profit."

WPP Group has four global advertising networks: Ogivly Group (which includes a number of individual branded agencies such as Ogilvy & Mather, OgilvyOne Worldwide, Ogilvy Public Relations Worldwide, Ogilvy Healthworld, OgilvyAction), Young & Rubicam Brands (including brands such as Y&R, Wunderman, VML, Burson-Marsteller, Landor Associates, Sudler & Hennessey, The Bravo Group, etc.), Grey Group and JWT. Agencies have individual specialized offerings as sub brands such as OgilvyOne Worldwide's Neo@Ogilvy, a search, digital media and performance marketing offering and JWT's RMG Connect, the agency CRM network.

Others include United Network as well as Bates 141, an Asian-only network. WPP Group has one media network, Group M, that maximizes the performance of WPP's media communications agencies and serves as a parent company to MAXUS, MediaCom, Mediaedge:cia (MEC) and MindShare. WPP Group has a number of Marketing Services agencies such as The Kantar Group, Hill & Knowlton, Fitch and many others.

As a parent company, the group's mission is to develop, manage, motivate, support, and ultimately apply talent for its operating units, releasing them of the majority of their administrative and financial responsibilities by achieving efficiencies in information technology, procurement, professional development, and client coordination that no single individual company would be able to achieve on its own. In return, operating units can focus their energy and resources on achieving their strategic and operational goals.

The group has managed its portfolio of investments and acquisitions through WPP Digital, a unit formed to provide direction in this critical area. WPP Group encourages its operating companies to work together, bringing their own disciplines to benefit clients in need of a more holistic service offering. WPP has appointed a number of WPP Global Client leads responsible for coordinating efforts on the client's behalf to leverage the full extent of what the group has to offer through its many operating units. WPP Group ensures there is a single ownership where it most logically resides.

WPP Group won global HSBC and Samsung accounts and many others using this approach. Perhaps one of the most publicized was WPP Group's approach to Dell's pitch in late 2007. WPP Group won the prestigious account after a 7-month long pitch against Interpublic Group by committing to build a brand new agency structured around the estimated $4.5 billion account. WPP agreed to build from scratch a 1,000-plus person agency (originally code named Da Vinci to be later formally named Enfatico) to service the massive account, across multiple disciplines and under one single P&L, rather than leveraging disperse network assets. Although the venture didn't deliver as originally planned (Enfatico later on ended up being folded into Y&R Brands), it signaled WPP Group's willingness to take risks, exploring new models to service demanding clients.[12]

Omnicom Group Inc.[13]

The Omnicom Group (OMC) was born in 1986 out of the merger of three United States advertising giants who played a predominant role in building the advertising industry as we know it today: BBDO as well as Doyle Dane Bernbach and Needham Harper Worldwide, now known at DDB Worldwide. OMC is a globally diversified conglomerate with thousands of clients from around the world in a broad variety of industries. It operates as the parent company for three separate and prestigious agency networks—BBDO Worldwide, DDB Worldwide Communications Group and TBWA Worldwide—as well as many independent agencies and the marketing services network, Diversified Agency Services.

Diversified Agency Services (DAS) includes a number of specialty service agencies such as branding, retail marketing, healthcare, multicultural, and relationship marketing. DAS includes Rapp, formerly known as Rapp Collins Worldwide, the leading direct marketing agency with both digital and data/analytics expertise. TBWA is made up of full service agencies around the world including direct/database and interactive services through Tequila, Agency.com and Integer. Tribal DDB is a digital marketing agency that is an independent division of DDB Worldwide.

OMC aligned several of its digital units with its traditional ad agencies in 2005: Agency.com was aligned with ad agency TBWA Worldwide and Organic was aligned with ad agency BBDO. OMC also has leading U.S.-based advertising agencies such as Arnell Group, Goodby, Silverstein & Partners, consistently ranked as one of the top interactive agencies, GSD&M, Martin|Williams, Merkley Newman Harty|Partners, and Zimmerman Partners. Originally formed out of the media departments of its three global advertising agencies, Omnicom Media Group (OMG) consists of three full service media companies, OMD Worldwide, PHD Network and Prometheus, as well as several media specialist companies in branded entertainment, print, outdoor, search, insert media, etc., and the digital arm of OMG Digital. OMC emphasizes organic growth, growing its existing businesses, so its acquisitions have historically been smaller in scale than its other main competitors.

Its largest and longest relationships have been Chrysler (with BBDO in 1944—no longer with BBDO today, but still working with some OMC companies), GE (with BBDO since 1920), McDonald's Corp (with DDB, TBWA and others and with DDB since mid-70s) and Fedex (with BBDO since 1989). Commonly referred as a "federalist" model, OMC is keen on preserving the autonomy and independence of its operating units. The company has had a hands-off approach that has been successful at attracting new companies to its federation while balancing the need to provide integrated offering to large clients through its multiple combined assets. The concept of "latitude within limits" is a big part of the company's philosophy.

As a holding company, OMC is set up to raise capital for its operating units, to give its members the tools they need to succeed and support the growth of the overall integrated client offering. OMC's focus and commitment to education through continued training and development programs (for example, Omnicom University, Omnicom Group MBA Residency Program, and Business Learning Program) has been instrumental in retaining, and motivating its talent pool, discussing business-building opportunities among units and non-proprietary trends and issues they face in everyday client situations. OMC's holding company sometimes pitches where an operating unit takes the lead.

Examples of successful OMC pitches include Chrysler, Bank of America, Motorola, and Johnson & Johnson's MD&D division as well as Bayer. In March 2006, OMC entered into an agreement with Motorola Inc. to give them access to the creative resources of various OMC agencies including BBDO New York, AMV BBDO, Goodby, Silverstein and Partners, and Siegel and Gale. BBDO New York serves as the central coordinating agency on behalf of OMC.

Interpublic Group of Cos[14]

Headquartered in New York City, the Interpublic Group of Companies, Inc. (IPG) is considered the grandfather of the global marketing communications companies. First incorporated in 1930 under the name of McCann-Erickson Incorporated, succeeding the advertising agency founded by A.W. Erikson, and in 1911 by Harrison K. McCann, IPG was born in the early 1960s with a network of two agencies, McCann Erikson Worldwide and

McCann-Markschalk. Today IPG is the parent company of advertising agency McCann Erickson and media company Universal McCann. IPG operates in two fundamental disciplines called "Integrated Agency Network (IAN)," comprised of Draftfcb, Lowe and McCann, media agencies, stand-alone agencies and Consistuency Management Group "CMG," which is comprised of the specialist marketing service offerings.

IPG has three global advertising networks: Draftfcb, Lowe Worldwide and McCann Worldgroup, and full-service United States agencies (Campbell-Ewald, Campbell Mithun, Deutsch, Hill Holiday, The Martin Agency and Mullen). McCann Worldgroup includes McCann Erickson Advertising, and MRM Worldwide for relationship and digital marketing, Momentum Worldwide for experiential marketing, McCann Healthcare Worldwide for healthcare communications, Futurebrand and Weber Shandwick.

Introduced in 2006, Draftfcb is a newly formed company resulting from the merger of Draft and Foote Cone and Belding (also one of the earliest advertising companies, founded in 1873). IPG also has two media specialists, Initiative and Universal McCann. Although they operate independently, these two media companies have been aligned to Draftfcb and McCann Erikson to improve cross-media communications and integrated delivery.

IPG has a number of specialist firms across a full range of marketing services: FutureBrand for corporate branding, Jack Morton for experiential marketing, Octagon for sports marketing, Regan Campbell Ward for healthcare communications, digital marketing by R/GA, WeberShandwick for public relations and several multicultural (Hispanic, African-American) agencies.

R/GA, McCann Erikson and Universal McCann have been considered to be IPG's most valuable and profitable brands within their network. IPG offers a number of client solutions among which is their "virtual network models" where the client relationship is held with the holding company to steward multiple IPG specialist companies. IPG's priority has been to reinvigorate its offering and improve its overall financial strength as a result of a major and disastrous financial restatement that was followed by the implementation of rigorous and vital financial controls previously lacking. The SEC opened a formal investigation in response to the restatement announced by IPG in 2002.

The network holding company responded by revamping its structure and eliminated a large number of its legal entities, streamlining its company portfolio by consolidating or closing operating units. In 2006 IPG reorganized its media operations to align its strategic communications planning process more closely to its global network agencies and create a closer relationship between the two disciplines.

Publicis Groupe[15]

Publicis ("publi," the abbreviation of "publicité," "advertising" in French and "cis" for the number six as in 1906, the founder's birth year) was founded in 1926 in a poor neighborhood of Paris by a 20-year-old French advertising pioneer, Marcel Bleustein-Blanchet. After opening a N.Y. office in 1957, through a merger and strategic alliance with Foote, Cone and Belding in 1988, Publicis attempted to enter the vast and prosperous United States market. The adventure ended in 1996.

Publicis Groupe was created in 2000 when Publicis, the Paris-based agency, acquired Saatchi & Saatchi for $1.7 billion. It only gained a solid foothold in the U.S. and became the fourth largest marketing communication company in the world after merging with Bcom3 Group under the leadership of his CEO Maurice Lévy. Publicis Groupe also formed a strategic partnership with Japan's largest group, Dentsu to strengthen its global reach in Asia.

Perhaps the most talked about event in the world of Publicis has been its most recent $1.3 billion acquisition of Digitas (the fourth largest marketing services agency in the United States and the third largest interactive agency at the time) in Dececember 2006 to improve Publicis's digital capabilities and providing a stronger U.S. based operation.

Today, Publicis Groupe is one of the world's largest communications group. Publicis Groupe's slogan is "Viva La Difference," cultivating and celebrating how they are different from the competition based on culture, methods, and approach to communication. Publicis Groupe includes three global advertising networks (Leo Burnett, Publicis, and Saatchi & Saatchi), two multi-hub networks (Fallon Worldwide and Bartle Bogie Hegarty), regional agencies such as Kaplan Thaler Group (NY), Beacon Communications (Tokyo), Marcel (Paris). Publicis has also two global media consultancy and buying networks (ZenithOptimedia and Starcom MediaVest Group) and a wide range of marketing services. Considered the "founding pillar," Publicis has been the largest agency network within Publicis Group, with a particularly strong footing in Europe.

Founded in the mid-1930s, Leo Burnett has worked with prestigious clients over the years. Leo Burnett integrated with Arc Worldwide under the Leo Burnett Worldwide brand name. Among its largest and longest relationships: L'Oréal (with Publicis since 1934), Toyota (with Saatchi & Saatchi since 1976), HP (with Publicis and ZenithOptimedia since 1993), Nestlé (with Publicis since 1954), Whirlpool (with Publicis since 1986). Publicis Groupe is a large family of companies who have the autonomy to foster their own culture but participate in the group community.

The network holding concept has proven to be a competitive advantage for its members, for example allowing Fallon Worldwide to expand internationally with global clients like Nestlé and United Airlines or for Starcom MediaVest Group and ZenithOptimedia to invest in people and infrastructure to strengthen their current offering. A group called P12, consisting of senior employees representing each major operating group, provides oversight and helps establish standards such as compensation and incentives across all business units. Publicis Groupe invests in its staff by providing training and professional development resources such as the Peak Performance program, Leo Burnett University, or the ZenithOptimedia University.

Publicis Groupe's prime objective has been to become a leader in digital. Publics Groupe's approach to the digital agency model was to establish one shared interactive operation for the entire group (using acquired Digitas) separate from its core agencies (versus being integrated directly into traditional agency structures) but available for them to leverage. Its acquisition of Boston-based Digitas (founded in 1980) and Razorfish (from Microsoft's prior acquisition of aQuantive) were strong confirmations that it intends to be a major player.

The Perfect Storm Agencies can grow by winning new business, organically or through acquisitions. The industry consolidation has been the undeniable trend of the past decade as agencies realized that the globalization of the marketplace required them to evolve their offering and meet the needs of even more demanding global clients. Client consolidations became prevalent in many industries. How do agencies keep up? They consolidate to stay in the game, mostly in the media space where economies of scale translate into a competitive edge as clients look for greater media buying efficiencies. This is a sign that the agency business is blooming in vitality and is considered a critical industry of the future. Perhaps the largest acquisition ever seen on Madison Avenue was the $4.7 billion acquisition of Young & Rubicam in 2000. WPP's deal to acquire Grey Global Group for $2.5 billion in 2004 was certainly a major event as well, outbidding Havas (Publicis dropped out of the auction), managing to keep P&G and Unilever under the same agency umbrella. In 2000 Publicis SA bought Saatchi & Saatchi for $1.8 billion, creating what is now known as Publicis Groupe.

In 2002 Publicis Groupe acquired Bcom3 Group (Leo Burnett, D'Arcy) for $2.2 billion, moving Publicis in the lead pack of the Big Four. There were rumors of further consolidation, with the speculated acquisition of Interpublic Group by Publicis (playfully named "Inter-Publicis") which never materialized. The $6 billion acquisition of aQuantive by Microsoft set the tone by its scale alone, following the multi-billion dollar acquisitions of 24/7 Media by WPP, Digitas by Publicis.

The Big Four made a number of sizeable investments in digital ventures. Consolidation is also happening as clients look for one or fewer agencies to manage their media and creative assignments. These account consolidations (for example, in 2005 General Motor's $3.2 billion and L'Oreal's $1.5 billion media reviews) resulted from perceived fall off of agency performance, cost cutting efforts, changes in client leadership, client mergers and acquisition, among other reasons. For clients, this dynamic industry phenomenon has its fair share of pluses and minuses. Advertisers see their agencies acquire capabilities and talent that were both unavailable previously or were handled by other agencies, leading to severe integration challenges and excessive overhead.

Clients benefit from agencies merging but expect their services to be fully integrated into the agency's suite of services. However, as smaller, nimble, low overhead specialized agencies are acquired, costs for services suddenly and unavoidably go up once fully immersed into the larger operating structure.

It also creates a number of unexpected client conflicts that do not always end up in their favor. This being said, looking at cost alone is short-sighted. In the end, clients have more to gain than to lose from the industry consolidation. A few, large companies eventually emerge and set direction, bringing together a richer set of integrated capabilities to the marketplace that benefits advertisers. The top holding companies are continuing to strengthen key competencies, expanding their footprint, and investing to improve their talent base. They have no choice with the rest of the industry breathing down their neck. After all, this is a highly dynamic industry that continues to place new demands on these companies. And not unlike the epic battle of the young David and the Philistine warrior Goliath, the big guy is not always the one standing up.

David vs. Golliath

Independent agencies such as Wieden + Kennedy and Mother continue to show up as nimble contenders to global agencies for creative assignments. These nimble indie shops have idea-centric approaches to solving client problems combined with agile organizational structures, reduced overhead and middle management, and a culture of collaboration and partnership that translates for clients into lower cost delivery, fast turnaround, and highly creative solutions that can come from anywhere in the agency. Ask them to scale, however, and things can get a bit more complicated.

There are a few other organizations worth mentioning, given their reputation and influence: Dentsu, headquartered in Tokyo, Havas, headquartered in Paris, Aegis Group, headquartered in London, MDC Partners (headquartered in Toronto) and Sapient Corp (headquartered in Cambridge, Mass.). The remaining share of the business is divided up between smaller agency networks, large and medium-size independent agencies, and small (and "want-to-be-and-want-to-remain small") advertising boutiques. The continued industry consolidation, accelerated by the race for digital marketing supremacy, has energized the industry and encouraged the emergence of small, new agencies hoping to get on the bandwagon and either find a niche or get acquired by traditional agencies anxious to stay in the competition. These independent shops end up being acquired by hungry holding companies or private equity investors.

Many small boutique agencies like Mother are making themselves powerful adversaries of the big firms, finding their "Achilles' heel" and building direct relationships with big brand advertisers, many of which discreetly outsourced complex digital assignments to these shops. It's cyclical in the end. Boutique agencies are acquired or grow to become large ones, opening room for the small shops to promote less cookie-cutter work, and more nimble, personalized, agile services. For example, award-winning creative shop Crispin Porter + Bogusky was acquired by MDC Partners in 2008. Previously independent firms Digitas and Razorfish were acquired by Publicis Groupe, leaving a few rare and truly independent, privately-held shops like AKQA and Firstborn, especially in digital, which has seen a rapid acceleration of mergers and acquisitions.

Client Viewpoint

"Small independent agencies can sometimes be driven by budgets and maintaining a tight scope of work. If they are too rigid in that approach, it can end up eroding the relationship over time. From my experience, larger agencies are often more flexible to work with. As long as the scope of work and budget are within the ballpark and both parties treat each other fairly, the focus can be on the work, not on the agency financials."

Delmar Wyatt
Director Advertising Operations, Qwest Communications

Many of these agencies vividly proclaim their desire to remain fully independent, hoping to avoid the financial pressure of a group P&L that may require them to be less selective about the clients they bring on to meet revenue or profit targets. They also want to maintain their creative freedom that is particularly important to their founders and creative leadership. In reality, few are those who resist the temptation of a financially sound business arrangement that could reward its owners and provide access to capital that could be invested in the agency's growth.

There are a few independent agency networks, mostly led by companies like ComVort Group (headquartered in Barcelona), Worldwide Partners (headquartered in Denver) and IN (headquartered in London). These networks were created based on the belief that advertisers benefit most from small, local entrepreneurial agencies. They offer services for a fee to their members, some of which include pitching for new business that would otherwise be out of reach of these small agencies. Some of them go as far as allowing each agency to own shares by incorporating their network. Agency networks like thenetworkone™ or Transword Advertising Agency Network offer clients the ability to build an "on-demand" network of independently operated creative agencies and cross-discipline specialists from around the world.

Small agency boutiques are typically created by former ad agency executives hoping to bring along former clients. That was the case for United Airlines, for example, who shifted its ten-year relationship with Fallon Worldwide to a brand new agency, Barrie D'Rozario Murphy (BMD) after a former Fallon executive formed its own agency with a few associates.[16]

These creative boutique agencies are even challenging the big guys, demonstrating leaner overhead, more attractive pricing, and flexible models that make them attractive to accounts such as Heineken who assigned his $150M global branding business to StrawberryFrog in 2005 (whose roster in recent years included Wieden & Kennedy, TBWA/Chiat/Day, AKQA, and Euro RSCG most recently as agency of record for its flagship brands).[17]

Although we are likely to see clients continue to experiment with small, agile, innovative, independent boutique agencies to challenge themselves, it is clear that most small independent shops do not have the backbone and muscles to support a large, demanding global client. Dell parted ways with Omnicom Group's BBDO, which handled a large portion of its advertising work, and assembled a number of agencies from independent Mother to large agencies such as DDB (Omnicom), Carat (Aegis), and MRM Worldwide (IPG) while working on a larger plan to move away from its 800+ marketing firms globally to more centralized marketing. It was short-lived. Dell eventually moved its estimated $1.5 billion to WPP in late 2007, defeating IPG. The David and Goliath battle has been going on for a while and it is of epic proportions.

The Big Four will continue to furiously battle for supremacy, aggressively pursuing new clients, protecting existing ones, and acquiring new assets and competencies that complement their integrated client offering. Smaller, nimbler boutique agencies will continue to emerge and blossom. What is most certain is that tomorrow's agencies, regardless of their size, will be increasingly versatile, innovative, and "customer-centric." Forrester Research calls it the

"Adaptive Marketing Era"[18] where consumer to brand interactions must generate conversations that in turn prompt audience participation.

As Jeff Goodby, the talented Co-Chairman and Creative Director at Goodby, Silverstein & Partners puts it so eloquently: "Marketing will be, of course, carried out in the digital spaces, by people quite different from the ones who inhabit today's agencies. They will first and foremost be thinkers, capable of coming up with ideas that clients can't imagine themselves—or else their agencies will no longer exist. They will be aggressive learners about what is new and interesting in the world. And they will be what Thomas Friedman calls "versatilists," able to write and draw and program and read research. Agencies that are able to offer a staff that is like this will resemble Pixar more than they resemble the big agencies of today."

The agency community is often a maze that is difficult to navigate without getting lost in its complex of web of partnerships and affiliations. Although further consolidation is likely, it's likely to remain a confusing world. The agency landscape is now permanently transformed as a result of lasting changes in technology, media, and consumer habits. Having a basic understanding of the agency service taxonomy and of the major agency players and holding companies is a requirement for any company that decides to hire an agency. Once you do, you'll realize that the world of Madison Avenue is not so mysterious, after all.

{Taking Immediate Action}

TOP 5

BEST PRACTICES TO HARNESS THE MADNESS

❶ Don't be intimidated by the rapidly changing and often confusing world of advertising and marketing communications agencies. After reading this book, you are likely to be one of the most knowledgeable employees in your company. Ask your agency about their growth plans and how you fit in.

❷ Pay particularly close attention to the big network-holding companies as well as the top agencies in each of their respective marketing communications disciplines. By their sheer size, they influence and shape the entire agency community.

❸ Always keep an eye on dynamic, independent boutiques that challenge the status quo and come up with new, innovative approaches and business models.

❹ Use valuable industry resources such as trade magazines, and dedicate some time to stay abreast of new developments in the industry such as mergers and acquisitions, agency awards (Cannes, Effie, Clio, etc.), client reviews, key account losses and wins in your industry, talent on the move, and more.

❺ Attend key industry events to network with peers and learn best practices and success stories that can then be applied to your own client/agency relationship(s).

3 "THE BUCK STOPS HERE"

Mastering the discipline of agency management

> "Each problem that I solved became a rule, which served afterwards to solve other problems."
>
> —RENE DESCARTES
> *Philosopher, mathematician, scientist, and writer*

It's late Sunday evening and you just received a phone call from Mark, the company's Chief Marketing Officer (CMO), in a state of panic. The latest creative concepts produced by the agency are still not hitting the mark. Mark is growing concerned about the competition's recent gains in brand awareness and favorability as well fourth quarter's aggressive revenue targets. After numerous rounds, the concepts are still off-strategy. Wendy, the agency's Group Account Director, alerted you that the agency's run rate was too high and that there were growing concerned about the account's shrinking profitability. The agency's CFO is on his case and she's now asking for a budget increase. This is coupled with the fact that the agency raised concerns weeks ago about the lack of clarity about the campaign's objectives.

There appears to be overlap in responsibilities with another roster agency. The agency is confused about who the decision-maker is. There were too many reviewers to please, diluting the initial concepts presented. The agency staff is burned out and is becoming de-motivated. The agency recently hired a new hotshot Creative Director after the agency's creative product was identified to be a weak spot in last agency performance assessment. The situation is tense. Contract is up for review. Budget is tight. Time is of essence. Mark is asking you to either turn the situation around or move the work to another agency. Sound familiar?

Suddenly you wish you had taken Agency Management 101 back in business school. You aren't to blame ... it simply didn't exist. C-level executives haven't typically intuitively thought about actively managing agencies as a formal role within their organization to improve both the effectiveness and efficiency of client/agency engagements. Although they appreciate that unique skills may be required, they don't often think about agency management as a distinct business function or discipline they need to build in their organization. Then again, *"Why should we?"* some wonder. The most skeptical would ask:

Clearly reality is far different. Agencies have never been in the commodity business (at least not the ones you want to work with). To the contrary. It's absolutely insane to see so many brand advertisers treat them as such, ignorant of the golden egg potential at their fingertips. However, agencies do require active client management and consistent oversight to deliver optimal value. Thankfully, most clients have come to realize that these strategic partnerships require a higher level of direct, ongoing engagement than traditional vendor relationships.

Client Viewpoint

"We work very effectively with other parts of the company. There are no silos when dealing with our agencies. The large majority of the time, we can walk in a room with stakeholders from marketing, procurement, finance and legal and make a decision."

SHERRY ULSH, Director Global Marketing Finance and Procurement, Burger King Corp.

For advertisers wise enough to consider agencies a strategic extension of their marketing organization, it's no less important or demanding than getting top performance from internal staff. A CMO is accountable for having the right mix of marketing skills on his or her team, setting clear goals and metrics to measure team performance, continually recruiting, developing, and retaining key talent, and ensuring that these critical human resources are managed, motivated, and rewarded. Common-sense principles of managing a company's human capital apply to external talent agencies as well. Whether in good or difficult economic times, Wall Street rewards companies that manage their human investments wisely. Wall Street also rewards companies that use their marketing and media budgets as aggressive growth engines for their company.

Companies no longer award their trimmed-down budgets to agencies tasked to handle company-critical marketing efforts then cross their fingers and hope for the best. Not if they need to deliver market results to the CEO, the board and shareholders—and certainly not if they intend to stay on the company's payroll. There is way too much at stake these days. Agency spending is one of the largest non-payroll expenses any company has. And marketing is too critical to a company's ability to compete and sustain continued growth not to strategically manage this investment. Advertising and marketing communications agencies are simply too instrumental to a company's ability to build great brands, grow revenue, and gain market share.

From Art to Science: Agency Capital Management

Like an orchestra, you need more than talented, well-trained musicians to perform a concerto. You also need a conductor with an intimate knowledge of resources at hand and the right music sheets—the equivalent of a blueprint for how to get most of your agency—to get to the right outcome. Even the most skeptical companies have come to realize that wisely assigning experts time and resources in managing agency relationships yields stronger dividends than a portfolio of unmanaged investments.

Expectations are often non-linear in a business environment where external and internal conditions are dynamic and are hard to predict. Luckily, in this instance, there is a clear relationship between cause and effect—over both the short and long term. The performance of an agency is a direct function of the energy invested by the client in making sure the relationship is properly set up and the partnership is adequately supported on an on-going basis. Garbage in, garbage out: Clients get out what they put in. The reverse is true as well.

Agency Viewpoint

"Too many clients rely on their procurement organization to drive the conversation about value. It's a dangerous way to go about this, because procurement can measure costs but not value."

DAVID KENNY
Managing Partner, Vivaki

Former VP, Online Experience of Safeco Insurance, Randy Wise said it best: "The quickest path to a bad agency is a bad client; the quickest path to a bad client is a bad agency." Well orchestrated yet flexible agency capital management is the key to strong marketing and communication delivery and effectively competing for customers in an increasingly fragmented marketplace.

Working with an advertising or marketing communications agency is far more complex, vastly more demanding than most vendor relationships a typical busy purchasing department is accustomed to. The role of agency management still suffers from a lack of consideration in some marketing and procurement organizations, even though it is far more rewarding and strategically beneficial to companies if the agency is managed properly. This means that the right agency roster has been picked, the metrics for success are clearly understood, the agencies have been thoroughly briefed, the teams are partnering effectively, the right agency resources are working on the right assignments, and so on.

The complexity of the agency world comes from its large number of interactive and connected elements that draw from a number of corporate functions within a company, including corporate and product strategy and planning, scope of work management, fee negotiations, agency training, and agency monitoring and assessment.

No matter how much rigor and thoughtfulness clients put into it, effective agency management remains a balance of art and science. The concept of "science" is introduced when results are not only verifiable but also predictable and reproducible. Although fitting that litmus test at times, the up-and-coming nature of agency management, combined with the changing media frontier, requires finding new ways to creatively solving for business challenges. The discipline of agency management is arguably still immature in most companies and prone to experimentation for the years to come. Best practices, professional standards, and tools are beginning to emerge in this area, giving advertisers what they need to make the best use of their agencies.

Finding the Fulcrum of Efficiency and Effectiveness

The 15% commission system that privileged large media buys is long gone but not the important role media plays as a discipline. Savvy media planners and buyers now have a shot at trading their cubicle for a window office next to their creative counterparts who have always enjoyed this brass ring, something not envisioned even a few years ago. Their star is rising. After all, media buyers and corporate procurement professionals speak a common language: they know how to save money and efficiently leverage a company's budget.

Agency compensation agreements are now usually based on "cost plus" labor agreements where profit is negotiated separately on top of labor costs; these have for the most part completely replaced the commission based contracts. Agency fees have been fiscally "commoditized" by procurement's forceful entry into the marketing spend category.

New agency CEOs, skilled in finance and operations, are set to reinvent their agencies into highly successful profit-driving businesses. This is a challenging undertaking for these industry captains who face pressure from higher client expectations at the same time as increased cost pressure from the client's number crunchers, and from their finance and procurement departments.

Whether the client's department is called Purchasing, Procurement, Supplier Management, or Strategic Sourcing, the sudden emergence of this expense-management role in the corporate world is highly debated as it relates to the management of agency services. Yet procurement's growing influence in the industry in recent decades is undeniable. The end result is acute pressure on agency pricing based on competitive benchmarks, and on audits and procurement-led financial negotiations that can squeeze agency profits and potentially threaten their ability to sustain the very business that are helping clients drive their own growth and profitability.

Compensation was certainly easier for agencies twenty to thirty years ago! To the agency's despair, the client's procurement department is historically known for purchasing manufacturing parts and other highly commoditized "buy it anywhere" products where materials and shipping costs trump breakthrough creative thinking and strategic counsel. This tension is touching a sensitive nerve in marketing and agency executives who have historically handled this by using a broad palette of buying criteria.

Agency Viewpoint

"Too many marketing managers are not properly trained to manage agencies. They are often promoted to marketing from finance, operations, or sales functions. As for procurement, I wish they would understand the art and science of advertising and creating ideas, and not view it as a commodity. Procurement is killing great thinking, and clients are going to get mediocre results, since they cannot afford to put the best talent on accounts that are under-paying their agencies. Successful relations are born when clients provide access to agencies, and the agencies behave and communicate and advise in a candid and transparent manner."

MARC A. BROWNSTEIN
President and CEO, Brownstein Group

Today there is a very apparent shift in roles played out in different corporate functions relating to working with agencies. Not so long ago, agencies would often conduct business over cocktails, on a golf course, between speeches at an awards ceremony, or at a non-profit auction event with the CMO with whom they had strong years-long personal relationships.

Today, agency executives are increasingly dealing solely with tough procurement professionals in their business transactions. The same procurement professional they are negotiating with might be responsible for budgets for

PCs, travel and office furniture and want a bottom-dollar deal. They might be willing to trade a long-time agency partner for another to save a buck. This may be slightly exaggerated but you get the point. Not everyone in finance or procurement is sensitive to the powerful social media buzz of a compelling new online community; the insight and value brought to bear by a top-notch Account Planner just hired away from a competitive agency; or the agency's breakthrough use of emerging media campaign that exceeded revenue objectives. *"What did you say your overhead was again?"* is painfully echoing through the walls of Madison Avenue, fearful of e-sourcing or "Online Reverse Auctions" or other techniques used to further drive down prices.

Client Viewpoint

"To be a good client means that you carefully think about what your agencies can do and focus them on the right problems. Agencies need a strong partnership with their client to do their best work. The greater the expertise at the client, the better off the agency is."

AMY FULLER, Group Executive Worldwide Consumer Marketing, MasterCard Worldwide

Agency expenses represent a sizeable portion of a company's marketing budget, so it hasn't gone unnoticed by CFOs and procurement executives seeking to get all vendors to re-examine and justify the pricing of their services. Procurement's primary objective is typically to maximize shareholder value by pursuing maximum productivity from a company's external spend, consolidating the supplier base whenever appropriate and handling common transactions such as requisition to purchase order processing. To fulfill their efficiency agenda, they are increasingly partnering with their business counterparts to source agency services at the right cost. Appropriately, they foster a culture of fiscal accountability, setting spend control targets.

The concept of "Marketing Procurement" has emerged as it own discipline, led by savvy professionals, providing marketing departments and senior leadership a valuable and well-informed internal partner to frame and support well-crafted agency relationships.

Unfortunately the agency business is not often well understood outside of the company's marketing department. It is frequently associated with the outdated stereotype of charismatic entrepreneurs with large expense accounts and excessive overhead at the cost of large, sluggish clients. The world has changed, even though perceptions have not, and the continuing cost pressures inflicted by CFOs on their organizations have not spared the marketing function—as evidenced by the preeminent interest of this topic at industry events. As the growth in digital media has made this sector of marketing spend more accountable, expectations for tight cost control and rigorous marketing budget management across all agency functions has only accentuated procurement's role.

However, simplistic approaches such as indiscriminately reducing agency-related expenses and fees may result in unintentionally reduced work quality and talent, and therefore in lower marketing effectiveness and business impact. Like any business, agencies assign their best resources to profitable clients with long-term potential and those who know how to fairly compensate them for their services.

In other words, as in any other industry, agencies will pursue, invest in, and protect their higher-profit clients. Advertisers cannot viably compromise quality of their market presence and long term business value for short-term cost savings over the long haul. Marketing leaders and traditional procurement professionals don't always see eye-to-eye on how to set the right compensation balance point or how to measure agency value. Their agendas are often aligned but their priorities might not be, occasionally creating healthy tension. However, in economically challenging times, enthusiasm often concedes to pragmatism. Spend-control becomes a necessity that even talented agency executives and marketing leaders can't argue with. A more rigorous process, involving formal requests for information (RFIs) and requests for proposals (RFPs), overtakes informal courting previously handled over dinner by marketing and agency executives.

Agency Viewpoint

"Procurement and agency management are useful endeavors. A lot of money and effort is wasted by ignoring these things. However, clients have gone far overboard with this stuff, and they are now in the process of costing themselves big money, even as they think they're saving it. Cost consultants often don't know that their criticisms compromise creative product, make it less effective, and thus cost companies millions in future benefits. Pitch consultants never advise clients to hold anything less than full-fledged, all out pitch processes. This is often expensive and wasteful, both in terms of time and money. Push-back is already happening and it will build, believe me."

JEFF GOODBY
Co-Chairman and Creative Director, Goody, Silverstein & Partners

Adept advertisers can apply healthy cost-pressure without negatively impacting the agency's work or damaging valuable business and personal relationships. It's not surprising that agencies are resetting the dialog to focus on value-add, creativity, and ideas they bring to clients and less on the material nature of time and resources needed to accomplish client goals. Agencies have figured out that what applies to their clients also applies to them: Differentiation is the key to unlock the potential of a brand.

To overcome procurement's mechanistic decoupling of services as commodities, agencies are investing in differentiating themselves and their services from the competition and building value to justify higher pricing. They feel strongly that they are in the business of building top-line growth, not solely to help advertisers reduce cost. This is the balancing act of driving marketing efficacy, not driving your relationship to the edge of a rocky cliff. This is where the Agency Management function comes in.

The Multi-Dimensional Role of Agency Management

The Agency Management discipline provides a much needed balance to a traditional procurement or cost-driven approach to buying marketing services or a more casual "fair exchange value" approach to deal-making with agencies. Agency management savvy professionals can shift the conversation from purely a cost management to an opportunity growth discussion, leading to better decisions and collaborative tradeoffs with agency partners. In the world of advertising and marketing communications services, known for its intangibles and "soft" subjective business propositions, judgment calls based on the price-value equation are arguably better made by the business function ultimately responsible for its business outcome.

Agency Viewpoint

"Improving internal operations and having strong agency alignment goes hand in hand."

DAVID KENNY
Managing Partner, Vivaki

After all, agency-spend is an investment. It doesn't mean, however, that these decisions shouldn't be informed by and made in concert with finance and procurement departments. To drive business results that clients can take to the bank, advertisers must treat agencies as strategic business partners, not merely suppliers.

Client Viewpoint

"The continued growth of digital and advancements in technology are having a profound impact on the agency landscape. Clients are asking more questions. They want to understand the economics behind these changes. They are getting savvier. They are also pushing agencies to innovate and stay current."

CLAUDIA LEZCANO, Director of Advertising, Burger King Corp.

Agency Management is therefore a business discipline focused on the development, management, and nurturing of a company's partnership with its agencies with the goal of improving the tangible business impact of its advertising and marketing communications. The agency management function is responsible for the optimal allocation and use of agency talent to support the company's objectives. In other words, it's about making sure that the company has the right agency, doing the right type of work at the right investment level and in the most efficient ways. Where the agency management function sits organizationally and what its actual responsibilities are will vary based on whether the company has a centralized or a decentralized approach to marketing, and whether it is a large multinational or a small, domestic company.

It's absolutely insane when under-informed clients investing substantial budgets are not training budget owners or formally assigning that responsibility, even partially, to someone in the organization. These advertisers are effectively shooting from the hip, aiming with all the precision of a shotgun and hoping for the best. They glaringly fail to realize the full benefits inherent in their partnerships. Marketing or procurement leaders with past agency experience are by far more inclined to invest time and resources in these critical relationships than those without it. They have a much better appreciation of what can be accomplished and what it takes to get things done.

Individuals or organizations that enjoy enduring success have core values and a clear sense of purpose. The role of agency management is about getting better work and greater value from the company's advertising and marketing communication agencies. Agency management must therefore operate based on a disciplined and predictable approach to driving measurable business impact through agency partnerships.

To realize most value from these partnerships, clients must master both the business of astutely managing agency relationships (aka agency strategy and operations) and the demanding business of getting work done through agencies (aka client/agency engagement). Client/agency engagement activities range from briefing agencies and daily project-level interactions to planning for and facilitating productive exchanges between client contacts and agencies in order to get the work done. These important assignment-based activities are fulfilled by all project and budget owners throughout the client company.

Agency strategy and operations ensure the consistent and disciplined management approach of the contractual, economical, and operational aspects of the relationship. These important management and enablement-based activities are typically fulfilled by a few select individuals within the company.

Over the years, I've seen the many ways companies of various sizes choose to fulfill these agency management responsibilities, choosing whether these responsibilities are centralized or distributed within the organization, or both. Sometimes best practices are centralized but execution is decentralized—and if it is centralized, the choice is whether or not the function resides within a marketing procurement or becomes a marketing operations function.

Although promoting accountability for working effectively with agencies must be shared with anyone in the company interfacing with them, some functions of agency management such as Strategy and Operations are better handled centrally by one or multiple subject matter experts. This particular role requires a strong understanding of the science of working with agencies. The charter of this team of experts or individual—we will call the person fulfilling it the Chief Agency Officer for now—is to devote time to implementing and continually refining the right agency partnership model for the company to produce measurable results for the company.

In a multi-agency environment, this individual is also expected to coordinate relationships among the different agencies and ensure productive collaboration and partnerships between them. Ideally, he or she has agency and client experience, sound strategic planning skills, and a solid track record partnering with other company departments he or she will come to depend on, such as legal and finance. It's important to note that although some responsibilities are typically centralized, everyone in marketing or procurement—whether they directly or indirectly interface with the agencies—must have a basic understanding of the company's core business and operating and engagement principles in order to steward the tremendous financial and human investment most companies make in these partnerships.

What are the core expectations from agency management? Agencies must be carefully selected, aligned and organized to provide the right competencies to the business. Agencies must have rock-solid contracts in place along with motivating and fair compensation. Agencies must be briefed effectively and have sufficient view into the workload to staff the account with key talent. Agencies must also be evaluated. Although they may vary in scope and in complexity, typical responsibilities of the agency management function include the objectives, priorities, and primary purposes shown in the following chart.

Agency Portfolio Management

Agency strategy is about carefully planning the framework in which a company chooses to work with one or more agency partners based on the outcome it wants to achieve through its agency model. This is by far one of the most high-stakes agency management responsibilities and yet is often absent or handled informally. It first ensures the client's advertising and marketing communications needs of its agencies are well-defined and documented, and regularly vetted with internal stakeholders. It then helps determine which type of agency model (integrated, lead agency, open-sourced) and portfolio is best suited to serve the unique needs of the company both today and over time. Given the foundational nature of agency management and its importance in a company's ability to generate compelling return on its agency investments, senior leadership must answer similar questions:

- What agency skills are most needed today for our specific situation?
- What are our medium-term and long-term agency needs?

<table>
<tr><th>Objectives</th><th>Priorities</th><th>Functional Areas</th><th>Primary Purpose</th></tr>
<tr><td rowspan="6">Development, management and nurturing of the company's partnership with its agency(ies) with the goal of improving the measurable business impact of a client's advertising and marketing communications</td><td rowspan="2">The best agency competencies and resources to support client needs</td><td>Agency Portfolio Management</td><td>Determine client needs, understand market offering, lock on the best agency resource model and roster.</td></tr>
<tr><td>Agency Search and Selection</td><td>Identify, review, select, onboard a new agency.</td></tr>
<tr><td rowspan="2">The best contract and compensation agreement to motivate and align agency and client interests</td><td>Agency Contract and Auditing</td><td>Determine contract terms and conditions. Ensure full compliance.</td></tr>
<tr><td>Agency Compensation</td><td>Determine best approach to fair and equitable compensation, negotiate agency fees and payment terms.</td></tr>
<tr><td rowspan="2">The right input and feedback process to yield optimal results and value from the partnership</td><td>Workload Planning and Agency Briefing</td><td>Define scope of work and workload. Monitor and improve consistently.</td></tr>
<tr><td>Performance Evaluation and Management</td><td>Conduct regular performance evaluation and drive joint improvement plans.</td></tr>
</table>

Typical Agency Management Responsibilities

- Should the agency responsible for our creative also be chartered with media planning and buying?
- Will the same agency approach for PR work for social media?
- Should we consolidate all activities under one integrated, full service agency? Or should we diversify and hire a stable of highly specialized agencies?
- Should we concentrate our work with agencies from the same holding companies? How would we want to benefit?
- Do we need a separate agency to handle digital marketing?
- Should we consider doing some of that work in-house?
- How often should we re-evaluate our approach? Against what criteria?

- Which agency should be assigned to what brand or line of business?
- Should we pursue retained or project-by-project relationships?
- How do we best support our go-to-market requirements across all the regions in which we do business?
- How will we define success for the company's agency model?
- Should we optimize for flexibility or efficiency?
- What's the contingency plan if something were to quickly go sideways with the agency/ies? How do we mitigate the risks?

Whether advertisers are in financial services, packaged goods, or pharmaceutical, whether they are part of a large multinational or a medium-size domestic company, have a centralized or decentralized approach to marketing, or market to consumers or businesses, their agency needs will vary significantly. Some companies may even require multiple agency models and a unique portfolio of agencies to serve the many, diverse needs of their organization.

Answers to these questions will provide insight into the type of agency model(s) best suited to support each distinct circumstance. Further, they will inform the way these relationships must be contractually, financially, and operationally managed. This is where critical decisions are made on alignment of agencies to business needs by discipline or brands.

Client Viewpoint

"Clients must be as integrated as they expect their agencies to be. There are too many silos today on either side. Everything must be integrated. Agencies tend to mirror their clients but if the client doesn't lead in this area, then agencies won't follow."

SUSAN MARKOWICZ, Global Advertising Agency Manager, Ford Motor Company

Agency management is responsible for establishing clear objectives, and for selecting and implementing the best agency solution for the company. For example, an advertiser may choose to designate a lead agency for a particular brand or for a particular discipline. Following up with clear rules of engagement for agencies and for the marketing organization is particularly important as well. Agency management decides how agency partnerships should be managed and the company's operating principles on how to work effectively with them. For more information, see chapter 4.

Agency Search and Selection

Searching for and selecting the best mix of agencies on your roster is another critical agency management responsibility. It requires a solid understanding of what the company needs from its agencies and how to conduct a rigorous, efficient, and collaborative search that gets to the right outcome: an agency partner with the best competencies, experience, talent and resources to meet or exceed expectations. For companies with high agency turnover or expanding needs, having well-honed skills in-house or a strong, independent consultant to help with this pivotal task, proves to be an especially handy skill when it turns into an activity undertaken more than once every couple of years. Agency reviews and searches have become so frequent in today's dynamic environment that some best practices have emerged, setting up standards to which both clients and agencies can adhere.

Client Viewpoint

"We want to be considered our agency's preferred client. We want their people to say 'I want to work on the Campbell Soup business.' This means treating them with respect, as partners, and giving them challenges that inspire them to think in fresh terms. This is how you get the best possible talent on your business."

KEVIN PARHAM, Director Global Advertising, Campbell Soup

Clients must consider the most important criteria, whether they are core competencies, experience, the client portfolio, the culture and personality of the agency or any other criteria, by which they plan to review and select the best possible match for their needs. Assign this responsibility to someone with inadequate experience and your search can turn into a disaster, a wasteful exercise for everyone involved with a questionable and often unsupported outcome.

Clients may decide to hire an agency search consultant with an intimate knowledge of the marketplace. Doing so can speed up the search process, introduce efficiency and increase the client's likelihood of finding the best agency match. Yet search consultants will still need to interface with the multiple contacts at the client and receive strategic guidance and responsive support. Regardless of whether a search consultant is involved, someone senior will need to be appointed to orchestrate the entire review process, ensuring partnership with key internal stakeholders. It is imperative that this role be played by subject matter experts in agency management since this is where ownership and accountability for that relationship will ultimately reside. Once an agency has been hired, agency management is on point to ensure an efficient and streamlined on-boarding of the new agency. For more information, see chapter 5.

Agency Contract and Auditing

Like any other business relationship, the financial and service agreement between clients and agencies must be captured in a contract of some sort. No matter how tempting, no work should ever be initiated without a contract in place. The contract is typically supported by a number of addendums which flesh out the details such as scope of work, staffing plans, rate cards, and other relevant documentation.

Taking time up front to establish clear shared expectations and legal parameters for the newly formed relationship ensures that the partnership can quickly move into execution mode with confidence that both parties' interests are protected. It may also prevent both parties from falling into potentially costly litigation proceedings over misunderstandings that could have been prevented from the start. Often negotiated as multi-year contracts, contracts and their addenda provide clarification and protection about a number of important business and legal considerations including confidentiality, competitive conflicts, code of conduct, and insurance.

Client Viewpoint

"The whole industry is facing a number of challenges, from dealing with the issue of IP ownership but also value based compensation and sequential liability. In the end, it's about having clear expectations, scope and roles with your agencies."

SHERRY ULSH, Director Global Marketing Finance and Procurement, Burger King Corp.

These clauses based on the size of the relationship can be fairly complex and will require careful business and legal consideration. In the best scenario, the agency management team member directly interfaces with the company's legal department and facilitates the back and forth process between the respective legal teams and the agency relationship owners. If there are disagreements about the business terms, agency management leads intervene to hopefully reach mutually satisfying terms. Typical contentious terms such as termination clause, noncompete, and IP ownership or licensing are often business requirements, rather than legal in nature. As a result, they may require further input or decisions from the company's business stakeholders.

Although finalizing a contract can require the active involvement and support of other internal departments like IT and finance, having the right contract terms in place will ultimately fall under the agency management team's responsibility—whether it sits within Procurement or Marketing. Ensuring full contract compliance through occasional audits is also a key responsibility of agency management. For more information, see chapter 6.

Agency Compensation

There are numerous ways to structure agency compensation agreements. Companies often ask themselves such questions as: "Which compensation method is most beneficial to both parties?" and "What compensation method will encourage both parties to behave in the best interest of the relationship?" or "How do we ensure agency compensation motivates the agency to do what's right for the client?"

Why is it so challenging for clients and agencies to come up with the perfect answer? There are many permutations of compensation methods, all with distinct advantages and potential tradeoffs that must be carefully evaluated. Clients must model and evaluate a range of scenarios to decide which path will yield the best outcome short and long term for the relationship. In doing so, the agency management team must reconcile the needs of different parts of the company such as marketing and finance in order to derive most value. In the end, both parties must feel that the agreed compensation is fair, competitive, and motivating. Clearly, what's fair to the client and to the agency can be diametrically different.

Similarly, what seems reasonable to finance and marketing might also be diametrically different: Marketing wants a Lamborghini V10-powered coupé to win the competitive race but finance would rather deploy a fuel-efficient Toyota Prius. These can be controversial topics and subject to endless internal and external negotiations. In the end, no two contracts are alike. The agency wants terms that are conducive to the agency doing its best work and assigning its best talent to the client account. Getting it right often requires benchmarking and arranging to audit agency expenses to guarantee a certain level of cost competitiveness. As new performance and value-based practices emerge, the agency management team must assess the company's alternatives and find the best compensation methods to get to the right outcome.

Agency compensation is also about how clients manage agency-related expenses, a responsibility shared with the finance organization. Because cash flow is a vital bloodstream for agencies, the flow and timing of payment significantly influences the relationship. Small client relationships may only require tracking agency expenses and ensuring prompt payment. For large, multi-national relationships, agency-related expenses require additional management supervision to handle efficiently and in a timely manner a sizeable number of transactions in multiple worldwide locations as well as dealing with financial concerns such as foreign exchange rates, VAT, hedging, AVBs, media credits and pre-payments. For more information, see chapter 7.

Workload Planning and Agency Briefing

Workload planning is the essential process of identifying and cataloging the work to be done, articulating client expectations as precisely as possible through the agency briefing process, and ensuring that the agency is able to assign resources where they are most needed to carry out the mission at hand. It also happens to be one the most challenging tasks faced by clients today. Clients are 100% obligated to accurately define their objectives, spell out their marketing plans, and scope the work asked of the agency. If they don't, clients will end up with unnecessary levels of re-briefings and creative rework that will burn through the budget and cost them dearly.

According to a study conducted by marketing consultancy Jones & Bonevac,[19] the majority of agency executives surveyed said less than 40% of client briefs communicate clearly what's expected of the agency, and of that number roughly one out of three said only 1% to 10% of briefs provide clear performance or success metrics. According to the survey briefs are also constantly changing. It points out that 75% of agency execs see client briefs go through an average of up to five significant revisions after the project has been kicked off. This can result in significant inefficiencies, higher agency fees, and budget waste. Why is the potentially most impactful thing a client can do to gain most value from its agency relationships also the most difficult to do?

Client Viewpoint

"As part of Campbell Soup's training, we use a variety of tools to improve the quality of our engagement with agencies. For example, we conduct role-playing exercises so everyone gets to be the agency. Everyone laughs when we start, but soon they realize how challenging the job of pitching creative ideas can be. This is very enlightening."

KEVIN PARHAM, Director Global Advertising, Campbell Soup

Many companies have a very difficult time planning, prioritizing, and scoping what they want their agency to do in advance of the work's commencement. This is often for valid reasons, such as delayed product launches, sudden competitive threats, or unexpected budget cuts. However, workload planning must be completed early enough to allow the agency to adequately staff the account with the best talent for the business and be ready to handle the work volume and type of services required.

Effective Agency Briefing is equally critical. A successful agency/client engagement hinges on a clear definition of what is expected, when it is to be delivered, and how the work will get done. This is the essence of a solid engagement and this is why agency management is instrumental in establishing an efficient process to enable the exchange of information between the two companies. This ensures that the agency is client-ready and the client is agency-ready before the start of any engagement. For more information, see chapter 8.

Establishing a Framework for Success

Is the relationship living up to its promises? As in any relationship, it is expected that issues will arise from time to time; a few things will need to be tweaked to run more efficiently. Since we're dealing with human beings interacting with each other, the intangibles are a very real part of what we consider when evaluating the quality and effectiveness of a relationship. It is the responsibility of agency management to monitor the overall agency/client performance and relationship health by instituting a standard and regular performance review process with the agencies based on key performance indicators (KPIs) that have been agreed upon by both parties. Based on these results, improvement areas can be identified on both sides and action plans put forward and monitored to ensure continual improvement and healthy productive relationships. For more information, see chapter 9.

Client Viewpoint

"Agencies help manage the complexity of the work going through the system. Agency Management plays a significant role in making sure that the work is being done well and those partnerships are evaluated fairly."

MOLLIE WESTON
Director Agency Management Operations, Best Buy

Although these functions outlined on the previous pages are the most common responsibilities held by the agency management discipline, its role does not end here. Agency management has direct and structured accountability to the company's senior management internally and to leadership at the agencies. As such, it's a vital, albeit less obvious, charter to conduct regular reviews of the account, organize cross-agency summits, and keep an eye out for other relationship building events that help ensure everyone is on the same page.

The client's agency management team may conduct regular meetings with senior management on either side of the fence to discuss the health of the whole relationship—what's working well, what could be working better, the overall quality and business impact of the work, agency vitals such as payments and cash flow, key hires and departures, team morale, and other operational details. It is an ideal time to discuss business priorities, any shifts happening internally or externally, and to check in on long-term goals for the partnership.

Agency management also partners with its agency partners to guarantee that the account is consistently staffed with the right mix of qualified, client-ready staff with sufficient training and experience to help the company achieve its goals. The agency business is primarily a talent business. This is why clients must pay close attention to the experience, seniority, and skills of the staff that the agency assigns to the relationship.

Hiring and retaining key talent is what makes or breaks agencies and their ability to keep accounts. Agencies are only as good as each of their people. Clients want minimal disruption or personnel turnover in their business. Is the account fully staffed? Are the account resources too junior, too senior, or too distracted to carry out the work? Do we have the right mix of talent? Weak or frequently changing agency staff results in poor outcomes for the client and loss of institutional knowledge. It causes inefficiencies with sizeable financial impact (severance and legal expenses, on-boarding and training costs, learned lessons forgotten, and so forth).

It is the agency's responsibility to staff the account with the best mix of agency resources, a difficult task often lacking rigorous methodology. Agencies have to translate the client's scope of work into a well-tuned yet profitable staffing plan and must factor in a number of variables when determining the right mix of resources. Many of them are subjective at best, such as how efficient or inefficient the client is at approving work or the degree of clarity about a particular client initiative.

In turn, reviewing and approving the way the account is staffed and trained, making sure its people have been carefully prepared, and monitoring the effective use of these resources, is the client's responsibility. A company's ability to ramp up agency personnel quickly and effectively will directly impact the quality of the agency work and client/agency productivity.

Agency staff needs frequent and unfettered access to information relevant to the work they are doing on the client's behalf—guidelines, policies, brand assets, product briefings and research, internal tools, and any information that can facilitate a seamless and productive engagement. Providing training to new and existing agency staff must be paramount to keep all staff refreshed and updated on potential changes to the company's business, competitive environment, strategic initiatives, standards, and policies.

"The Buck Stops Here"

President Harry S. Truman's desk in his White House office bore a sign with the phrase "The Bucks Stops Here."[20] Originated from from a phrase used in the game of poker and made in 1945 in the Federal Reformatory at El Reno, Oklahoma, the sign mounted on its walnut base left no doubt as to who was in charge and who had ultimate responsibility for making and dealing with the consequences of important decisions. As it relates to the management of agencies, the accountability question remains: Who has "the buck stops here" responsibility within a client organization for the vibrancy and efficacy of business-critical partnerships?

All too often, the lack of ownership and accountability for agency performance is itself responsible for the failure of an agency relationship. Either no one seems to be on point or too many people have conflicting agendas, leaving agencies wondering which decision maker to turn to. One individual or a designated agency management team to coordinate and facilitate the effective management of the relationship will minimize confusion and increase ownership for success, which in turn will significantly strengthen the partnership.

Client Viewpoint

"The marketing procurement role is to act as a strategic buffer between the agencies and the needs of the company, answering to both. We like to think about ourselves as another informational point for the agencies and for the business."

JEFF DEVON, Director Global Marketing, HP

The discipline of agency management is based on a set of fundamental concepts and best practices that anyone in the company should become familiar with, regardless of company size or functional responsibilities. Everyone in the company has some responsibility for fully leveraging the investment made in its agency partnerships. This is an opportunity every project or budget owner must take seriously to make the best use of company resources and deliver measurable business results.

Agency management must be treated as an essential business, procurement and marketing discipline, regardless of whether a company feels it can afford to dedicate resources to it or chooses instead to add that role to someone strategically placed within the company.

Important agency-related decisions are often vetted and approved by a senior leadership team or by a virtual team of key stakeholders from multiple client organizations and corporate functions. From hiring a new firm, negotiating a contract, to effectively briefing the agency on a new project or getting the best possible work from them, agency management responsibilities require a mix of fundamental skills in business, marketing, people management, and finance. The agency management function has often historically lacked proper structure, planning, and operational rigor, leading to time-wasting reviews, disappointing results, and a host of other inefficiencies that can end up costing companies as much as a third more of their total agency spend.

So who within your organization are the best suited candidates to take on the agency management role? What skills do they need to succeed in the role? A candidate is likely to be more successful in the role when he or she has extensive client and agency experience under his or her belt. Having worked for an agency at some point in their career will provide them with a unique perspective that is difficult to obtain otherwise.

It also reassures agencies to know that they are interacting with someone who understands their perspective. These range from understanding the marketing challenges faced by the company to keen insight into the primary levers that drive revenue and profitability. Having operational knowledge of what it takes to get things done helps ensure the role is tuned to the requirements that the agency solution must be designed to meet.

The agency management role requires a diverse set of business skills and professional experience, on both the client and agency side to enable smooth, profitable, results-driving operations between the two organizations. The last thing any advertiser needs is an agency distracted from doing its best work because of inattentive briefings, personnel clashes, or payment delays due to lack of thoughtful planning and anticipatory internal coordination. The role requires people of well rounded experience, with a solid reputation for building strong partnerships and a passion for designing a state-of-the-art agency capital management system that drives business and financial performance and improves operational effectiveness.

Client Viewpoint

"A procurement professional has a different perspective than a marketing professional may have. Procurement meets with the agencies perhaps a few times a year and their focus is on reducing costs. They think of marketing as an expense to the business. The marketing organization offers a very different perspective. We engage with our agencies almost daily. We think of marketing as an investment in growing our business. In the end, we are buying creativity, not just a hard commodity. From our point of view it's not only about cost. It's about the quality of the talent the agency provides. The challenge is in reconciling those two different perspectives."

DELMAR WYATT
Director Advertising Operations, Qwest Communications

Advancements in the Field of Agency Management

The recent emergence of discipline-specific technologies in the field of agency management is hugely promising and is likely to see accelerated adoption in businesses of all sizes, harmonizing processes and automating tasks that were previously manual and labor-intensive and prone to error, such as:

- Agency compensation and financial management
- Workflow management systems
- Content/asset management and distribution systems

- Agency performance evaluation and scorecards
- Scope of work management and agency briefing.

These powerful tools and solutions are now coming of age, fueled by innovation in the field of cloud computing, system integration, software-as-service marketing automation, and business re-engineering and productivity improvement. As they evolve they have the potential to dramatically reduce the time and effort required to administer these activities. By reducing administration costs, improving controls and traceability, increasing productivity, enhancing transparency and executive decision-making capability, they can free you to focus on strategic priorities and outcomes.

They can also increase agency information accessibility to a wider number of stakeholders with the company, further advancing the understanding and practice of responsible agency management inside client organizations. However, simple access to these solutions is no substitute for common-sense practices and sound business judgment.

As in any relationship, agency management is more a journey than a destination. Companies are encouraged to take a "crawl, walk, run" approach to building their own agency management function to avoid any missteps and to ensure a balanced investment of time and resources. The function is inherently deeply influenced and shaped by the work of other departments. It requires cross-group collaboration and aligned commitments.

In the end, getting greatest value from agency partnerships is not only about agency management but about leadership. Leadership of both agencies, and what the company organizes itself to ask of agencies, is about inspiring and motivating talent. It's about pushing the limits, focusing on what truly matters, taking occasional risks and creating an environment that makes smart people want to go the extra mile to fulfill a shared vision. Leadership in agency management is what drives greatness and delivers meaningful results that both client and agency can be proud of.

{Taking Immediate Action}

TOP 5

BEST PRACTICES TO HARNESS THE MADNESS

❶ Build an agency management competency within your company, by assigning a seasoned individual or team to fulfill that role. Encourage everyone in the company—whether in marketing or procurement—to take accountability on how to realize most value from these investments and relationships. Ensure complete management support to make and enforce agency-related decisions.

❷ Define roles and responsibilities with key stakeholders. Partner with senior executive management, marketing, procurement, legal, IT and finance to understand their requirements and dependencies and ensure a smooth integration with internal stakeholders groups.

❸ Set clear objectives and success metrics to ensure all parties are working toward the same goals, and effectively leveraging each other Review results and insights together and identify shared action plans to drive constant improvement.

❹ Take full accountability for the partnership. Serve as an internal advocate for the agency. Mediate or arbitrate as needed. Showcase the great work done by the agency and draw attention to the results generated from the partnership.

❺ Never compromise business performance, creativity, or staffing quality for arbitrary, short-term cost savings. Focus instead on driving up the value-add equation and turn agency relationships into powerful growth engines for your company.

4 MARC, CATHERINE, AND JOHN

Building a sound agency strategy

"Strategy is the art of making use of time and space. I am less concerned about the latter than the former. Space we can recover, lost time never."

—Napoleon Bonaparte
Political leader and military strategist

Marc Pritchard of Procter & Gamble (P&G), Catherine Coughlin of AT&T, and John Stratton of Verizon Communications all have something in common. Sure, all three of them have been long-term company employees with impeccable track records before taking on their current roles. Sure, they are well-respected marketing leaders of global marketing powerhouses in their respective industries: Marc Pritchard is Global Brand Building Officer for one of the world's largest and strongest portfolios of trusted brand names (Pampers, Tide, Ariel, Crest, and Olay) in over 80 countries around the globe. Catherine Coughlin is Senior Executive Vice President and Global Marketing Officer of the world's largest telecommunications company. And John Stratton is Executive Vice-President and Chief Marketing Officer of Verizon Communications, one of the global leaders in delivering innovation in communications, information, and entertainment.

For a few consecutive years, they have been the top three marketers in terms of ad spending in the United States. Together they invest hundreds of millions of dollars in advertising, marketing, or communication activities in the global marketplace, handled by a handful of talented agencies. But what they share is immensely more critical to their companies' success: Despite the constant business frenzy, they have developed a sturdy agency strategy that serves all their communication needs and enables them, through the use of carefully selected and managed agency partnerships, to fully flex their marketing muscle and aggressively compete. How do Marc, Catherine, and John actually do it? They have carefully assessed their agency needs and determined the ideal roster of agencies to lead them to success. They are not alone.

How are P&G, Johnson & Johnson, Macy's, Wal-Mart Stores, Inc., AT&T, MasterCard, Burger King, Verizon, Intel and other brilliant companies harnessing the madness and getting most value from their investment? They have chosen an agency strategy that has been engineered to support their business goals. The essence of strategy is clarity of purpose and designing a clear path to achieve that purpose.

It's truly insane to think that billions of marketing dollars are still channeled through randomly selected agencies by clients of all sizes without a clear agency strategy, and with no clear path to turn their agencies into powerful allies. Developing a sound agency strategy is by far the most critical ingredient to implementing a successful agency model that drives short and long term results. A successfully-implemented agency model in turn ensures that clients get the most from their agencies. Surprisingly enough, clients often make poor, on-the-fly decisions—and then justify them using an episodic set of criteria—because they lack a well-throughout plan on how to accomplish their objectives. Until recently, companies have rarely invested the critical time and effort needed to define and agree on an overarching strategy before making important decisions such as starting a new agency search or determining the right mix of agency services needed.

Client Viewpoint

"I've seen agency/client relationships going on for decades. Marketers are not always satisfied. It is challenging to get fresh thinking. Agencies may also act as if there are entitled to the business. How many people do we know have been married for 25 years? If agencies experience high turnover, how do clients benefit from the continuity of a long term partnership?"

BRETT COLBERT
Global Manager, Procurement Advertising, Anheuser Busch InBev

As a result, they end up losing in-market time they can never recover. They find themselves without the luxury to build for the long term when they just have weeks or months to make their mark. The fanatical Chief Marketing Officers' (CMOs) high turnover phenomenon leads to short-term marketing strategy which, in turn, results in short-term agency decisions. The absence of a clear agency strategy can only slow a company down, adding confusion and uncertainty at a time when the entire enterprise needs to be aligning behind one common vision instead of random tactics.

Where is Your Mountain? Are You Climbing It?

The concept of Agency Strategy and Portfolio Management can be best defined as the company's key priorities and associated actions that contribute to a quality, effective, and efficient agency resource plan that drives desired business outcomes in a prescribed timeframe (for example, 12-24 months). In

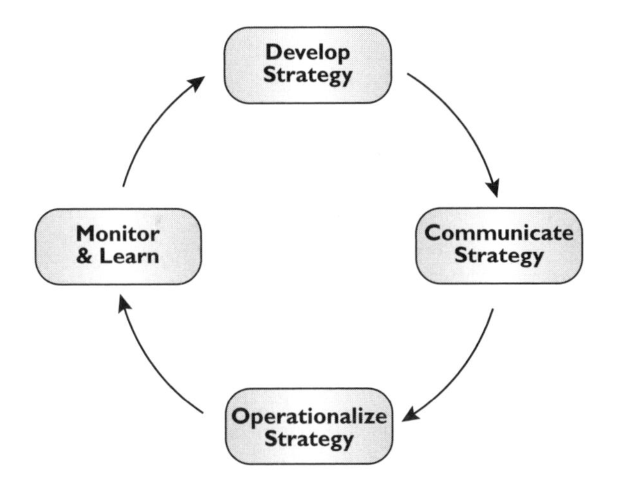

Closed-Loop Agency Strategy Life Cycle

short, strategy provides clarity, focus, and direction and aligns people and projects behind a common goal. It is also the process by which clients articulate measurable objectives and lock in resources to achieve them.

Without a clear and compelling strategy, any agency-related decision is doomed to be sub-optimal or, even worse, fail miserably down the road despite the large sums invested. Continued underperformance in this area is commonly due to objectives not being clearly spelled out or agreed upon, and disconnects about how to best support company priorities resulting in breakdowns between strategy and execution.

The diagram above describes how to maintain a firm and continuous link between the different components of a successful agency strategy.

A closed-loop agency strategy makes certain that at least a minimum set of procedures and controls are in place end-to-end to deliver according to the agreed strategy. You don't need to be a Macy's, Burger King or MasterCard to apply these basic fundamental steps toward having a sound strategy. A client starts by assessing its marketing needs, developing measurable objectives, and then translating them into strategic initiatives and tactical action plans. Once objectives are set, the client absolutely must communicate internally to align all stakeholders and ensure buy-in to the strategic direction. Then the client maps out the operational plans and resources to catalyze the plans into motion. The client must ensure plans are on track by continuously monitoring progress made according to objectives and learning from successes and failures. A periodical (quarterly or bi-annual) reassessment of the strategy is necessary to reevaluate assumptions, assess marker dynamics, and refine understanding of key success factors. Here's how.

Strategy Development

Advertisers want to capitalize on the value of a consistent, well coordinated agency strategy that allows them to meet their business and marketing objectives. Developing such a strategy requires at least a minimum level of research and exploratory work and more importantly, clarity about what one is aiming for. How do we get started?

Companies must first conduct a thorough assessment of their agency needs. You should ask: What do we need the agency to do that we cannot effectively do for ourselves? Interview stakeholders. Find out what competencies are needed. Discover what clients will value most in agencies, how they plan to leverage the agency's skills and talent. Draw upon insights gained from past successes and failures. Anticipate potential roadblocks such as talent gaps or budget limitations. Collect, analyze and apply this information to make better, smarter decisions about what kind of agency you're looking for. Having visibility into key competitors' agency rosters can also be helpful to understand potential agency conflicts and risks.

Client Viewpoint

"We have the responsibility to do strategic category reviews every 12 to 18 months. We are constantly looking at the quality and performance of our agency, the changes in our business needs, and changes in the marketplace, to evaluate whether or not we have the right number and the right type of agencies on our roster."

MICHAEL E. THYEN
Director, Marketing and Sales Global Procurement, Eli Lilly and Company

There are a number of ways by to collect competitive data, including trade publications and agencies' Websites where case studies and client rosters are openly posted and available. You might want to know which agencies are working with your competitors, what the nature of their relationship is, (exclusive or not, retained, or project based), their scope (geographic or functional, domestic or global, PR, digital, or events, etc.) Who knows? If you see a magical combination, you may want to attempt to hire away an agency from the competition. By forcing an agency to resign a competitor's account to take on yours, one can potentially capture years of category knowledge and transferrable best practices to undermine the competition.

Client Viewpoint

"The most strategic agency relationship these days is with the media agency. Because it is so complex and so much money is involved, clients think twice about moving their business."

LYNNE SEID, Partner Global Marketing Officers Practice, Heidrick & Struggles

On the other hand, great work in an adjacent category can suggest potential success in yours. Are you willing to train up an agency on the dynamics of your category? Or do you need to hit the ground running, with talent already versed in what it takes to win in your segment? The result of your analysis is the initial development of a strategy and agency model—a construct of the mix of agency services needed and their alignment with the business—that delivers according to the company's collective needs, and that the internal stakeholder team can rally behind. Often easier said than done, developing an agency strategy typically results from clients answering these fundamental questions:

- What business or marketing priorities will the agency model be supporting? What measurable objectives are most important to the client?
- What professional or specialty skills are most needed to complement and deliver on internal marketing talent and resources?
- Should the company assign a "lead creative agency" to rally behind one idea across disciplines? Should the company consider doing some of its work in-house?
- Should the company seek to work with a large network-affiliated agency or a small independent boutique agency?
- What criteria should be used to align an agency to a product/brand? Who will be the ultimate decision-maker?
- Where should digital, interactive and social media expertise come from in the existing roster? Should the company invest in building this skill set internally or externally, or both?
- Is there adequate endorsement and support of the agency strategy and selected agencies at the executive level and a relatively consistent level of investment?
- How will the company measure the success of its agency strategy?

Clear, well-supported answers to these questions are essential to develop an agency plan for long-term success and to assemble a roster of agencies that will become the in-market firepower the company can rely on. The upfront time invested will always prove to save time and money and will be hugely beneficial in the end. It becomes the company roadmap to a shared definition of success with the agency/ies, no matter how big or small your company.

Aligning the company around a single agency strategy is not only a sound logical approach; it will prove to be vital to mutual success. It will become a priceless reference point when tough decisions will undoubtedly have to be made. It may lead to actions designed to strengthen the quality of the work, improve the client/agency engagement, drive greater cost-efficiencies, and build new agency and client team skills and capabilities.

However, if the chosen agency strategy doesn't address and deliver on real business challenges faced by the company, it will not receive the level of executive and staff attention and support it needs to flourish. Ideally, measurable objectives are established at the beginning of the fiscal year based on the business priorities required to achieve market, investor, or business expectations. Objectives focus on what needs to be done, when it needs to be done, how much needs to be invested in getting it done, and how to enforce accountabilities, increase transparency, and inform partnership opportunities.

Client Viewpoint

"We promote team collaboration with our agencies. Having key agency people here on site means that they are an integral part of our business and our culture. Agencies are always plugged in to what's on going here at Burger King Corp. That's the way we work."

CLAUDIA LEZCANO, Director of Advertising, Burger King Corp.

The annual agency plan—often a subset of the overall marketing communications plan—articulates how the company proposes to achieve its objectives, what agency model it will implement, and how to highlight specific activities that will be needed to carry out the mission. It's about making sure the right agency(ies) are doing the right assignments, effectively and efficiently.

It also provides actionable insight into the challenges faced by either the client or the agency. Clients need to give themselves at least one year to see the results of their agency investments before deciding if further agency adjustments are necessary. Any timeframe shorter than a year is likely to be premature and wasteful. A lot can happen in a year. However, if you do not set your sights on a spot on the horizon, you may never effectively leave port.

Agency Viewpoint

"Agencies can no longer afford to house every possible service under one roof. When agencies try to stand for everything, in the end, they stand for nothing."

TIM WILLIAMS, President, Ignition Consulting Group

The purpose of a sound agency strategy is to equip the company with an understanding of its top priorities that require external talent, and a clear plan for how the company will align itself to focus the energies of its agencies to achieve those goals. It's about driving the internal organizational alignment, clarity, and focus as well as mindfulness about choosing and readying the right agency/ies to achieve its goals. More importantly, it's about being one step ahead of the competition at all times.

Finding the Right Agency Strategy for Your Business

To determine the right agency model, clients will want to evaluate the breadth of options available and the implications each scenario may have for the company's marketing effectiveness, and for marcom integration, costs, speed to market, agility, process efficiencies, brand/message control, and internal resourcing, before deciding on the right one. Building a sound agency strategy comes down to the following considerations: the use of bundled or unbundled agency services, and determining whether these come from centralized or decentralized agency resources. Are you choosing to optimize for simplicity, seamless agency-led integration, and economies of scale, or are you choosing to optimize for choice and flexibility, client-led integration, and loosely controlled competition?

Client Viewpoint

"We invested in a portfolio approach to our agency roster, organized by discipline. The roster is the go to list for every brand in the company."

A LARGE ADVERTISER

Clients may choose to establish a relationship with an agency holding company, an agency network, an integrated agency, or a roster of independent agencies. Bundled services include holding-company or network-led models as well as integrated agency models where multiple expert services can be accessed through a single umbrella relationship. These centralized resources "under one roof" tend to organize themselves around streamlined client coordination and integration. Unbundled services include "lead agency" or "free form" agency models that provide more flexible agency options. Decentralized resources tend to focus on maximizing client flexibility and building best-in-class functional specializations.

Large agencies are built on economies of scale which can be critically important to clients with a global footprint or ambition. They can cross cultural lines, balancing client needs for global strategy with requirements for local relevancy and flexibility. But is flatter and leaner better? What do top brand advertisers such as Procter & Gamble, AT&T and Verizon Communications have in common? All three have formalized agency-of-record relationships which are aligned with one or multiple network holding companies to manage and optimize their multi-billion dollar advertising budgets.

Large companies have matrixed businesses with diverse needs. They cannot put all their eggs in the same agency basket. As a result, they use a number of agencies they align with according to business group or product category, either in or off network. They diversify their agency roster to test new capabilities, spread the workload, provide controlled competition, and motivate agencies to deliver their best product at all times. Whenever possible, they centralize their media buying needs through one agency media partnership to capitalize on economies of scale.

This led John Stratton at Verizon Communications to rethink its agency model and consolidate its agency roster from thirty-eight agencies to eight in 2007 with Interpublic taking the central stage with McCann Erickson Worldwide and Universal McCann.

Given its scale, is no surprise that one of the world's largest global advertisers, Proctor & Gamble Co., has chosen to tap into the largest network holding companies to run its advertising and marketing communications. Today these range from Publicis (Leo Burnett Worldwide, Publicis USA, Saatchi & Saatchi, Kaplan Thaler Group, MediaVest USA and Starcom MediaVest Group), to Omnicom (BBDO Worldwide, TBWA/Chiat/Day, DDB Worldwide, Integer Group) and WPP (Grey Worldwide) to share the majority of this gigantic account, with a few others such as Havas (Arnold Worldwide), Wieden & Kennedy, and Carat. AT&T's multi-billion agency business has done a large volume of work with Omnicom (BBDO Worldwide) for most of its brands including corporate and WPP (Mediaedge:cia) for media communications services and buying.

A number of smaller specialty agencies also have been reported to work on the account, including Razorfish, Digitas, Interbrand, Integer Group, and others. Verizon's Communications' account has been led by Interpublic Group of Companies. McCann Erickson Worldwide, MRM, R/GA and Universal McCann in addition to Publicis' Moxie Interactive, Zenith Media and others. Their roster of discipline-focused agencies is continually changing; the examples given are in constant flux, and are only meant to be illustrative of historic agency strategies.

Client Viewpoint

"Ford Motor Company has a network-holding based approach to its agency roster. The consolidation of agencies under the WPP virtual umbrella gives us single accountability, a single P&L to worry about, economies of scale and a single point of coordination."

SUSAN MARKOWICZ, Global Advertising Agency Manager, Ford Motor Company

In the end, building a sound agency strategy is a matter of setting a clear direction for the way a company is planning to create the most value from its agency partnerships and making sure it delivers according to its objectives. These decisions will typically be based on two dimensions: the options desired (both in breadth and depth) according to flexibility necessary in the agency roster and the type of cross-agency coordination desired, and whether this will be handled by the client internally or by the agency externally.

Deciding on the right agency model will mean that the client has conducted a self-assessment, has a reasonable understanding of what is required

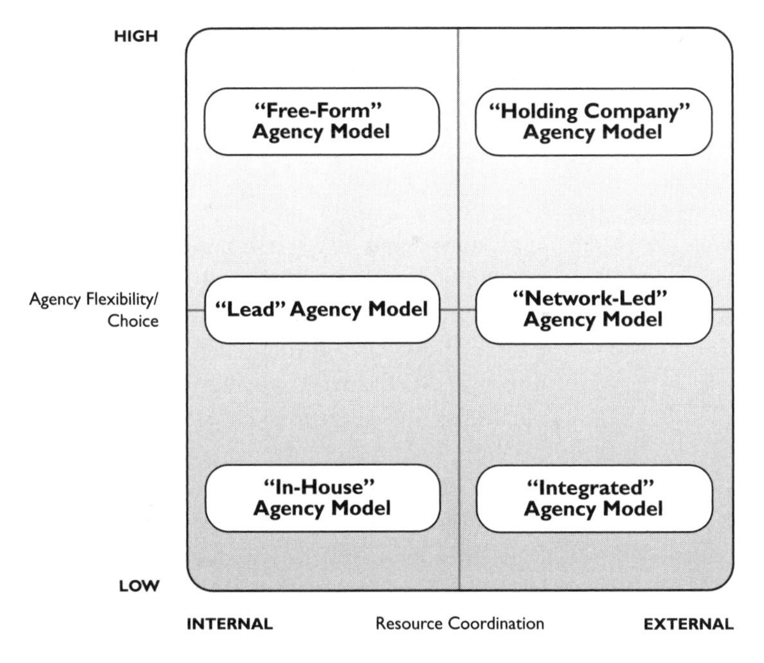

Key Considerations for Selecting the Right Agency Strategy

to meet its marketing objectives, and the agency management team has complete senior executive buy-in.

A number of alternatives for agency strategies have emerged and taken a strong foothold in recent years to meet the ever-changing and diverse needs of advertisers. Solutions dramatically vary from one holding company to another; they may even label them differently. Although there is no industry standard taxonomy for agency models, in the end they tend to all fall within one of the options shown in the figure above.

"Holding-Company" Agency Model

Holding companies serve as financial shells, designed as a model to avoid competitive client conflicts that have historically prevented them from pursuing business within a particular industry or product category due to current client rosters. The holding company also acts as a parent company, overseeing a portfolio of agency resources to meet the needs of a global mix of clients in need of multiple agencies. Under the holding company agency model, the client partners with a holding company (e.g., WPP Group, Omnicom Group, Interpublic Group of Cos, Publicis Groupe) to capitalize on the full range of discipline and segment-savvy capabilities offered across all of their agency networks and their operating units.

The holding company takes an active managerial role, managing the relationship, identifying needs, and bringing together the optimal mix of talent from anywhere in the holdings to service the client. This approach helps overcome organizational silos and disparate profit centers. The holding company handles the complexity of coordinating multiple agencies, networks, and disciplines across all geographic areas.

This agency model is best tailored for those global companies operating in multiple continents with large marketing spend, and that want (and can afford) choice, scale, and flexibility. Although it can be a powerful solution to clients requiring a vast and rich set of capabilities, the model's efficiencies must outweigh the cost of managing the inherent risk and complexity of this operating model. Holding-company led reviews by clients like HSBC, Bank of America, Nokia, Samsung and Intel have generated much interest over the years.

Client Viewpoint

"We have relationships with agencies as well as long last standing relationships with some agency people who have moved agencies to agencies. It's a people business after all."

CLAUDIA LEZCANO, Director of Advertising, Burger King Corp.

In the Dell $4.5 billion global marketing services review in 2007, different network holding approaches were at play to consolidate the client's existing roster of 800 agencies: IPG's standard approach of bringing together different agencies from varied disciplines vs. WPP's approach that involves the creation of a cross-discipline unit dedicated to Dell. In the case of Dell, on Sunday, December 2, 2007, after a seven-month battle between the two agency holding company titans, the decision was announced: WPP won over IPG for Dell's three-year contract. Then followed the announcement by WPP that it was creating a brand new agency, ambitiously called "the greatest agency in the world."

Client Viewpoint

"Agencies must embrace cross-agency collaboration. At the holding company level, it means tapping into the best possible talent to serve the needs of the client. Motivating the best talent to not just work our business but really drive our business is what we're interested in at J&J."

JAMES R. ZAMBITO, Global Marketing Group Controller, Johnson & Johnson

Although the enthusiastically-conceived project ultimately appeared to face a number of challenges, the creation of the highly-hyped agency, eventually named Enfatico, spoke creatively to the needs of sophisticated global clients like Dell which couldn't be easily met with any collage of current agencies.

In a different approach, in August 2005 Bank of America selected Omnicom to handle its marketing and media services business based on a core team of Omnicom agencies including Live Technology, Organic, BBDO Worldwide, Javelin, OMD Worldwide, and others. Two years later, Bank of America decided to end its exclusive relationship with the network holding company and put its media planning and buying duties into review, signaling that clients such as Bank of America may occasionally break the model and seek instead a roster of best-in-class outside of their existing resources.

In the case of HSBC, the company's brand position demanded agencies who could deliver local executions that reinforce the global strategy. WPP's proposed ability to offer a global solution ("teamHSBC") that leveraged the resources of its multiple operating companies as well as their shared knowledge allowed them to capture the $600M HSBC account.

Holding companies have a compelling opportunity to tap into their network to assemble teams of individuals suited to best meet the needs of their prospective clients. They can create new units dedicated to service clients by combining efforts and resources from multiple agencies, as in the case of Kraft Foods "One Team" that included MediaVest and Digitas and was created in early 2010 to handle the client's global media account, or Blockbuster's DDB Entertainment Unit that combined youth-marketing agency Uproar with other various DDB properties. Under this model, holding companies seek efficiencies across their operations, encouraging their operating units to work together to further strengthen their capabilities. If they don't perform to the client's expectations, the holding company is accountable to secure alternatives within their broader network.

The primary client benefits of the holding company model are:

- Brand consistency
- Breadth and depth of agency talent
- Consistent and streamlined processes
- Elimination of overlap and redundant activities
- Resources and infrastructure
- Volume discounts and economies of scale
- Simplification (for example, one contract, one P&L, consistent reports)
- Reduced client coordination (even more so if a client had multiple agencies in multiple regions)
- Staffing and operational synergies and efficiencies

On the downside, this type of agency model is usually a massive undertaking, highly publicized and scrutinized, and can be quite difficult to implement and support without major hiccups. They typically require long-term commitments on both sides. Furthermore, clients have less flexibility, switching costs are higher, and the lack of competition can limit a client's ability to benchmark and negotiate effectively. Holding companies often acquire agencies for their clients to move the partnership forward by combining a broader suite of agency assets. Holding-company models are popular for large global-scale clients with competitive conflicts that cannot be easily resolved within existing agency or network offerings.

Client Viewpoint

"Agencies should find ways to make it easy for clients to work with them ... Large agencies have to figure out how to better leverage their portfolio on their client's behalf. Clients want to have access to top notch "out of the box" thinkers without having to struggle through a series of one-off contract negotiations."

JEFF DEVON, Director Global Marketing, HP

"Network-Led" Agency Model

The network-led agency model is most appealing to somewhat larger clients that need a strategic partnership with an agency network (such as Ogilvy & Mather Worldwide, DDB Worldwide, McCann Worldgroup) but do not need to go beyond a particular network and tap additional resources from a global holding company. The agency network is typically composed of multiple, unified, specialized operating units that the client can easily access, providing access to a large range of agency services and key assets within a given agency network under one contract. One agency leads the account, typically the "creative" agency (the agency that develops the core messaging with the broadest exposure) in that particular agency network, and coordinates behind the scenes how to leverage their network resources in a smooth and effective way for the client. It may wrestle with operational silos at times, depending on how well integrated and cohesive the network is in practical terms.

The holding-company and network-led model both present very similar benefits to clients: a one-stop shop to drive brand consistency and marketing integration, and economies of scale while still offering access to a wide set of competencies and talent.

Both models can reduce the coordination and orchestration role played by the client in other more decentralized models ... at a cost. For clients concerned about the holding-company's ability to bring together disparate agency resources and operate the new combined entities effectively, a network-led model can be a great alternative. Agency networks are set up to operate this way by design and can quickly assemble resources to service a client's evolving needs.

"Integrated" Agency Model

Also referred to as a "full-service" model, this is the most popular agency model among clients of all sizes looking to better orchestrate all their marketing and communication activities with a single agency, under one roof, with increased brand clarity and consistency in look, feel, and messaging. An advertiser typically relies on one fully integrated agency of record (AOR) to service all of its needs and realize organizational efficiencies by minimizing duplicative client-side efforts. The integrated AOR is a full-service agency at the core, with multiple departments fulfilling the services that might otherwise need to be sourced individually.

Client Viewpoint

"Cross agency collaboration can be an on-going challenge, because agencies are highly competitive by nature. However, we continually reinforce the need to operate as one team. All agencies should be involved in the ideation stage. It must be a collaborative, team effort."

MICHAEL FITZGERALD
Associate Director, Business Advertising, AT&T Inc.

Contrary to the holding-company or network-led model (which are also one-stop shops, with the holding company or the network agency connecting the dots in the background to make it seamless to their clients), all the services are sourced from within one single multi-disciplined agency. Integrated agencies (for example, Saatchi & Saatchi, DDB Worldwide) bring cross-functional disciplines—advertising, media, interactive, direct response, PR, promotions, and so forth—together under one branded offering and within a single agency. They might occasionally elect to go outside the agency to outsource work they might not have deep enough expertise in, but they handle these contractors and vendor relationships directly.

Working with and trying to manage multiple agencies can dilute a company's brand equity over time. This sort of command-and-control approach allows clients to manage all agency activities centrally with greater brand consistency. Prestigious account consolidations such as Sears' $600M+ account with Young & Rubicam have made the front pages of newspapers as global companies look to a few large-scale agencies to consolidate all their work under one umbrella. The primary objective is to bring brand consistency to their portfolio of communications, speak as one voice to their numerous audiences around the world, reduce the noise associated with random messaging, and harmonize customer communications.

Dealing with a single agency relationship allows clients to invest more time on clarifying objectives. This eventually leads to a better agency product by not having to spend a large amount of time coordinating multiple agency relationships, looking for ways to foster collaboration among them, and having to deal with separate entities with different operating processes. It also provides better economies of scale, an increased cost efficiency obtained by leveraging resources within a single agency, avoiding staffing redundancies and consolidating overhead.

Having one single point of contact can significantly reduce complexity for the client, reducing administrative efforts and costs on the client side. Small- to medium-size clients may have only one agency they rely on for all their advertising, marketing or communication needs. If all of their needs are adequately addressed through an integrated model, this is a good way to go since it is less labor-intensive for the client and less demanding. Having more than one agency may not ultimately make sense economically or practically. The concept of "agency monogamy" is not for everyone. It is particularly of great value to small to medium-size clients under constant pressure to drive brand consistency, and land fully-integrated campaigns while streamlining the use of client and agency resources.

"Lead" Agency Models

Often called "unbundled" agency model, clients may consider partnering with multiple agencies if the business is large enough to justify it and if the client wants to maintain a healthy level of competition among its agencies. Clients are increasingly exploring multiple agency relationships vs. the single end-to-end full service lead-agency approach of prior decades. It's nothing new to large global companies like Walt Disney, Sony, Motorola, and Coca-Cola that have for years had multiple agencies working on their business. It's relatively new to smaller size companies who are willing to trade off the ease of one-stop shopping for multiple "best-in-class" agencies.

Client Viewpoint

"We have retained agencies of record. This is a part of what we call the agency partnership. It goes beyond the single agency model. We have deep partnerships across a number of agencies. Our agency structure is evolving as our needs are changing. We want the right mix of generalists and specialists in our roster."

SHERRY ULSH, Director Global Marketing Finance and Procurement, Burger King Corp.

Many companies want to have the ability to load-balance the work, pick the right agency with the right skills for a given assignment, and keep the agencies on their toes so no one takes their business for granted. Under this model, the client has already selected a number of individual agencies in various and often complementary disciplines.

But occasionally they may rely on the main lead agency to lead the outsourcing of the work when needed, as a general contractor would. Clients hire a lead agency (typically a "creative" agency by trade) or multiple ones to act as the brand steward(s), the core integrator(s), responsible for owning the creative idea, coordinating the creative development process across all touch points, and managing all aspects of the campaign with other discipline-specific agencies. The lead agency might play the role of the architect and general contractor, setting strategy and steering other agencies throughout the process but you will still need plumbers and electricians to get the house built. The lead agency can be a network-affiliated agency or an independent shop.

This is what Motorola asked BBDO NY to do in early 2006 as their "central coordinating agency," working with a number of other shops for product-specific assignments or complementary skills like digital executions. Prior to that, Motorola's global creative duties were consolidated at Ogilvy & Mather (WPP). Under a "lead agency" model, although it is the responsibility of the lead agency to orchestrate with other agencies, the client must still provide oversight and support to ensure effective collaboration among the agency roster. Great ideas can come from anywhere.

When clients need a particular agency capability, they often want to work with the best-in-class agencies in a particular discipline. This is what motivated Nike to expand beyond its decades-long partnership with independent lead agency Wieden + Kennedy to complement it with talented digital-native agencies such as AKQA and R/GA.

It is rare to find truly integrated agencies with world-class services in each and every category. Clients are required to assign lead agencies to different disciplines. P&G has built a similar agency strategy it calls Brand Agency Leader (BAL) that is designed to support its approach to value-based compensation.[21]

To avoid talent duplication, overlapping agency capabilities, and poor cross-agency collaboration that eventually results in operational inefficiencies, P&G moved away from its decentralized agency model. This was done to improve spend efficiencies, reduce coordination time, and promote more holistic and consistent communications.

Their previous approach was inefficient, too demanding to adequately scale to their needs, and compensation was a barrier to enabling collaboration. P&G's BAL model ensures one agency is assigned a "lead" role (and specifically one individual) on each particular brand and is on point to coordinate all other agency efforts with a single master plan, a single fee, and a +/- 10% value-based compensation adjustment that ties to brand sales, share, and qualitative metrics, and is then typically shared among all agencies.

Although P&G approves the agency partners, the "lead" agency (BAL) is directly contracting with the P&G approved agencies, effectively acting as a general contractor. A sort of bill of rights, a set of principles that agencies agree to (for example, share ownership of the work, working as a team, ideas can come from anywhere, consumer at the center) ensures complete alignment.

Because some agencies specialize in building expertise and skill sets in one particular area, it's most difficult for mainstream agencies to deliver superior results to those that dedicate their passion and efforts on being the very best in a particular discipline. Intel selected independent agency Venables Bell & Partners based in San Francisco as their lead creative agency following a $150-$300M global creative account review in 2008 that signaled the high tech giant was moving away from the network-led approach of working with a leading global marketing communications company McCann Worldgroup (which includes major agency brands such as McCann Erikson and Universal McCann) to a model that gave them flexibility in their choice of agency.

Client Viewpoint

"The Brand Agency Leader Approach is working very well for P&G against our primary objective to deliver more integrated brand building to our consumers and to do that with less time and touches for all involved. This has been a very positive change for us that could not have been accomplished without the support and long standing relationships of our agencies."

RICHARD C. DELCORE
Director, Global Branded Entertainment, P&G

Clients will typically have multiple specialized agencies: one for general advertising, one for events, one for PR, one for retail promotions. These agencies might have "AOR" status for their specific discipline (Agency A is the agency of record PR agency for the company). This is especially common in the media space where advertisers will typically assign one AOR for media planning and buying to realize the benefits of greater economies of scale.

However, the "lead agency" model can present some challenges as well. Streamlining processes, reducing internal and external overhead, and seeking cost efficiencies, proves to be especially challenging when working across several agencies. Large companies with a multitude of products and customer segments may likely require multiple agencies. They may need agencies in PR, advertising, media, digital, packaging. They may require an agency focused on the Hispanic or other specific target markets. And one specializing in social media or mobile advertising. It's not uncommon for large advertisers to have a half-dozen agencies, if not more. This can be a bit like aligning agencies with multiple individual companies with their own distinct requirements.

Client Viewpoint

"The objective of our agency open source model at Intel is to ensure we work with best of breed agencies in all facets of our business. Innovation and flexibility are at the core of our agency model."

MARIANN COLEMAN
Director, Global Media Relations and Performance, Intel

Typically, agencies are primarily aligned with product groups that have synergies with their experience or are chosen for the unique capabilities of the talent of a particular agency. Of course, this type of consideration may vary based on the organizational structure of the company on which agencies are mapped. Ideally, you will want to see agencies aligned with client organizations based on audience, brands or customer segments so they can build a deep understanding of the individual businesses they serve.

For example, one agency might have built expertise in a particular audience such as the youth or Hispanic market. Or a particular discipline such as PR or retailing. Agency alignment is often based on the way budgets are split and managed on the client side as a matter of practicality. Aligning the right agency with the right piece of business is a challenge for both the client and the agency. Poor performance on one piece of business can lead to a full account review with the client which can jeopardize the overall relationship. As a result, agencies have the incentive to do well across the entire relationship, especially in the areas of critical importance to the client.

On the other hand, managing relationships with multiple agencies can prove to be challenging for the client.

First, the agency management team must often play the role of the referee, making important decisions and bringing agencies together between the different disciplines and encourage team work and collaboration. Second, the client must ensure all agencies "play nice" and truly collaborate, acting as marriage counselor as needed to keep the agencies working together at their best. The discipline of agency management adds complexity, intensity, and resource requirements when choosing a multi-agency environment.

Client Viewpoint

"Best of breed is our philosophy and approach to agencies, picking the best agencies rather than consolidating under one or more network holding companies. Our internal Agency Management Council ensures that key stakeholders in marketing and procurement are involved in the selection of roster agencies. This grass roots approach facilitates buy-in and accountability."

TOM CHETRICK
VP Advertising and Marketing Services, Bristol-Myers Squibb

"Free Form" Agency Model

Some clients, unable or unwilling to commit to a particular agency, are selecting a varied roster of agencies across product lines, geography, and practice disciplines. Under this type of "open-source" model, the roster of is a pool of approved agencies that any budget owner can engage. It requires heavy internal logistical coordination, vendor management, and operational oversight.

Quality control is limited. It also often results in lack of or unstructured cross-agency collaboration that can weaken the consistency and effectiveness of the client's work. Under this model, a client gains flexibility and variety of choice at the expense of efficiencies, client time and integration. This type of tradeoff can be made when the client chooses to play an especially active role in seeking efficiencies through triple bidding and other methods to drive cost efficiency.

This model tends to be short-term focused and somewhat transactional in nature. Given its fragmented nature, it does not build the type of strategic partnership that generates most value in client/agency engagements.

A "free form" approach predominantly supports project-based engagements, providing the roster of agencies a limited line of sight to future business and therefore limiting their ability to secure and retain top agency talent. The agency must gain internal mind-share, grow organically, and drive to upgrade the client relationship to a more exclusive status, which can denigrate necessary collaboration and integration across agencies and disciplines. In this model, the client is solely responsible for ensuring the integration of the various pieces of the puzzle, clarifying roles and responsibilities to avoid territorial issues, and keeping a sharp eye peeled for redundancies and randomization of resources.

Agency Viewpoint

"Some large clients think they want a small/mid-size agency, so the client will remain important; the reality is that large clients often need the resources of large agencies. But small, independent agencies often provide smart, nimble thinking that can be game-changing. Clients are best served to understand the strengths of agencies and surround themselves with an A-Team."

Marc A. Brownstein
President and CEO, Brownstein Group

Client Viewpoint

"Our full-service, in-house agency competes with external agencies for creative assignments. Our model requires our in-house group to win each project while recovering all costs needed to complete the project."

Tom Chetrick
VP Advertising and Marketing Services, Bristol-Myers Squibb

"In-house" Agency Model

Under the "in-house" agency model, a client decides to bring or build in-house some of the work that would otherwise be conducted by agencies. By deciding to take on that responsibility, it seriously limits a client's ability to tap into the breadth and depth of external agency resources otherwise available. But it has the advantage of offering absolute control. This model does require heavy internal coordination of the various services provided by internal teams, and builds a vulnerable cost center within companies whose core business is typically well outside the core competencies necessary to deliver compelling marketing communications designed to attract and grow profitable customers. In-house agencies tend to be best suited when limited to specific competencies.

The choice of agency model is a function of a client's desire to have access to a large or more limited number of agency competencies, as well as a client's preference for managing these resources internally or externally. Some clients have the resources and have built the depth and operational rigor to manage all of these resources to have one unified end.

Others do not want to deal with the complications, time and efforts required to coordinate and bring together the various agencies within the roster. They choose to outsource that role to one company, hoping to reduce the waste associated with managing the complexity of multiple agencies and various cross-agency engagements.

Client Viewpoint

"An effective way to foster cross-agency collaboration is to conduct agency summits. It is an opportunity to bring the agencies together to improve communication between them and the client. It has been my experience that these summits must be initiated by clients or they are unlikely to happen."

DELMAR WYATT
Director Advertising Operations, Qwest Communications

Large advertisers with sizeable budgets, many brands to support, and sound agency management practices, might use a combination or permutations of these models to find the best agency model for each brand or simply to experiment and learn which is optimal to complement company resources and return the most dividends on their marketing communications investment.

For example, they might have an "integrated" agency model for brand A and a "free form" agency model for brand B. Agencies are every day coming up with new ways of organizing and packaging themselves to meet client needs. Johnson & Johnson, one of the world's largest advertisers, has used a variety of creative agencies to service its numerous brands, from large agencies such as JWT, DDB, and BBDO to smaller indie shops, in addition to a host of carefully-picked specialty agencies.

Agency Viewpoint

"When clients have a roster of agencies, you never get rid of territorial issues but some competition is healthy. All the agencies must be incented for the outcome. You cannot reasonably align agencies unless everyone, including the client, is aligned around the same goals."

DAVID KENNY
Managing Partner, Vivaki

A client may also rely on one agency to address its core needs and yet, hire a few specialized agencies to complement its roster where it has current gaps.

Although the agency models covered above are among the most commonly used, we are likely to see a number of alternative models emerge that draw from creative approaches and industry best practices.

Global Consideration

As companies expand internationally, they must also consider the best agency model to support their global brand and marketing efforts. Brand uniformity, campaign synchronicity, efficient global deployment, and speed to market are vital considerations. As companies expanded their business abroad, so have the agencies to support them. Many agencies have built or acquired offices in all countries and regions where clients have a need for their services, as an alternative to clients disseminating brand/campaign guidelines and letting their subsidiaries work with uncoordinated, disparate local agencies.

Today these agencies land global campaigns that carry one voice globally but are adapted locally to resonate with local audiences. A much better outcome is achieved than the cacophony and brand devaluation that could result from messaging inconsistencies. In optimal cases, clients use these local offices not only to land the work in the field, but also to check for local cultural sensitivity during the idea and concept development stage so there are no surprises when the campaign breaks. Often ideas are generated from the global teams working with corporate headquarters, but the most sophisticated agencies embrace ideas and best practices coming from anywhere around the world and share them with all the offices. Talent to serve client needs is globally shared as well across offices.

Client Viewpoint

"How do we attract the best talent on our business, especially in smaller (yet emerging) markets where marketing investment is not large?"

CHARLIE SILVESTRO
Vice President, Global Agency Operations, MasterCard Worldwide

Some companies such as Adidas, Sony, and Jaguar use specialized global production and deployment agencies that partner with them and with their creative agencies to create, translate, localize, adapt, manage, and deliver campaigns in local markets through more efficient in-market resources or a "hub and spoke" model.

A good example of this approach is Intel. In early 2009 Intel moved away from its agency network-led model with McCann Worldgroup to a lead agency model with Venables and a number of agencies playing leads in key disciplines such as media, production, interactive, retail, events, and brand strategy. Venables partners with OMD and Tag Worldwide on their successful campaign "Sponsors of Tomorrow."

Rather than building their own network, some agencies are partnering directly with lower-overhead, streamlined global production and transcreation companies to bundle services and bring a one-stop competitive solution to their clients. Whether advertisers are relying on their global agency network or specialized production and deployment resources to go to market, they realize that in order to achieve business goals, global campaigns must go beyond "take and translate" models that simply speak the local language.

Client Viewpoint

"At Walmart U.S., we use a mix of open source and agencies of record. We firmly believe in building strong partnerships with our agencies. However, due to the nature and volatility of our business, we use a core set of agencies as AOR and have an open sourcing model to meet other business needs."

Carla Dodds, Director, Multicultural Marketing and Marketing Vendor Management, Walmart U.S.

Having copywriters and art directors that are fluent in multiple languages might be a plus, but it's about understanding the cultural and local nuances of each individual market to land work that makes campaign investments credible, affordable, and effective. And finally, global advertisers need agency partners that can manage the sophisticated asset trafficking, distribution, tracking, and optimizing of creative assets using the latest Digital Asset Management (DAM) technology and processes.

Communication Plan

Having a sound agency strategy is imperative. But it's not enough. It also requires rolling up sleeves and making sure the strategy is well understood across the organization and fully supported internally. No strategy can be successfully implemented without a robust communication plan that aligns the entire company behind a common approach and communicates these benefits through the banner of a unified mission. The reality is that not everyone internally may agree with agency decisions made by the agency management team for and by the company.

Budget owners and marketers may be told to work with a particular agency they didn't choose. These same employees may have worked with other agencies in their past lives and are likely to push to continue to hire those at will. After all, this is a relationship business and relationships are what matters. Understandably, clients move from company to company and often hope to leverage their own, well-trusted agency partnerships rather than the ones mandated by the company. To complicate matters, these rogue agencies may not have to subject themselves to the demands and expectations imposed on larger ones, making themselves even more attractive to inexperienced marketers looking for shiny new deliverables and easy wins to propel their carrier.

A rogue agency may also appear to be more responsive and cost-effective than the company's agency of record, free of any centrally defined process and perhaps free of having to comply with what could be perceived as inconvenient and inflexible corporate standards. Small agencies are also willing to temporarily give up profits to secure a marquee client name on the front door that might help them secure other, more profitable businesses down the road. The combination of the two can be very appealing to marketers who frequently work in silos and are not overly committed to a model that might appear, at first glance, to predominantly benefit the corporation at large. Independent marketers often need to be reminded that these rogue agency relationships can prove to be highly inefficient for the marketers themselves, exposing the company to potential legal and PR risks, and may in turn suck a disproportionate share of corporate resources and prove to be counter-productive.

Client Viewpoint

"Agencies should get better at self-promotion. They are often too conservative and must be bigger advocate for their work and for themselves. They need to remind clients: This is why you hired us, what sets us apart from the competition."

SUSAN MARKOWICZ, Global Advertising Agency Manager, Ford Motor Company

Agency Viewpoint

"Agencies need to do a better job of creating differentiated value. They should do fewer activities perceived to be commodities by their clients and focus more on their core competencies. They need to identify what they do well and focus on the services for which the client is willing to pay a premium price."

TIM WILLIAMS, President, Ignition Consulting Group

Those responsible for defining and promoting the agency strategy are likely to meet some resistance from pockets across the organization, even with the best intentions and a robust strategy. Hence, a robust agency strategy communication plan becomes vitally important to success. Because agency decisions are often perceived as secretive if not subjective, it is important to educate the entire organization and encourage employees to support the company's overall agency strategy. Clients should consider the wide range of internal communication vehicles at their disposal to explain the company's approach, agency decisions, and highlight the excellent work done and results achieved in partnership with the agency(ies).

Executing a carefully crafted communication plan doesn't mean going deep into every agency-related topic or over-selling the agency. By exaggerating the likely benefits of the agency model and ignoring potential pitfalls, companies could come short of meeting expectations and endanger the viability of the overall agency model. So communications must be anchored into reality and must be backed up with demonstrable evidence of the value it generates.

To effectively communicate the benefits of an agency model, clients should consider partnering with their agency to implement a regular communication plan that includes a variety of "proof-points." This can be a combination of case studies, reports, sample portfolio, executive summaries, Web seminars, and training and speaking engagements that are venues to carry the message loud and clear that the model is delivering its intended benefits. Every marketer within the client organization must also be reminded of the important role they play in making sure the company leverages these agency resources wisely and optimally so the agency can do their very best work and achieve the marketers' objectives. Accountability goes both ways.

Client Viewpoint

"At Bristol-Myers Squibb, we reward agencies for their strong, sustained performance on our business. In the end, top performing agencies get to stay in the roster and are considered for almost all new assignments."

TOM CHETRICK
VP Advertising and Marketing Services, Bristol-Myers Squibb

Similarly, marketers must be reminded of basic engagement principles and best practices trained in effectively working with agencies: consistently providing thorough, clear direction to the agency, investing time and resources to drive great strategy and ideas, and aligning feedback internally so that the agency can efficiently do its best work. Celebrating joint successes will ensure that client project leads and agency staff are acknowledged for their performance and set an example for others in the relationship to follow. Successfully managing the relationships also necessitates frequent and timely communications about important decisions about the company's strategic direction or key priorities. Agencies should communicate information to key clients on the account and announce important milestones, such as key new agency hires and staffing changes, acquisitions, and new client accounts.

In the end, mindfully planning for communications is key to getting employees to care, become engaged, support the company's approach to agency management, and eventually turn them into active supporters and advocates of a streamlined agency strategy.

Operating Plan

A strategy has been defined and agreed upon. Everyone involved with the agencies is clear about what the company is trying to accomplish and what the priorities are. It's still too premature to declare victory. A strategy is only as good as one's ability to execute it. Any company function must determine the resources required to carry out their mission.

That's true in agency management as well. The company must develop a robust operational plan that spells out the actions it will take to bring the strategy to life, defining clear roles and responsibilities for all agencies, articulating key operating principles and requirements that the agency (and employees) must adhere to, stating expected client/agency engagement practices and the operating budget required, aligning scope of work to staffing plans, and encouraging effective team collaboration and management of resources.

Here are a few standard operating principles that clients must consider:

Client Viewpoint

"To foster cross-agency collaboration, we host an agency summit twice a year to bring internal business partners and agencies together. It's important to break down the walls of territoriality."

MOLLIE WESTON
Director Agency Management Operations, Best Buy

Mandated Versus Optional Use of Agencies Is the usage of the company's agencies a mandate or simply recommended? If the choice is left to individual budget owners, a client's ability to realize some of the benefits of its agency model, such as economies of scale or consistent, coordinated go-to-market, strategy will be seriously compromised. The choice is yours and typically dependent on your company's culture or go-to-market process. An optimal model requires constant monitoring and support. If the use of certain agencies is mandated, it might be limited to specific disciplines or the policy might allow for some flexibility (for example: 3/4 of total marketing spend must be within an agency or a network of agencies). A corporate mandate will require unconditional executive management buy-in. The company policy might state that it expects the use of these relationships. Any justifiable exception might require approval from the CMO.

Client Viewpoint

"Everyone has to play nice in the agency sandbox. Effective cross-agency collaboration is vital."

BRETT COLBERT
Global Manager, Procurement Advertising, Anheuser Busch InBev

Centralized Versus Decentralized Access to Agency Resources Does the company want a central team or specific individuals to interface with the agency(ies), offering a single point of contact to kick off projects and prioritize workload? Or does the company want to offer unfiltered, unstructured access to its agency(ies), so anyone can initiate a project, with minimal company supervision? Typically, the larger the company, the more problematic is a decentralized approach to engaging with agencies. This decision is likely to be based on the type of agency services (perhaps media services tend to be more centralized than creative services), organizational considerations, company size, and a number of other variables.

Global versus local scope This is a major design point if the client has international offices and intends to launch marketing campaigns in more than one market. The operating considerations for global clients are far more complex (such as how to manage global input, how to create global assets, the approval and distribution process, localization and adaptation of global assets, and so forth) when work must be executed and delivered internationally.

Other typical operating considerations might involve the way these resources will be funded (centrally or by division), what internal processes must be followed, what agency training is required, and engagement roles and responsibilities. Once the operating principles have been agreed to, a number of processes have to be established internally and in partnership with the agency, specifically around the governance of the model and engagement rules. These processes and rules of engagement range from describing a standard process and tools for kicking off a project with an agency to handling potential disagreements during the course of a project.

Clients must determine the right escalation process for their company to facilitate valuable and timely conflict resolution. The most common operating process involves the end-to-end management of a project from strategy development and agency briefing to campaign measurement and optimization, documenting each step and the expected role played by the different roles at the client and the agency, respectively.

Another important consideration is determining the resources and budget requirements to operate the company's agreed agency strategy. Some agency models require light operating support, while others require heavy support and funding. For example, a mandated global agency model with centralized agency resources may require greater client and agency staff commitments and an adequate operating budget, while a local model enabling decentralized access of agency resources will operate with minimum resources.

Client Viewpoint

"I often get asked whether longevity in client/agency relationships is important to us. An advertiser can be with an agency for 10 years. Or only 10 months. In the end, it's all about performance. Are you getting a high performing agency team on your business? This is what's truly important. If your agency delivers consistently for 10 years, then longevity is a great thing."

MARTINE REARDON
VP of Marketing, Macy's

Continuous Improvement

The company's agency strategy cannot be set in stone. It must be based on the culmination of the insights, feedback, best practices, and dialogue that occur throughout the year. It is likely to evolve, adapting to changing market conditions. But we can't improve what we can't measure. As in any strategy, it must allow for input and on-going feedback. Employees on either side of the fence should be encouraged to constructively and openly make recommendations on how to improve the partnership, improve the quality of communication between the parties, and effectively encourage ownership of accountability in the relationship.

Agency Viewpoint

"We need to rethink how we work with clients. Agencies must now engage beyond the communication layer, with product, distribution and P&L owners who are the real owners of the 360 degree customer experience. Clients shouldn't silo marcom as much as they do. Many of our clients are becoming more marketing centric, with differentiation in the product, distribution, and experience. Communications alone are not enough differentiation as consumers get transparent information faster than ever before."

David Kenny
Managing Partner, Vivaki

This is what Kaizen (the Japanese equivalent of "continuous improvement") in agency strategy is all about. There are a number of ways advertisers can fine-tune their agency strategy. These range from shared agency performance dashboards to informal business reviews with the agency to assess how well things are working.

Regardless of the particular measurement systems used, whether formal or informal, advertisers should ensure that these metrics are part of the company's regular rhythm of business and that they closely tie to other operating metrics the company relies on to determine the health of its business. It's not easy to do. It depends on the company having come to the realization that a solid client/agency relationship will yield good work and a weak one won't, therefore choosing to pay close attention to the health and quality of that relationship.

Business reviews with the agencies, whether semi-annually, quarterly or monthly, are golden opportunities for the client and agency leadership to discuss the health of the relationship, review the work, identify threats, roadblocks, and opportunities, raise visibility to potential issues that will require proactive management, explore ways to improve the partnership, and more importantly, ensure that both parties are staying closely aligned and focused on key priorities.

Clients should conduct these business reviews at least twice a year or even quarterly with their agencies. The type and size of the relationship may not justify a higher frequency, so every client will need to determine what makes sense for their own situation. At the very least, the agenda must allow for ample discussion and ideas exchange as well as a thorough review of score-cards and key performance indicators.

Agencies are greatly valued for their creativity and know-how. A business review is the perfect occasion for an agency to shine and demonstrate their value to the client's business. It is also a perfect opportunity for clients to evaluate how effectively their strategy is playing out. Advertisers should also consider conducting internal business reviews without agency participation to candidly discuss the status of these pivotal relationships and anticipate potential concerns.

Client Viewpoint

"The longer you can maintain a relationship that is healthy and is working, the better off you are. It's true professionally and personally. It certainly is true for client/agency relationships."

JULIE GIBBS, Director, Corporate Brand Marketing, Campaign Management, Adobe

These business reviews can be facilitated by drawing upon agency dashboards. These dashboards are like an automobile dashboard, containing instrumentations and data pertaining to the successful operation of the agency model. They may include critical data points based on the nature of the relationship. These activity-based, performance-based or relationship health-related metrics may include business and campaign results, the number of projects handled or assets created by the agency and the manpower required to bring them to market, agency attrition, new hires, burn rate, and qualitative metrics such as satisfaction and team morale.

These management tools for clients and agencies keep an objective pulse on the relationship. They can encourage fact-based discussions between clients and agencies by analyzing purposeful and actionable metrics that, ideally, have been jointly defined and agreed upon. As a result, action plans for continuous improvement can be initiated and progress can be made in key relationship areas over time.

Building a sound agency strategy and agency portfolio is paramount to any company's ability to compete and win against the competition and make strategic use of the agency's competencies and resources in advertising and marketing communications. Marc, Catherine, and John have built a sound agency strategy that enable them to make the best use of time and space in maneuvering decisively against the competition on the cut-throat chessboard that is their marketplace. They have assembled a robust roster of agencies to meet their demanding marketing needs. Marc, Catherine, and John have also mastered what it takes to make great agencies do excellent work.

{Taking Immediate Action}

TOP 5

BEST PRACTICES TO HARNESS THE MADNESS

❶ Carefully assess and rationalize your company's needs of its agency partner(s). Do not make decisions about your company's agency portfolio without seeking input from those directly impacted by it.

❷ Pick the best agency model to meet the needs and unique circumstances of your business. Determine the level of flexibility and agency choice desired and whether coordination between agencies be handled internally or externally. Secure adequate budget and resources to successfully bring the strategy to life.

❸ Partner with your agency to regularly showcase the work, campaign results and value generated from the partnership by using internal communication tools and company events. Regularly celebrate joint successes and recognize top agency performers and internal clients.

❹ Conduct regular business reviews with agency partners to foster a healthy, productive relationship. Discuss what's working and what's not, opportunities and potential roadblocks to success, and agree on joint action plans to drive immediate improvements and higher performance.

❺ Decide which operating principles should best support the company's approach to working optimally with agencies. Prepare for the unexpected by developing a contingency plan.

5 ASSORTATIVE MATING AND THE SWEATY T-SHIRT THEORY

Conducting a successful agency search

"He who would search for pearls must dive below."

—JOHN DRYDEN
Writer and poet

As in everyday life, individuals and companies can sometimes jump quickly into a relationship, without having a true sense of self or without thoughtful consideration. Tabloids made fortunes telling the stories of celebrities like Jennifer Lopez, Colin Farrell, and Pamela Anderson whose marriages didn't last more than four months.

And when you thought you'd seen it all, celebrities Dennis Rodman and Carmen Electra's highly publicized marriage ended after only nine days in November 1998. In this culture of "speed-dating" or even "speed-marriage" how can we be expected to act any differently with business partners? A privileged society, deeply rooted into a pervasive society of speed, convenience, and instant gratification, has made it easy for companies and the people that lead them to embrace this growing cultural phenomenon.

Yet it is common knowledge that selecting the ideal agency partner, whether in creative, media, digital, public relations, or any other communication discipline, is by far one of the most impactful decision clients make. It's insanely easy to pick up the phone and on the spot, hire a new agency. It's insanely more demanding to find the ideal strategic partner to reshape the company's marketing approach and propel the business forward. Finding compatible agencies is no longer good enough in the highly competitive environment of 21st century.

Perhaps the dating and marriage partner metaphors has been over-used when describing the "do and don'ts" of finding the ideal business partner. Countless cultural anthropologists and experts in human psychology counsel us on how to find the right partner. It usually involves a series of somewhat logical steps, from assessing personal needs, matching candidates based on key criteria, conducting chemistry and reference checks, to the actual dating. Then if you plan to turn your date into something more, you can get terrific advice from marital experts and couple counselors on how to preserve, grow, and nurture this relationship over time.

When applying these same kinds of strategies to the business world the complexity is exponentially greater. Clearly it's a more involved process than the one of a fish who uses electric signals to find the right mate. We wouldn't be so lucky. Regardless of the type of services sought, most clients don't look for a "brand" agency or a "PR" firm for their next assignment. What they look for is a strategic partner that can drive measurable business results and give them a competitive edge. When searching for a true marketing partner, how do we know we are looking in the right places? If birds of a feather flock together, aren't we searching for agencies that mirror our companies?

Everything I Know about Agencies I Learned from Biology

In a study known as the "sweaty t-shirt study" conducted by Claus Wedekind, a biological researcher at Bern University in Switzerland, men were asked to wear the same cotton t-shirt for 48 hours.[22]

They were not to wear any deodorant, cologne, or use scented soap. They were asked to avoid smelly environments, products or activities. The t-shirts were to be placed into a plastic bag. Once returned to the scientists, the t-shirts were then placed into boxes equipped with a smelling hole. Women were invited one at a time to smell them, describe each odor and indicate which one they were most attracted to. Half of the boxes included t-shirts from men with similar Major Histocompatibility Complex (known as MHC) genes. The other half included t-shirts from women with dissimilar MHC genes. The women who volunteered to participate in this study did not know which t-shirts where which.

Agency Viewpoint

"Clients should ask themselves: Are these people offering us anything we can't do ourselves? What difference will they really make?"

JEFF GOODBY
Co-Chairman and Creative Director, Goody, Silverstein & Partners

Surprisingly enough, Claus Wedeking concluded that women were most attracted to men with MHC, the most dissimilar from their own. The preference was stronger as the likelihood of pregnancy increased. The rational? The more diverse the genes, the stronger the immune system to fight potential diseases.

The key take-away here is that clients should consider agencies that are compatible, whose values match their own but are intrinsically different enough to extract most value from the work they produce. They should look for a trusted partner with the required skills and capabilities to meet their needs, often diametrically different from the core competencies of their company but that complements them. It's another way to say something we've known all along: opposites attract. Just like in real life, it's often for the best. But why are relations so hard to maintain?

It's nonsense that so many clients have been getting into the sad habit of hiring and firing agencies as they would commodity suppliers. Perhaps it's because, sadly enough, some agencies are behaving as if they were. It's insane that so many agencies are missing the opportunity to establish themselves as inseparable allies and vital assets to their clients. But clients must also resist the temptation to launch into search after search looking for a bright new shiny pearl. They must resist RFP scope creep, or as what some agencies call "RFPs from hell," inviting too many agencies to participate in poorly orchestrated, months-long discussions during which agencies are asked to fill out insanely long questionnaires and share their ideas for free.

Client Viewpoint

"Agencies bring strategy and creative thinking to the table. We don't want cheaper versions of ourselves."

BRETT COLBERT
Global Manager, Procurement Advertising, Anheuser Busch In Bev

Clients with agency responsibilities may be naively criticized internally for looking like they are sleeping at the wheel, or resisting change, having the same agency partner for years. Instead, they must be increasingly discerning if they are to build a reputation of integrity and partnership that attracts the best agency talent to their company.

Savvy clients must make sure they are judged internally on what truly matters to the business. It can prove to be quite challenging to launch a comprehensive agency search and find that new agency partner. Or to add a new strategic agency partner to an existing roster. Or simply to add a specialty agency where there is a gap in capabilities. So clients should carefully consider all their options before deciding to put an account in review. They may end up wasting precious time and resources on-boarding new agencies and going through learning curves. Only when they have decided that this is the best course of action should they move forward with a review.

Agency Viewpoint

"The pitch process is out of control and about to experience a big backlash by conscientious agencies. It's going to be ugly."

JEFF GOODBY
Co-Chairman and Creative Director, Goody, Silverstein & Partners

Ask Visa. They had been working with their agency BBDO Worldwide for nothing less than 25 years before moving their estimated $600M global creative and strategic marketing account to Omnicom Group's TBWA Worldwide, following a holding-comp pitch for its business. Unfortunately for agencies, most clients are no longer committing themselves to such long partnerships. The world of marketing is changing too fast. So are their needs. Yet too many clients are focused on the short term, conducting excessive agency reviews that end up undermining their long-term efforts and their ability to attract top talent.

Bold agencies like Crispin Porter + Bogusky are now taking strong positions, as in the case of Volkswagen, by turning down invitations to participate in existing account reviews.[23]

Although history proves them right—chances to retain an account once in review are pretty lean—few can realistically afford to take a "no defense approach" by letting a client go to the competition without a good fight. Clients must also follow industry best practices if they are to conduct an effective and efficient search project.

Client Viewpoint

"In a business environment changing as fast as it is and technology advancing by the day, doing a "landscape" review is often more effective than doing an agency review every three to five years. Are we asking agencies the right questions? Do they have the right competencies? Clients have to work as hard as their agency partners to stay abreast of what's happening in the industry so they can have these informed conversations."

JEFF DEVON, Director Global Marketing, HP

Common Reasons for Starting an Agency Search

A successful search is never guaranteed. Like you, I've seen my fair share of questionable searches with questionable results. Read the press and you will realize that, despite the number of agency reviews constantly under way and years of experience on both the client and the agency side, no process is ever bulletproof. Arguably the most important step in this process is the one that ends up receiving the least attention: it is "self-discovery." It is common sense: Clients must have a clear understanding of what business problem they are solving.

What sparked this agency review? What are the business circumstances that led to this particular search? It forces clients to look deep inside and answer questions truthfully. It requires a comprehensive, honest self-assessment of the company's marketing strengths and weaknesses. For instance, is the brand strategy hitting the mark? Are we adequately leveraging new, emerging media with the current agency? Are we confident in the lead agency to successfully launch the new brand campaign? There are many valid reasons for a company to seek a (new) agency relationship. However, contrary to popular belief, an agency search is not only the result of performance issues.

Here are the most common reasons to start a search:

Change in Business A company may require new or incremental agency resources as a result of a new business, brand, or product line being launched, or business divisions being split. Having a new agency partner can be seen as a positive change by some companies if there is a material departure from the prior brand positioning, execution, and work style, as Sprint concluded when moving its $1.2 billion account to Goodby Silverstein & Partners in 2007. It could also result from a decision to dismantle an in-house creative team like Best Buy did after 20 years handling its advertising budget in-house. It could result from clients being merged or acquired, such as the Procter & Gamble's 2005 acquisition of Gillette, forcing multiple incumbent agencies (Publicis, Omnicom and WPP agencies such as BBDO, TBWA, Grey, Saatchi & Saatchi) to defend their share of the estimated $6 billion advertising account.[24]

Client Viewpoint

"Usually a new CEO comes in. Within six months, the CMO is held to scrutiny or leaves. Six months later, a new CMO comes in and puts the agency in review. We see this over and over."

LYNNE SEID, Partner Global Marketing Officers Practice, Heidrick & Struggles

Leadership Turnover Many reviews are initiated as a result of marketing organization overhaul and higher turnover among Chief Marketing Officers (CMOs) that we have seen with many large advertisers over the years. The appointment of a new CMO often triggers an agency review, within weeks or months. In the case of Chevy, newly hired marketing chief Joel Ewanick shifted the entire $600 million account to Goodby Silverstein & Partners from Publicis only a month after Publicis won the account and without meeting with the incumbent agency.[25]

The pressure of increased marketing accountability and higher returns on marketing investment has significantly reduced the average tenure of CMO. The next CMO has very limited time to prove himself/herself to the CEO and board of directors. Working with an agency the CMO is unfamiliar with and with whom the company may have had questionable results under the prior leadership, is undesirable. This is the opportunity to get a fresh start, either working with agencies that the CMO built a strong work partnership with

Client Viewpoint

"How you deal with agencies speaks to what kind of client you are. If you get divorced once, you may blame it on your former spouse. If you get divorced twice, you may find yourselves blaming your spouse once again. But if you get divorced three times, you have to start looking inside. It now says something about you. Clients are not always good students of history and end up repeating mistakes over and over.

A LARGE ADVERTISER

over the years in a prior role, or simply to turning up the heat on the incumbent agency. Clients should certainly refrain from doing reviews as a way to keep the agency on its toes. There are many effective and less costly ways to keep agencies motivated.

Conflicts This is a common issue for clients. A conflict may come up as a result of a new multidisciplinary account win by an agency pitching an integrated offering, forcing a client to reconsider its relationships with agencies now in direct conflict with their competitors. An agency may wish to pursue a significantly more attractive (either larger or more profitable) client opportunity and deliberately resign its current account to pursue it. Discover Financial Services selected WPP Group's MediaCom to handle its planning and buying duties after Publicis Groupe's Starcom, the incumbent agency, decided not to defend the account because of a conflict with its new Bank of America account. Agency mergers also tend to create account conflicts. In the case of IPG Lowe New York and sibling Deutsch merger in 2009, it created a conflict for Johnson & Johnson's Tylenol business, a key account for Deutsch. Lowe's clients Matrixx Initiatives' Zicam cold remedy and Sepracor's Lunesta sleep aid put their business for review.

Client Viewpoint

"Conducting agency reviews every three to five years allow sclients to keep their creative fresh and agencies on their toes."

BRETT COLBERT
Global Manager, Procurement Advertising, Anheuser Busch InBev

Performance Issues Perhaps the most common reason for a review is poor agency performance. The client decides that its agency has repetitively failed to meet expectations (missing deadlines, quality of the work, inadequate staffing, costs, etc.) and that attempts to improve the performance have been unsuccessful. Either party may conclude that the relationship is no longer performing at acceptable levels. It's time to move on. No client has the luxury to waste time and resources with under-performing agencies. Under this type of scenario, the incumbent agency is unlikely to be invited to participate in the review.

Client Viewpoint

"Clients have a vested interest in sustaining a successful partnership with an agency. It's costly to switch agencies and there is a huge learning curve. Plus, clients often end up facing similar problems with the new agency."

A LARGE ADVERTISER

Transparency is the key here. There is no point inviting them if they do not have a chance of winning. If every attempt has been made to fix problems and save the relationship, why waste further efforts and resources on either side with an agency review? Clients should be transparent about the status of the relationship with the incumbent agency before the search/review gets initiated.

Missing Competencies A client decides that new skills and competencies are needed but are not currently available through the current agency roster. This is often the case in digital marketing where new capabilities emerge frequently and agencies struggle to keep up on all fronts. The client may want to beef up their marketing muscle in social media, analytics, mobile advertising, or paid/organic search marketing.

Or the client may decide that the creative is no longer where it needs to be to capture audiences. Client needs change and evolve constantly based on market conditions and innovation. The incumbent agency (if there is one) might be invited to step up, and build or acquire the missing expertise. Or they may lose to a new agency that can demonstrate they are a better fit.

At the risk of stating the obvious, there is no "perfect" partnership. Even clients showing signs of obsessive–compulsive personality disorder with their agencies are unlikely to find the answer to their challenges by systematically jumping from agency to agency. I fondly refer to those clients as "Rocket Frogs," named after the Australia frog that can jump over two meters or up 50 times its body length. Jumping is easy. Landing is harder. But working joint issues diligently is most rewarding. Most clients don't anticipate the significant opportunity cost associated with a search. If the incumbent agency is invited to participate and has a reasonable shot at keeping or expanding the account, it might still negatively damage the relationship.

Client Viewpoint

"I've had the privilege of working at companies with long standing relationships with their agencies. As in every aspect of life, relationships are based on a genuine understanding on how to best work together, a high level of trust which proves to be extremely efficient. Any company with a relatively complicated business knows that the cost of re-educating a new agency can be quite high. So if you decide to change agencies, it better be worth it."

AMY FULLER, Group Executive Worldwide Consumer Marketing, MasterCard Worldwide

In the book *Adland* James P. Othmer gives a humorous, provocative view into the incumbent agency psyche: "Being put up for review is akin to having your spouse announce in front of everyone you know that he or she no longer loves you and for the next several months he or she will be seeing other people—dozens of smarter, younger, cooler people, many of whom, by the way, you know quite well—and then having all sorts of experimental sex with the most interesting and promising of them, probably no more than six, often doing many of the things that you may have once suggested but were never allowed to."

Given typical switching costs, delays and potential challenges associated with on-boarding a new agency, savvy clients carefully evaluate their options before making the decision to initiate a search. The investment in time and resources to conduct a search, to find, hire, and on-board a new agency is consequential. Not to mention what it takes to fully transition out the incumbent agency: transitioning assets and doing financial reconciliations.

In the event of competitive conflicts or continued, unsolvable performance issues, the decision to search for an agency partner doesn't leave much time for consideration. It is a critical mission and must be conducted swiftly. Any irreconcilable performance or relationship related issues require much more careful consideration by both advertisers and agencies. Like a divorce, they must weigh the implications and often complications associated with parting from each other. Perhaps they can seek the assistance of a third party and give each other the opportunity to work on their differences before throwing down the towel and calling it a day.

Agency Viewpoint

"One of the challenges faced by the industry is that switching costs are often too low. Changing agencies should be highly disruptive if agencies are doing their job and truly delivering value."

DAVID KENNY
Managing Partner, Vivaki

Although it may be that alternative agencies appear as shiny objects from a distance, not adequately working on the issues until the point of no-return is ground for simply displacing problems from one relationship to another. Logically, this is one of the first questions any agency executive would ask during the preliminary stage of the search. As they say, the grass is always greener on the other side of the fence. However, changing agencies will inevitably negatively impact current priorities and productivity during the review and potentially the transition time (should a new agency be selected), so one must ensure that the problem is irreconcilable and that the client/agency relationship is beyond recovery.

Handled Internally or by an Agency Search Consultant

As part of its self-assessment, a client must decide if the search/review will be handled internally or by a neutral third party. Companies should ask themselves: "Do we have the right skills and expertise on our team to conduct a comprehensive review and assess existing and prospective agencies? Do we have the time and resources to do so internally without disrupting the normal course of our business?" Often the answer is "no." Searching for the right agency is a demanding process that requires a good amount of experience and professional expertise. This is why it is common practice for brand advertisers to call for the help of an experienced client/agency matchmaker, specialized in assisting companies conduct a thorough agency review/search.

During the continued growth of digital services with new shops opening door every day, it's increasingly harder for marketers with limited time bandwidth to invest much time in the selection process. Agency search consultants typically save precious time for clients who don't have a deep knowledge of the agency industry, need help to narrow down the search to a few qualified candidates with the right credentials, and don't have the know-how to manage a search effectively. Clients tend to invest the majority of their time in the initial and final stage of the search process, leaving the bulk of the responsibilities and communications to the consultant.

Client Viewpoint

"When conducting an agency search, best practices are to be fully engaged throughout the process with the search consultants to ensure that the company's best interests and requirements are met."

CARLA DODDS, Director, Multicultural Marketing and Marketing Vendor Management, Walmart U.S.

It is equally difficult for procurement organizations that have incomplete visibility of the full breadth of the marketplace to step in and run the search. The project lead may not have the depth of knowledge, working experience, resources, objectivity, or even bandwidth necessary to successfully manage the search project from beginning to end. Beyond the expertise and best practices agency search consultants bring to the table, they can prescreen agency candidates anonymously, a key benefit to brand advertisers who need confidentiality. Their objectivity can be of tremendous value to clients with very divergent opinions.

Some of these consultants have built proprietary databases with proven quantitative and qualitative evaluation methodologies and systems to help brand advertisers find the perfect match based on client experience, competencies, talent, and overall cultural compatibility. These consultants keep themselves up to date on agency capabilities by conducting regular visits and keeping in constant contact with top agencies.

So, one might amusingly wonder: How do you actually search for a search consultant? Clients should leverage industry resources like the Association of National Advertisers (ANA), American Association of Advertising Agencies (AAAA), and Adforum.com for a comprehensive list of search consultants. There are a few consulting firms with dedicated resources and vast expertise in this field, such as Pile and Company (Boston, MA) and Select Resources International (Santa Monica, CA). Clients will want to evaluate search consultants based on the following criteria: industry experience (health care, insurance), client profile and affinity, recent assignments, type of agency services (creative, media, digital PR), seniority and experience, reputation in the agency industry, domestic versus international resources, client references, and cost/value.

Some of these search consultants have international offices or partnerships overseas to handle global clients. To avoid any potential conflict of interest it's highly recommended that the contract with the search consultant should clearly state that they are not to accept financial incentives from agencies. Clients should seriously consider whether or not they are capable or willing to handle a search on their own. These talented match-makers are valuable resources to novice and sophisticated clients alike.

Client Viewpoint

"Using external resources to assist in an agency search can be quite helpful. Clients don't typically have the time to search the marketplace, spot competitive conflicts, check references, or have the time, bandwidth, and expertise that search consultants offer. Effective search consultants have a broad view as to what agencies are good options for a client's needs and they will have insights into an agency's performance record with other clients. Using a search consultant can save significant time in the search process."

DELMAR WYATT
Director Advertising Operations, Qwest Communications

A Methodological Approach

A well-conducted agency review/search is expected to result in the establishment of a highly productive and hopefully long-term partnership that translates into more effective work and better business outcomes. Some best practices are emerging as a result of years of practices among clients, search consultants and industry consortiums.[26, 27] Finding the right agency to support your business can turn out to be risky, time-consuming, frustrating, and daunting. But well worth the investment in time and efforts if it is done properly. It requires a fair amount of research and preparation.

The activities can be divided up in two primary groups: internal and external. The internal phase (inward) consists of defining objectives, getting the project organized, and the initial research and

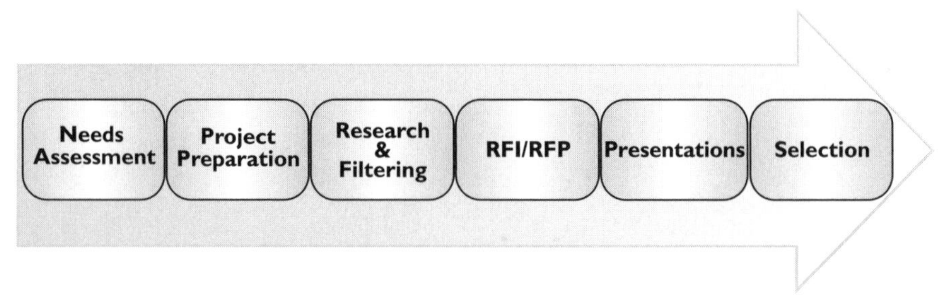

Agency Search/Review Process

filtering under way to identify potential agency candidates. The external phase (outward) consists of reaching out to the candidate agencies, exchanging information, and having them show-case their capabilities in credentials and/or creative presentations.

In the last phase of this process, the client can finally reach his or her decision, select the agency, and initiate the on-boarding process. It's insane to see clients initiate a search without having clear expectations about the process or the outcome and without the necessary experience to make this a productive exercise for all involved. A search demands discipline and absolute commitment to allow for a thorough probing and assessment of agency capabilities.

Client Viewpoint

"Over the year, I've learned that clients must allow enough time to conduct an effective search. They need to have the right decision makers and get buy-off from management about the selection criteria before anyone gets into a room."

SUSAN MARKOWICZ, Global Advertising Agency Manager, Ford Motor Company

Demonstrating basic know-how and skills goes both ways. It's absolutely insane to see inexperienced agencies consistently fail at avoiding common pitfalls that systematically turn off clients. For example, many agencies still fail to adequately prepare or research the company or the client's category. Many agencies still fail to bring the staff that will be working on the account for client face-to-face meetings. Instead, they show up with their executive team knowing full well that none of them will be touching the business in a meaningful way.

Too many agencies fail to listen and to ask questions to deepen their understanding of the client. It's "show and tell" and they lose sight of what matters to the client. Too many agencies over-commit in the spur of the moment, providing an unrealistic picture of the agency's true capabilities and resources back at the home base. Too many agencies present under false pretense integrated offerings with multiple offices that have little experience working together.

Phase I: Needs Assessment

Launching a new product line before finding out why the last one flopped is a bit like going into a second marriage without understanding why the first one failed. This phase of the agency search process is about coming up with a clear definition of services and competencies being sought by the client as well as the breadth and depth of resources required to carry on the work. What agency traits are most desired? If having breadth of services is an important client requirement, agency networks might be better suited than independent agencies. The selection criteria used to evaluate candidates can only be determined if the client is clear about its needs: Is the client looking for a full service agency or for unbundled specialized marketing services? Is this an exclusive relationship? Is the client looking for one or multiple agencies?

There is no magic silver bullet here. Investing the time early on to do this well will pay off and avoid wasted time and efforts down the road. The procurement and legal teams may provide a few of their own to complement those developed by the marketing organization to address some fundamental requirements: credit rating, overall financial health such as balance sheets, income statement, and cash balance (for publicly traded companies), past and potential open litigation, and public records about the agency.

Client Viewpoint

"Finding a new agency is not only about the search and matching exercise. It's about the process of understanding each other, setting clear expectations, defining roles and responsibilities and agreeing on protocols internally and with a new agency partner."

MOLLIE WESTON
Director Agency Management Operations, Best Buy

Checking the financial health of prospective agencies is not only critical to ensure they stay in business while servicing your account. It also guarantees that the agency can invest in staffing the account rapidly enough to serve a new account. The answer to these questions will yield a "go/no-go" decision in the preliminary phase of the process. Once the initial filter has been applied, client needs will be determined based on a pre-determined set of criteria that are unique to each client. Some of the most common ones are shown in the figure below.

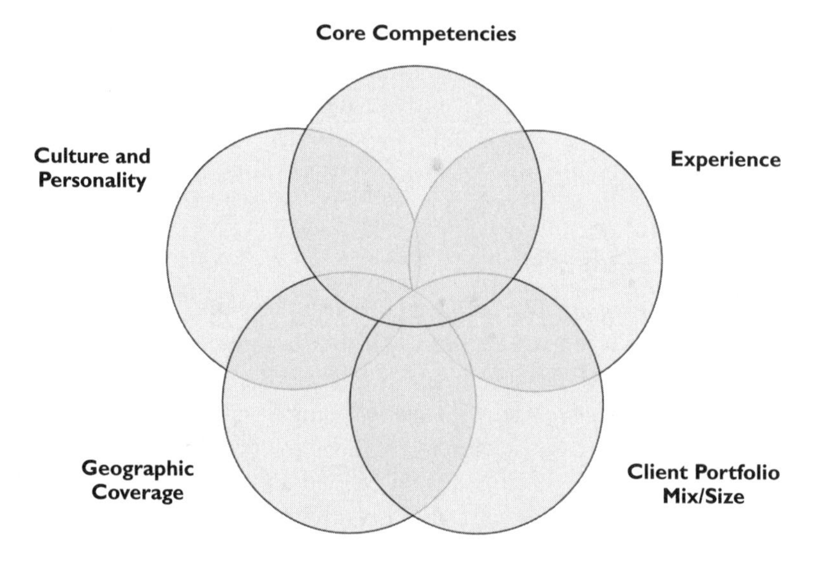

Agency Selection Criteria

Core Competencies Clients must articulate the particular strengths they are looking for to complement their marketing organization or their existing agency roster. Is this a search/review for creative or media duties? Is the client looking for a one stop shop with full-service capabilities? Or is the client looking for a specialized agency to handle specific activities such as PR, retail, events, or diversity marketing? Clients must be transparent about what they are expecting the new agency to do as well as what they are not expecting it to do, which is sometimes equally important. If this is a review, the candidate agencies are likely to examine the incumbent agency to gain as much insight as possible on how they compare in terms of competencies.

Experience Clients must determine the depth and breadth of experience they require on the account: Is the client looking for an agency with experience in a particular functional area (creative, media), industry (telecommunications, travel, for instance) or audience segment (Youth, Senior, Women, Children, Hispanics, and so forth)? Is the client looking for an agency with a minimum number of years of experience? Is the client looking for an agency with global experience as well as international offices in particular regions or countries?

The work performed for past and current clients will speak credibly to their experience. The client must decide whether or not that experience must originate from the agency's client portfolio (current and past) or from the staff's collective experience that might have been gained working for other agencies. Do they have the right people on staff?

Client Portfolio Mix and Size The makeup of the client portfolio of an agency is quite important for cross-polarization and best practices. For example, a packaged good company may want to select an agency with retail clients to leverage their understanding of packaging and merchandising. Is the client list synergistic? Another important criterion is the length of relationship within the existing client pool. Agencies can grow through acquisitions as well or organically through existing client relationships. It is indicative of the agency's aptitude to retain clients. Some agencies are in constant search for new business, speaking to their aggressive growth agenda or to their inability to keep clients. Agencies constantly participating in searches can be easily distracted. Clients should stay away from "hot-shot" agencies, eager to win new business but unable to build long-term partnerships.

The size of client accounts is also an important consideration from a risk and critical mass standpoint. The agency must be big enough to handle the account but not too big that a relatively small client wouldn't get noticed. An agency with one predominantly large client might be concerning as well. Agencies have learned that overdependence on a large client can be devastating when the client resigns the account. The sudden loss of a large account could seriously destabilize the agency and its ability to fulfill its other client commitments. The size of the prospective account in context of existing client accounts will directly impact the level of attention, the quality and seniority of the talent assigned to the account.

Large accounts (in revenue and profits) get A talent. Small accounts are likely to get C talent. It's common sense. Agencies invest their top resources on their best clients. It's always best for clients to be a big fish in a small pond. And it's not just about revenue. Being a big fish means being one of the largest and most profitable clients in their portfolio. Being a small client can present some benefits as well. It means that a large portion of the agency overhead is picked up by large clients. And the client has access to best practices that wouldn't otherwise be available.

Geographic Coverage Is the client marketing domestically, regionally, or internationally? Does the client need access to agency resources in specific countries? Most agencies have international offices or partnerships but there are still few agencies with extensive international presence. Proximity to the client might be an important consideration as well for some clients. A client headquartered in San Francisco might be hesitant to hire an agency in New York City. Regardless of the advances made in technology and telecommunications (cell phones, email, instant messaging, workflow management systems, video conferencing), regular face to face interactions are still highly valued by both parties.

Agency Viewpoint

"One client took our proposed team from Brownstein Group out to lunch to get to know us, as a step in the review. If they didn't enjoy eating lunch with us, they certainly weren't going to enjoy working with us day in and day out."

Marc A. Brownstein
President and CEO, Brownstein Group

Being on the opposite sides of the country, or being even separated by multiple states, might make travel too cost-prohibitive (high cost of airfare travel) or simply too inconvenient (time difference, availability of resources, meeting style preferences, willingness to travel). The reality is that clients prefer to work with agencies that can be at their offices at very short notice. Long-distance client/agency relationships are rarely sustainable, pushing agencies to open offices within proximity of their clients.

Agencies tend to gravitate toward large cosmopolitan cities such as New York, Chicago, San Francisco, Tokyo, Paris, and London that are known to attract and produce talent. So agency proximity might require talent tradeoffs. Unless a client is lucky enough to be based in New York, of course. That's the case for Heineken USA, which limited its creative account review to local shops specifically in Manhattan near their offices.[28] It's not uncommon for agencies to separate the account management and business development functions by operating satellite offices close to clients, balancing the need for proximity and access to talent.

Culture and Personality Although often overlooked at first, the culture and personality of an agency can be a determinant for the long-term fit of a relationship with a client. Some clients or agencies will even conduct a cultural audit to identify and understand the nuances in corporate cultures and how they might impact the quality of an enduring client/agency relationship.

Are you looking for an agency with a more traditional, conservative culture or one that excels in creativity and innovation? Do you embrace a culture of entrepreneurship or do you emphasize a culture of team work and collaboration? Are you willing to tolerate a high degree of creative freedom or do you want an agency partner that plays by your brand playbook? Do you want an agency partner that priorities quality over speed? There are many facets of an agency culture that can foster a very productive or antagonist relationship if mismatched.

Client Viewpoint

"Clients should always ensure upfront and tight alignment at a senior management level as to the criteria on what to look for in an agency prior to initiating a search. This is about leadership but this is also about being respectful about the time and resources agencies are investing going into a pitch."

JENNIFER BERGER, Director, Marketing & Advertising Services, Starbucks

Phase II: Project Preparation

Time has now come for the client to prepare internally and to assemble the resources required to carry out the search. Although there are some best practices worth considering, most of which have been published by the Association of National Advertisers (ANA), American Association of Advertising Agencies (AAAA), and World Federation of Advertisers (WFA), the way to approach this process should be tailored based on the unique requirements of a client. At the offset of the search, a team of hand-picked individuals is usually put together from multiple departments—marketing, purchasing and legal.

Key stakeholders from the business units or subsidiaries concerned may also be invited to get their input and buy-in. It's important to make this a collaborative process from start to finish, especially if they are expected to actively embrace and evangelize the chosen agency.

Too often, client teams that weren't invited to participate, end up rejecting the relationship afterwards when issues arise, as they inevitably do. The more upfront buy-in, the more likely the decision is to stick, and support to be provided. The team is formed, composed of a Project Lead and a Core Team. The project lead is first appointed by the Project Sponsor who oversees the entire project. The project sponsor is either the final decision maker or the arbitrator, should the Review Team be unable to reach a decision.

Given the strategic importance of an agency search, the CMO or VP of Marketing is often the project sponsor, if not the project lead in smaller organizations. Once the "go-to" project lead has been assigned, he/she is responsible for assembling the core team, a virtual team typically composed of representatives from around the company and relevant business groups. The core team typically includes select clients—typically marketers—as well as key representants from legal, procurement and PR. The core team meets on a frequent basis to make sure the project objectives are met within the defined parameters, keeping the project on time and on budget. Having the right individuals on the team, with relevant experience and the right sphere of influence is essential to gather meaningful feedback throughout as well as to the credibility of the selection process.

The core team will sign off on all documents produced, so everyone is working from the same sheet of music. The final decision may be reached unanimously or by the majority of the team. They may make their recommendation to the project sponsor who is the ultimate decision-maker.

Once all key individuals have been engaged, the search methodology and timeline have to be defined and agreed upon. The project schedule is often a source of tension since the need for an agency to take on work immediately has to be tempered by the need to follow a well-orchestrated process that delivers a viable long-term solution to the company. The duration of the project will vary significantly based on the nature of the review, its scope, and the client itself. Global agency searches can take up to four to sixth months, in some cases even longer, especially if it involves a large number of participants around the world.

A domestic search can take up to two to three months depending on the complexity and scope of the search, but most clients will target an eight weeks window. Clients looking to hire a new agency for one particular assignment may need an accelerated search to get a new agency hired within weeks, not months. Clearly, the process for a much more simple search wouldn't require nearly as much effort and due diligence as a search for a long term partnership. The schedule has to be vetted internally to ensure it provides sufficient time for all parties involved to contribute. No one wants to start over simply because the decision was rushed or there wasn't any internal buy-in.

An agency search consultant can speed up the selection process and save the company precious time. Before the process is formally kicked off, members of the core team must commit the time to participate in all key milestone

Roles	Responsibilities
Project Sponsor	▸ Is accountable for the overall project ▸ Is the final decision maker or arbitrator in the event of a tie-breaker
Project Lead	▸ Assembles the Review Team ▸ Defines the schedule and associated milestones ▸ Is responsible for the successful completion of the project. ▸ Is the spokesperson for the project inside and outside the company ▸ Is the direct interface to other departments
Core Team	▸ Represents the interests of the company ▸ Screens potential agency candidates ▸ Participates in agency visits ▸ Reviews agency materials and responses to RFI and RFPs ▸ Participates in agency presentations ▸ Provides input to inform decision ▸ May be asked to cast a vote
Consultant (Optional)	▸ Provides project management and coordiation support ▸ Shares knowledge of the agency market, identifies potential candidates ▸ Interfaces with agency candidates ▸ Facilitates agency fact-finding, pre-screening, reference checking ▸ Weighs in on the selection ▸ May be asked to handle post-selection activities, e.g., negotiations, on-boarding

Typical Agency Management Responsibilities

meetings and decisions, or agree to delegate. Revisiting decisions that have already been made can be disastrous and demoralizing. If there is an incumbent agency, the agency leadership must be notified in a timely manner to allow them to handle PR and employee inquiries.

A communication plan will need to be established that include internal FAQs, email announcements and press releases. Agency searches/reviews always generate buzz and press inquiries. A PR plan ensures so that any leakage to the press can be handled in the best interest of the company and the agencies (should those be publicly disclosed). Having clear expectations and objectives is of upmost importance to best prepare for a search.

Phase III: Research and Filtering

At first, the options may seem endless or somewhat overwhelming with countless agencies to choose from. There are thousands of talented agencies around the world with unique credentials and competencies. Finding the ideal partner among those is a bit like finding a needle in a haystack. Where do you start? This is where a search consultant can be handy. He or she can quickly and objectively come up with a preliminary list of potential candidates based on his or her experience and knowledge of the industry alone. Clients can also leverage a variety of industry references, business journal listings, and other resources that provide robust multi-criteria searchable agency directories and services with in-depth agency profiles such as the Advertising RedBooks™, Adforum.com, Agencyfinder.com, ANA, 4As and any other relevant organization. Annual lists of top agencies are published by trade magazines such as *Ad Age*, *AdWeek*, and other specialized trade publications.

It's absolutely insane to see ill-informed clients invite large numbers of candidate agencies to the process without first attempting to reduce the list to a reasonable number, wasting their own time and valuable resources and those of the agencies in the process. Clients are encouraged to identify no more than ten to fifteen agencies at this stage of the process. Although there is no magical number, common sense calls for a number that is large enough to provide sufficient choice but small enough to be manageable. Once RFI responses have been received and evaluated, no more than six to eight agencies should be invited to next phase and respond to the RFP at which point, only three to four agencies are then participating in face to face presentations. The 4As calls this the 15-8-4 rule.

To narrow down the list to qualified agency candidates, the core team should consider filtering agencies with competitive conflicts that are unlikely to be resolved favorably (the competitor's account is significantly larger than yours, so there is no way the agency would jump ship). The agency will need to decide whether or not they would consider drop their existing client(s) if/once awarded the business.

The concept of "conflict" has evolved in recent years. Lack of industry standard definition has led clients to decide for themselves what is tolerable or not. Holding network companies have broadened their offering through multiple branded agencies within it to deal with those conflicts and give themselves an opportunity to pursue multiple clients in a same category. If you are Burger King, do you have anyone in the food industry on your list of competitors or only those in the fast food business? This is a subjective judgment call for brand advertisers to make. Clients would typically produce a list of their key competitors at the beginning of the project.

Once the preliminary list has been compiled, the selected agencies are asked to participate in the review process. At that point, the client must provide some basic information about their search. The intent is to offer sufficient information for an agency to decide if they want to participate in the review. The agency packet might include an introduction to the company (vision and mission statement), a business and financial overview, an overview of key business objectives as well as marketing challenges, and a description of prior marketing service provider arrangements.

It can include current agency rosters and tenure (including any recent additions and terminations), what is expected of the agency, scale and scope of the relationship, expected marketing expenditures/budgets, prior compensation methods, reasons for the review, timing and key milestones, number of agencies invited (is the incumbent agency invited?), selection criteria, decision making process, access to resources and key contacts, process for work approval, existing program and research measurement, and success metrics.

If one of the agency candidates works for one of the client's competitors but is considering resigning the account, it becomes a much more delicate situation given the confidential nature of their involvement. This would need to be managed with the upmost level of confidentiality to avoid any leakage that would jeopardize the search and the agency's relationship with their client. Once the agencies have received their packet of information, a phone conversation can be scheduled to answer any additional questions they may have.

Thankfully, the AAAA published a paper on agency search agreements to provide agencies with best practices on how to obtain formal agreements between an agency and a prospective client or for handling a client's request for proposal. The paper provides some useful guidance on sensitive topics such as confidentiality, information disclosure, need for transparency, ownership of agency ideas and work, and reimbursement for agency activity and expenses. Questionnaires such as the "AAAA Standardized Marketer New Business Questionnaire" and the "AAAA Standardized Agency New Business Questionnaire" facilitate up-front discussions, putting the agencies on a more equal footing and improving the agency's understanding of the client's needs. A client should target to have three to five highly qualified agencies to the next stage of this process.

Phase IV: Request for Information (RFI)/ Request for Proposal (RFP)

The American Association of Advertising Agencies (4As) recommends that clients and agencies enter into a formal agreement at the outset of every agency search, covering key topics such as confidentiality, ownership of agency ideas and work, and reimbursement for agency participation and expenses. Since clients and agencies are very likely to disclose proprietary information about how they do business (process, technology, approach/methodology), they recommend that access to and use of such confidential information should be protected by a mutually binding confidentiality agreement which protects both parties.

The concept of ownership of agency ideas and work can be more controversial. The agency is likely to produce ideas, concepts and share recommendations that have intrinsic value to the client. AAAA therefore recommends that the agency preserve ownership of those ideas and work in a written agreement. Finally, the agency may expect to be compensated for its time participating in the review in addition to the costs associated with the review (travel expenses, etc.). The reimbursement of expenses is pretty common but compensating agencies for their time participating in an agency search is less common and sometimes debated by clients who expect agencies to eat the cost as part of their new business development efforts. Some agencies may choose not to participate in a review based on these terms. Clients must weigh the pros and cons accordingly.

Client Viewpoint

"While conducting an agency search, probe deeper than case studies from credential presentations. Check references; dig deeper using your connections. This is a small community. You will gain tremendous insight from hearing about other's experiences with an agency or team."

KEVIN PARHAM, Director Global Advertising, Campbell Soup

Once agencies express interest in participating in the review, a more involved information gathering process will start to validate and complement the information already collected about the agencies. The purpose here is to further reduce the list of qualified agencies to the very few final candidates. To make an informed decision, the client will require participating agencies to fill out a Request for Information (RFI) document.

Be reasonable, however. Limit the number of questions to the most relevant and insightful ones. It's insane to see clients send very extensive RFI templates with everything question imaginable that agencies have then to fill out. Sadly enough, most of these questions will probably not be read in their entirety by the client.

In some rare cases, the RFI is not restricted to a particular set of pre-determined agencies. For example, in 2009, the French Interprofessional Center for the Dairy Industry broadly advertised in *AdWeek*'s Services and Resources section its search for a communications agency as part of a three year assignment to develop, coordinate and put together a mix communications campaign in support of the presence, consumption, and sales in the U.S.A. of cheeses from France.

The purpose of the RFI is to provide detailed information about the agency's profile, management team, organizational chart and operating structure, business approach, financials, credentials, client list, and potential conflicts (and more importantly, how they would be resolved), core and extended capabilities, and so on. It typically requests case studies and creative work samples that might help understand the agency capabilities. It is pretty standard documentation that agencies are accustomed to providing. Agencies must be cautious however about the claims made, and avoid overstating account wins and status of relationship with other clients.

A very effective way of gaining insight into a particular agency is to speak to the agency's existing clients. The RFI should include a reference section, requesting the names of at least two or three existing clients, with similar account size and services. This type of conversation can prove to be the most valuable part of the screening process. The team will learn much about the strengths and weaknesses of the agency as seen from another client's perspective.

Another way to gather information is to visit the agencies' Websites. In today's environment every agency has a Website, and given the increasing importance of digital in our communication mix, the quality of the Website experience may tell you quite a bit about their understanding, appreciation, and abilities in this area. Have you ever heard of the story of the shoe maker who never wore good shoes? Or the hair stylist with his/her hair always messed up? Not a confidence-builder, is it?

A Website can provide very helpful information about the agency's ability to talk about itself and gives access to press releases that speak to major events in the agency's history or annual reports for publicly traded companies providing much insight on how each agency within the network is doing overall. However, if it's obviously biased, sometimes outdated and pretty limited in content, it tells you something else, doesn't it?

Instructions will need to be provided to the agencies on how to fill out the RFI. Clients will want to make sure to remind agencies of the confidentiality of the information exchanged between the two parties, that any news release or any disclosure regarding any aspect of the selection process cannot be made without the client's written approval; whether or not you will be responsible for any the costs they will incur during this process; the client's policy regarding document retention and disposal; how to submit questions and to whom; how to treat any pre-contract discussions; how one plans to treat intellectual property and any other similar considerations. So the RFI fills a major gap in information gathering and it is highly recommended during a review. Still some companies will bypass this step and directly get into a Request for Proposal (RFP).

The purpose of the RFP is to describe the way the agency would meet the needs of the brand advertiser, how they would structure the team to serve the account, what resources would be involved, and how they would approach the business overall and what their proposed financial arrangements would be. It provides deeper insight into the strategic approach taken by the agency. It is very specific to this particular client situation and therefore requires a bit more prep work for the agency. The RFP will include questions such as:

- "What specific actions would you suggest the client take to meet its marketing objectives?"
- "How you characterize the client's efforts today?"
- "What do you see as they key issues, challenges, and opportunities faced by the company?"
- "What are your views and opinions on their industry?"
- "How would you structure your team to most effectively serve the account?"
- "How would you propose to collaborate with other roster agencies?"
- "How would triage the work?"
- "How would you suggest we measure performance?"
- "How would you stage your growth to meet those demands?"

Finally, the agency should be asked to provide the most compelling reason for the client to choose it over another (arguable equally capable) agency. Given the amount of information covered in a typical RPF, a client will want to minimize the number of agency candidates at this stage of the process to avoid crawling under pounds of carefully organized paper reports that may, even worse, never be read. As in prior stages, the agencies may have clarifying questions about the RFP. I strongly encourage clients to invite questions from agencies. As the 18th century French philosopher and writer Voltaire suggested: "Judge a person by their questions, rather than their answers." Clients will learn tremendously about the agencies by the way they formulate their questions and the type of questions they ask.

However, it's absolutely insane to think that some clients will answer questions but then turn around and share those with every agency candidate. If an agency is not asking the right questions, they shouldn't benefit from getting answers from agencies clever enough to ask them. There are different schools of thought about whether or not a client should level the playing field. In my opinion, clients should not attempt to artificially level the playing field to save themselves time and efforts.

Once the information has been carefully reviewed, the consultant or project lead may require every team member to fill out a scoring sheet to then aggregate all the responses on a simple table or scorecard so that agency responses can be evaluated side by side. If you are using a consultant, they will provide you a standard template that has been customized for your individual needs. Summarizing the data supplied into a readable format is imperative to help the team evaluate the responses provided. It requires everyone to use a common taxonomy and definitions. In addition to the table, a simple scoring methodology will facilitate the ranking and sorting of agencies.

The scoring methodology can vary from scoring each attribute on a scale from 1 to 5, For example, 1 being "the lowest" and 5 being "the highest" for each question on a similar scale, or 1 being "strongly disagree" and 5 being "strongly agree." Each attribute or question should be weighted and agreed upon by the team. Then the results can be tabulated and calculated based on the score and weight. The analysis can be conducted in a number of different ways to evaluate the strengths and weaknesses of each candidate. After this initial rating, a first cut can be conducted and the list of agency candidates reduced to the final few.

Phase V: Presentations

The RFI/RFP phase misses a vital component: the human experience. It's incredibly difficult to get a feel for what it would be like to work with an agency based only on the way they answered questions and without getting to know the individuals that provided them. Some would argue good agencies can be particularly bad at filling RFI/RFPs. Perhaps. It's almost certain that those good at filling out RFI/RFPs are not always the best agencies to work with. The point here is that the RFI/RFP phase is about collecting meaningful information that can be used to inform the face to face discussions that will result from this phase of the process. It's rarely sufficient to form a decision at this phase and marketers should be wary of making one now.

The next logical step is meeting with the agency to check the chemistry between the agency and client team, clarify any potential gap in the RFI/RFP, and give both parties the opportunity to ask questions, and ultimately assess their understanding of your business and their ability to think about it strategically. The chemistry check is a critical component as it says much about the future partnership from the outset.

Client Viewpoint

"One of the most common mistake companies make during an agency search is to not invest enough time to get to know the account team that will actually work on their business. In the end, this is less about the agency itself as it is about the people working on your account."

TIM WHITING, Senior Director Global Marketing, Motorola

This opportunity obviously goes both ways. During the stage of "courtship," both parties find each other very engaged, willing, and positive about the future, sometimes at the risk of de-emphasizing negative perceptions and magnifying positive ones.

The agencies will need a reasonable amount of time to get prepared for the final stage of the review process, especially if it involves a creative shootout which is more time-consuming. The credential presentations may be taking place at each agency, sometimes in multiple locations per agency for global clients. It is highly recommended to conduct the meeting at the agency's office rather than at the client's corporate headquarter, which seems more appropriate for a creative shootout.

Client Viewpoint

"During an agency pitch, ask for the people that will be working on your team. The client might fall in love with the pitch team, then a bus load of new people show up the following day at the door."

JULIE GIBBS, Director, Corporate Brand Marketing, Campaign Management, Adobe

It's always tempting for clients to conduct the meeting at their office to minimize the burden of travel and coordination. Visiting agency offices, however, gives clients the opportunity to experience firsthand the true personality of the agency and validate whether or not it is consistent with the materials they provided. There is nothing like seeing how they treat a client at the front desk. Check the atmosphere and layout of their workspace, get a feel for the culture and energy level, and see how they interface with other in their own element.

It is of upmost importance to meet the core team that would be actively engaged in your business at those meetings, not just the management team that you may not see much of after the selection process. Agencies tend to put their best talent upfront for this type of meeting, even if those resources won't be involved as you move forward. Make sure the folks that will work on your business are the ones presenting. Half a day is a standard time allocation for these onsite visits, giving everyone enough time to participate, usually followed by a smaller group dinner to become more familiar with the agency management team and the key people involved in the business.

The review team is encouraged to take notes on the presentations but their feedback should be requested only when all agencies have presented, to give them a chance to compare all presentations before stake-ranking them.

It's now time for the "pony show." There are two types of meetings: credential presentations and create shootouts. Some clients may require both, if time and budget allows. If a creative shootout is expected, the credentials presentation is unlikely to be a decisive factor in the selection process. So it makes sense to schedule those within proximity to get a full picture of the agency candidate.

Credential Presentations

For credential presentations, the objective is to go past the documentation and ask questions about the information that has already been submitted. It also gives the agency an opportunity to show their proprietary tools and solutions, some of their work and client case studies that speak to the hot buttons and pain points experienced by the prospective client. The review team should judge both the content and the form. The content will include questions about their ability to understand their client's business, to provide strategic insight and create impactful ideas, to leverage the brand, find innovative ways to speak and engage their audiences, to measure, optimize, and analyze performance.

The form will include questions about their ability to present their work effectively, to leverage each skills, seek buy-in, invite input and manage client feedback. It also includes more subjective criteria like passion and energy level expressed by the agency during the presentation, as well as how approachable the team members are and whether or not people would feel comfortable working with them.

Client Viewpoint

"Creative is where you establish emotional connections between people and work, and between a company and its customers. It is a fundamental part of any meaningful agency review."

JULIE GIBBS, Director, Corporate Brand Marketing, Campaign Management, Adobe

Creative Shootouts

The purpose of the creative shootout is to assess how the agency would address a real client marketing challenge and demonstrate how they would apply their skills in a real-life scenario. It gives the client a better understanding of the agency's listening and reasoning capabilities, how the agency likes to engage with a client, and how they communicate their ideas and receive input.

The participation in "creative shootouts" is a highly debated topic since some agencies do not believe that this type of creative real-life assignment, sometimes referred as a "beauty contest," is conclusive. It's a worthwhile argument. But what other options do clients have besides credential presentations? How would they get to know the team and see them perform? Hiring a couple of agencies and giving them different paid assignments is not only unrealistic, it would be even less objective.

Typically, the same marketing assignment would be provided to the agencies, allowing the core team to compare the respective approaches and creative solutions. A creative shootout usually requires more time and resources since it will require the client to brief the agency and be available to answer any follow up questions. The specific assignment should be relatively well defined and well contained to help the client assess the candidate agencies compared to their most important selection criteria. Therefore, it is common for the creative shootout to be limited to rough concept to avoid the often unnecessary production expenses to bring it to life. It is recommended to put the emphasis on the idea development process and less on the tactical execution process, which is typically not a differentiating and therefore deciding factor in agency reviews.

Although the client will need to allocate enough time to answer any questions about the assignment, unlike a real assignment, the project lead is likely to shield internal contacts from the barrage of questions an agency would usually ask. A briefing document will be submitted with all appropriate supporting documentation (research materials, branding guidelines, etc.). Once again, the way the agency interacts with the client during that time will be very telling, a close approximation to how both parties would work together and should ultimately reflect on the end product delivered by the agency.

Client Viewpoint

"Agencies don't make money on clients they don't have. It's increasingly hard for agencies to do a good pitch these days given the lower margin levels. You will get a more honest piece of work if you pay for it."

JULIE GIBBS, Director, Corporate Brand Marketing, Campaign Management, Adobe

Equal time (say one or two conference calls with the client) and access to information should be provided to the agencies.

For global accounts, the client may require the candidate agencies to demonstrate their capabilities on a global scale as well as in-market, with their ability to adapt a global concept into specific markets. This is what Visa requested of TBWA before the company decided to appoint the agency as its creative global agency around its global brand campaign "Life takes Visa."

Perhaps the most common issues faced by the industry are related to the ownership of ideas and whether or not agencies should be compensated for all or some of their expenses, regardless of whether or not the work will be used by the client. Agencies like Euro RSCG Life have been known to decline participating in reviews where the client wants to keep pitch ideas and materials. No agency wants to give away work.

Participating in a creative shootout can be an expensive proposition for an agency as it will require a number of resources to work on the project and out of pocket expenses.

Some clients will offer to compensate for the agency's travel expenses; some will offer to compensate for a portion of the expenses associated with the assignments. This is commonly known as "pitch fee." If the client offers to compensate the agency for some of their time and/or expenses, a written agreement should be signed by the agency and the client that stipulates ownership of the work. This type of compensation issues are typically addressed early on in the review process.

Although most agencies consider business development as a "cost of doing business," the most prestigious agencies may still decline to participate in the overall review if the client won't agree to compensate the agency for all or some of its expenses. They certainly get a point. For many of them, it can turn out to be a wasteful and expensive exercise. And it might distract their existing team from servicing existing paying clients.

In advance of conducting search meetings or presentations, it is recommended that the client and participating agencies discuss how ownership, license, or usage rights of agency-developed ideas, plans, and work will be handled.

It's insane for a client to assume that an agency would agree to enter a pitch if the client has the ability to own the work of that agency and hire another one to launch the campaign. Unless specified otherwise, the agency keeps ownership of the work presented, regardless of whether or not a fee is paid to the agency. Once again, the core team will be asked to provide feedback about the presentation(s), and about the agency's ability to perform in the context of a real business scenario.

Client Viewpoint

"One of the most common mistakes made by clients when conducting agency reviews is to underestimate the value of keeping stakeholders informed throughout the process so there are no surprises and everyone understands the decisions and their consequences."

MARIANN COLEMAN
Director, Global Media Relations and Performance, Intel

Phase VI: Selection

The assessment of the credential presentations and creative shootout (if applicable) complements the RFI/RFP already conducted. Further conversations may be needed to address any outstanding questions or concerns by the core team. The methodology has already been defined and agreed upon, the qualitative and quantitative information has been collected, so it is now only a matter of consolidating the assessment of the various team members. Trust and integrity are of upmost importance throughout the process.

The DraftFCB's now infamous honeymoon with Wal-Mart Stores, Inc. which hired DraftFCB in October 2006 after a comprehensive review, only to re-pitch the business two months later amid concerns over the handling of the review by Wal-Mart Store's SVP of Marketing Communications Julie Roehm, will probably remain the most publicized agency review of all times.[29]

The lawsuits that followed between the company and its former employee shed lights on the importance of strict adherence to corporate policies (not

Individual Scoring Submissions by Individual Members				
Client Team Member: John Smith				
Criteria	Weight	Agency A	Agency B	Agency C
Broad Strategic Thinking	15%	5	3	4
Understanding of Business/Industry	10%	3	1	5
High Impact Creative	10%	2	5	3
Innovative/Outside of the box ideas	5%	4	4	2
etc.	etc.	etc.	etc.	etc.
TOTAL	**100%**	**3.5**	**2.8**	**3.2**

accepting gifts from candidate agencies, for example) and code of conduct. Using the same scoring methodology and taxonomy for the credential presentations and creative shootout allows for consistency and builds trust in the fairness of the evaluation. The core team adds their scores against the weighted attributes and any appropriate commentaries as in the above example.

The results will be once again compiled and summarized anonymously for the team. The reason for keeping results anonymous is to save face for team members who may not have picked the lead agency and to avoid putting them into a defensive position that could derail the process. Once the results are available, the core team should meet again to discuss the findings. If everything went according to plan, the team has reached consensus and a winner has emerged. If not, the project sponsor may need to arbitrate the decision. The discussion is centered on remaining gaps or weaknesses that the agency will be asked to address. The client then contacts the selected agency to congratulate them.

It's advisable to notify the chosen agency that it is considered as the company's number one choice but that the final decision is pending reaching agreement on payment terms and the contract. The client is then in a much stronger position to negotiate favorably when the final decision is contingent on mutually agreed terms.

The prospective agencies should not be contacted yet since failure to reach an acceptable agreement with the lead agency candidate may require the client to pursue an alternative solution. Although rare, given that financial arrangements have been discussed during the course of the review, the agreement has not been a key focus area until now and it now may go side-ways after extensive contract deliberation cycles. The decision is then communicated internally (email announcement, newsletters, etc.) and externally (press release, articles). Internally, the company will need to provide some justification for why this particular agency is a better fit than any others and what the company is doing to get the agency on-board and ready to take on business. At the very least, it should provide a rudimentary Q&A with engagement rules and contact information for all agency offices concerned.

The non-selected candidates will need to be notified prior to any internal or external communications, preferably by phone, followed up by a formal communication from the company. They will most likely ask for feedback about where they fell short on meeting expectations, especially in light of the numerous hours they invested to get to this point, which is understandable. This may be a highly sensitive topic since your legal department will advise you to keep it high-level and focus on tangible criteria the agency didn't meet to the client's satisfaction.

If handled professionally, the defeated agencies might gain some insight that would be applicable to future reviews. It's critical to avoid burning bridges. You may be reaching out to them a few years later to pick up another piece of business or participate in a new agency review. Be decisive, be direct, and be fair. As in personal relationships, always stay true to your values and you will find the pearl you deserve.

Client Viewpoint

"Most clients say they want a partnership but it must be set that way from the beginning."

JULIE GIBBS, Director, Corporate Brand Marketing, Campaign Management, Adobe

Conducting an agency search has become an incredibly valuable skill set for clients to acquire in light of the continued fragmentation of marketing services and even greater demands and expectations on existing relationships. A well-managed agency search is a demanding process that requires the involvement of significant resources at agencies and clients. Having a rigorous process mapped out and assembling a strong internal team will increase the quality of the end product: the right agency to meet current (and hopefully future) client needs. Having clear objectives and requirements is a must before investing any time and resources. Having executive buy-in and support is vital. Transparency and communication are key. Clients must also remember that agencies pay close attention to the way they handle reviews and searches. The way they conduct themselves and the way the process is handled says a lot about the type of client they are. The 4s created Review Central on its site where report cards and comments on RFPs and pitches will be posted, shedding bright lights on good and bad search practices.

Clients will continue to experiment and find more effective, streamlined ways to find and hire the best agency partner for their business. An agency partner that hopefully brings a unique and distinct offering that complements and strengthens the company's core marketing muscle. Some like Mtn Dew, are even turning over the selection of their agency to brand advocates and fans, asking them to review video postings and cast their vote online for the agency of their choice.[30]

No matter how much time and resources have been invested in this process, finding a new pearl and hiring that agency is only the beginning. The overall success of an agency search should also be measured by the quality of the on-boarding, staffing, training, and briefings that will follow that selection. It's now all about getting the agency quickly up and running so it can prove itself and make the clients highly successful. Only time will tell if you found the right agency pearls for your business.

{Taking Immediate Action}

TOP 5

BEST PRACTICES TO HARNESS THE MADNESS

❶ Conducting an agency search is costly for everyone involved and doesn't always lead to a better partnership. So don't start a search unless you are absolutely certain that you need to, and have a clear idea of what you are looking for.

❷ Hire an agency search consultant if you don't have extensive experience in this area, if this is a large scale project, or if you simply want to accelerate the speed of the project without compromising the quality of its outcome.

❸ Set up a collaborative process with agency candidates that encourages open discussions, exchange of relevant information, as well as provides reasonable access to key stakeholders. Set a reasonable schedule.

❹ Be transparent about the selection criteria and the decision-making process. Determine upfront if you will compensate agencies for their participation in the review. If you are asking agencies to participate in the creative shootout, be clear about expectations as it relates to ownership of IP. Don't communicate your decision until you have negotiated competitive terms with the chosen agency.

❺ Look for compatible agency partners doesn't mean looking for a mirror image of your company. To the contrary. Look for partners that enrich, expand, stretch, and strengthen internal skills and ultimately complement you as a client.

6 Pacta Sunt Servanda

Setting up a rock-solid agency contract

> "There is no such thing as inclement weather, only inappropriate clothing."
>
> —Ben Zander
> *Boston Philharmonic Orchestra Conductor*

I am no attorney. If you read this, chances are you're not one either. Not to worry. You don't need to have a law degree to have a basic understanding of agency contracts and to play an important role in setting up one for your company. Yet there are many legal factors to consider. It is critical that you have a contract in place that clearly outlines the obligations of both parties. If you speak Latin, you may have picked up that Pacta Sunt Servanda means "agreements must be kept." If you have a well thought out and negotiated contract, both parties are more likely to keep up their end of the bargain. Simply put, a contract helps define what is expected of us.

While most agency agreements are likely not to end up in court, if agreements are not kept then this is considered a breach of the agreement and the courts can step in to make sure that "agreements must be kept." There are a few things typical legal departments might not be accustomed to deal with when setting up a contract with an advertising or marketing communications agency. It's crazy to think that so many clients and agencies are getting "married" so eagerly that they don't even read the fine line of their prenuptial agreement. It's even more insane when they wake up with a headache months or years later, dazed by what was so quickly agreed upon when their current circumstance seemed to be a remote possibility.

What do clients *really* need to know about agency contracts? What risks are they trying to manage with the contract? How does a client set up a contract that provides adequate coverage and protection? How should a client deal with intellectual-property rights for the work produced by the agency during a pitch or during the course of a relationship? How should they handle the termination of a contract or competitive conflicts should they arise? What are some of the most common mistakes and best practices in contract negotiations today? Why should they care?

I debated whether or not I should include a chapter in this book dedicated to agency contracts. And if I did, whether it should be less than a page long. Most legal-related matters and contract language have the unavoidable effect of sleeping medication on most people. Yet, without them, we might expose our respective companies to potentially disastrous and unintended results. So I decided to take on the challenge and provide the reader a succinct, yet insightful and actionable overview of the fundamentals of advertising and marketing communications contracts. This chapter describes some of the most critical sections that anyone in marketing or procurement should be aware of as well as common pitfalls both clients and agencies must avoid before tying the knot.

Using Contracts to Strengthen Relationships

A well established and structured contractual relationship is more likely to yield positive results and strengthen the partnership. In its purest form, a contract is a legally binding exchange of promises or agreement between parties that the parties are expected to follow on a continuing basis but that the law will enforce if needed. Naturally, agencies need to understand what is expected of them (scope of work) in exchange for a financial return (compensation) that must be agreed upon from the start.

There are a number of advertising or marketing communications contract types available to companies meeting different client and agency business requirements. These requirements are based on the unique needs of a particular client/agency relationship—Website design and PR contract requirements are different from media contracts, for example—and the nature of the agreement both parties intend to enter varies accordingly. These contracts all have something in common: they set legal boundaries for all to obey and help state mutual expectations about the services provided and the method by which they will be delivered.

Client Viewpoint

"Don't use the contract from the old agency and dust it off for the new one. In that contract might be hidden the reasons why you are looking for a new agency in the first place."

JULIE GIBBS, Director, Corporate Brand Marketing, Campaign Management, Adobe

Having a contract in place with your agency is not only common sense, it is the legal means to manage mutual expectations once it has been signed. It also protects both parties when they need it the most. Clients should determine and agree on contract terms and conditions at the outset of the relationship but should be prepared to revisit those occasionally, especially when the relationship has matured and mutual needs are better understood or more clearly articulated.

There is much that is critical to any relationship that cannot be captured in a legal document, to most attorneys' despair. Albert Einstein was right when he said that "Not everything that counts can be measured and not everything that can be measured counts." That applies to agency contracts. Fortunately, legal departments can help clients come up with standard terms and conditions that adequately protect the company's interest. After all, these contracts are a bit like insurance policies. You don't really need them until something happens in the relationship that makes you wish you had explicit terms to clear the path to solving a particular problem or addressing misaligned expectations. A breach of contract can also have severe implications for the party concerned. This section provides an overview of key issues and considerations before putting together a solid contract with an agency.

This is not however a substitute to the legal services required successfully finalizing a contract and providing adequate protection for both parties. It is highly recommended that any contract be reviewed by the company's legal department or a qualified external law firm before signing it, entering in any type of business relationship with an agency, or even starting any work.

Too often, clients jump in and start doing work with agency without a contract in place, at significant risk to both the company and the agency. It is particularly important to check industry references[31,32] and get legal counsel as contract complexity has increased significantly with the expanding and complex nature of advertising services rendered, especially in digital media. With that said, how does one get started? Let's find out.

Getting a Rock-Solid Contract in Place

Companies and agencies should not underestimate the time and effort required to get a sound contract in place. It's not uncommon to see this process significantly shrunken to accommodate pressing business demands which in turn, may lead to challenges in the relationship moving forward. It's wise to invest the time to get it right the first time around. This process can take anywhere from three weeks or less to over three months depending on the scale and nature of the work relationship pursued. More importantly, the timing will be mostly impacted by the willingness of both parties to move decisively and compromise on elements of the contract where they may have initially

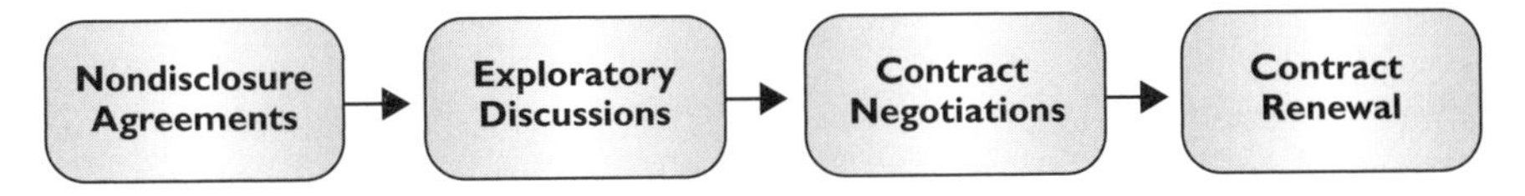

Process for Getting a Rock-Solid Contract in Place

taken adversarial or simply opposing positions. A number of steps should be followed to get the desired outcome from these negotiations.

From the beginning to the end of this process, both parties are actively negotiating to ensure their interests are being adequately represented in the forming partnership. Let's walk through each step.

Nondisclosure Agreement Typically, a client will start conversations with an agency after signing a mutually binding nondisclosure agreement (aka NDA). An NDA is designed to protect the confidentiality of any information shared between the parties, including at the initial phase of the "meet and greet" process. A client may need to reveal their marketing challenges or priorities to the agency. An agency may be asked to disclose their existing relationships. An NDA is designed to protect both parties until a decision has been made to move forward.

Client Viewpoint

"The most important parts of a contract are the scope and staffing, as well as the transparency of the costs for those two areas."

CARLA DODDS, Director, Multicultural Marketing and Marketing Vendor Management, Walmart U.S.

Exploratory Discussions This next phase typically involves a number of discussions with management teams from both companies about the nature and scope of services the agency will be asked to provide. The more specific, the better. There is no point going further into negotiations until those have been clearly defined by the client and adequately understood by the agency. It will be the basis for the conversations on expectations and compensation that will follow. Anything short of getting absolute clarity on the full range of services the agency will provide to the client is likely to end up being wasteful to both parties.

In absence of clarity, perhaps because it remains uncertain as to the agency capabilities in every service area, it might be wise to be as inclusive as possible and incorporate a description of all services that would be potentially be used by the client. Although this particular phase tends to be led by business stakeholders you would definitely benefit if you coordinated with your lawyer even if their contribution at this stage is limited.

Contract Negotiations If the corporate legal department has experience in handling this type of contracts, they may have a template that incorporates the unique terms and conditions associated with such services. If the corporate legal department does not have experience in this area, they should hire outside counsel with expertise in this area of adverting and marketing communications to help with the process and ensure adequate terms are included. Similarly, agencies bring years of experience working on similar contracts and can be expected to drive their agenda. They may use their own legal resources or subcontract these services to a law firm specialized in these services.

Both parties will go back and forth to seek consensus on open issues. Common roadblocks and issues will be addressed in the following section. The draft contract and redlined versions are reviewed and discussed extensively by both parties. This is where negotiation skills become handy. This process is generally led by attorneys with close input by the business, helping to inform important contract decisions. Some compromises might be necessary on both sides to get closure. Once both parties have reached an agreement on the totality of the contract, it can be signed by the individuals with appropriate decision-making authority. The contract is not effective until signed, so both parties should get it signed before any work is initiated.

Contract Renewal Agency engagements typically last many years. You do not, however, want to negotiate all the terms of the agreement every year. As such, many agreements remain in effect until terminated by either party or are renewed with minimal changes. Any change must be captured in writing and submitted once again for signature. The renewal contract will likely include a number of important addendums such as scope of work and staffing plans, financial and compensation terms, affiliated companies and other contract details that may be revised on a periodic basis but wouldn't necessitate a full contract review.

While these terms may appear in an addendum, they are the most important terms in any contract since they define what the agency will do and how much it will be paid. For this reason, these terms are often segregated in separate addendums from the basic terms and conditions governing the relationship. This way, addendums can be revisited annually without requiring a potentially lengthy or costly legal review of the entire agreement.

Standard Terms and Conditions in Advertising and Marketing Communications Contracts

Every relationship is different. So every relationship will require unique consideration when deciding which terms and conditions are most suitable for that relationship. A client may appoint the agency to be its agency of record for all or a portion of the business (also known as "exclusivity"), either domestically or internationally. A client may only contract with an agency on a project basis and with a number of other agencies under non-exclusive agreements. These nuances impact the nature of the agreement and the terms that will need to be negotiated.

In principle, both parties are agreeing to enter negotiations to establish fair and equitable terms for the relationship. But unless they both work hard at it, where they end up may not hold up to their original goals. The amount of legal considerations in an agency contract is enough to make anyone's head spin a few times.

Client Viewpoint

"Agency contracts have changed drastically over the past few years. More often contracts involve some aspect of system compliance or integration as part of the scope of work. Technology and Marketing have converged."

MOLLIE WESTON
Director Agency Management Operations, Best Buy

Fortunately, there are a number of contract terms that are considered fairly common to advertising and marketing communication services, and can be applied to virtually any client/agency relationship. The following section highlights the most common issues and why they matter. The most critical and most debated part of a contract is often the one about compensation. Prepare with your legal and corporate affairs department or contract with a specialized legal firm before having in-depth discussions with your agency.

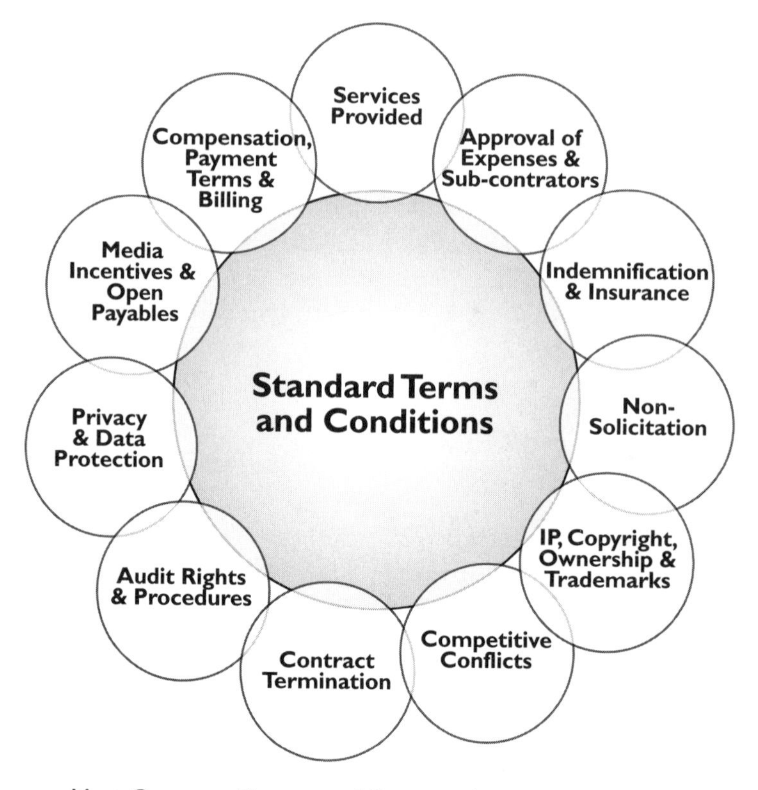

Most Common Elements of Contract for Agency Services

This figure shows terms of standard contract clauses that should help you get the conversation started, from general business terms such as copyright ownership and trademarks, privacy and data protection, and termination to more financially-oriented ones such as compensation, payment terms and billing.

Services Provided by Agency

What it is: A description of the services performed and delivered by the agency. These services will vary based on the type of services provided. A typical contract, for example, may include the following top-line description: analyze client requirements; provide account planning services and develop communication strategies; formulate and submit for approval concepts and recommendations; prepare recommendations and plan to meet them, and so forth. It may also include a list of additional agreed-upon services provided, such as social media, PR, promotion, merchandising, analytics and the range of media used by the agency, such as television, radio, printed advertisements, Websites, and so forth.

I suggest that clients aim broadly at first in this area. The list has to be exhaustive enough to not limit the range of services covered by a particular agency to the point where it is overly restrictive. But it should also be limited to those that are current core-agency competencies and agreed services. The list can always be updated as the relationship evolves when the agency decides to expand its service offering or the client transfer responsibilities from one agency to another. This is where the client must state clearly whether or not the agency is acting as an independent contractor or as an agent that is likely to change based on the type of services rendered.

Why should clients care? This is where the scope of services provided is defined. Perhaps more importantly, it can also define what's out of scope to avoid any confusion in the relationship moving forward. If the list of services is too broad, it is not prescriptive enough and can lead to scope creep or false expectations on both ends. If the list of services is too narrow, it may be slow you both down and not be flexible enough to accommodate ever-changing and growing client needs. If the agency acts as an independent contractor, the client cannot be held responsible for the personnel hired by the agency and the agency is responsible for all staff costs and contractor expenditures.

Compensation, Payment Terms, and Billing

What it is: This is where the contract will describe the structure of the compensation, payment schedules, approval process and (if appropriate) incentive compensation terms, cost allocation methodology such as overhead, and production and media expenses. This section should address how freelancers are handled financially, how overhead (if appropriate) is defined and calculated for the purpose of this agreement, how payment for production and media expenses (billings and invoicing) should be handled.

For example, what should the payment schedule be? How much of the costs should be paid upon award of the project or at its completion? Is the client requiring a non-use fee clause for music and talent contracts? Is there a policy for talent exclusivity? It addresses the approval process for such expenses: the type of information required for processing, the timing for payment, the handling of taxes and exchange rates, and other important financial provisions. It also states the type of financial reporting and frequency required in support of the relationship. It is likely to include a section on taxes (different types of taxes, ownership), especially for international contracts where there is a fair amount of complexity.

Why should clients care? This is the section that usually gets the most attention from both parties since it deals with financial transactions and impacts cash flow and payments. Detailed payment and billing terms are most important to ensure clients and agencies establish the back end processes and operating guidelines for prompt and timely payments. Clients should make sure that what is agreed upon is in line with their financial processes and internal regulations. The next chapter covers agency compensation in more details.

Approval of Expenses and Subcontracting

What it is: This section should stipulate what expenses are covered by the contract, what information is deemed necessary by the client, and how these expenses should be approved and by whom. There are a number of expenses associated with doing business with an agency that must be detailed out in the contract from media to artwork and production (artwork, mechanical, printing, proofreading, digital distribution,), talent (talent and production rights including right to use names, voices, music and so forth), collateral support and merchandising material related to advertising, marketing or communication campaigns, packing, shipping, delivery, research (competitive analysis, advertising concept testing) and media reports/ratings.

Some expenses like production may require the agency to competitively bid the work to multiple vendors. The agency may expect pre-payment to minimize cash flow for large expenditures. Payment terms may vary based on the type of expense and will need to be agreed upon. Penalties may be sought by the agency for continued late payments since it represents a serious financial burden. If expenses end up higher or lower than budgeted, a financial reconciliation process should articulate how those are to be handled. Typically, the agency is not allowed to subcontract any part of the work to any subcontractor without the client's prior written permission. If the client approves it, then the agency is held responsible for the performance and obligations of the subcontractors.

This section should also specify how travel expenses will be handled during the course of business. The client may have a detailed travel policy that it wants employees and vendors to adhere to. The travel policy might include specific guidance on allowable expense categories.

Why should clients care? It's in everyone's best interest that there are no surprises about what's included and what's not when first invoices come through the client's desk. How to best manage cash flow is an important consideration for the agency as well as for the client. No one is expected to profit from it and if set up properly, a neutral cash flow (aka "float") position is in everyone's best interest in the long run. What information is needed and clarity about who approves them should make the approval of expenses equally smooth for the client and efficient for all involved. The subcontracting approval makes it clear to the agency that they will need to apply the same rigorous process and controls with all its resources.

Travel can be a sizeable expense item when dealing with remote offices (client and agency do not reside in the same city), network coordination for agencies with international offices and out-of-town shoots. In other words, if a client is expected to spend a fair amount of its budget in agency travel, it's in their best interest to be as prescriptive as possible about the company's travel policy.

Media Incentives and Open Payables

What it is: If the agency is on point to manage media expenditures, clients have to clearly spell out how any discounts, rebates, incentives, paybacks, barters, credits collected by the agency, whether directly or indirectly related to the agreement, are credited back to the client within a particular timeline. It will also define how those media incentives are tracked and reported. Open payables are all media purchases that have not been invoiced by the third party media provider in excess of one year for any reason, something more commonly found in digital media which still lack the rigor of traditional media operating efficiencies. Although the client indemnifies the agency and remain liable for any funds, these funds should be returned to the client once that time window has passed.

Why should clients care? This is earned by the agency based on the total volume of spend and as a client, you are therefore entitled to those credits. Having clear rules on how those are treated ensures a smooth process for processing credits and open payables associated with aged media buys.

Indemnification and Insurance

What it is: This is a standard contract clause stipulating who is financially responsible and must defend the other party in any suit or proceeding against the client or its contractors, vendors, agents and other roles, holding the client harmless against any costs, damages or settlement awards which arise out of or are related to the breach of the contract. Mutual indemnification regarding claims of implicit or explicit breach of duties guarantees that each party will fulfill its obligations. In this section are also listed all insurances the agency must obtain and maintain throughout the entire term of the relationship.

Insurances may include commercial general liability policy, automotive liability, workers and employers' liability, professional liability/errors and omissions liability, workers' compensation and full compliance with all applicable laws, statues and regulations. It often requires the agency to provide certificates of insurance. These insurances can quickly add up to millions of dollars a year. For international contract, exchange risks and responsibilities will need to be spelled out based on the currency in which the agency will invoice the client.

Why should clients care? There are increasingly more examples of costly litigation over advertising and marketing activities these days. It's clearly better to be safe than sorry. An indemnification clause is a prerequisite. Your attorney shouldn't let you sign a contract without it anyway. If you are lucky, you will never have to find out know why it was so important to include in the contract. This clause is a must-have as well. Agencies have typically obtained the appropriate insurance policies to put the client at ease and to protect themselves. Tax liabilities can add up quickly, so having clarity on who pays certain taxes is important from the start of the relationship. Tax provisions are often complicated, so it is highly recommended that the tax and finance department weigh in on these provisions.

Privacy and Data Protection

What it is: Data protection is of paramount importance, especially when dealing with "personally identifiable information" (PII), something increasingly more common in a digital media environment. The clause clarifies the agency responsibilities as it relates to the collection, storage, usage, monitoring, security, and eventually destruction of client data. It should reference any relevant corporate guidelines the agency must follow.

Why should clients care? When providing PII, customers trust that the information is adequately safeguarded. Privacy laws around the world require clients to apply more vigilance and rigor to the handling of customer data. Giving access to sensitive data like customer data to a third party vendor like an agency is a risk that can mitigated with the appropriate level of disclosure and information sharing. It's especially important when the agency is responsible for handling large volumes of customer data on the client's behalf or is handling digital assignments where consumers are invited to provide their contact and profile information for promotional purposes or to access certain services and offerings, a growing share of client's marketing budget.

Audit Rights and Procedures

What it is: It's important that a client has full access to transactional and payment data handled by the agency on its behalf for a given time period. The type of documentation and records required should be listed (payroll records, timesheets, media placement, production bids, and books of account, to name a few).

Another important disclaimer is how audits will be paid for, especially if discrepancies are revealed through this process and how any overcharged or undercharged amount will be handled. It also clarifies who is authorized to conduct such audit. Some data such as individual agency salary is typically off limit and any audit of related data can be conducted through an independent third party to avoid compromising the sensitive and confidential nature of this information. If the audit reveals discrepancies in excess of a certain percentage of the total (usually 10% to 5%) of the total audited amount, the agency can be made responsible for paying for the cost of the audit.

Why should clients care? Clients will want to conduct an audit from time to time and having the requirements spelled out from the beginning will expedite the process when the time has come. It will also reduce the possible confusion and uncertainty around the way the audit will be conducted.

Non-Solicitation

What it is: The client and the agency agree to not solicit employees of the other party. Because a no-hire clause is generally not recommended based on labor laws, a non-solicitation clause is considered its second best cousin. A non-solicitation clause may continue for a number of months following an employee's termination or resignation to avoid having folks potentially "gaming" the system.

Why should clients care? It presents a number of benefits to clients. It's not uncommon for some clients to excessively hire from its agency roster, depleting an agency of its raw talent. Agencies find such practice to be potentially destabilizing for their operations and very costly (recruiting, on-boarding, and training costs of replacing that talent). And what is not financially sound for the agency over time is likely to impact the client relationship one way or another.

There are three common clauses that are particularly important to advertising and marketing communications contracts and require special consideration from a business and relationship perspective: intellectual property ownership, competitive conflicts, and contract termination.

Intellectual Property, Copyright Ownership and Trademarks

What it is: There are also different concepts of ownership. For example, the contract clause may give the agency access to all names, marks, logos, and designs for the sole purpose of performing the services already defined. The agency is not held responsible for the information provided by the client but the agency is held responsible for getting licenses, permits and other usage rights that fall within the agreed scope of work. From a client perspective, this section should stress that the work created by the agency is considered "work made for hire" by default for copyright purposes, including inventions, ideas, techniques, software and such. Whether or not an idea or a concept is ultimately produced should not alter its ownership.

Agency Viewpoint

"Clients should first ask if the agency has a standard contact. Many clients insist that their contract be used, without seeing what the agency typically uses. Most common roadblocks are about ownership of intellectual property. Clients want to own the agency's work; so do the agencies."

MARC A. BROWNSTEIN
President and CEO, Brownstein Group

Although different agreements can be pursued (such as rejected ideas that can be repurposed by the agency on another client, software and applications), most clients are retaining ownership of any work produced, regardless of its outcome. This remains a controversial topic in the industry. I expect continued tension on this subject in the years to come as the line between branded content and creative continue to blur and agencies build innovative customer experience-enhancing applications and tools they might want to repurpose for other clients.

Due to the popularity of labor-based compensation models, clients typically want to maintain full ownership of the work developed by that labor, even if concepts and materials are not being used immediately or are used for a different purpose from the in-scope services described in the contract (for example, using a concept developed for advertising into an internal promotional campaign). The issue tends to come up frequently when clients are making agencies pitch for their business and the agency expects to retain creative ideas and ownership of intellectual property rights presented.

It is common practice for the agency to keep ownership of the ideas produced during a new business pitch until the client hires the agency to execute the work or some reasonable financial arrangement can be made for the client to use a particular idea without formally hiring the agency to execute the work.

Why should clients care? The concept of ownership in advertising and marketing communications is increasingly more sensitive as dynamic digital experiences, software, and interactive solutions are built above and beyond traditional forms of communication, which may be appealing for agencies to repurpose and offer to other roster clients. Should all content created by agencies be treated equally? Are current agreements unnecessarily restrictive, inadvertently prohibiting the agency from using software that is not a specific stand-alone client deliverable? Should agencies and clients re-evaluate the standard ownership and intellectual property provisions of their contract to end up with more equitable agreements?

Most agencies are willing to explore creative financial arrangements that give them skin in the game, pushing the limits of "ownership" in the work produced for a client. The American Association of Advertising Agencies issued a position paper in early 2010 to address ownership, intellectual property and indemnification provisions when creating digital, online and mobile content.[33]

The 4A's position is that agency agreements with clients should be written to "preserve agency ownership and agency right to use agency developed software and tools." They assert that unlike a creative asset or commercial which is only of value to the client for which the agency created it, software and software related materials often produced by agencies as a by-product of services provided to the client have applicability and significant value to other potential agency clients. Therefore, agency/client agreements should be revisited to take this into consideration.

In the context of a new business pitch, it is important for the client to know what's off limit and what's not as it relates to creative ideas and concepts presented by candidate agencies after an agency has been selected. As far as trademark standards are concerned, this section must insist that all materials be reviewed by the client for explicit approval and how that process should be handled.

Competitive Conflicts

What it is: Setting clear expectations about the companies that the agency is restricted from working with is an important consideration when both parties agree to work together. Too often, the contract doesn't clarify with enough specificity the level of exclusivity the clients seek to enforce, leaving it to personal interpretation or prolonged, painful after-the-fact negotiations. Both parties attempt to find the right balance between an agency's desire to grow business where it has relevant experience and a client's desire for exclusivity. Clearly, agencies working for Burger King are very unlikely to also work for McDonald's or Taco Bell.

For the agency, agreeing to limit its business to one client in a given category is often a difficult decision. Agencies will consider this type of competitive conflicts clause when the client's account is sizeable enough to warrant such restrictions. There is no true industry standard on how to handle competitive conflicts, which often results in vague contract terms, subject to interpretation. How restrictive is the relationship? Is the conflict defined at the company, category or brand level? Is the agency handling the entire client's entire business (packaged goods) or a specific brand or category (Cereal brands X and Y)? Is conflict defined globally or on a country-by-country basis? How often is the list updated? How broadly is the client defining its competition?

In the past few years, this type of policy is increasingly more flexible and less restrictive, especially among large multi-brand companies that potentially compete with a substantial number of companies. It may be that the agency is already working with their key competitor and would need to resign the account upon a contract signed. Or it may be that the agency is planning to expand its client's portfolio in a particular industry segment. It might even be accidental on the part of the agency, as the result of mergers and acquisitions, for example, making it impractical for agencies and their holding companies to run their business.

Some exceptions are now commonly granted by the client at the agency's explicit and written request as long as certain criteria are adhered to: dedicated team structures so no staff can work for both accounts at the same time, restricted staff movement from one account to the other to a minimum period of time, housing of staff—in different offices or different floors, establishing proper technology firewalls and User Rights Management to secure access to documentation, directories, servers, and setting policies to ensure the strictest levels of confidentiality and security.

There are expectations in global accounts as well, where direct conflicts on a country-by-country basis are tolerated and competitors can co-exist under one agency banner because the global client has limited billing in that particular office. According to the American Association of Advertising Agencies,[34] "statements of agreement and trust are in favor, replacing formal conflict policies." It goes on to make the point that "conflicts are in the eyes of the beholder. Senior executives place high value on relationships and might endorse arrangements that less senior management might not feel empowered to approve."

Ultimately, the client, defined as the relationship owner, has to be comfortable (and that goes both ways). An agency should expect some latitude to pursue client opportunities that do not directly compete with their existing client. Those criteria should be defined and agreed upon for inclusion in the contract. Agencies typically will reach out to clients before entering a pitch to clear the way or decide to walk away. After all, relationships are based on mutual trust, which both parties play in a role in defining when drafting a competitive conflict clause.

Why should clients care? This issue can occasionally be a deal breaker. There is a lot at stake, so clients are understandably worried about the potential information leakage or conflict of interest an agency may have by servicing competitive businesses under the same roof. Although client rules seem to relax a bit about competitive conflicts, the concerns that led to this type of clause must be addressed by the agency to the client's satisfaction. Or the agency must decide if dealing with it is worth the trouble and run the risk of potentially losing the account.

Agencies gain deep industry experience when working for a particular client, which could easily be offered to another client in a similar category, eager to tap into a knowledgeable agency partner who can immediately deliver value to their business. Are you willing to potentially see the confidentiality of your work, all your past efforts, campaign learning, business intelligence and marketing best practices be taken to the competition? Similarly, a client must decide if they want to run the risks of having the agency resign the account due to a so-called "competitive conflict." Once again, it is about finding the right balance point between been vigilant without being unnecessarily restrictive with an agency.

Contract Termination

What it is: Any client/agency relationship eventually comes to an end. The termination clause describes the protocols and procedures associated with termination of the agreement and the transition period that follows. This includes but is not limited to: prior written notice, number of days for termination to be effective, the rights, remedies, duties and responsibilities in the event of termination, the transfer of client work, property, materials and assets, how to deal with non-cancelable commitments such as production and reservations, and contracts and arrangements with advertising media and vendors. A 60-90-day termination notice is the norm for most contracts giving everyone enough time to transition out of the relationship with minimal disruption. The actual terms vary based on the nature of the relationship and its overall scope. Large, retained-based, global contracts tend to offer more cushion than small, local project-based arrangements.

For the client whose agency walked away, it gives it enough time to look for another agency to pick up the work where the incumbent agency left it. For the agency whose client walked way, it gives it enough time to replace the account with a similar-size client, or layoff employees and reduce operating expenses at a speed that doesn't prevent the agency from transitioning the work without unforeseen hiccups. Agencies will often leverage for as much time a client is willing to agree to, giving them a safety net that allow them to hire key talent where it's needed.

Clients with labor-based agreements have been pushing for even shorter termination notice than 90 days to reduce the financial constraint of having to pay for a new agency to ramp up while paying for the incumbent to exit. Clients should carefully weigh the financial benefits of short termination periods against the potential waste or opportunity losses that can result from overly aggressive and potentially messy transitions. An extended termination date can be granted at the agency's request if the given termination takes place within the first year of the relationships. This additional protection invites the new agency to move aggressively with staff hiring without having to worry about the return of their long-term investment.

Why should clients care? It's a semi-sour topic, a bit like negotiating a pre-nuptial agreement with your soon-to-be spouse. Unlike a marriage, however, an advertising agency agreement will inevitably end. It's simply irresponsible not to define what happens when the time comes. The larger the account, the greater the pressure agencies are likely to exert to convince clients to agree to lengthier termination notices in an attempt to minimize their financial exposure.

Clients should apply good judgment to find the right balance point. A lengthy termination notice can prove to be expensive at the time of separation. A short termination notice might be financially beneficial to clients but might de-incent the agency from making staffing commitments that in turn benefits the relationship and the work itself.

Other standard clauses worth mentioning include code of conduct, business and employment practices, confidentiality and proprietary information for its adequate safeguarding, contract survival, procurement and subcontracting policies (related to non-discrimination, off-shoring, etc.), record retention and disposal, and how agency staff should conduct themselves when interacting with clients or on the client's behalf with third party vendors, freelancers and subcontractors. Clients should decide which ones are most relevant to their situation and ensure compliance with all relevant client policies and applicable governing laws. Issues such as insolvency for example tend to be more important with less established or small agencies and should be given some consideration.

A number of exhibits or addendums will be incorporated into the main contract. These exhibits and attachments should receive equal attention before being included in the final draft. They typically cover contract clauses that must be revisited or updated on an annual basis including but not limited to annual scope of work: fees and staffing plan, competitive businesses, list of designated countries (for global accounts) or affiliated agencies covered under the agreement (if applicable), rate cards, service level agreements, and more. Service Level Agreements may include important joint expectations such as the process for getting creative approvals, business reporting and asset management requirements, and company policies and guidelines that agencies are expected to follow.

Client Viewpoint

"We have solid contracts in place with our agencies based on years of best practices. We are constantly updating our contracts to reflect the reality of the marketplace. But what truly matters is turning a piece of paper into something you can live with and making it practical for both parties."

SHERRY ULSH, Director Global Marketing Finance and Procurement, Burger King Corp.

Remember, if a client is discussing terms and conditions with an agency, he/she's negotiating. If you are not ready to do that, just don't. Ask the opinion of an attorney about how to apply the above terms and conditions to your business situation and the answer is likely to be: "Well, *it depends*!" Well, you know what? It does depend. There is no magic contract template and no silver bullet either.

At the very least, as clients initiate discussions with the agency, clients should state their intentions, requirements, and concerns and see how the agency responds. Clients should listen carefully to the agency's perspective. It will likely provide great insight about the way they conduct business, what they seem to care most about and how diligent they are about managing their own business.

So prep as much as possible with an attorney with knowledge of agencies. Once the contract is signed, it will supersede and replace any prior agreements between the parties, any prior written or verbal negotiations, communications, understandings, or agreements. By the time clients are done asking clarifying contract-related questions, they will soon start to realize that a more meaningful answer perhaps lies in the company's risk tolerance level and a judgment call as to where to draw the line between the need for business flexibility and rigorous control.

Conducting Audits to Ensure Full Compliance with Contract Terms

Clients are seeking to improve transparency to more efficiently and accurately manage expenses handled by their media and creative agency partners. They ask themselves: Are contract terms being followed consistently? Where is my greatest exposure today and how will I manage that risk? Audits often reveal that agencies consistently earn revenue or profit in excess of that understood by their clients and this can go unnoticed. These discrepancies often result in financial restitutions to the client, in addition to improved process and controls. Preliminary compliance audits and risks assessment tend to be performed—to ensure agency compliance to contract T&Cs and as a result, identify existing or future risks that require immediate actions.

Transparency and an open-book policy are key to the long-term viability of the partnership. There have been a number of scandals and news breaking stories about occasional conflicts between clients and their media agencies about their level of transparency provided about their dealings with publishers and media companies, and specifically, whether agencies should be entitled to profits from negotiated discounts and credits when acting as brokers rather than agents on their client's behalf.

For example, large global advertiser and French dairy Danone Groupe, accused the media agency Aegis Media's Carat of failing to pass on millions of dollars in discounts obtained from media buys. As a result of this dispute, a highly publicized court battle followed in Germany where a judge asked to open Carat's book from a few years back. Clients are strongly encouraged to hire skilled auditors with intimate knowledge of the agency industry, Sarbanes-Oxley and other industry specific practices and tools.

As part of the audit, clients are encouraged to ask for observations regarding issues that might not be captured in the contract but might still be considered best practices and relevant to this exercise. Both the agency and the client will need to provide relevant data to the auditor. The auditor will determine the sample size and methodology based on client guidance, such as high spending areas, known problem issues, or potentially high risk topics. Audit findings are reviewed and discussed with the agencies. Any findings that must be remedied are in timeframes determined by the severity and financial value of the findings. (Higher risk and spend areas usually require remedies within 30-60 days).

Although the client has audit rights, typically detailed in the contract, random or too frequent audits can potentially disrupt business, delay client projects, put a strain on the relationship, raise concerns about the agency's trustworthy nature, and can negatively impact the partnership if the audit is not managed properly. It is advisable to set an audit schedule that summarizes the type of audit conducted and the timing and countries involved. This audit schedule may be shared with the agency so proper advance notice is provided to the agency. Clients should consider putting in place a multi-year rolling plan, by agency audit type and geography (if appropriate) based on a common set of guiding principles and procedural protocols. This type of audit plan does not prevent random audits from being conducted if the contract allows for it.

Diverse Functional Scope Areas

Audits are usually financial or operational in nature. Operational audits are designed to ensure operating guidelines and processes are adequately followed and executed to determine if information flows effectively and efficiently to the agency. Operational audits review procedures and test the approval of media plans, job reconciliations, and client reports, for example. In the case of pay for performance agreements they determine whether the agency achieved the performance objectives identified to earn a bonus contained in the agreement, whether the bonus was awarded, whether support for the decision to pay the bonus or not to pay the bonus was communicated in writing, and whether the bonus payment was actually paid to the agency in a timely manner.

Financial audits are designed to ensure financial terms are applied consistently; billings and other agreed-upon financial transactions are handled according to the contract. They help identify duplicate payments, pricing errors, missed media/production credits and refunds never returned to client, excessive costs, miscalculations of sales tax, commissions and other related costs, non-compliant travel expenses, payments not reconciled with actual costs, excessive costs. Financial audits are most common with media agencies since they may lead to sizeable client credits for over-payment or inaccurate billings. There are three primary agency financial audit types:

- *Fees:* verify compliance to contract and pricing terms and conditions (revenue, staffing plans, fee calculations, overhead, margins, open payables, invoicing). Findings may reveal that the agency is charging fees resulting in profit levels in excess of that agreed with clients.

- *Media:* verify compliance to media related contract terms and conditions, as well as the quality and cost effectiveness of media placement done by the agency and other financial-related transactions (cash flow, billings, media spend and related controls). Clients want their agencies cash neutral. Many agencies are not as diligent or timely enough when reconciling media credits, rebates, and discounts.

- *Production:* verify compliance to production related contract terms and conditions and competitiveness of rate cards (production spend and related controls, production credits, and adherence to competitive bids).

How the audit is funded can significantly influence its outcome or even its integrity. Audits are typically funded by the client as a priced fee. But a typical agency audit can be priced differently: as a one-time fee to the client (the most common alternative), on a contingency basis (as a percentage of cost-recovery) or as a discounted fee and capped commission on recovery funds. In a challenging and cost-cutting business environment, clients may not always be able to secure the budgets they need to conduct desired audits. The alternative is to conduct an audit on a contingency basis under which the auditor assumes the risk (no recovery means the auditor doesn't collect any audit fees) and any associated costs but is potentially paid a percentage of recovered funds.

The last two compensation alternatives, although popular for those who want to have this cost fully recovered or don't have any room in their existing budget, may create some tension and be damaging to the relationship since the auditor is financially incented to aggressively find and recover funds to offset their own costs to hopefully make a profit. Clients tend to work with audit firms with a specialty practice in the field of advertising and marketing communications, bringing very tangible benefits to the companies they work for. These audit firms usually have deep experience in agency-side financial and operational functions, a very strong knowledge of agency accounting systems such as DDS, Adman, Adware and others, and have access to best practices to share with clients.

Audit Process Overview

Once the client has notified the agency of its intent to conduct a particular audit at a particular time, both parties will determine what data is needed, what sample size to use, and will provide a list of key contacts to help coordinate the project.

▸ *Access to data:* A typical audit requires the exchange of information among three main parties: the client, the agency, and the auditor. The client will need to provide a copy of the contract. The agency will need to provide a summary spreadsheet of all billings and accounts payable data during the established audit time period. The client will need to provide copies of the executed contracts among the parties as well as any supporting documentation used to validate and cross-reference the agency data.

▸ *Sample size definition:* It typically doesn't make economical sense to audit all activities conducted by an agency. Selecting a sample size (say 20% of all jobs) is therefore what is necessary, minimizing time, efforts, and costs. The sample, once selected, can be provided to the agency for additional information gathering such as client bills, job detail reports, estimates, timesheets, authorized statements of work, invoices, and bids. The auditor will now proceed with the actual execution of the audit and conduct the fieldwork at concerned agency offices. The audit often starts with the agency contract and baseline requirements. This is a review of the agency contracts and scope of work to make sure a contract was signed before the work was initiated, that a purchase order or statement of work was executed, a brief was submitted to the agency and agreed upon before any work was started, addendums and appendixes are completed, and established policies and procedures are adequately followed. Here is a list of most common audit activities:

▸ Verify all vendor invoices were submitted to client and the amount billed to the client (at actual cost for pass-through expenses) or expenses agree with the total amount paid by the client or paid to vendors.

▸ Determine whether the agency collected any annual volume bonuses (AVBs), vendor rebates or volume discounts and make sure those are passed back to the client in a timely manner.

▸ Verify that any bid policy is followed and exceptions, if any, are documented.

▸ Determine if the agency is regularly reviewing suppliers and how competitive their rates are.

▸ Compare the date that the client paid the agency to the date the agency paid the media vendor to determine if the agency is in a positive or negative cash flow position.

▸ Verify that the total amount billed to the client does not exceed the total estimate amounts agreed to for expenses incurred by the agency.

- Confirm agency's time reporting policy, timeliness, and accuracy by reviewing staffing plans and ensuring staffing/fee reconciliation is conducted as planned.
- Identify any cost elements prohibited per the contract.

Once the fieldwork is completed, the audit findings are reported back to the client and agency, preferably in writing as a formal wrap-up and in a group meeting for lively discussions. It's recommended that the auditor review preliminary results with the agency so that findings are vetted and the agency has a chance to provide additional input and clarify any outstanding issues. If restitution is required, the auditor will facilitate the process. Financial audits can lead to the restitution of various forms of payments, credits, sales tax, cash flow, and other possible over-charges.

Audits help define compensation guidelines, enhance contract language, limit litigation risks, provide accounting transparency, and build trust. It's insane to think that some agencies have not established rigorous enough processes internally to come out of this process clean. It's equally insane to see clients conduct audit after audit with little regard to the impact on the relationship or agency resources. Audits must be fact-based, not opinion-based. Keep in mind that audits are not designed to be punitive in nature. If a client doesn't trust the good intentions of its agency, it's time to move on.

In this particular instance, the audit serves as a joint opportunity to look for greater efficiencies in the relationship and uncover where things may not be run optimally. This is why the audit findings do not systematically need to be revealed to the client first. After the agency has a chance to provide additional input to the audit findings, a meeting is scheduled by the auditor to review those with both the agency and the client. By that time, there should be agreement on improvement areas and both parties should discuss an action plan with a specific timeline to address them.

Client Viewpoint

"Clients and agencies should make sure they are aligned on the same principles and goals before they structure their contract and relationship. Having the right foundation and measurements in place to separate personal relationships from the performance of the business is critical. Don't let personal relationships get in the way of the goals of the businesses."

MICHAEL E. THYEN
Director, Marketing and Sales Global Procurement, Eli Lilly and Company

In the end, Pacta Sunt Servanda implies more than saying contractual agreements must be kept or that one must always prepare for rainy days. It means that clients and agencies' contracts and audits must be performed by each party in good faith, which is absolutely critical to establishing trust and maturing any business relationship.

{Taking Immediate Action}

TOP 5

BEST PRACTICES TO HARNESS THE MADNESS

❶ Use the contract to strengthen the relationship with your agency partner. Clients should invest the time to get the contract right with their agencies and enter negotiations with the explicit goal to establish fair, equitable, and mutually agreeable terms.

❷ Clients must include most common clauses in their agency contract, such as indemnification and compensation, but should pay close attention to critical clauses such as ownership and intellectual property (especially in the context of software and digital tools developed by the agency), as well as contract termination and competitive conflicts.

❸ Use addendums for the variable parts of the contract, such as fees, scope of work, and staffing, that must be updated periodically.

❹ Set up an audit schedule and hire skilled auditors with intimate knowledge of advertising, media, and marketing communication disciplines and common industry practices.

❺ Avoid conducting audits on a contingency basis. Clients shouldn't use audits with punitive intentions in mind but rather use audit to identify improvement areas in operational and financial transactions and processes.

7 JUST SIX NUMBERS

Determining the right client/agency compensation

"Fortune favors the prepared mind."

—Louis Pasteur
Chemist and microbiologist

Always complex, sometimes frustrating, often contentious are words people might use to describe their income tax return. Some might even use more colorful words. Well, the Internal Revenue Service (IRS) may have finally found its match. "Client/ agency compensation" is a topic that stimulates similar feelings among high-ranking clients and agencies. This is due in large part to inconsistent and, from time to time, inequitable practices that have people pulling their hair. Over the years, agencies have painfully discovered that negotiating profit margin with clients feels a bit like what I fondly call the "hair loss syndrome": you have less than you think and you lose more each day. Yet compensation, when it is done right and fairly, is known to be a critical part of any successful business partnership.

Clients do not always have the required knowledge, tools, or resources to assess the fairness of existing agreements or to anticipate what's next in compensation. As a result, they tend to rely on old-fashion negotiation techniques, pressuring agencies to reduce overhead costs and shrinking profit margin. Traditional client/agency compensation agreements are, for the most part, obsolete. Luckily, new approaches to compensation such as incentive-based or value-based agreements drive greater shared accountability and enhanced performance from the relationship by focusing on what matters the most: not cost but the value realized from their multiplier effect.

Altering the Future of Client/Agency Relationships

In his ground breaking book entitled *Just Six Numbers*,[35] English science writer, cosmologist, and astrophysicist Sir Martin Reese, also known as Baron Rees and Royal Astronomer of England, discusses how mathematical laws underpin the fabric of our universe. According to Sir Martin Reese, just six numbers govern the shape, size, and texture of our universe. And what's most amazing about his assertions is that if the values of these six numbers were only fractionally different, stars and galaxies would not form, complex chemistry would not be possible, and life could not evolve. In other words, we would not exist.

What has a British cosmologist and astrophysicist to do with the controversial topic of client/client/agency compensation? I believe everything. I cannot help wondering if the logic that is true in astronomy could also be true in client/agency compensation: If a starting point is specified with clarity, is the outcome most predictable? How many values or financial metrics, if changed slightly, would with most certainty alter the future of a client/ agency relationship?

As clients enter negotiations about compensation with their agencies, clients must consider which of these numbers, whether it is margin, overhead, headcount, cost per unit of work, cost per qualified prospect, return on marketing investment, a specific revenue target, year over year sales growth, market share, or another factor will keep their relationship with the agency in balance and make it all worthwhile in the end. Client/agency compensation may not be rocket-science; it certainly borrows from the world of logic and numbers: the right numbers can lift a relationship to excellence or keep it on the ground. As in astrology, it encourages people to look up, not down.

Why is it so hard then? Both parties enter discussions in good faith, but soon negotiations derail for a number of reasons: mistrust, friction, misunderstandings, or the absence of industry standards. Both sides get caught into circular arguments, pulling the bed sheets to their side and trying to extract further tiny concessions from each other. Yet they are often missing the big picture.

At its core, this assumes that both parties will reach an agreement on the value that is being created and share a common desire to reach a fair and equitable agreement. As Molière, the 17th-century French playwright and actor, so rightfully captured: "Things only have the value that we give them." Value is highly subjective by nature. Clearly, "fair and equitable" is in eye of the beholder. Do clients really know what they are truly getting for their money? And if they did, would they compensate their agencies any differently?

The chronic pressure on client "non-working" budgets in the past few decades, mainly from agency fees and profits, combined with increasing client demands in a far more challenging business environment and labor-intensive digital world, the industry has been forced to pause to reexamine how much clients pay for agency services. It has a tremendous economical and operational impact on their relationship. It is commonly accepted that the era of commission-based compensation is flat dead. And the existing era of labor-based compensation is slowing coming to extinction, after years of shrinking agency profit.

The significant growth of digital as one of the most complex, high volume disciplines in the media mix is also a paradigm shift that has broad implications on how budgets are set and how agencies are compensated. In lieu of these changes, clients and agencies are scratching their heads wondering what's next in compensation. Large brand advertisers such as The Coca-Cola Company and Procter & Gamble are challenging the status quo, experimenting with new approaches and promoting new compensation standards with their agencies. They are hoping to finally end the debates about equity and profit sharing and incentive compensation that have been raging for years now. But are we anywhere close today? If you look in the mirror, you will realize that we've certainly come a long way, from commission based to labor based compensation to now pay for performance with value-based compensation.

It's insane that client/agency compensation has historically been based on how much clients spend in media (that is, commission-based). Yet it worked for a long while. There was logic to the madness of the time. It's crazy that it is now, for the most part, based on the agency's time and efforts, irrespective of performance or the value realized from the work. It's insane to think that so many agencies still don't have skin-in-the-game. And when they do, agencies are eager to share any upside, but are far less enthusiastic about sharing the risks.

It's absolutely crazy that the client pays whether or not the work is any good or accomplishes the campaign objectives. Activity-based compensation is nonsense in the long run. This is not the way successful companies manage their human capital. When agencies go beyond the call of duty and find creative ways for clients to drive measurable business results, agencies don't get necessarily get paid more either. It's equally insane.

But how do they accurately define performance or value in a given relationship? Frankly, clients haven't always made it easy for agencies, allowing cost-cutting efforts to take center-stage and often undermining themselves in the process. They have negotiated aggressively, pushing agencies to apply unusual financial pressure on their organization and operational rigor on how they do business to eliminate inefficiencies. There is nothing wrong about that at face value. But too often they went as far as forcing fees down to unsustainable levels, allowing scope creep, but shooting themselves in the foot by negatively impacting their agency's ability to hire/retain the right talent and serve their clients effectively.

Agencies found themselves unable to deliver value-generating ideas that their clients most desperately needed to drive their business forward. Steamrolled by some overly-aggressive procurement teams unaware of the counterproductive effect of their actions, many agencies ended up on their back, weakened and with bruises, broken bones, and unwanted talent attrition.

Conversely, some agencies have failed to stand to clients. They failed to drive value-based partnerships focused on the big picture and measurable business results. Some of them failed to avoid turning into commodities.

As Jean-Marie Dru, Chairman of TBWA Worldwide declares "We are paying the price of belonging to an industry which has not learned how to protect its own interests. We are our worst enemies."[36] What will compel the right behavior and make it a true partnership? What is truly equitable? What will make clients feel good about what they get for their money and yet allow agencies to invest in technology and talent and improve the value they provide? It's time we demystify common beliefs and explore more effective methods of client/agency compensation.

Overcoming the Inherent Complexity of Agency Compensation

Why has it gotten even more complicated in the past few years? Figuring out what to pay an agency is not a simple task. The stakes are great. And it's not getting easier, either. For clients that require agency resources around the world or have multiple agencies in their roster, the added complexity is unavoidable. Unless managed centrally, such services may have to be provided by entering one or multiple contracts with potentially different compensation agreements.

Client Viewpoint

"In today's environment, there is strong momentum to drive compensation down as the market softens. But be careful what you buy and for how much. Especially when you want the best people working on your account. Before 'cutting the agency fee', be an informed buyer and understand the dynamics of the marketplace. In the end, you'll get what you pay for!"

KEVIN PARHAM, Director Global Advertising, Campbell Soup

The specialized and labor-intensive and therefore costly nature of digital marketing forces us to reset expectations. As strongly advocated by the AAAA,[37] the complexity and interactive nature of the digital process, the often expensive, scare-technical talent required, the rich set of technologies, tools and service-providers needed, and the high number of creative assets that must be produced, placed, refreshed, tracked, and continually optimized in a vast number of ad sizes and platforms, cannot be accommodated by existing, rigid, and linear compensation agreements.

This cannot happen until at least significant improvements in industry standards and new technology enable greater automation at every step of the process, in workflow and traffic management, asset development and data mining, and campaign analytics and performance optimization. Agency resources are tighter than ever before. Expectations for innovation are greater. Qualified talent is scarce. Work volume is increasing. Speed to market is accelerating. How are clients dealing with these challenges? How do they know if they are compensating their agency fairly? Should they shift budgets from lower media to higher agency fees and production as it relates to digital? Where should they start?

Most agency contracts are carefully negotiated arrangements that vary based on the nature and complexity of the work, the agency workload, and the respective company cultures and leadership profiles, The client and the agency should first discuss their respective goals, philosophies, and expectations about compensation. All of that should be done prior to selecting a particular compensation agreement. Then both parties have the opportunity to choose among a wide set of compensation methods to meet their unique requirements.

In reality, this is a bit more challenging to accomplish. Few on the client side have broad enough experience to determine with some precision what's reasonable and what's not, leaving everyone guessing: What is the right compensation for our relationship? This is perhaps why it remains such a popular and highly debated topic at industry events: finding the right balance without paying the agency too much or too little, rewarding for the right outcome, and yielding the most possible value out of the partnership. Clients might ask themselves:

- Are terms competitive relative to industry norms?
- What profit level is deemed reasonable? Do both parties feel that the agreement is fair and equitable? Is it motivating?
- How much compensation should be put at risk to drive meaningful change? Based on what metrics?
- What should the payment terms be? Should the client be entitled to a discount if payment terms are expedited?
- Should the client allow markup on production expenses?
- What costs should be included in overhead calculations?
- How much time and efforts can a client afford to spend on administrating its client/agency compensation plan?
- How do I make simplicity a key ingredient of my compensation model?

Although savvy clients have answers to these questions, client/agency compensation remains a multifaceted code that is not likely to be deciphered anytime soon.

Moving Toward Greater Transparency and Equitability

In compensation agreements, one should never assume that agencies will subordinate their interest to their client. Why should they? Agencies know too well that the reverse is true as well. The chosen method is less important in the end than making sure the parties' interest and priorities are completely aligned. Compensation agreements must be designed to align the financial commitment to the strategic marketing goals of the client. But they must satisfy the needs of the agency to earn a fair profit and grow its business. Without it, the agency is unlikely to attract talent and deliver its best.

Client Viewpoint

"We believe in allowing agencies to earn a fair profit. Nothing more, nothing less. If you pay less, agency talent may go down and work quality may suffer. If you pay more, you haven't done your due diligence."

TOM CHETRICK
VP Advertising and Marketing Services, Bristol-Myers Squibb

Many clients have hidden behind the growing role procurement is playing in their organization, allowing their counterparts to choke agencies by cutting margin to the bone and not realizing in the process that they were shooting themselves in the foot. To be a good client, and more importantly a good partner, one must therefore have a basic understanding of the agency business: how agencies generate revenue, bill for their services, manage expenses and ultimately yield a decent profit like any responsible for-profit organization. Understanding and even acknowledging that simple fact will go a long way with agencies and will set the right mindset for internal groups such as legal and procurement, who are usually involved in these negotiations.

After years of having companies compensate their agencies by paying a commission on their media expenditures, this form of unpredictable, controversial compensation method is, for the most part, long gone. The growth of non-traditional channels combined with the continued cost increase of media placements have increased the perceived—and sometimes real—gap between what agencies delivered and what they got paid for it. In the end, it has led the way for labor-based fee agreements in a concerted effort by clients to more closely link service delivery with compensation, by paying for the actual resources needed plus profit.

Greater marketing accountability at the boardroom level and the laser focus on return on marketing investment has put pressure on the way agencies are compensated for their services. This has led to the growing involvement of procurement type of functions in pricing negotiations. CFOs are now challenging CMOs: Are we over-paying our agencies? Are we getting value for what we are paying them? Agency fees are often the largest marketing spend category in advertisers' budgets, so it's no surprise that it has received growing attention in the past few years.

Advertisers' trust in agency billing and cost accounting has been shaky to say the least. It has been fueled by agencies' lack of financial disclosure, ambiguous business models, and well publicized cases in the news like ONDCP accused of unethical practices such as over-billing and other fraudulent behavior.[38] As a result, clients have been driving to obtain more financial transparency from agencies and pushing for compensation terms grounded into real operational expenses, effectively driving costs down and reducing agency margins to a visible, known entity.

The United States federal law, Sarbanes-Oxley Act of 2002, also introduced a set of new or enhanced standards for all, which certainly impacted the way network holding companies manage and report revenue and expenses, ultimately improving internal controls and increasing client and stakeholder confidence.

In the end, the compensation agreement will need to be considered equitable to both parties to be conducive to a successful partnership. Yet clients and agencies often differ on what constitutes a reasonable profit. Clients want the best of the talent the agency can offer but are they willing to pay for it? Anything short of terms that are mutually agreeable but also sustainable will eventually derail the relationship and lead to wasteful litigious discussions about the long term viability of the partnership. But the concept of equitability is known to be quite subjective. Clients and agencies are naturally coming at it from different angles and often have divergent definitions for what is "fair."

Not all agencies are created equal, and therefore command different agreements based on their unique capabilities. Clients want to give the agency a reasonable deal without breaking the bank. The agency wants to increase (or maintain) the profitability of the account and move toward the higher end of the range. They all have good and valid intentions. Negotiations will take place to move the needle somewhere close to the middle of the range, allowing both parties to compromise but hopefully feel good about the outcome of the process.

Agency Viewpoint

"*Compensation remains a central issue in client/agency relations. Too many client/agency compensation models are still built around time and efforts instead of business outcomes. Agencies must promote approaches that align the economic incentives of both parties.*"

TIM WILLIAMS, President, Ignition Consulting Group

A friend of mine once compared the premium car segment of the economy to the ad agency industries, stating that they both face monopolistic competition. For both there are many producers and consumers, neither business has total control over the market price, and buyers perceive that there are non-price differences among the competitors' products. For all intents and purposes services can be substitutes for one another and there are few barriers to entry and exit. It is a client's willingness to switch that keeps agency compensation in touch with reality, that is: the market. He's absolutely correct.

However, clients might be tempted at times to play on agency insecurities, threatening to put their account in review in order to land a better deal. And agencies may under-resource their clients to meet short-term profit targets or come up with other ways to make up for their concessions. But clients would be unwise to flex their muscles without thinking about the implications. Experience shows that if one party walks away feeling that it has lost, it means both parties have lost in the long run.

Client Viewpoint

"When I was on the agency side, I always thought 'You work for your client, you get paid by the agency.' Agencies can make themselves more valuable to their clients by sharing the client's culture, being forthcoming and strategically looking for the client's best interest. If cost effectiveness is a key priority to the client, then be it."

BRETT COLBERT
Global Manager, Procurement Advertising, Anheuser Busch InBev

Lack of Industry Standards

There is no standard or universal compensation agreement marketers can pick up from the template rack at Office Depot. This is a sweet spot for agency consultants eager to help clients sail through these unfriendly waters. Client/agency compensation agreements vary widely in nature and scope as do cost accounting methodologies they often rely on. Experts on either side still debate what is deemed acceptable non-working media, and more specifically, what reasonable profit margins are, what should be included in overhead and pass-through expenses, and ultimately what constitutes a fair deal. Compensation is often based on scope of work, resources, value, or a combination of the three. The scope of work is often the initial basis for determining the required agency resources and agency fees.

Although all compensation agreements inherently include all the same financial elements of labor, overhead, and margin, their definition and the way they are calculated will vary significantly from one agency to another, leaving marketers scratching their heads for comparability and benchmarks. Clients feel that they are likely to overpay when they are not sure what things should cost. Should they agree to post-termination rights and compensation contingencies? Should they push back on non-advertising usage right provisions, territorial, or media limitations? They want standards or guidelines, especially in contentious areas such as IP and digital.

Digital typically calls for lower media investments but higher fee and production budgets. Digital requires more creative units than traditional media due to its higher refresh rate and rotation of creative across a wider range of media. Campaigns tend to change frequently, requiring greater upfront but also more flexible media planning and buying, analytics, trafficking, designing, and programming agency services to refresh and update. There is ongoing tracking, reporting, and analysis to optimize campaign performance. Programming and back-end requirements are far greater as well. Production-related costs are often embedded into agency fees contrary to traditional media. Digital marketing is more labor-intensive.

All of these reasons increase client costs exponentially, and if those were unexpected, can create huge tensions among clients and agencies. This is particularly challenging for clients given the degree of variability in digital assignments. Thankfully, organizations like ANA and AAAA have collaborated to remove some of the guesswork. They come up with common guidelines to help their members effectively manage compensation, promoting more consistent implementation of compensation arrangements that result in more productive agency relationships.[39, 40] This is a first good step to educate business leaders involved in such negotiations.

Understandably, the ANA and AAAA do not endorse or recommend any particular approach because of the multitude of business scenarios, but they reinforce basic principles that apply to most situations. Some clients have established digital rate cards to improve budget predictability and to control production expenses. P&G, for example, pre-approved a short list of production houses that its agencies must pick from on their assignments.[41] Without a solid understanding of the varied choices available to them, clients are unable to develop and negotiate pricing terms that effectively motivate agencies. Keep in mind that compensation agreements significantly impact the way an agency services an account, what talent and resources are assigned to it, how responsive they are, how they perform, and the level of investment they are willing to make to grow and nurture the relationship. Make no doubt about it. Whatever compensation agreement has been chosen, it will deeply affect the dynamics of the relationship and therefore, should not be under-estimated.

Client Viewpoint

"We believe agencies are in the business of making a reasonable profit."

CHARLIE SILVESTRO
Vice President, Global Agency Operations, MasterCard Worldwide

As more marketing dollars are shifting to non-advertising agencies and the media landscape completes its deep transformation, the need for alternative compensation methodologies emerges and takes a strong foothold in client/agency relationships around the world. Less dependent on media activities, also perhaps less dependent on the popular labor/fee-based model, these alternatives are more focused on business outcomes, performance, and value.

Unfortunately, even hugely popular labor-based agreements are complex by nature and require some understanding of cost-based components. Each of these alternative models has pros and cons as it relates to the economics, with varying degree of sophistication and administrative requirements that clients must carefully evaluate before deciding on the one that is most applicable to the relationship being pursued. In the end, there are no industry standards. There is also no right or wrong compensation model as every situation is different but some best practices have emerged for clients to learn from and take into consideration.

How to Determine the Most Relevant Compensation Model

Negotiating compensation is an incredibly important organization competency for companies to develop and refine. Clients must rigorously structure their approach to compensation and get internal buy-in about their strategy and overall philosophy about risks/rewards and operating principles. They must develop pricing benchmarks and cost databases to better inform their decisions. They must develop formal guidelines and negotiating training, and dedicate skilled resources to materially increase their chances to yield a positive outcome from agency negotiations.

There is no universal compensation approach that meets the needs of every client or every agency. To decide on the right compensation agreement, clients must first acquire a rudimentary understanding of the way agencies operate as a business, and look at the way they generate revenue, manage costs, and yield profits.

The clients must educate their agency on their business category, the company's existing and potential challenges and opportunities, and give a detailed description of their short and long-term marketing and business objectives with metrics for success. The must explain the type of talent and competencies needed, levels of service expected, budgets/resources available, and the nature of the involvement of other roster agencies involved. Finally, they need to discuss what constitutes, in their opinion, a successful partnership. This exchange of information constitutes the framework on which negotiations, tradeoffs, and compromises will be made.

Then, they need to determine what the most suitable compensation model for their needs is. The right type of compensation may vary based on account size, client expectations, duration of the agreement, type and scope of services provided, as well as the stability and predictability of the account. Some clients may use a hybrid of different compensation approaches for different marketing services, geographies, or business units.

There is tremendous momentum to shift client/agency relationships and compensation agreements to a more outcome, performance-based model. Finally, once the compensation method has been chosen and their mutual approach and objectives have been shared openly, both parties enter into negotiations to get terms finalized. Only then can back-and-forth negotiations effectively take place to reach a consensus. The end result is a contract with compensation terms that are hopefully fair and equitable, and aligns agency and client interests and priorities.

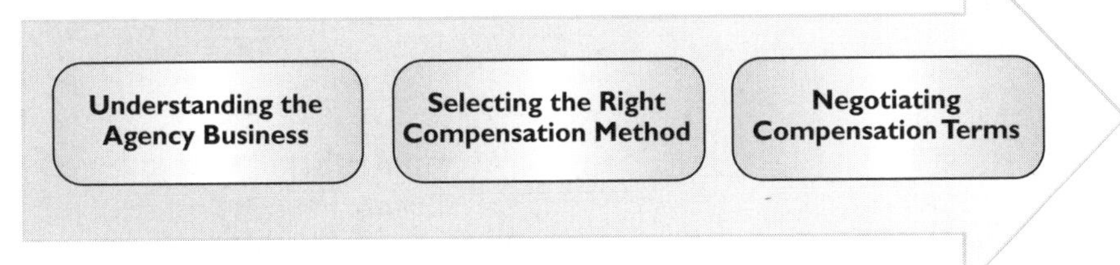

Client/Agency Compensation Development Process

Step 1: Understanding the Business of Agencies

In principle, agencies offer their knowledge and expertise to clients. How they provide such value is through qualified and motivated teams of experts.

The agency business, like any other consulting professional service, is a business of people. The agency's primary asset is its talent base—how to find, retain and motivate it. So relentlessly increasing the output and productivity of employees is vital to their success. The agency economical model is relatively simple in concept. At the risk of over-simplifying: Agencies generate revenue for their services through commissions, markups, and fees. They subtract their largest operational costs, namely salaries and benefits. They also subtract their costs of doing business, aka overhead, leaving them a profit margin or markup, which typically ranges from single digits to 20% or higher. Profit margin is expressed as a percentage of all up revenue, while markup is expressed as a percentage multiplied by all up operating expenses.

There are nuances between disciplines, especially in those where media is an important part of the relationship. Media and PR agencies, for example, have different service models and, therefore, varied pricing menus that are specific to the nature of services provided. Understanding how agencies turn a profit and manage costs is a prerequisite to clients effectively negotiating with agencies. Revenue is typically defined as fee income, markup on billable items, and advertising commissions if media is part of the picture. Agencies often use a combination of revenue sources to grow their business.

Agency revenue is not very predictable by nature and is often subject to massive fluctuations. Marketing expenditures are subject to economic conditions. In a growing and healthy economy, a client's marketing budget will be adjusted upward to stimulate demand. In a declining economy or recession, marketing budgets tend to shrink to keep operating at minimal cost. And when marketing budgets are reduced, so are agency expenditures.

Client Viewpoint

"I wouldn't want to run a business for anything less than a decent margin. Would you? You can't expect to have your agency operate a less than a reasonable profit margin."

JULIE GIBBS, Director, Corporate Brand Marketing, Campaign Management, Adobe

It is also a very highly competitive industry. Agencies have to compete in a highly fragmented environment with attractive pricing to maintain existing client relationships and attempt to win new ones. Profitable agencies tend to share a common set of operating principles: they hire world-class talent, have clients that are happy to pay for them, and those clients feel that they are getting full value for their investment.

Agencies are efficient at doing capacity resource planning; they have designed and implemented a strong time, media, and production tracking, with a billing and financial reporting infrastructure giving them timely, accurate, actionable information to manage cost and therefore profitability. Most agencies will ask employees to fill out timesheets to help them run their agency as effectively as possible, even if the compensation agreement is not hourly based. It allows them to measure client profitability, whether agency staff is at full capacity and have the bandwidth take on another client.

Agency Viewpoint

"We believe contracts should be simple and straightforward, with bonuses offered only if the agency outperforms very specific goals. There's still nothing wrong with charging by the hour, with overhead congealed in the hourly rates."

JEFF GOODBY
Co-Chairman and Creative Director, Goody, Silverstein & Partners

Another important aspect of agency profitability is submitting billings to clients on a pre-determined schedule and making sure clients are paying their invoices when they are supposed to. Whenever they can, clients will push for extended payment terms as part of the compensation package being negotiated. Reviewing the profitability of a given account is standard practice for the agency (and jointly with the client), regardless of the chosen compensation agreement. This information proves to be useful to run their business more efficiently, deciding which relationship is profitable and which one is not, and what actions must be taken to improve profitability without impacting the quality, speed, or effectiveness of the work produced. Profitable agencies attract top talent. Nonprofitable agencies are undesirable to both prospective employees and clients in the long run. As agencies lose or fail to attract talent in critical roles, they run the risk of eroding work quality and effectiveness.

Common Sources of Agency Revenue

Fees By far, fees have been the most common source of agency revenue in the past few years. "Fees for services performed" are paid in return for the agency services. Fees are typically calculated based on projected hours by approved hourly rates (cost per hour). Fees can be retained if there is a clear scope of work and mutual desire to commit to assign dedicated resources. Retained or project-based, hourly rates are expressed by combining direct labor costs, overhead, and a markup, and dividing that number by workable hours per year (1680 in most countries). The compensation is based on the notion of full recovery of the agency costs and a fair and equitable profit. Direct labor and overhead are considered pass-through expenses (benefits and social costs can be included in overhead or direct labor).

The markup, or profit margin is negotiated independently with the agency. The majority of compensation agreements are likely to fall within a 10-25% profit margin range, based on supply and demand as well as a number of other partnership considerations (the popularity of the agency, the scope of the relationship, the size of the account, and so forth). Large clients like Unilever have so much buying power that they can dictate to their agencies reduced upfront profit margin (5%) and extended payment terms, with the opportunity to earn more via a performance bonus.[42] Ultimately, profit margins are subject to the laws of demand and supply: what both parties are willing to live with.

If the agency is paid on the basis of time and material, tracking time accurately becomes critical. A growing number of agencies now rebel against timesheet reporting. While it may be good for certain professions like attorneys, they argue it is not for advertising and marketing communications. Most agencies feel strongly that compensation should not be determined based on activity level but rather be determined based on performance or value, allowing them to generate additional revenue when they meet or exceed expectations.

Commissions Agencies pay for the media placement for advertising time or space that they place on the client's behalf. Historically, they made a commission—15% has been the standard commission for a number of years—on these media placements as a primary form of compensation. The agency would handle 85% of the media payments, a pass through expense, and bill the client for an additional 15% pre-determined commission, considered agency revenue. Today, paying commissions is no longer a very common form of compensation. It used to be a lucrative way for agencies to generate revenue as commissions were loosely tied to the resources required to effectively plan, buy, and place media, leaving much room for agencies to be creative on how they managed their engagement.

If traditional media used to generate commissions in the 15% range, digital media typically required an effective commission rate ranging from 25-30%. To reduce the risk associated with a small client not fulfilling its contractual payment obligations, some agencies will usually pay media after they have received payments from the client—a method often referred to as "pre-pay," acting as the client's agent rather than the primary obligator.

Although rare among large accounts, examples like BBDO's position as second-largest unsecured creditor as a result of Chrysler's Chapter 11 bankruptcy, which adds up to $58M, have served as painful reminders of the agency risks involved. These payments, made on behalf of clients, are commonly referred to as billings. Commissions can also be generated from clients paying a gross rate billed by media and the agency paying for media at a lower rate, generating a net difference commonly called commission. The nature of the agreement will dictate whether or not the agency is keeping the commission as part of its revenue or whether commissions are paid separately.

Production Markup Markup is a percentage allocation on top of pass-through production costs that is passed on to the client. Marking up production is a common form of compensation for agencies. In fee-based compensation agreements, however, the agency is not permitted to mark up production. Agencies are now seeing production in a digital world has another source of potential revenue, creating their own production studio vs. contracting production through third party production suppliers. As a result, we have seen a shift from external third-party production resources to in-house agency resources, resulting in higher scale and volume of projects. Agencies have hired digital talent such as developers and programmers to realize greater cost efficiencies, improve execution quality. They are rethinking how production can be monetized.

Other Derivative But Often Controversial Sources of Revenue

Agency Volume Bonification (AVB) AVB is a credit or bonus received by the agency from media vendors. It can take the form of free airtime/space in media, media upgrades, cash or credit notes, typically negotiated on an annual basis and paid the following year. The practice has been in existence in Europe for a few decades and exists in many countries around the world. This payment of credit does not exist however in a few countries, including the United States, Canada, France, and Australia. AVBs are not client specific. AVBs are earned by the agency based on the total agency volume of media-spend with a particular vendor and may vary based on a variety of criteria (performance, timeliness of payment, key relationships). For agencies handling large media buys, this may represent a substantial volume of credit (from 1% to 3% on average) and therefore, a sizeable financial benefit to the agency if the client is not diligent about requesting it.

Float/Account Receivables Most clients will seek a float-neutral situation with their agencies. Cash management is an important part of effective financial management for agencies. Most agencies will perform a risk analysis for every client on their roster before deciding if they agree to float media expenditures. Agencies are not banks. Agencies are not expected to turn a profit (or a loss) from having a sizeable amount of cash at their fingertips when clients prepay media (or when they do).

The reality is that some media and production firms have payment terms that are less preferential that those negotiated by the agency, giving the agency the opportunity to sit on a pile of cash until payments are due to their third party providers. When they do this, they are simply generating interest from any large pre-paid media or production expenses sitting in the agency's bank account. The reality however is that clients are now asking for delayed payments to media owners, requiring media agencies to take on the added expense risks on their client's behalf. Regardless of the approach both parties agree to take, the larger the client budget, the more knowledgeable both parties must be about how to handle float.

AVBs and Float are rare sources of revenue for agencies whose clients have adequately addressed them contractually. Finally, the nature of the work provided by the agency will dictate whether or not one particular source of revenue or multiple ones apply to a given client/agency relationship. Payment terms (for example, net 30 days) are another important consideration. An agency's lifeblood is in its cash flow. So it must be satisfactorily addressed in the financial flow between the client and the agency so it minimizes the agency's potential exposure.

Agencies have identified alternative sources of revenue over the years, going outside of traditional forms of compensation such as revenue-sharing deals. Now that we have reviewed the many ways agencies generate revenue, let's examine how they manage costs and ultimately profitability.

Standard Agency Costs

Typically, agencies incur "direct" and "indirect" costs as part of running their business. Direct costs tend to be mostly labor-related and include salaries (base, bonus, benefits, merit, vacation, payroll taxes, and any other employment related expenses). Indirect costs include overhead costs required to run the agency. Overhead is comprised of all agency operating expenses which range from insurance, space/facilities, maintenance, and utilities to office supplies, IT, hiring fees, property taxes, severance, and indirect non-billable salaries (human resources, reception, accounting, etc.). The list goes on. Overhead, however, excludes direct labor and client costs. Direct client costs (travel, materials, couriers, etc.) are usually billed to the client as pass-through expenses.

It's important to note that agencies use different accounting methods to calculate overhead rates. Because there are no industry standard overhead rates or cost accounting method, it is recommended for labor based agreements that both parties first agree on a list of allowable overhead expenses. ANA and AAAA publish a list of standard overhead expenses.[43]

Actual costs vary by discipline (such as advertising vs. PR), geographic location or city and ultimately, by agency. Overhead typically is allocated to clients based on their proportionally share of client direct labor (100% overhead rate means that for every dollar in direct labor, another dollar in overhead is charged to the client). A few are occasionally debated by clients. "New business" falls under that category along with "bad debt" (billings not paid by advertisers). In the case of new business expenses, agencies argue that these costs ultimately benefit clients: By having a healthy and diversified client portfolio, they are in a better position to make preemptive investments, hire talent, share agency resources, and in the end make their offering more valuable to existing clients.

As far as bad debt is concerned, some agencies are asking for up-front payment of media and production expenses to minimize risks. In early 2009, Omnicom Group standardized its contracts with suppliers, including a sequential liability clause, to insist on the fact that they won't assume financial liability until a client pays.[44] Overhead should not be considered independently of other cost elements when negotiating with an agency. A client might want to compromise on some of these costs but fully loaded hourly rate remains the benchmark costs between similar agencies. How far should clients go at understanding agency costs? Are internal agency costs potentially irrelevant to pricing discussions? A basic understanding of the agency's business can make you a better, more informed client. This being said, clients are always better served by focusing on the performance and value created from the relationship than by scrutinizing costs.

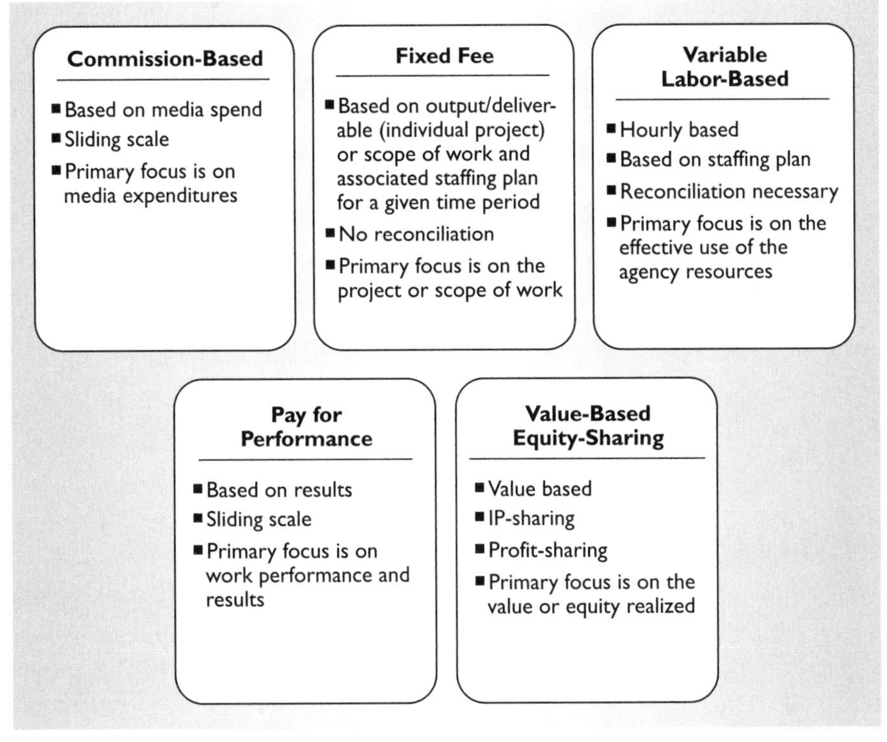

Client/Agency Compensation Agreements

Step 2: Selecting the Right Compensation Method

Fee-based agreements are now by far the most common form of compensation because clients have a reasonably sound understanding and visibility into the tangible resources agencies are putting toward their business. Large clients tend to use a combination of methods. Smaller clients consider compensation agreements that are simple to set up and administer. Clients are encouraged to explore the pros and cons of various compensation models before deciding on the one that leads to the best outcome.

Commission-Based Agreements

Although there are different types of commission-based models, such as fixed or variable based on volume of spend (aka sliding scale), they are all based on the concept that agencies are compensated based on a commission applied to the cost of media. Commission-based agreements are naturally limited to relationships where media plays a big role in the services provided. They therefore have more limited applicability than fee-based or incentive-based agreements.

The oldest form of agency compensation, the commission system, presented some unique benefits: Clients only spent media on campaigns that performed well. So arguably, agencies were highly motivated to produce successful campaigns that would be in media outlets since they were paid a commission on all media placements. This being said, the commission system has limited applicability and questionable value today. They no longer have the favor of clients who do not want to subject themselves to the bias of agencies promoting higher-spend or media-based activities when other alternatives might be more appealing. Given the fragmentation of the media landscape and the growth of digital and earned media that result in smaller but more targeted media buys (or no buy at all), commission-based agreements are considered to be too precarious for agencies. Although those are in rapid extinction in most developed countries, calculating commission rates is still a common metric for check-and-balance purposes.

Fixed-Fee Agreements

Under this type of agreement, the client agrees to pay a fixed amount to the agency to deliver according to a specific project or an agreed scope of work for a given time period. The fee is fixed regardless of whether or not the agency will require slightly more or less (or a different set of) resources to get the job done. So payment is pretty much guaranteed, pending completion of the work. Fixed agreements are used for project by project relationships (project-based agreements) or for a body of work over a given time period (retained fees typically set annually).

Fixed fee agreements are perhaps the simplest form of compensation and the most common one for clients with "open source" agency models that emphasize choice and flexibility, at the expense of cost efficiencies that can be realized by the economies of scale of retainer-based agreements. A project is priced for a set of deliverables. The negotiated fee does not vary. There are no strings attached on either side. There is no reconciliation in the backend. If the agency used more or less resources to get this done, they will either pick up the difference or drop it to the bottom line. Project-based relationships are the least preferred by most agencies. There is no upfront financial commitment and limited line of sight into workload, so the agency is hard pressed to guarantee continued access to top resources.

"Upon completion" agreements also put much pressure on agencies as payment is done when the services have been fully completed. Fee revenue recognized on a completed contract basis contributes to higher seasonality. Straight-lined contracts are usually preferred by agencies as they guarantee a predictable revenue flow. It also makes it easy for clients to anticipate and book expenses. This type of compensation is mostly common with agencies that are on a trial basis before a clients further commits.

Another fixed fee agreement (labor-based fixed fee) assumes that the work is well defined for the full year. The agency has a solid understanding of scope of work and staffing requirements and the client agrees to a fixed annual retainer. Similar to project-based agreements, the negotiated fee does not vary either, no matter what the circumstances. Considered relatively more simple than variable labor-based agreements, once the fixed fee has been agreed upon, no reconciliation is needed to track individual cost elements or resource utilization. This is particularly popular among agencies that do not believe in asking employees to fill out timesheets. Simplicity is one of the main benefits here. It doesn't however allow much flexibility, which proves to be challenging for clients in highly volatile or unpredictable industries, requiring them to set bare minimum staffing and fees with their agencies.

Variable Labor-based Agreements

The most common form of payment for professional services of all types is in the form of billable hours. Labor-based agreements have been in place for a number of years in advertising and marketing communications where commissions were not applicable or undesirable. It has received the favor of many clients who, under cost and financial pressure, realized that the commissions paid were in large, an unjustifiable excess of agency costs to deliver these services and ultimately, would provide agencies a disincentive to be media agnostic. The concept is fairly understood as it is standard in other professional services. The client agrees to a fee amount to deliver against an agreed scope of work, for a given time period, in return for a forecasted number of agency resources at a given hourly rate.

The scope of work includes a detailed description of the deliverables, schedule, and other agency responsibilities. Variable labor-based agreements are based on the notion that an annual financial commitment by the client enables its agency to staff the account with the best resources while realizing economies of scale, which are then passed on to the client as discounted rates.

Client Viewpoint

"A retainer based client/agency compensation model can give clients more flexibility and eliminate waste by allowing clients and their agency partners to spend more time doing the work and driving the business forward."

JENNIFER BERGER, Director, Marketing & Advertising Services, Starbucks

Full Time Equivalent (FTE) is a term used to express a unit of client labor that is equivalent to one full time employee or multiple shared employees adding up to the equivalent of one individual. The hourly rates by function

(Creative Director) or by individual (Joe Smith, Account Director) are calculated based on direct labor, overhead and the agreed margin. A rate card is produced which summarizes rates by job function which is used by the agency to determine staffing plans based on set budgets. Some may use average functional (vs. individual) salary to simplify an already complicated approach. The number, type and percentage of time allocated per individual (whether dedicated or shared resources) are determined based on scope of work requirements.

The number of FTEs required is based on an agreed baseline of annual work hours (which typically exclude vacation, sick time, and holidays). The denominator for annual work hours may vary as the contract must comply with local laws. For example, France and Germany have more restrictive labor laws than most countries.

Agencies can generate additional profit to the bottom line when a billable employee works more than the typical average work hours. For that reason, client typically request than the agency not pass on charges to the client for more than the determined number of hours per year for a particular individual, which would equate to 100% of billable time for that individual. Any time spent over a typical work day benefits the client.

The agency and the client monitor utilization of billable hours against the contracted number and decide if some type of financial reconciliation is required. Labor utilization is traditionally defined as the percentage of billable hours utilized relative to the number of hours contracted. Typically, an allowable band is determined and as long as utilization falls within that band (says plus or minus a few percentage points), no financial adjustment is needed.

Agency Viewpoint

"The industry is still struggling on the topic of compensation. Client/agency compensation is about aligning accountabilities to the outcome. We all do better work when we do. We share the same goals and the risks together. The incentive should be aligned with growing share and revenue, or more specific marketing outcomes."

David Kenny
Managing Partner, Vivaki

Unlike the fixed fee compensation model, the client or the agency agrees to monitor utilization of resources and reset staffing and fee resources based on pre-agreed reconciliation terms. The actualization of costs or resources used typically takes place at the completion of a project or a determined contract period (often annually). The annual reconciliation can be conducted by a third party to ensure the client is getting what it paid for and that no one unfairly benefits from the arrangement: a client could request higher paid employees once staffing and fees have been determined; an agency could delay hiring of key talent or by bringing on lower paid employees on the account, effectively improving margin. For agencies, capturing time might be a business necessity to make optimal use of their resources.

Getting staff to fill time sheets accurately is also challenging, adding to the skepticism shared by clients about the accountability of time-based arrangements that often result in financial audits. Clients must also take into consideration that these agreements require greater administrative efforts. Some might argue that the significant time and resources an agency spends in recording, tracking, and reporting labor utilization might be better spent servicing clients and driving business results.

In a fee-based agreement, clients typically spread payments evenly throughout the year. By making recurring monthly payments, the agency is benefiting from a predictable revenue flow from the client, regardless of potential "peaks and valleys" in terms of agency workload. Fees should be reviewed periodically and adjusted based on material changes to the scope of work and associated staffing plan. Both parties must agree on the number of acceptable change order and restatement periods.

Finding the right balance between revenue/fee predictability for the agency and scope of work flexibility for the client is at the core of typical agency fee negotiations. It has been increasingly challenged by clients and agencies alike because it is based on the notion that the clients pay for time, regardless of how effective that time might be spent and regardless of performance. Rance Crain, a columnist for *Advertising Age*, said it best: "So nowadays, agencies get paid for their work like accountants and attorneys do, based on a negotiated fee. They get paid whether their ads run or how much their client spends. In most cases, they get paid the same for good or bad advice—just like lawyers do."

Client Viewpoint

"Mutual accountability means everyone must have skin in the game. At J&J, we have been proponents of pay for performance type arrangements with our agencies since 2001. Agencies respect and want that accountability."

JAMES R. ZAMBITO, Global Marketing Group Controller, Johnson & Johnson

Another disappearing form of labor-based compensation is "cost-plus," implying that the client will compensate for actual (vs. estimated) agency expenses plus an agreed upon margin. This is mostly beneficial to agencies guaranteed to be compensated based on actual costs, even if those increase unexpectedly. This is unpopular among clients due to the lack of budget predictability and lack of incentive for cost-control.

In recent years, we've seen new and creative models emerge from innovative agencies and clients who pave the way, from Pay for Performance to IP-sharing or sales-based royalties. Such models already exist in other service industries such as the music business, software development, and photography. They challenge conventional wisdom and traditional compensation methods in which they operate as "agents" on the client's behalf. They are simply rejecting what they consider to be the "ancestral" principles of hourly billing and labor-based agreements that reward regardless of business output. They are viscerally opposed to the notion that agencies all have to contribute to clients are their time or efforts. Agencies want more ownership.

Ultimately, agencies want to see radical changes in the way they are to be compensated for their work. They want compensation to be based on the results they help produce, the value they provide, the intellectual property they create, not the time they spend or the costs they occur. For the most part, clients concur.

Pay for Performance Agreements

The idea behind Pay for Performance (aka PFP or P4P) is quite simple in theory, but putting it into practice can prove to be challenging. It comes from having any part of the client/agency compensation, above and beyond the baseline compensation, contingent on meeting or exceeding agreed upon performance metrics, similar to the ways a sales organization might be compensated. Or an attorney hired on contingency, hoping to receive a percentage of the damages awarded in favor of his client

The concept is far from being new to the business world but it was new to the agency community until P&G pioneered the idea of tying client/agency compensation to business results based on principles familiar to the packaged goods giant. As a matter of fact, P&G introduced a profit-sharing program giving employees an ownership stake in the company as early as 1887. Today, P&G's P4P are reported to be split between sales and share and performance evaluation, with sales being the biggest driver. Also commonly known as "Payment by Results" or "Performance-Based" agreements, these bonuses are now common to many relationships. Variable pay outcome is mostly about getting active involvement in driving toward the desired outcome. Failing to reward employees, or even vendors, for outstanding performance and superior results might be one the greatest missed opportunity of all times in business management.

When compensation and results are disconnected, and there is no upside for agencies going above and beyond, why should they? Arguably, at the essence of any business partnership is risk taking and upside sharing. At least, on principle. The fear of losing a client should motivate agencies but it may not be enough on a consistent basis to ensure it meets or, better, exceeds expectations. Frankly, agencies can become complacent knowing that seeking a new agency can be an expensive endeavor and a major distraction for a client's core business. They need something else to provide compelling incentives and go the extra mile. The concept of partnership is doubtful until both parties have skin in the game and the financial success of the agency is tied to client results or service levels.

Giving agencies a stake in the performance of the work itself or the company's performance encourages "media-neutrality" and "discipline-neutrality" among specialty agencies, perhaps overtly focused on what they do vs. what's needed. It also encourages agencies to focus on what truly matters to the client. Clients typically rely on business metrics such as revenue growth or market share, leading indicators such as brand awareness, perception change, and relationship metrics, like ones captured in performance reviews. Those companies who use performance incentives report that it does result in greater agency performance.

Client Viewpoint

"There are pros and cons to Pay for Performance compensation agreements. The key question is 'Are we compensating them fairly?' Not whether or not we should pay more. The jury is still out as to whether or not incentive based compensation is delivering on its original promise."

BRETT COLBERT
Global Manager, Procurement Advertising, Anheuser Busch InBev

In the ANA Client/agency compensation Guidebook, Stanley and David Beals state that "A major impetus for the use of performance incentives has come from advertisers challenging the idea of having to pay the same for mediocre work as for outstanding work. Looked at another way, many advertisers are willing to pay a premium for work that proves itself in the market." They make an excellent point. Marketers want to reward excellent work, as long as that work is yielding the desired results. Who wouldn't? P4P programs are set up based on the principle that a noticeable and impactful shift in interest, attitudes, and behavior can be expected from the agency when operating under this type of compensation agreement; there is a greater level of focus on things that matter most. As a result the client is not taken for granted. Everyone on the account seems to try harder, everyone is well informed about their contribution to the business, and so forth.

Simply stated, paying more is fine when you are getting equally more as well. Of course, incentive based program go both ways even if agencies tend to resist any uncertainty in their business. It means that for any potential upside, there is a potential downside, balancing rewards and risks accordingly. Clients and agencies must ultimately agree on the objectives, the risks and potential earn out, and the measurement and evaluation system. Setting up this type of compensation agreement is a collaborative process that must be based on complete transparency and trust. There are some best practices every client should consider:

Objectives are clearly defined, agreed upon from the outset, and signed off by senior management on both sides. Typical objectives are: (1) quantitative based on business performance (sales, profits, growth, share, stock value, customer satisfaction, etc.) AND marketing communications metrics (awareness, perception shifting, recall, engagement, site traffic, profiles, response and conversion rates, cost per click, cost per lead) or (2) qualitative, such as thought leadership, creative, innovation, customer service, or ideally, (3) a combination of both to provide a comprehensive view into how well the agency is performing. Most common criteria are sales awareness, perception shifting, and response rates. These are more easily attributable to the agency's performance compared to metrics such as company profits, stock value, or brand equity that can be, in some industries, outside of the direct span of control of the agency. If the performance evalution includes multiple metrics, these should be prioritized and weighted accordingly.

Client Viewpoint

"Too often, the agency is not being told upfront that they will be measured based on business results. Clients often pick agencies based on how much they like the work but they often fail to take a hard look at whether or not the work is delivering against key metrics."

JULIE GIBBS, Director, Corporate Brand Marketing, Campaign Management, Adobe

Not all agencies are comfortable with business metrics weighted so heavily with the high number of variables, many of which are out of their control. Should Toyota's agencies be penalized for its massive recall and product quality issues? Maybe not. But if they are not, they shouldn't expect the agency to be rewarded for product awards, distribution deals, and other business events that might drive their bottom line. Clients often take significant risks. Agencies should only receive rewards if they share client risks. If the agency is highly dependent on the client to accomplish its goal, these dependencies should be clearly spelled out, and failure by the client to meet them doesn't necessarily disqualify the agency from earning its potential bonus. Clients should ask themselves:

- Are the objectives clear and specific enough?
- Are they realistic?
- Do they stretch the agency enough?
- Can this be adapted globally?
- Are those objectives within the agency's control or influence?
- Are they promoting shared accountability?
- Are they too subjective?

- Can they be effectively and accurately measured?
- Are the goals time-bound, so performance can be assessed within a time-window during which the agency can positively impact them?
- How do we handle long-term goals that cross over multiple fiscal calendars?
- Is the agreement flexible enough that goals can be reset if mutually agreed?

Stay away from intangible metrics that might be too vague or arguable, leading to endless, wasteful debates with the agency as to whether or not the objectives were accomplished and the agency should be paid. Give yourself enough time to measure progress by the time you have to determine what the agency is entitled to.

Determine profit targets at different levels of performance in good faith. It assumes that the client has already a solid understanding of compensation benchmarks across the industry. It also assumes that the incentive is meaningful enough to positively impact the relationship. For the purpose of this discussion, if you assume 15% margin as the industry norm (numbers tend to vary significantly by type of agency and client), the agency might be willing to risk all or some of its profit (typically in the 5%-12% range) in return for a potential uplift deemed appealing enough (typically in the 18-22% range) upon meeting jointly agreed objectives. Clients should set a base level compensation that is fair relative to industry standards. All agency costs—whether direct and indirect—should at the very least be covered.

Typically, a minimum margin level is guaranteed to the agency, preventing agencies from staffing at the bare minimum to reduce expenses in the event it is unsuccessful. But some clients have been pushing for all profits to be based upon performance. Some may risk all their profit but few will risk doing work at less than break-even since it effectively threatens the viability of the agency. Either way, the upside must be somewhat proportional to the risk taken and vice versa. It must be perceived equitable and fair by both parties.

Agency Viewpoint

"We are open to incentive-based compensation; however, in our experience, few clients are willing to share sales and other data that are used to measure performance. We believe that value-based compensation is the most equitable compensation method. Fair pay for a the value of the idea, rather than how much time it took to create it."

MARC A. BROWNSTEIN
President and CEO, Brownstein Group

Metrics and measurement have been mutually agreed upon. The metrics that will be used along with specific target goals, such as how the information will be collected, by whom, for what time period, when it will be reported, and how it can be validated. For qualitative objectives, who makes the final call on whether or not a goal was met or exceeded expectations is also critical. The computation of results may vary based on the level of specificity sought: Some criteria may be weighted more heavily than others (business metrics such as sales might represent one third of the incentive budget, marketing communications metrics such as favorability might represent another third, and qualitative assessment such as customer service or collaboration might represent the remaining third). The qualitiative assessment must be conducted objectively. The agency's incentive can be then calculated and distributed based on a basic scoring system (for instance: needs improvement, achieved, exceeded).

Conduct regular reviews. Training employees on both the client and agency side ensures that everyone understands what is expected of them and how the process works. Setting up a regular cadence to monitor performance gives the agency an opportunity to react before the end of the time period if results are not trending positively. It clearly takes special meaning when the agency's profitablity is at risk. If both parties agree to reset on the metrics or targets due to significant scope of work changes or material events (acquisitions, economic conditions)it can be done at such time. Communication and transparency are key, from start to finish.

Set adequate budget and payment schedule. Clients should budget assuming the maximum payout and have the reserve in place if/when full payment is due. Clients can effectively pay the full amount on the regular payment schedule and ask for a credit at the end of the year if the agency didn't earn all of the incentive. Or the client can set aside the incremental budget to pay for the incentive at the end of the year, a preferable scenario from a cash flow perspective.

P4P models are always challenging to implement for clients without prior experience in this area. But it should not deter you from implementing it or at least experimenting to get a feel for it. Agencies are likely to question aggressive, even punitive, P4P models where all or a sizeable portion of the agency's profit is at risk. Clients are likely to question bonuses that do not get systematically passed on to the actual staff working on the account. It assumes a good track record at rewarding high performance employees and measuring verifiable, indisputable results. Once objectives are set, the agency must have a seat at the table whenever important decisions are made that might impact the performance of the program they have shared accountability for.

New relationships benefit the least from P4P agreements because they usually require a certain degree of familiarity with the account. Agency performance is highly subjective without quantifiable metrics, exposing agencies to undue risks due to mergers or acquisitions, or frequent changes in management. Regardless of the level of rigor and integrity applied to this process, it requires a fair amount of trust between the client and the agency. After all, the client is often on point to collect and to report and compare results with objectives. Trust is earned over time; so well established client/agency relationships seem to be best positioned to use P4P.

In my experience, this type of compensation model also tends to work better with clients that have implemented a similar bonus program for employees and/or upper management based on company and/or individual performance for two primary reasons: (1) It demonstrates that the company has already bought in into the concept of P4P, which is that the work will generate a measurable business benefit and (2) It indicates that the company has already identified the metrics by which performance will be measured, making this a shorter ramp up for everyone involved.

Client Viewpoint

"I find it amusing to hear folks ask about the 'right level of agency profits.' Guess what, if you want to reconcile hours and rates every month, that's old economics. It's about who can find the right balance between great creative people who deliver, an optimum mix of media platforms and sales/share growth. The faster you figure that out, the quicker you will win. Clients need to experiment and learn more. We should focus less on agency profitability and more on the work—how to make it more compelling, how it can motivate customers to act."

JAMES R. ZAMBITO, Global Marketing Group Controller, Johnson & Johnson

For the most part, it is a philosophical approach that typically is anchored into a company's culture and ways of doing business. If a company hasn't set an incentive pay program internally for its employees, the chances for such incentive program for vendors to work are limited. P4P agreements are also more commonly found among large advertisers. It has nothing to do with risk tolerance but has to do with complexity and client bandwidth.

Large companies are more likely able to afford the time and resources to set up, manage, and administer this type of elaborate compensation agreement than small ones. The benefits must outweigh the time, resources, and costs required to manage it. An independent consultant might be a valuable resource to busy clients for the heavy-lifting, facilitating the selection of goals and metrics, as well as reporting results and payout. Bad, good, or excellent work should not be compensated the same. As labor-based agreements grew in popularity, so did the perception that agencies are in the business of selling time by filling timesheets. We know however that agencies are in the business of driving measurable results for clients. Clients prosper or die based on a few key performance metrics. So should their agencies.

P4P compensation is recalibrating the relationship to be results vs. activity focused. It encourages agencies to engage with clients upstream and more strategically about what they can control and what they might be able to influence, including timing, pricing, and retail and channel distribution. The greatest value realized from P4P is clarity of goals, aligned priorities, and stronger synergy. In the end, P4P agreements are intended to increase shared accountability and strengthen the strategic relationship between clients and agencies.

Value-based and Equity-sharing Agreements

A new type of compensation agreements has recently emerged, suggested by agencies looking for creative ways to overthrow traditional cost-based compensation philosophies considered flawed and grossly inadequate. They argue that the ingenuity of what they do is in the approach they take and the value they create as a result, not how many bodies they assign to the account. Staples's "Easy Button" idea developed by McCann Erickson was so successful that the company ended up producing the buttons and selling them in their store.[45]

Agencies are licensing technology and applications they built for some clients and now offering them to others. Entrepreneurial independent agency Mother New York created and sold a hot-dog business called Dogmatic, inspired from their travel through Europe. Other agencies like Euro RSCG, which create songs for their clients, also generate revenue from in-house record labels. Agency Schafer Condon Carter created and sold a low-carb, low-calorie brand named Hogwash to a bottler company.[46] Agency Anomaly incubates and creates joint ventures ranging from skin care products to fashion and music.

For agencies willing to go outside their core offering, the revenue opportunities seem endless. These innovative concepts are putting emphasis on value, not cost, answering a fundamental desire by clients to see their agencies laser-focus on what matters most to them.

Value-based If P4P is predominantly focused on results, another form of compensation is making waves centered on the ultimate end goal of any partnership: "value." Value is the worth expressed in monetary terms of the benefits (however it is defined) a client receives in exchange for the price it pays for a given market offering. Clients genuinely know that their agencies add tremendous value to their marketing efforts. But how is that value defined? By whom? And how is it measured? Naturally, it comes in different flavors depending on who is defining it. Here's the challenge: for agencies, it is based on the principle that they should be entitled to a portion of the value they create on their clients' behalf. For clients, it is based on the principle that clients should pay for the value they believe they are receiving from their agency which may or may not be based on in-market results. They might receive a royalty for the life of the work produced. It is a highly subjective measure and works best when the value created can be sustained over time. It is therefore extensively debated and difficult to agree on. Some call it Utopian: admirable but impracticable. For that reason, it will take time for this type of compensation to go "mainstream."

Agency Viewpoint

"Agencies must take more risk for their own sake and for their client's sake. Agencies don't have enough skin in the game today. I want to partner with my clients and invent products and new brand experiences and own some of the residual. The risks and rewards come together. The work gets stronger when they do."

DAVID KENNY
Managing Partner, Vivaki

Consultants like Ronald Baker and Alan Weiss have published books on the subject of value-based pricing (*Professional's Guide to Value Pricing*[47] and *Value-Based Fees*[48] respectively), vividly promoting an alternative to existing compensation methods and moving beyond the old "time plus materials" concept employed by so many professional services. Although their views are not specifically focused on advertising, marketing, and communication agencies, they are emphasizing the need for anyone in professional services to change their views on how to price their services, from selling time to generating profit from their intellectual capital, and in the process, permanently get rid of time sheets.

It's important to distinguish value from price in this concept. Raising or lowering price does not in effect change value but, instead, provides an incentive or disincentive to purchase. So the incentive to purchase must exceed the one from the competition, which implies that clients must gain visibility into market rates. Value-based compensation is based on a powerful idea.

In 2008, the Coca-Cola Company (TCCC) designed an elaborate value-based compensation model with deliverables price based on historical pricing and perceived value and with profitability solely contingent on meeting performance goals.[49] The company piloted the model and the following year rolled it out to key markets hoping to replace its labor-based approach and create incentives for agencies. Previously TCCC agencies were guaranteed a profit which now must be earned.

TCCC compensation model is based on two principles: investing in outputs based on scope of work deliverables and rewarding outcomes that are based on actual performance. The scope of work deliverables establishes the base fee, with no markup and is submitted to roster agencies. The pay for performance component, which replaces discretionary bonuses, adds on to the base fee 30% or higher in bonus markup. The scope of work is broken down into discreet creative and media deliverables by various campaign development stages from research and brand strategy to proof of concept, adaptation, trafficking and measurement. A database of cost per deliverable is helping TCCC figure out what things have historically cost them and the highest and lowest they would be willing to invest in per deliverable.

The TCCC model assumes a base value range is determined per deliverable based on historical cost per deliverable (the price paid for similar work in the past) and value perception based on past work and project parameters (budget, strategic nature of the assignment, talent requirements, and so on). Over time, Coca-Cola built a comprehensive data base of spend information based on different types of assignments that allow them to determine the "value" of a particular project. Once the value has been defined per deliverable, then the pay for performance amount is defined along with metrics and weighting. Although the model has received mixed feedback, it has certainly generated much interest among the client and agency community eager to explore better, more rigorous ways to define value in compensation agreements.

Profit-sharing Sales-based royalties or profit-sharing agreements are fundamentally transforming the nature of the client/vendor relationship to a business partnership. They introduce the notion of risk and reward-sharing by giving the agency an opportunity to invest in building value that can be monetized or in sharing sales associated with the activities driven by the agency.Or the agency might introduce a new product line on the client's behalf by giving up its time in return for a share of the revenue and profits.

It might also consider being compensated by taking ownership into a new business venture, officially becoming a business partner to the client as Haggar Clothing did with its agency Crispin Porter + Bogusky. The concept is based on whether or not an agency and its client are willing to incorporate a certain level of risk and reward in the compensation that tie back to not only performance but business ownership and long term profitability. The possibility in this area is endless.

I suspect however that clients will not move in that direction on their own. Agencies might find it possible to monetize the value of their engagement with consumers, above and beyond their client assignment, developing and distributing surplus entertainment content. Smaller clients who want to subsidize some of their agency costs might be more open to this type of arrangement.

Another type of related compensation approach is shared ownership, also popular in the corporate world where employees are eligible to earn stock or ownership of the company. As in profit-sharing agreements that are based on sales, the potential earn-out is based on how well the company is performing (or is perceived to be performing in the case of public companies). Once an employee or an agency has equity in a company, it suddenly changes the nature of the relationship as both parties share the financial outcome, good or bad.

IP-sharing: Agencies are now challenging the client's outright ownership of intellectual property rights and pushing for alternative limited-ownership licensing arrangements that give them skin in the game. IP-sharing agreements tend to focus on the value of the intellectual property generated by the agency as part of a client assignment. Under the concept of IP-sharing, an agency might develop a Web experience with functionality (automated reminder service) that it intends to resell to other clients or customize for them at a profit. In this instance, the agency would agree to restrictions by agreeing to not make this solution available to companies in the same business to protect their client's interest without limiting their ability to profit from it.

In a digital world where agencies are asked to write code to develop engaging digital experiences, the temptation for agencies to fully or partially own the IP is increasingly higher. Clients are not likely however to agree to sharing the IP of innovative, creative ideas that are natural extensions of the brand identify or brand assets for which they want to retain full ownership. I also suspect that digital agencies are more likely to seek this type of partnership opportunities. This type of compensation agreement is far more complex to set up and presents higher risks for business conflicts with continued pressure on the relationship. It is, however, likely to become the norm, especially for client assignments that require a fair amount of Web development and innovative applications.

Step 3: Negotiating Compensation Terms

As Chester L. Karrass's book title explicitly states: "In business as in life, you don't get what you deserve. You get what you negotiate." Negotiations often start with familiar rituals: The clients insist on laying out their company policies, with justifications based on vague or inconclusive competitive benchmarks, boilerplate terms and conditions, and other non-negotiable issues. Agencies counter with "we are unique" arguments, guesstimates, case studies, references, and pages-long disclaimers. Both parties operate with little insight or trust. They do know how to align to their mutual interests. We've all seen this movie before. There is a better way.

- First, client/agency compensation should be based on the total cost of the ownership, which means going beyond the typical agency costs, calculated by a fair and equitable profit margin, to also take into consideration the overall investment made by the client, the real and perceived value of the services received, and the potential long-term value of the relationship as a whole.

Client Viewpoint

"Best practices in regards to negotiating compensation, as all negotiators will tell you: don't negotiate on a single point/position; start discussing mutual interests and the options which may satisfy those interests. By doing so you'll find that there are several ways to satisfy both client and agency needs."

CHARLIE SILVESTRO
Vice President, Global Agency Operations, MasterCard Worldwide

- Second, negotiations should be for the most part finalized before any internal or public announcement is made about the selected agency in the case of a search, or before any work gets initiated in the case of a contract renewal. A client runs the risk of losing a strong hand at the negotiation table if it fails to lock on compensation early on. Once the announcement is made public or the work has started, all bets are made and leverage has been lost. In some unfortunate cases, endless, wasteful negotiations by individuals that have not been empowered to make decisions may shorten the honeymoon and perhaps even deteriorate the relationship.

- Third, both sides must assign that responsibility to someone with adequate authority to make decisions. Most client contracts are individually negotiated and therefore, the terms and conditions, engagement profile, and the basis on which they generate revenue and profit vary significantly from one relationship to another, making it hard to apply best practices for clients in search of guidance.

- Fourth, clients must have a clear understanding of the expense classification, definitions of compensation terms, direct and indirect agency costs included, and the cost accounting methods associated with various forms of fee agreement. They need to lock on payment terms. They should also agree on reporting, year-end reconciliation and audit requirements and associated administrative costs.

- Finally, reporting requirements have to be comprehensive enough to satisfy clients' need for agency transparency and reasonable costs. Agency financials should be reviewed annually at the very least. A financial reconciliation of payments ensures that the compensation model is adhered to and gives the opportunity for modifications of compensation terms in subsequent years if appropriate. Anything more frequent may not be needed.

In healthy client/agency relationships, transparency and trust are critical success factors and signs of longevity. Some agencies go as far as sharing detailed profit and loss statements to show clients how profitable (or not) their account is to them, which in turn might be taken into consideration for future negotiations. This open book approach builds trust in the relationship and shows that both parties want to establish a fair and equitable partnership.

Needless to say, the specific compensation terms and conditions must be kept confidential at all times as those tend to vary from one relationship to another. How often should you review compensation agreements? The short answer is how often you deem it is necessary. If the client or the agency experience major changes in business conditions that justify reevaluating client/agency compensation terms, then be it. Otherwise, it is recommended to review those only every two years, depending on the economic climate.

Client Viewpoint

"Payment terms in agency relationships are often about who is acting as the bank when it comes to third party costs. Clients do not want to pay the agencies sooner than necessary and agencies don't want to be carrying the overhead of third party costs. Ideally, it's about being cash flow neutral for both parties."

DELMAR WYATT
Director Advertising Operations, Qwest Communications

In a period of economic uncertainty, clients should revisit compensation terms at least annually to keep terms competitive and on par with industry standards. The process can be a major resource tax for both the agency and client, so more frequent re-evaluations might be wasteful and distracting for everyone. Compensation by its own nature is never static. It is subject to change based on the evolving nature and requirements of the relationship. The reality in client/agency compensation is that every dollar in their bottom line is a dollar not ending up in yours. So clients are rightfully being diligent about compensation agreements. Unless a dollar in their bottom line has a multiplier effect on yours.

In that case, it's worth the investment you are getting back. Clients must work with agencies in very close partnership to identify potential efficiency improvement. It is known that conditions of scarcity often produce more creative and innovative results than conditions of abundance. Any efficiency improvement should be considered to be mutually beneficial to the relationship, whether or not it leads to adjustments of compensation terms.

Ending the Debate?

The compensation model of the past is no longer suitable to either party. Clients pushing for further margin-squeeze, while the agency workload becomes more complex and more demanding, is preventing agencies from hiring and training great talent. There has been too much abuse on either side for too long. As a result, there is too little transparency and virtually no trust. It has led to the continued weakening of relationships between clients and their agencies, which as a result undermines a client's ability to succeed in the marketplace. Clients no longer want clock-watchers on their business. Agencies no longer want to die by a thousand paper cuts. Too few are getting what they want from their existing relationship.

It is time for change. It's time to end the debate, move toward a bi-partisan approach and change compensation agreements to focus on the sheer measurable value and results produced by agencies. It's one thing to pound our chests with pride that we cracked the code when at industry events. It's another to make it an effective and sustainable way of driving greater value from the partnership every day. Compensation must reward results and value, not activity, efforts, labor or costs.

The agency community is enthusiastic about new forms of compensation that no longer set a ceiling on a profit indexed to cost. Some agencies have established incubating departments/teams to collaborate with clients on creating new products and services. They range from new lines of consumer products such as skin care, shaving cream, juice drink brand, books, and candles, to paid Web services and software tools such as virtual conference software, Twitter analytical tools, and computer/video games.

In addition to these there are many other potential sources of revenue outside of conventional client assignments[50] that can be sold directly to consumers or even licensed to other agency clients. Agencies like Anomaly created departments to incubate IP and invest in new business opportunities and joint ventures like i/denti/tee, its fashion and music joint venture involving iTunes, and other business partners such as Hard Rock Café so music lovers can buy t-shirts that allow them to wear their favorite lyrics. The list of business opportunities pursued by agencies appears endless. In return, the skepticism expressed by some clients about the entrepreneurial nature of some agencies is understandable: Where does an agency start and end? The concept of partnership clearly takes on a new meaning.

These concepts introduce a new level of complexity that often make them impractical to negotiate, set up, and administer, at least for now, until industry standards and best practices emerge and lead the way. Clients must consider a number of criteria that will play heavily in their decision: How predictable, measurable, simple, scalable, flexible, and equitable is the proposed compensation plan?

Large clients or ones with established agency relationships can have privileged compensation models that are measurable, predictable, and scalable. Predictability and scale are both critical for securing discounted rates based on economies of scale. Small to medium size clients or new relationships may pursue simple, yet proven models with a high degree of flexibility. Large companies might be able to deal with the administrative requirements of more complex compensation models. Does it allow agencies to be adequately rewarded for the risks they are willing to take? Are interests and priorities clearly aligned? Well established and mature client/agency relationships are well positioned to experiment P4P and value-based models.

Client Viewpoint

"Negotiate before falling in love. It's good practice for clients to negotiate terms with an agency before they are coming to pitch the business. It ensures better alignment and is easier for all involved."

Brett Colbert
Global Manager, Procurement Advertising, Anheuser Busch InBev

Global clients typically work with multiple agencies to accommodate scale and coverage that may not be available through a single relationship. A few global agencies have access to a network of local offices in the countries their clients operate. Unfortunately, the level of sophistication or uniformity of compensation practices is still widely spread around the world, making it challenging for global agencies to come up with a standard compensation model. The global agency takes on the challenge of coordinating of the various accounting systems under a single profit and loss management of the account, making it seamless to the client. The client still can gain visibility into these practices by conducting occasional audits.

The large majority of global accounts are handled as labor-based agreements. The contract stipulates the requirements that must be followed by all offices to avoid any confusion or misalignment. Once the profit margin is agreed upon for the relationship globally, overhead and labor costs for each geo concerned must be negotiated (often with the assistance of local agency and client resources). The end result is a global rate card that is the basis for staffing decisions and billings. As expected, P4P is harder to manage in global contacts because of cultural differences and business practices. IP-sharing agreements are few, given the added complexity of multinational offices. Labor-based (fixed) agreements are popular as they greatly simplify the administration of the account.

Finding Common Ground

Aligning compensation philosophies is common sense, so it's a good place to start. If the agency is simply an extension of the client's marketing team, whatever compensation agreement you contemplate should ideally be aligned to the way the client handles employee compensation. That includes principles on how a client remunerates employees, and what their benefits, culture, and retention philosophies are. It's easier to implement a client/agency compensation based on the guiding principles of a client's approach to compensation, and it's easier to explain because everyone in the company is fully aware of it and hopefully supporting it. If it's a good idea for employees, it's probably a decent idea for agencies. There shouldn't be a double standard. I am not implying that it must be identical. But it can be based on a common set of principles.

Client Viewpoint

"Marketing executives have target bonuses based on the company's performance and their individual contribution. Performance is typically determined based on quantitative (sales, profitability, etc.) and qualitative metrics. The agencies that understand this about their client/marketing partners have probably the most productive partnerships. Their client's bonus is about meeting goals. When agencies start the discussion about "big ideas" that are not anchored into tangible business priorities, they get a very negative response from clients. Executives want their agencies to be paid based on the same criteria. They want agencies to have more at risk. That's true partnership."

LYNNE SEID, Partner Global Marketing Officers Practice, Heidrick & Struggles

For example, clients with a strong culture of accountability, that also offer bonuses to employees based on the company's performance (business, financial, marketing), are more inclined to institute Pay for Performance pricing than those who don't. Similarly, clients that foster an employee culture of long working hours may not be receptive to client/agency compensations that are hourly based. The compensation agreement will not to be tailored to the needs of both parties, but essentially cannot be diametrically opposed to a client's philosophy on employee compensation if it is to be successful and take root within that relationship. Finding and implementing the right compensation agreement is critical to the success of that relationship.

In the end, clients must face the legendary "fast, good, and cheap" triangle, well known in software engineering, which states that it's virtually impossible to get all three and that one must choose: If you pick good and cheap, you might compromise speed. If you pick fast and cheap, you might compromise quality. But if you pick good and fast, don't expect it to be cheap. There are a number of scenarios to pick from, so advertisers must carefully evaluate their options, and avoid compensation agreements that fall short of motivating the agency to do their very best when servicing your account.

In the end, clients and agencies must share risks and rewards, and pick just the numbers that matter if we are to truly end the debate. Agencies like Omnicom Group's TBWA/Chiat/Day have decided to raise the bar and assign real expertise to this area in response to clients' desperate efforts to reduce expense at all costs.[51,52] Agencies are creating Chief Compensation Officer roles to lead fee and contract negotiations with existing or potential new clients, exploring ways to create greater value while protecting an agency's ability to grow and prosper rather than relying on busy and ill-prepared executives. Clients must also play their part.

CMOs must reaffirm their commitments to healthy agency relationships that emphasize value over cost, and results over efforts, which is not much different from the way they want consumers to buy from them. They must enable agencies to invest in the talent they need to succeed and focus their resources and energy on delivering great work that drives business growth. To do so, they may need to stand up and vigorously push back against unfair payment terms, unreasonable cost cutting demands targeted at agencies from Finance.

CMOs and business leaders must advocate for their agencies as drivers of growth, protecting these valuable resources as they do internal ones, and keeping their goals and respective economic interests aligned. They must educate key internal partners about the business value generated by their agencies, explaining how digital will profoundly change the mix between media, production, and fees in the years ahead and how shared economic incentives between a client and an agency yields greater return.

Agency Viewpoint

"At Publicis, we believe in a P&L structure aligned around clients vs. agencies."

DAVID KENNY
Managing Partner, Vivaki

Beyond Financial Incentives

For years, brand advertisers have used extrinsic motivators like money—the carrot-and-stick approach—to motivate agencies to perform well on their business. Even today, clients incentivize agencies to consistently meet or exceed certain expectations of particular value to them. But is that sufficient? Drawing on four decades of scientific research on human motivation including experiments in behavioral science, Daniel H. Pink in his book *Drive: The Surprising Truth About What Motivates Us* shows a different way to motivate and achieve high performance. He argues that the reward-and-punishment approach so popular in routine, rule-based, yet essential left-brain type of work, doesn't work any longer and can even do harm in today's fast growing right-brain type of environments where cognitive thinking is prevalent. Why?

In his memorable speech at TED he suggests that "reward actually narrows our focus and restricts our possibility," especially in a business environment where there are no clear set of rules and no single solution to a problem. To sharpen our big-picture thinking and accelerate creativity, are material, financial incentives the way to motivate? Dan proposes intrinsic motivators organized in three major elements: "autonomy, mastery, and purpose."

Client Viewpoint

"In the end, there is no silver bullet to compensation. Client/agency compensation should be first and foremost aligned to a company's philosophy. It's about identifying what's important to you then managing the agency relationship fairly and consistently."

JAMES R. ZAMBITO, Global Marketing Group Controller, Johnson & Johnson

I've come to believe that his argument also applies to client/agency relationships, especially among agencies where cognitive thinking, creativity, and innovation are core to their offerings. Agencies want some autonomy and creative freedom to think proactively about a client's business, something many of them feel challenged to do in an environment where they are asked to manage a narrowly focused scope of work and tight budget that leaves little room for anything else. They want to be rewarded with work that allows them to refine their craft.

And finally, they are motivated first and foremost by assignments because those are what truly matter and have strong emotional relevancy or significance to the agency. Not every client assignment can meet all three criteria but thinking in these terms is a new way of looking at what motivates agencies and leads to higher performance partnerships.

If the value exchange is not only about financial incentives and is also not solely transactional, there are other ways to motivate an agency beyond pure compensation. A client can help an agency successfully expand its business in complementary industries or geographical markets, by providing access to research and insight an agency wouldn't otherwise have access to, and turn that insight into client value. A client can also contribute to case studies, becoming a valuable spokesperson about the partnership and an advocate for the agency at industry events for RPF or agency pitches. A client can contribute to developing greater talent at the agency by assigning agency staff to the right projects, developing new skills, attending internal training programs or events, or even partnering closely with internal teams on innovative concepts and ideas.

When done properly, compensation can turn into a powerful tool to motivate and restore confidence in client/agency relationships. The value exchange may be based on more or less than just six numbers. Whatever the right number might be to keep your client/agency universe in balance, keep in mind that pursuing equitable terms ultimately motivates people, builds trust, mutual respect and goodwill, and translates into outstanding success.

{Taking Immediate Action}

TOP 5

BEST PRACTICES TO HARNESS THE MADNESS

❶ Finalize compensation terms before making your agency selection. In year one of the relationship, do not overcomplicate. Pick a simple formula. Evolve compensation as the relationship matures.

❷ Prioritize compensation agreements that align your mutual interests and operating principles, and motivate the agency to act in ways that support your business priorities.

❸ Insist on rewarding agencies for outstanding business performance or value generated rather than based on activity, timesheets or efforts alone. Go beyond typical financial incentive arrangements and explore other creative ways to motivate agencies.

❹ Media discounts, credits, and float are potential sources of income and profit for agencies whose clients have not addressed those contractually. Make sure media discounts and credits are factored in your compensation agreement or, at the very least, consistently returned to the client.

❺ Don't ask your agency to act as a bank. Include equitable payment terms so cash flow does not become an unnecessary distraction in the relationship.

It was six men of Indostan
To learning much inclined,
Who went to see the Elephant
(Though all of them were blind),
That each by observation
Might satisfy his mind.
The First approached the Elephant,
And happening to fall
Against his broad and sturdy side,
At once began to bawl:
"God bless me! but the Elephant
Is very like a WALL!"
The Second, feeling of the tusk,
Cried, "Ho, what have we here,
So very round and smooth and sharp?
To me 'tis mighty clear
This wonder of an Elephant
Is very like a SPEAR!"
The Third approached the animal,
And happening to take
The squirming trunk within his hands,
Thus boldly up and spake:
"I see" quoth he, "the Elephant
Is very like a SNAKE!"
The Fourth reached out an eager hand,
And felt about the knee
"What most this wondrous beast is like
Is mighty plain," quoth he:
"Tis clear enough the Elephant
Is very like a TREE!"
The Fifth, who chanced to touch the ear,
Said: "E'en the blindest man
Can tell what this resembles most;
Deny the fact who can,
This marvel of an Elephant
Is very like a FAN!"
The Sixth no sooner had begun
About the beast to grope,
Than seizing on the swinging tail
That fell within his scope,
"I see," quoth he, "the Elephant
Is very like a ROPE!"
And so these men of Indostan
Disputed loud and long,
Each in his own opinion
Exceeding stiff and strong,
Though each was partly in the right,
And all were in the wrong!

—John Godfrey Saxe
Writer and poet

8 SIX MEN OF INDOSTAN

Successfully scoping work and briefing agencies

In his poem "The Blind Men and the Elephant" John Godfrey Saxe warns about common misperceptions when looking at the component parts, and not the whole. Without stretching the imagination too far, but to bring this home, one might think of the Elephant as a client and the Blind Men as the agencies. Playing on the metaphor, the agencies are simply seeking to understand the client, approaching it from multiple angles. However, without explicit guidance from the client, they are indeed blind. They are likely to misread the signs or make false assumptions, misinterpret the client, and ultimately, miss the mark and all be *in the wrong!*

The powerful lesson of this emblematic story is that agencies cannot deliver outstanding work without solid, comprehensive input from clients. Period. A comprehensive annual scope of work, combined with solid briefs, provides the agency with an inclusive picture of the client opportunity. It also guarantees absolute alignment by focusing on what truly matters.

This exercise involves adjusting the marketing lens from big to small, from planning to execution. Or more specifically, from the initial scope of work planning process—an aggregate, holistic view of all marketing campaigns and activities commissioned by client to an agency *(or the whole)*—to the individual project briefings, the act of providing directional input to an agency about a particular project or assignment *(or one of the many parts)*.

Client Viewpoint

"Agencies must be provided with good, relevant information by their client so they understand who they are talking to from an audience perspective and how to talk to them, to understand your business and customer set. You have to let your agencies become an extension of your organization."

MICHAEL FITZGERALD
Associate Director, Business Advertising, AT&T Inc.

Scoping work and briefing agencies are some of the most impactful activities a client must deliver to yield strong work and make optimal use of an agency partner. Effective scope of work planning and briefing are vital. It's so important to successful client/agency relations that it deserves its own chapter. To use the popular English idiom, now that the elephant is in the room, let's take a closer look at how clients can turn scope of work and briefings into highly productive endeavors.

Scope of Work Planning ("the whole")

A new fiscal year is around the corner. Everyone can feel the energy and excitement building up. The CEO sets the vision and business priorities for the company. The CFO provides financial guidance and distributes budgets. The CMO articulates the brand strategy and announces key marketing initiatives. The client's lead agency is anxious to staff the account and get ready to engage. Now what? The question resonates loudly through the hallways of marketing departments: What should clients do next? The answer: workload planning. Scope of work planning is about defining priorities and what a client expects from its agency(ies) for a determined time period (typically a fiscal calendar or a six month increment). It plugs right into the overall marketing planning process during which goals are set and budgets locked.

Client Viewpoint

"Our close partnership with BBDO including their involvement in early stage planning discussions has led to higher quality briefings and better deliverables. We want them to have a seat at the table."

JENNIFER BERGER, Director, Marketing & Advertising Services, Starbucks

The scope of work will include a top-level summary of all the marketing and communication initiatives, campaigns, and activities. It assumes a joint understanding of service levels such as decision-making approval and reworks and mutual expectations, typically covered in a Service Level Agreement. This critical systematic process ensures agencies are working on the right priorities, have adequate line of sight into the volume and complexity of the work they are tasked to do, and as a result, are in a position to make accurate staffing decisions. How else would agencies know whether or not they have the right staff in place to carry on the mission?

This is what agencies typically refer to as "agency resourcing." Also commonly known as "agency capacity planning" or "resource forecasting," it refers to the effective planning and utilization of agency resources, anticipating what's needed to successfully support a pre-determined body of work. Based on that information, preliminary resource plans will be determined by the agency. An agency may need to hire new talent, repurpose existing staff or pull resources from other sister agencies. They may decide to hire freelancers during low activity periods or to simply load-balance resources among multiple clients. There are a number of benefits clients get from scope of work planning:

- Guaranteed availability of agency resources
- Easier access to top agency talent
- Continuous, permanent knowledge of the account

- Easier to attract and retain good talent
- Reduced overhead
- Reduced non-billable time
- Reduced outsourcing, recruiting and on-boarding costs associated with unforeseen uptick in activity
- Reduced severance, legal expenses that may result from layoffs when activity stops or slows down

The media function also benefits greatly from workload planning:

- Better pricing when negotiating volume discounts
- Avoids premium pricing for random, ad hoc projects
- Better use of agency and client resources by avoiding last minute decisions and silo approach to negotiations
- Reduces inability to lock in strategic placements
- Penalty and/or rate adjustments for cancelations

The past few decades have shown us that there is a direct correlation between the degrees of involvement of an agency in the early phase of the client's planning process and the agency's ability to deliver strategic value and breakthrough ideas. This is common sense, after all: When agencies are involved early enough in the planning cycle, they can offer insight and recommendations that shape or strongly influence client decisions. Rather than being treated as "order takers," agencies seize the opportunity to shape the objectives that they will be asked to support. The end result is an agency better integrated into the company's overall strategy and objectives, more knowledgeable about what needs to be done (and why), more engaged with senior leadership, and better prepared to tackle their client's marketing challenges.

Client Viewpoint

"The scope of work goes to team Detroit which acts as a general contractor for creative talent or specialties needed to complete a project."

SUSAN MARKOWICZ, Global Advertising Agency Manager, Ford Motor Company

Defining an agency's annual scope of work is not a walk in the park: The strategy may not be fully baked, the decision as to which agency is doing what may not have been made, priorities may be conflicting or unclear, budgets may still be in flux, and yet work may need to be started immediately.

Sounds familiar? The myth of an agency with unlimited supply of superb talent standing by, waiting by the phone for a client to call, is hopefully long gone in people's mind. Frankly, it never existed, even in the most clement economic times. Agencies do not have endless resources or cash on hand.

It's especially important to realize this as agencies today face increasing demands of growing workload, greater complexity, and higher expectations from clients. They must work with their clients to map the effective use of their valuable but limited resources. Doing so requires them to actively engage in the process of setting objectives and coming up with ways to meet them. This is what a strategic partnership is all about.

Agencies should not only be on the receiving end of the planning process, they must be an integral part of it. They must be sitting at the table where priorities are set and decisions are made about marketing strategies. There are a few critical ingredients that contribute to a successful scope of work: transparency, customer insight, and flexibility.

First, clients do not mindlessly share confidential data with agencies they do not consider to be trusted partners. This point is not about nondisclosure; it is about clients investing valuable time and resources getting agencies up to speed on the company's strategy and big bets during a busy planning season. If sensitive, yet materially important information is not made available, it will seriously handicap the agency. In return, agencies must prove their trustworthiness if they are to be sitting at the strategic table.

Client Viewpoint

"At Campbell Soup, we follow a structured comment process called the huddle approach. Everyone gets a chance to discuss, share notes and have an open conversation so everyone's ideas and perspective are heard. We reach consensus and then consolidate our feedback, in writing, to the agency."

KEVIN PARHAM, Director Global Advertising, Campbell Soup

To respond to the challenge, the agency typically assigns its best account planning and senior management team, assembling as much agency brain and firepower as possible. Naturally, the agency is expected to be actively engaged in driving the marketing and communication agenda. It's no time to be a fly on the wall.

Second, the most valuable thing agencies can provide is consumer insight. We are talking about rich insight into customer audiences and segmentation, backed up by empirical data. Agencies can add tremendous value by sharing their knowledge of new consumer trends, innovations in media and technology, marketing best practices, insight that clients may not have otherwise access to.

Third, a certain amount of flexibility is often necessary as the scope of work changes to respond to rapidly changing market conditions or sudden competitive strikes. Flexibility must be part of the way the scope of work plan is engineered from the start, so agencies can quickly react and adapt. But no matter how diligent clients are about this process, it is known to be challenging, whether clients are in financial services, high tech, or in packaged goods.

So, if it is so fundamental to success, why is it so hard for clients to do? In an environment increasingly more volatile, continually subject to competitive pressure, companies may not want to set plans that are too rigid to accommodate for sudden change. Reversely, they may keep them too vague to successfully guide agencies. They may fail to engage the agency or may not invest the time to do the job properly. They may not be able to consolidate those into a comprehensive view. They may not solidify their plans until well into their new fiscal calendar.

Client Viewpoint

"An effective way to work with agencies is to develop an annual plan that gives the agencies a high level view of priorities key to the success of the business. In addition to the annual plan, I recommend that agencies be briefed 20 weeks prior to the beginning of each campaign window, if that window is shorter than the annual plan."

DELMAR WYATT
Director Advertising Operations, Qwest Communications

As a result, agencies may under-staff or over-staff the account based on how conservative or aggressive they want to be. In fee-based arrangements, agencies may lean towards having more, not less, resources assigned to the account in excess of what the client truly needs. They may also assign the wrong resources to carry out the work, leading to potential waste, inefficiencies and performance issues down the road. No matter how challenging, providing line of sight into the immediate future is the least clients can do to prepare their agencies. By doing so, they can ensure expectations are mutually understood, calculate resource requirements more accurately, focus on what truly matters and adds client value and come together as one to amplify their client's efforts.

Agency Briefing ("one of the many parts")

Once in a while, you run into these overly simplistic, yet essential questions. "What makes a good brief?" is one of those. The answer is priceless. Much of the responsibility for how much client efforts cost or how effective they are start with the direction provided to agencies. The client is setting the start and end points for a given assignment, supplying the agency with a solid foundation for strategy and creative development and vital information to complete it. A good brief exponentially increases the agency's ability to do great work. Perhaps no differently than a surgeon would.

Client Viewpoint

"I've known agencies that produced their own brief for internal purposes, hoping to emphasize what's truly inspiring about the assignment and remove the clutter. That's fine as long as the agency remembers clearly that the work will be measured against the original client brief, not their internal brief."

KEVIN PARHAM, Director Global Advertising, Campbell Soup

Imagine yourself for a second walking into an operating room, dreadfully hoping the surgeon was properly briefed about the procedure. As a client, you carefully selected the hospital and the surgeon, your service providers. The surgeon is competent, no doubt. But was he/she provided all the information needed to do the job? Are you both on the same page as to what a successful outcome is? Next time you brief an agency, think about it as if you were briefing a surgeon. You don't need to tell him/her what to do or how to do it. State the problem clearly. Give some background and focus on what's essential. Supply meaningful, actionable information. It's probably best he or she is aware of your allergies, has seen your lab results and is going in well informed. But once you agree with his/her recommendations, get out of the way and let him/her do the job.

How Clients Benefit

Client Viewpoint

"We demand cross-agency collaboration from our agencies. We gather all agency representatives together to get them briefed on new assignments."

KEVIN PARHAM, Director Global Advertising, Campbell Soup

In its most basic definition, a brief is the initiating point, the blueprint for providing the agency with all relevant insight needed to drive to the desired business outcome. It is the single most important phase of a working relationship with an agency. It is where it all starts. It facilitates the process of exchanging critical information with the agency, addressing the "what," "who," "where," and "why" of an assignment but not the "how." The "how" a project gets conceived and executed is for the agency to define. One thing is certain though: The better the brief, the greater the outcome.

A good brief informs but more importantly, inspires, motivates, and stimulates creative ideas from the agencies. If it doesn't get the agency hugely motivated, it's unlikely to ignite their creative juices and get the type of work they can produce. Providing clear and consistent direction, providing objectives and success metrics for a particular agency assignment, helps reduce significant waste. Even small improvements in this area can easily translate into millions of dollars in increased effectiveness or reduced expenses. So clients are wise to invest the time and energy required to produce the best possible brief before sharing it with their agencies. This investment will pay itself back over and over.

Client Viewpoint

"A good brief means clear goals and a vision as well as a constant, open dialogue between the agency and marketing owner. The client must communicate clearly but the agency is responsible for listening carefully to interpret what is being said accurately."

CARLA DODDS, Director, Multicultural Marketing and Marketing Vendor Management, Walmart U.S.

What It Is—What It Isn't

Over the years, briefs have gotten better, through trial and error and continued dedication, for those clients who understand the value of efficient briefings. But it can still be a clumsy process and clients universally agree: there is still plenty of room for improvement. Let's demystify common beliefs about what a brief IS and what it ISN'T:

A brief is not an order form. Often the solution for an advertising, marketing, or communication project has already been established upon briefing or is so baked that it leaves little room for the agency to play its role as a strategic partner and think tank. Many briefs are used as order forms, rather than inviting the agency to come up with solutions to the core business or communication challenge. Both parties may have to concede in order to find common grounds. The agency wants to show thought-leadership and they should be encouraged to do so.

A brief is not a one-way dialog. It is not just a physical object, a soft or hard copy of a document. A brief, also referred to as input document, is only a means to an end. The end is an agency that is highly engaged, excited about the assignment, knowledgeable, focused, and ready to get work started. It is a way to efficiently structure a rich and lively dialog between an agency (or multiple ones) and a client. A brief is usually best informed when agencies are given the opportunity to have direct conversations with the client.

Clients should set up a formal joint process requiring a review of the brief immediately after the brief has been submitted. A written brief submission is never sufficient to allow for the agencies to capture the intent of the project and can result in brief defects and additional costly review cycles. Some assignments will require a combination of agency skills from complementary disciplines (for example: PR, media, digital, promotion).

If multiple specialty agencies are involved, roles and responsibilities have to be clearly defined out of the gate. The opportunity for all agencies to be briefed simultaneously and to interact with each other is likely to produce better, more aligned and more integrated ideas that have far greater impact. The agencies might even bounce ideas off each other. Send the brief in advance of the meeting. The agencies will mostly likely need to seek clarification about certain aspects of the brief and perhaps even call out inconsistencies and gaps. Invite the dialog. Do not be defensive. This is a healthy process.

Client Viewpoint

"It's important to get full buy-in of the marketing brief across all levels, at the outset of a program, well before it gets to the agency. The information contained in the brief, needs to target-based, relevant, insightful and backed by research. Sometimes, organizations can fall in the habit of employing past templates and as a result, provide incomplete information to the agency. The marketing brief cannot fall short of providing clear direction.

MICHAEL FITZGERALD
Associate Director, Business Advertising, AT&T Inc.

A brief is not "The Provincial Letters" or a Pulitzer Prize. Keep it succinct. It's not about the quantity but the quality of information. Clients have the tendency to cram the brief with way too much information. Obviously, larger, complex assignments require lengthier briefs. But clients must spend more time on culling down pertinent information before sending it to the agency. To paraphrase French, and Blaise Pascal, "If I had more time, I would have written a shorter letter." Take the time. I've see clients produce brief documents 50 pages long coupled with lengthy and detailed research material and presentations, leaving it up to the agency to figure out what actually matters instead of making the tough choices. If you have relevant support documentation to provide, add it to the appendix. Keep the brief laser-focused on what needs to be done.

Client Viewpoint

"A brief is called 'brief' for a reason."

JULIE GIBBS, Director, Corporate Brand Marketing, Campaign Management, Adobe

A brief is not a substitute for the company's marketing plan. Too often, clients are tempted to incorporate all their marketing priorities into the brief instead of being specific about what is expected of the agency. The brief goes through multiple internal reviews before it is ready to be used as directional input to the agency. It is important to incorporate all internal input before the work has started. Too often, a brief will go through multiple rounds of revisions after it has been approved, adding unnecessary frustration, delays and costs. Clients often use the brief process to solidify their own strategy, test various ideas, and brainstorm with the agency for weeks before the brief is finalized and work can start. Although that process can yield tremendous value, it can also turn into a costly investment for the agency if not adequately budgeted by the client.

Client Viewpoint

"Any communication effort brings together Marcom, Marketing, Corporate Advertising, Corporate Communications and creative and media agencies to review the marketing brief as a team, discuss relevant customer insight, vet ideas and set expectations about 'who are we talking to,' 'what are we saying?' and how we envision saying it. Seeking internal buy-in, to ensure we are all on same page, is mission critical."

MICHAEL FITZGERALD
Associate Director, Business Advertising, AT&T Inc.

A brief is not about collecting data, it's about producing insight. Often some sections have not been well thought out or the brief is used as a data dump. Avoid the "copy and paste" from other documents. The brief is sometimes missing critical information like clear objectives and success metrics as well as important background on the core audience and key competitors. The brief should provide customer insight, insight that can get the agency thinking about how to best tackle the project. Otherwise, it is nothing more than garbage in, garbage out. Clients must provide meaningful, actionable insight, not raw, undigested data.

A brief doesn't have to be doleful or sterile. The briefing process is more involved than filling out a template and sending it to the agency. The end product must ignite and inspire the agency. It needs to invite storytelling by the creative team, get them to explore ways to bring a given campaign to life. It may also include videos, customer visits, testimonials, the participation in an event, or the actual prototype or demo of a new product giving greater depth to the assignment. If it doesn't get the agency's creative department energized, what are the chances they will, in turn, energize the target audience? A brief is not supposed to read like a company's earnings report or a grocery list. Spice it up. It must sell right off the page.

Client Viewpoint

"Clients may not always have clear plans or the right briefs to inform the agency. The lack of clarity about client assignments and continued change in direction are one of the greatest challenges faced by agencies today."

MARIANN COLEMAN
Director, Global Media Relations and Performance, Intel

What's in a Brief

Although briefs are likely to vary from client to client, and from discipline to discipline (disciplines like media and digital for example have unique requirements), there are a few topic areas that apply to virtually any brief:

> **Client Viewpoint**
>
> *"When agencies and brands are not aligned, things tend to fall apart. A robust scope of work includes a detailed description of agency responsibilities, deliverables and timing."*
>
> A LARGE ADVERTISER

Brief Essentials This section includes general project information and basic details about the assignment such as the project name or ID, the date the brief was created and the date of last modifications (for versioning control), PO number or related budget information, geographic scope, just to name a few. It also identifies key client and agency leads and contact details. Some clients may provide a precise or an approximate budget, some no budget at all, while others might provide some parameters or a budget range (such as $200K-$300K). Providing budget guidance prevents agencies from coming up with ideas that their client cannot afford.

> **Client Viewpoint**
>
> *"The most difficult part of writing a brief is to ask for one simple idea. A good brief is single-minded, easy to read, not filled with detail, with enough range and room for the agency to come back with ideas. If the agency needs to flip through multiple pages to understand (or not understand) what the ask of the agency is, then you don't have a clear brief. If everyone reading the brief sees the exact same storyboard in their head, then the brief is too narrow and prescriptive."*
>
> KEVIN PARHAM, Director Global Advertising, Campbell Soup

Timing is also key. Clients should be specific about any critical milestones (including in-market and out-of-market dates), campaign or product-related milestones (release date for a new product or an important corporate event), key milestones that will dictate the timing and tempo of communications and deliverables. If specific internal resources are needed (Privacy, Legal, Finance, and so forth), this is where they should be listed as well.

Key objectives and Success Metrics What does the client want to accomplish? How is success defined? What would be considered failure? What is the desired customer response or change of perception? Objectives must be defined in the broader context of the whole company's marketing and communication strategy and ultimately support it. It should reference which strategic objective or priority this assignment is aligned to. Clients are encouraged to set SMART (Specific, measurable, Attainable, Relevant, and Time-bound) business, marketing and communication objectives and call out the specific metrics used to measure success. Typical objectives range from business metrics such as growing market share or sales, generating a certain number of qualified leads and inquiries, return on marketing investment, to marketing metrics such as increasing unaided or aided awareness by X%, changing brand perception from A to B, increasing brand preference or retention by X%, etc. However, it shouldn't be a laundry list. One or two core objectives should be sufficient. Three or four at the most.

Only the most critical objectives should be listed and then prioritized. The timeframe should be clearly stated as well. The objectives must be reasonable in scope but stretched goals might be appropriate at times. Including past campaign performance as a benchmark might be helpful to determine the degree of difficulty of the campaign and its reasonableness. And of course, the more specific the metrics, whether quantitative or qualitative, the greater the chances are for the campaign to succeed. Clients should use standard metric definitions whenever possible.

Client Viewpoint

"Use the elevator test for agency briefings. If the agency brief cannot be summarized during the course of an elevator ride, from the bottom to the top of the building, then the brief is too complex. No one wants their agency to come back to them and say that the brief wasn't clear. Successful briefs are a top down process as they require initial management buy-in."

BRETT COLBERT
Global Manager, Procurement Advertising, Anheuser Busch InBev

If there are learning objectives as part of this assignment (such as determining the most impactful response vehicles for a particular audience), they should be clearly spelled out. The measurement system should specify how data will be collected and analyzed (response vehicles, social monitoring tools, position in search results, copy ad testing, etc.), by whom and how often results will be reviewed and whether results will be reviewed for ongoing optimization (if applicable) or performance evaluation.

Brand, Product, or Service The agency requires some background about the situation and circumstances that led to this assignment. They also need a minimum level of information about the brand positioning and the products or services involved. In this section, clients should include the product portfolio (if appropriate), value propositions, any relevant facts or history about the company, brands or products, a description of key features and benefits, claims and promises, the rational and emotional brand appeal.

In this section, clients should also describe the company's approach to distribution and channel strategy and pricing strategy. Any information that might help the creative team get intimate with the brand or with the end product or service that the client is promoting.

Target Audience and Customer Insight The client ought to provide a detailed description of the primary (or secondary if applicable) target audience including top level demographics, psychographics, lifestyle and behavioral data. Clients should also consider providing primary and secondary research as well as focus group results and customer testimonials in the appendix. For global campaigns, the brief should state in what countries or region the full campaign or some elements of it are expected to run. Any relevant customer insight and audience segmentation information should also be summarized.

Agency Viewpoint

"The more access an agency has, the better it will perform for the client. Clients are best served by bring agencies into their world, meaning: strategic planning meetings, sales meetings, trade shows, etc. The hurry up and wait syndrome can negatively affect how an agency performs for a client. Give your agency the proper time to think and plan, and you will get a more motivated, more creative agency relationship in return."

MARC A. BROWNSTEIN
President and CEO, Brownstein Group

Key Messages In this section, the client tells in his or her own words what they want to say to the target audience. This is a succinct list of key messages, prioritized and organized based on audience segmentation, on the mindset of the audience, the customer benefits, "reasons to believe" or similar proof points, what action they are expected to take (what do we want them to do), or what perception or behavior has been changed as a result of this assignment. This is where any overlap or dependencies on existing or upcoming advertising, marketing, or communication activities are identified and rationalized in a messaging context. If there are any offers, those should be included here.

Competitive Landscape and Market Conditions Any relevant competitive intelligence should be included in this section of the brief. All key competitors are listed along with their positioning and any comparative research results, as well as past, existing, or expected marketing efforts. Market conditions might include the social, political, or economical environment as well as current market or customer trends specific to the product or service offering. Potential threats and opportunities should also be highlighted. Market conditions might be specific to certain regions or countries.

Client Input and Approval A client may have a number of important stakeholders that are to provide input along the way, influence the agency work or simply drive the process forward. But someone must say: "the buck stops here." There should be only one final decision maker. Agencies require absolute clarity about who is the final decision maker, mostly for creative sign-off and for budget approvals.

Typical client roles include OARPs: an Owner (typically the budget owner), an Approver (who might be the same individual unless the Owner has delegated that responsibility), Reviewers (they provide input but have no decision making authority) and Participants (they contribute to the process or enable it). Everyone has a specific role. But there are often too many cooks in the client's kitchen. So pick the Chef. Once you do, stick to the plan.

Agency Viewpoint

"The ability to truly analyze the brief and client/agency communication process and then positively act upon those findings I believe holds the most promise to reduce costs in a win-win scenario for client and agency. It can also help squelch much of the conflict between client procurement and agencies."

ERIC SAMUELSON, VP, Production Procurement, Jack Morton Worldwide

Mandatories If there are specific requirements that the agency must adhere to, such as legal and creative/brand guidelines (use of logos, brands and sub-brands, trademarks, tag lines, tone, attributes, personality), the use of a particular media vehicle due to existing media commitments, the use of particular brand assets or images, certain time dependencies (sponsorship of a particular event), the use of specific vendors or digital solutions (the use of a particular Website, etc.), privacy policies and legal reviews (clearance), just to name a few, those should be all documented in the brief. If specific skills or capabilities (media planning, editorial services, localization, and so forth) are required, they should be properly called out. Apply good judgment. Those should not restrict the creativity of the agency.

A disclaimer about the confidentiality of the information should be added to the template, stating that the document is restricted to only authorized recipients. A list of supporting documents should be indexed and made available as appendix.

How to Cure the Root Causes of Inefficiencies

Successfully briefing an agency wouldn't be one of the most critical client accountabilities if that wasn't also the most challenging and eventually, the most rewarding. Agencies often complain about the poor quality of client briefs, for missing vital pieces of information or simply being unusable. It is amazing that one out of every three client briefs today is considered weak and, consequently, wasteful. According to a survey to agency executives commissioned by Jones&Associates LLC, now BriefLogic, less than 40% of client briefs provide clear direction about what's expected of them and at least 30% of agency's time and resources are ineffective or simply worn out due to poor client briefings. This ultimately translates into incredible waste, whether as a result of either excessive agency fees or lost opportunities from poor quality campaigns. Thankfully, clients can follow a few simple steps to eliminate common root causes of briefing inefficiencies:

Client Viewpoint

"Like a marriage, agency/client relationships require patience, fairness and honesty. In my career, I've seen colleagues complaining about the agency. I would ask "Is the work on strategy?"and, "Is it on brief?". And I would be told that the agency never got a brief. Everyone has to play their part or it won't work ... honest feedback, assuming the competencies actually exist, will correct most problems."

JEFF DEVON, Director Global Marketing, HP

Root cause #1: Unclear objectives or lack of transparency The client is eager to get the project started but has not done enough preparation or internal vetting to be able to provide the agency with clearly defined objectives. It's the equivalent of changing tires on a car that is still moving. Or asking a contractor to start pouring concrete while the floor plans are still being drawn by the architect. The goals are still vague, perhaps contradictory, somewhat confusing, or are missing all together. As a result, the brief is likely to change frequently, requiring a number of costly revisions--the equivalent of "defects" in the manufacturing world, well in excess of what would be considered an acceptable number of brief revisions (two or three at most). Engaging an agency without having properly and clearly defined objectives is likely to delay the campaign and increase costs.

Client Viewpoint

"Having different briefs to accommodate different assignments types is a best practice.

JULIE GIBBS, Director, Corporate Brand Marketing, Campaign Management, Adobe

The cure: Clients should invest the time upfront and be 100% clear about the objectives of the assignment before engaging an agency. Do not pick up the phone or schedule a meeting with the agency until the objectives are somewhat clear and the brief is reasonably complete. (Note: a client may infrequently ask the agency to help scope the project before finalizing the brief.)

Root cause #2: Lack of best practices and industry standards Few clients have taken the time to publish standard brief templates for their employees to brief agencies in very consistent ways, making it more predictable for both parties. In a world of accountability and performance-based engagements, "What we discussed over coffee the other day" is no longer acceptable. Since there are many different types of assignments (PR, social media, events, Website design, packaging, and so on), there should be customized templates to address their unique information requirements. Although there are many common elements, the type of information a PR agency requires is logically different from a Website agency. I've seen agencies that use "Conversation Briefs" for social media type assignments.

Few clients train their employees on how to effectively write a brief. This is a skill that must be learned. Unfortunately, agencies often deal with clients with varied degree of experience. No policy or procedure is in place to allow agencies to refuse low quality or incomplete briefs. Agencies do not always feel comfortable pushing back, leading to sub-optimal results down the road. There is no clear definition of what constitutes a finalized brief. The potential revisions due to poor or incomplete briefing may drag the process of getting the brief finalized, increasing agency time and leading to higher costs.

Client Viewpoint

"A good brief is about being clear as to your marketing objectives. Clients shouldn't be too prescriptive in dictating the tactics. They should let the agencies do what they do best."

DELMAR WYATT
Director Advertising Operations, Qwest Communications

The cure: Train budget owners and marketers on how to successfully brief agencies. Set company guidelines and quality standards for agency briefings. Agree on acceptable productivity standards. Encourage the sharing of best practices by posting briefs on a share accessible to others within the company.

Root cause #3: Too prescriptive client guidance Clients might be tempted to go beyond telling the agency what challenge they want them to address and also direct them on "how" to go about solving it. For the most part, the brief shouldn't mandate the type of deliverables the agency is to produce. Clients should think of themselves as music composers who set the vision and tempo but rely on orchestra leads to decide on how to build the best composition, with instruments are needed and how they come together for the music to come alive. At best, a client might recommend specific deliverables or media vehicles. Unless of course, this agency's sole purpose is pure execution and nothing more.

Client Viewpoint

"Sometimes the client wants the agency to help them figure out what direction to go in. If that's the case, the client should be clear about that.

JULIE GIBBS, Director, Corporate Brand Marketing, Campaign Management, Adobe

Typically, agencies are expected to deliver much more than traditional Websites, collateral or banner ads. They are expected to come up with innovative ways to address a marketing challenge. They are on point to determine the right media mix to support the campaign objectives. Clients who are too prescriptive end up burning people out, eroding the partnership which then leads to reduced quality of staff.

The cure: Clients should focus their efforts on accurately and comprehensively stating the communication challenge, providing all relevant data and then giving space to the agency to brainstorm and come back to you with recommendations on the most efficient and effective ways to accomplish that objective. This is their expertise and the client shouldn't do their job. As David Ogilvy once said, "Why keep a dog and bark yourself?"

Root cause #4: Lack of role clarity Roles and responsibilities within a client organization, between the client and the agency (or even among multiple agencies working on the same assignment) may not be clearly defined. There is either too much or not enough input by the right individuals. There is perceived or real overlap in responsibilities. There is ambiguity about who is accountable for input and who is accountable for decisions. Is it Matt the Chief Marketing Officer who occasionally drops in during creative reviews and is known to have veto power? Is it John, the opinionated brand manager, responsible for writing the large majority of the brief? Or is it Patricia, the director of marketing, considered the budget owner and the primary agency contact?

This lack of clarity around who does what can be a major source of confusion and frustration for everyone. As a major packaged good company who shall remain nameless put it to me humorously: "We sometimes have many final decision makers." The cure: Identify clear ownership and responsibilities for all participants. There should be a single decision maker or approver. The brief is written by the client, not by the agency. Each participating agency also has a defined role.

Root cause #5: Unreasonable client schedule or unfair expectations Time is of essence and a new campaign must be put in market as soon as humanly possible. The client is willing to cut corners, sometimes at the expense of providing a solid brief or a much needed campaign development process. Inexperienced marketers may not be aware of lead-time requirements for a productive briefing process and are setting unrealistic expectations.

The cure: Give adequate time to the agency to absorb the information, seek clarification, and respond with sound recommendations. Setting the bar high is a client prerogative. Too often, clients ask for the moon when they can only afford buy themselves a plane ticket to New York City. Set realistic objectives from the start.

All clients face these challenges at one time or another in their career. Agencies perform best when they know what is expected of them, are given room to come up with solutions on their own, and are held accountable for their work. The process goes smoothly when there is role clarity for all parties involved or when clients are following industry standards. Any improvement in the quality of agency briefs yields significant impact on the effectiveness of the work and the efficiency of the process to get there, the equivalent of millions of dollars in savings and upside opportunities that few clients can afford to ignore.

A good brief doesn't guarantee that the agency won't fail. But it certainly reduces the chances that it might fail because it's not properly aiming at the business challenge or opportunity. Clients should invest the time do brief agencies well as it will without a doubt pay off many fold, reducing wasted efforts and marketing budgets. Based on the nature and complexity of the assignment, agencies can then determine the type and number of staff needed to handle the project. In labor based or project-based agreement, this is how fees are then estimated and provided to clients for their approval.

Client Viewpoint

"To encourage cross-agency collaboration, we conduct agency share days during which agencies come together to be briefed and share critical information among their peers. One of them, often a creative lead agency, might be assigned as 'captain' and is on point to ensure the sharing of information among participating agencies on an ongoing basis.

TOM CHETRICK
VP Advertising and Marketing Services, Bristol-Myers Squibb

For most agencies, it's far from being a rigorous, scientific process. It is based on prior experience with the client (agency burn) and a robust understanding of the client engagement style and needs. As a result, it often results in lengthy back and forth negotiations to match the right resources to a particular brief or to the full scope of work. Clients often use benchmarks to ring fence negotiations to industry norms. Clients that are known to often change direction midstream, have inefficient approval processes, with too many stakeholders involved and excessive rework cycles are staffed more generously by their agencies in anticipation of these inherent inefficiencies.

Agencies are more likely to build buffers to avoid having to eat any resulting excess cost. In performance-based compensation agreements, this is where business and marketing objectives are captured. Clients should assess the accuracy of their scope of work planning and factor this in during agency staffing and fee discussions.

Agency Viewpoint

"Many clients are simply trying to settle petty differences within their marketing department when they brief agencies. ("See? I was right. They agree with me.") Try to set the agency up to teach you something new. To break new ground."

JEFF GOODBY
Co-Chairman and Creative Director, Goody, Silverstein & Partners

How can anyone be expected to deliver outstanding work without being provided good instructions and clear direction? Clients play an important role in reducing engagement inefficiencies. They must also reassure agencies so they do not fear that efficiency gains translate into lower fees (that is, revenue for the agency) but rather in win-win situation: The agency realizes higher margin and the client reduced expense. Clients are encouraged to benchmark and carefully monitor the quality of briefs submitted to agencies. They must initiate regular audits of briefing documents to determine what they can do to improve the quality and clarity of their direction to agency partners.

Unless the scope of work and the brief have helped the agency produce outstanding results, it is not doing the job, which is to point to the destination, provide maps and instructions, but let the agency figure out how to get you there. In the end, the performance of the work itself will validate the effectiveness of the client's scope of work planning and briefing. Then you might look back and conclude that both parties are in the right.

{Taking Immediate Action}

TOP 5

BEST PRACTICES TO HARNESS THE MADNESS

❶ Institute a comprehensive scope of work planning process to set top-line priorities and provide adequate line of sight to agencies about workload and staffing requirements.

❷ Invite agencies participate in upstream priority-setting discussions so they can advise senior management and strongly influence the company's strategy.

❸ Invest the time and efforts required to set clear, concise objectives in the brief before engaging an agency. Provide insightful, actionable data. Be transparent at all times.

❹ Set reasonable expectations. Define roles and responsibilities for everyone involved to avoid any confusion, duplication of efforts, and potential delays. Ensure client decisions are made decisively and in a timely manner.

❺ Tell the agencies what you need, not what to do or how to do it. Don't be too prescriptive or limiting. Empower agencies to do what they do best.

9 THE LOMBARDI RULES

Conducting productive agency/client performance evaluations

"If you are able to state a problem, it can be solved."

—Edwin H. Land
American Scientist and Inventor

Ask "Who is the best sports coach of all times?" and you are likely to get very different answers. In lockers around the world, you will hear names like Red Aerubach, Phil Jackson, Paul "Bear" Bryant, and many others, all equally worthy of this noble title. Regardless of who makes it to the top of your list, what they all have in common is a vibrant, resilient commitment to win as a team. Vince Lombardi is considered a legend in the NFL and a role model for his coaching philosophy and ability to motivate players.

Born in Brooklyn, New York, in 1913, Vince Lombardi is known for his infectious drive, perseverance, hard work, and dedication to the sport. Vince had remarkable work ethics that led him to graduate cum laude with a business major, working full time, and taking night classes in law school while playing semi-pro football. In his book *The Lombardi Rules: 26 Lessons from Vince Lombardi, the World's Greatest Coach*, he shares what principles he taught to motivate and lead to success:

- Ask yourself tough questions.
- Look the truth straight on.
- Lead with integrity.
- Build team spirit.

He led the Green Bay Packers who dominated professional football under his acute leadership that included nine winning seasons, NFL championships, and Super Bowls. He asked for dedication and commitment from each player. He gave nothing less to his team. His words of wisdom became legendary and his commitment to team success made him one of the most admired and respected coaches in the history of American football. These simple, yet powerful ideas apply virtually to any competitive team environment, whether in sports or in business.

The best sports coaches are known to be catalysts of team performance. They know that optimal performance can only be accomplished as a team and as a team only. They know that the whole is greater than the sum of the parts. And as a result, they expect much from each other and hold everyone accountable to do their part. Clients and agencies can learn a great deal from sports legends like Vince Lombarti who mastered long before us the art and skill of building high performance teams through structured performance management, direct, timely, and actionable feedback, self-criticism, trust, and mutual accountability. The fundamental shift in the way agencies and clients must engage in this increasingly fast moving, consumer-driven, complex, digital world is only reinforcing the critical need for ongoing, direct feedback that fosters a renewed sense of risk-taking, accountability, and partnership.

Purpose of Evaluating Mutual Performance

"How can we get most value from this relationship?"
"How can we be a better client (or better agency)?"

Every client and agency should ask themselves these two simple, yet essential questions. Given that both are investing a considerable amount of time, energy and resources to perform up to each other's expectations, building on existing strengths, overcoming weaknesses, and optimizing the partnership is of upmost importance. Client/agency evaluations are common among big and small companies. Providing or accepting feedback, from high to low ranks, is the best way to show that we care. Agencies are receptive to the opportunity of receiving (and sometimes providing) constructive input. After all, it makes the relationship more predictable. Early signs of dissatisfaction can be formally detected and addressed.

Agency Viewpoint

"The idea of branded message development with long timelines is long gone. Clients are asking agencies to drive customer engagements in real time."

TIM WILLIAMS, President, Ignition Consulting Group

It is common sense that identifying issues early on, before they get to be majorly disruptive to the relationship, is in everyone's best interest. Too often, either side goes on, leaving unresolved issues to grow like bacterial infections that eventually end up killing the partnership. Here are the primary reasons for evaluating the health of the client/agency relationship:

- It ensures both parties are getting optimal value from the partnership.
- It identifies strength areas and amplifies those. Recognize high performance relationships and celebrate successes.
- It identifies and improves under-performing relationships, points to non-compliance, or gaps requiring immediate attention.
- It points out areas where clarification, resources, focus, talent, and skill-building are most needed and must be applied to improve how both parties work together.
- It provides basis for managing incentive based compensation.

When performance evaluation is done at the offset of any new relationship, it sets up a baseline to compare future evaluations against. It encourages both agencies and clients to be mutually accountable to each other from day one. Most clients have established a formal performance evaluation program and have set clear performance targets for the relationship. They evaluate the work—the *what gets done* expressed as measurable business or marketing communication outcomes, and the relationship—the *how things get done* expressed as the quality of the delivery and the degree of satisfaction in the partnership getting to the end result. These two dimensions, the "What" and the "How," are natural complements. Both views are valuable.

Client Viewpoint

"Once a year, we conduct a 360 assessment of our partnership with key agencies. Designed to be flexible by nature, this process allows us to identify key improvement areas and fix them."

TOM CHETRICK
VP Advertising and Marketing Services, Bristol-Myers Squibb

Clients make the most out of their agency partnerships by investigating, diagnosing what's working and what's not, in order to yield positive change, improve mutual satisfaction, strengthen the partnership, and produce more impactful work. Then both parties need to act upon these findings decisively, so their investment in time and dollars pays off and is fully optimized, a requirement in a fast moving digital world where campaigns are launched within weeks, even days, and results known in real time.

A good performance evaluation program should be built on quantitative and qualitative criteria. These performance metrics will speak not only to the end goal of what must be accomplished, but also to how the work should be conducted. Relying solely on the end goal without setting expectations about how things get done may lead to inefficient behaviors and bad precedents that could be damaging to the relationship or to the work. The performance KPIs (Key Performance Indicators) must be exclusively composed of metrics that are under the agency's control. Common quantitative KPIs include campaign results such as gains in awareness and consideration. They also often include business results such as market share, and revenue growth.

However, it absolutely shouldn't include metrics that agencies have limited ability to impact such as stock performance. The metrics used are likely to be part of the company's own regular overall business metrics. The weight assigned to each type of performance metric varies by client.

Typically, quantitative metrics make up half of the performance evaluation, of which half of this is related to marketing communication metrics and half to business metrics. Qualitative metrics represent the other half. The quantitative aspect of performance evaluation is typically core to the way a company runs its business and measures success for advertising, marketing and communication campaigns. It is rarely consistent and frankly, varies significantly by client. This data will be used to inform findings-based conversations about how to improve the partnership through agreed-upon action plans. It might even be used to determine agency compensation.

Client Viewpoint

"Today we have qualitative metrics to conduct performance evaluations. We also have an open discussion every six months with our partners to review how they did. This is also a time to learn if we as a company are providing our partners with the tools for success."

CARLA DODDS, Director, Multicultural Marketing and Marketing Vendor Management, Walmart U.S.

Although there is clear acknowledgment of the benefits clients and agencies can realize from this feedback exercise, many still struggle in the design or implementation stages, falling short of reaping the benefits. They end up wasting precious resources in the process which is clearly counter-productive, a peril that can be avoided. Not every relationship is alike. So mutual expectations are to be jointly set at the beginning of the work relationship, leaving nothing to interpretation or guesswork. Everyone involved should have a clear understanding of how they will benefit from the assessment process and agree on the metrics before the evaluation ever gets fielded.

Once or twice a year, both parties should sit down and review how they are doing. This actionable insight can be then leveraged to strengthen success areas and to zero in on weaknesses that require attention. However, it is not in the best interest of the relationship to wait for this bi-annual or annual evaluation. Clients must provide feedback, preferably in a structured manner, on a regular basis.

After a project is completed, a new ad produced, a Website built, or an integrated social media campaign launched, agencies and clients should meet for a post-mortem to acknowledge positive outcomes and pinpoint opportunities for improvement. Some clients may choose to use a survey, offline or online, to capture the client and the agency feedback on each other's performance. Then both parties should review it, discuss it and agree on immediate actions they can take to leverage this insight or course-correct if needed.

I've highlighted earlier that agencies are natural extensions of their client's team. So it is no surprise to find similarities in the way employee performance is evaluated at a client and the way they evaluate their agencies. If a client conducts employee performance reviews twice a year, then it makes sense to align to the same schedule. Similar objectives would apply. Even the methodology itself, familiar to the client, can be easily picked up and replicated for agency evaluations.

Client Viewpoint

"We provide our agencies a work environment that is fostering collaboration. The client should always set the tone and expectations on how agencies should work together. The key is to facilitate the agency linkage to other agencies and internal groups."

CHARLIE SILVESTRO
Vice President, Global Agency Operations, MasterCard Worldwide

Potential Roadblocks to Performance Evaluations

Project-based snapshot views of performance can be used preemptively before an issue arises or gets worse. Regular ongoing milestone-based assessments significantly reduce the likelihood of a partnership falling apart. However, despite concerted efforts on advertisers' part, many still fail to accurately assess the health of a relationship before it experiences serious issues. Or they fail to provide meaningful insight on problem areas in the relationship, which in turn prevents either party from taking steps in the right direction. No matter how valuable the evaluation exercise, clients might still be facing possible roadblocks to improvement. They may ask: "Why is the evaluation process not working or producing the desired outcome?"

There are a number of potential issues: Clients and agencies may not be committed enough to the relationship to go through the process and realize its benefits. Client spend might not be large enough to justify it or to motivate either party to take it seriously. Assignments may be too sporadic. Some may think it's a wasteful administrative chore. Client and agency may not trust each other enough to be direct and transparent about the relationship. They may not see eye to eye on a particular issue. After all, similar to René Magritte's legendary surrealist painting "Ceci n'est pas une pipe" ("This is not a pipe"), the feedback received is only one's interpretation of the truth. The painting is not a pipe, it is an image of a pipe. If agencies and clients disagree on the feedback provided, can the relationship survive?

Another potential roadblock to the fruitful use of performance evaluations is that agencies may fear potential repercussions including losing the account or a portion of the business, or having clients attempt to renegotiate financial terms down to offset agency performance issues. They may not trust that the information will be used in a constructive manner. They fear the process will end up being a finger-pointing exercise or a witch-hunt.

Client Viewpoint

"We believe that agencies and clients do their best work when they provide each other feedback on how to work together most effectively. A 360 survey twice a year facilitates an objective and meaningful conversations about the relationship and how to improve it. We also conduct project debriefs so that both parties receive timely actionable feedback."

MOLLIE WESTON
Director Agency Management Operations, Best Buy

Another common issue is that clients may spend more time on collecting data and analyzing it than acting on findings and actually putting it to good use. They may not be asking the right questions. They may not be asking the right individuals, those who consistently interface with the client or with the agency. They may not be clear on what actions to take. They may not know how to prioritize issues or simply know how to get started.

Performance evaluation is the topic of many vivid debates at industry forums, especially when it ties back to compensation as we saw in prior chapters. I do not expect the heated discussions to phase out in the years ahead. We may not agree on what constitutes an effective evaluation program but there are some best practices worth adopting. A comprehensive agency assessment should be 360-degrees, allowing both the client and the agency to provide balanced feedback about the relationship. As far as the client-side is concerned, it should provide a voice to the troops on the ground, budget owners, senior management, and anyone interfacing regularly with the agency.

To broaden their perspective, clients may also want to familiarize themselves with third party resources like *AdWeek*'s Annual Agency Report that reviews top agencies across a number of criteria, such as creative, management, and clients. They should also consider reaching out to other clients of their agencies to share their respective experience and learn from each other on how to get most value from their relationship with that agency.

Five Easy Steps to Effective Performance Evaluation

To successfully conduct open client/agency evaluations, clients should follow five simple, intuitive, consecutive steps going from survey design, training, fielding, reporting and analysis, to the actual discussions and action plans that will contribute to sustainable improvements.

Performance Evaluation Process

Survey Design (duration: one to two weeks)

This is the part of the process where objectives are set and questions are agreed upon. Both parties will achieve greater results from the exercise if fully transparent during the design phase with both client and agency teams actively engaged in providing input to the attributes and KPs that will be measured. At the very least, agencies should validate the assessment criteria so both parties are completely bought in and therefore, receptive to the feedback received. It would be highly unproductive to have folks arguing about the validity of the results and the way a particular question was phrased after the fact. The survey may need to be adjusted annually to reflect the evolving nature of the relationship or changed expectations.

> **Client Viewpoint**
>
> *"Clients should consider evaluation agency performance quarterly in the first year of the relationship. In the second year, a client may only need to conduct the agency performance annually or semi-annually."*
>
> JULIE GIBBS, Director, Corporate Brand Marketing, Campaign Management, Adobe

Who should participate? Preferably participants who are the core people working most directly with their counterparts on the client or agency side to ensure responsible evaluations. In order to facilitate the gathering of names, a scrubbed list should be created as a starting point for the agency and client to use and compile names. Naturally some people have moved on or changed roles. In the arena of client/agency performance evaluation, less is often more. Participation should be limited to those who directly and materially interface with the agency or with the client, including but not limited to senior management, marketing, finance, operations, and procurement.

Those who do not directly interface with the agency or the client, or those who do very infrequently, should be excluded. Resist the temptation to turn this into a company-wide proxy vote. For example, it is best not to invite folks who have been working together less than six months. Their limited exposure can potentially skew results. Once the list has been finalized, one must ensure adequate participation so the sample size is statistically representative for results to be conclusive.

How is the right measurement scale determined? What a client uses as measurement scale is far less important than being consistent about it. Keeping the scale identical year over year is critical to produce a meaningful benchmark or monitor trends over time. For illustrative purposes, here is an example of a basic 4-points scale:

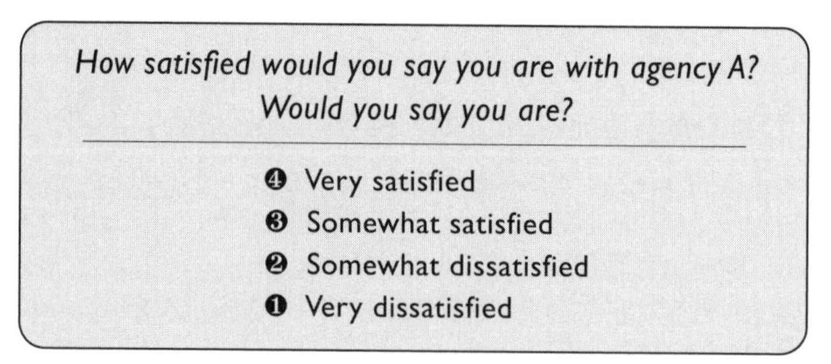

Some companies use a 5-point scale, with 1 meaning unacceptable/poor and 5 meaning extraordinary/outstanding. Survey participants are asked to rate each attribute on that scale. A target should be set, and communicated broadly to all stakeholders. A target performance marker on the survey itself may also help ensure participants are using a consistent mental model for their assessment, fully aware of whether they are scoring the agency above or below target expectations. This is particularly helpful in some parts of the world where cultural norms may lead participants to either score on the higher or on the lower end of the scale. Not only will the results be compared with the target, it will help set expectations for the level at which the agency is expected to perform.

An optional comment box associated with each question should be provided to generate actionable insight as to why a particular good or bad score was provided. Easy to use, open text fields for individual commentary will help illuminate the rationale behind particularly high or low scores. It's best to keep the survey to a manageable length. The survey should be designed to take no more than 20 to 30 minutes to complete or the drop off rate might be too great to generate statistically valid results.

Communication and Training

Once the survey form has been finalized, clear guidelines and instructions have to be provided to the participants. At this stage, it's most important to remind them that they have carefully selected to participate and set expectations about the way the information will be used once the survey has been completed. Having a robust communication plan laid out for all participants and stakeholders ensures everyone is clear about the purpose of this exercise and the role each one of them play. Put on your marketing hat and think about those whom you're asking to participate in the performance assessment as your target audience. Why is this exercise important to them, to the company, to the agency? What is their role? How will results be used? By whom? When will the reports be available and who will see them?

It might be wise to have the initial communication to assessment invitees sent from top management and co-signed by senior leaders at both the client and at the agency to show their support and commitment to the process. The training should communicate how to use the survey to provide feedback, how the feedback will be used and for what purpose, how data will be analyzed and reported, how to use the reports once distributed, how to review those with the client and agency teams, how to encourage a constructive dialog that ultimately yield joint action plans, how to put those in action and monitor progress. The objective is to diagnose both the health and performance of the partnership, to celebrate successes and action improvement areas and get most out of the relationship.

Participants should be told at least a week or two prior to the fielding how the process will unfold, when they are expected to participate, and what will happen as a result of it so there is no surprise or confusion throughout the process. Recruit key influencers to encourage invitees on their teams to participate. It might be wise to conduct training sessions and set up Q&A sessions ahead of time to give participants the opportunity to ask questions and prepare themselves, and provide context for this survey so participants understand what's expected of them. Ask them to be fair and objective in their feedback, providing commentary wherever appropriate to illuminate the reason for the ratings—especially for high or low ratings.

Tips for performance reviews are:

- Ask them to apply a balanced point of view. If one circumstance in a full year was especially poor, avoid over-penalizing for that one transgression.
- Similarly, don't give inappropriately overly-glowing ratings.
- Don't place all of your ratings in the middle of the scale. We need to tease apart the strong areas of performance from the weak.

- Give credit where due: If they've done a really good job, don't hesitate to use the higher ratings.
- Conversely, if performance is especially weak in some areas, use lower end of the scale.
- Ask participants to devote the time necessary to provide thoughtful, accurate, and actionable feedback.

Fielding

The survey is sent to assessment invitees. Make sure that only those who are on the pre-vetted list of those most engaged in the relationship can take the survey. No forwarding should be enabled and no additions should be allowed once the list has been finalized. Using a Web survey is probably the easiest and most effective way of collecting input. The link to survey contained in invitation email can be customized to the invitee's profile, making which agencies or client groups the participant is reviewing very clear. The Web survey should allow for multiple sessions per user, so users can save their responses if they are interrupted during the appraisal process. They should be able to save their work if they cannot complete it during one session and come back to the survey during the allocated time window and make changes they deem appropriate.

A clear deadline should be provided with ample time to participate. Giving participants two weeks to respond should be sufficient, giving everyone the opportunity to reflect and provide meaningful feedback. Track participation: Multiple reminders should be sent to non-responders as the deadline nears. Assuming normal conditions and sufficient time for the surveys to be completed, participation rates should be in excess of 75%. Anything short of that might be indicative of deeper relationship concerns and require individual follow-up with non-respondents to understand the underlying issues.

Reporting and Analysis

Once the input has been gathered, organized, and reviewed, insights gained from the results of the summary synthesis and analysis are shared. Both parties should simultaneously receive summary insight into overall aggregate results and information about which performance attributes were given the highest and lowest scores. Results should be provided within a reasonable timeframe, so they remain actionable and relevant. Three weeks after ending of survey is an acceptable turnaround time depending on the survey's complexity, scope, and reporting requirements.

Analyzing such a vast amount of information can be intimidating. The results should be summarized in simple to read charts that emphasize key take-away and high/low ratings. Statistical techniques like regression analysis allow advertisers to single out the attributes that have the most impact on overall satisfaction and analyze which improved performance can be highly correlated with a higher overall satisfaction score in the future. Candid commentary and feedback should be easily searchable and sortable by key work, attribute, agency, or any other relevant dimension. Assessment results should be reviewable on any particular criteria vector (topic, agency, business group, geographic group if applicable, product line). The level and depth of reporting may vary significantly from one relationship to another.

Client Viewpoint

"We evaluate our agency relationships and each other once a year, but maintain an open dialogue all year long. We put performance plans in place when issues are identified and provide clear and specific examples to help resolve them. We are willing to make that commitment and our agencies are grateful in return because they feel that they end up being a better agency as a result."

SHERRY ULSH, Director Global Marketing Finance and Procurement, Burger King Corp.

The survey and back-end data collection process should be set up to allow for customized queries and top level reports, including historical views (this year compared to prior years), comparative views (client vs. agency, self-assessments), by attribute, by low or high scores and a number of other pivots based on the nature of the survey itself. These reports, ideally available online, should allow participants to search for comments/verbatim as well by attribute or score, giving access to a rich data set to be used for action plans. Special consideration about the way the information will be distributed within the client organization or to the agency should be given before the process kicks off.

Agency Viewpoint

"Clients and agencies should sit down at the beginning of a relationship and agree to specific metrics. And then measure them consistently, every quarter. When this is not done, both sides are set up for failure. When it is done properly, both sides enjoy a healthy, prosperous long-term relationship."

MARC A. BROWNSTEIN President and CEO, Brownstein Group

It's important that both parties get access to the information at the same time. Failing to do so will erode trust. In the spirit of the partnership, I highly recommend that results are made available at the same time to both parties and be delivered preferably in person. Using a third party vendor to conduct the assessment can facilitate this. For clients with multiple agencies, results should be kept confidential and not referenced or shared with other agencies. It might be tempting to push an agency to do better by telling them that others received better scores or to compare them, but it would only create further animosity between agencies in the roster.

Turning Insight into Action

Participants should be given the option to print a copy of their numeric scores and comments for each attribute, which may be helpful when discussing and preparing action plans. Once the information has been collected, it will help inform a findings-based conversation between the client and its agencies about how the relationship is working and action plans for improvement overall. Creating an open, collaborative forum to review the results and debate and agree on next steps is strongly encouraged. A lot can get lost without the benefit of having key stakeholders answering clarifying questions.

This entire process has no intrinsic value, and is a complete waste of time and resources, unless both parties are both 100% committed to take action. Mutually-agreed corrective action plans with clear owners and due dates should be developed as a result of these discussions and progress toward those should be monitored so there is a clear indication that history won't repeat itself. The agency and client should ensure key lowlights and identified areas of improvement are addressed as part of the regular meeting cadence.

Examples of Action Plan components:

Client-Agency

- Improve timeliness (within 24 hours) and details of summary meeting and calls.
- Reduce attrition by creating quarterly team and individual award.
- Hire additional copy-writing resources with technical background and category knowledge.

Agency-Client

- Improve quality of briefing information, with an emphasis on competitive intelligence.
- Improve accessibility and availability of key client stakeholders.
- Reduce number of client contacts.

What Feedback Should Clients and Agencies Share with Each Other?

What information should agency and client share with each other that will improve performance? Measurement criteria must be carefully defined, but put away your engineering or research degree: This is not rocket science. That's the good news. What's important to the client and to the partnership drives what will end up in the actual survey. There is no standard form. There are commonalities but clients must tune the basics with a customized set of questions that address their unique requirements.

The questions must focus on whether or not each party is fulfilling its obligations. They should be worded positively so it doesn't promote finger-pointing, but rather encourages constructive feedback. It's often easy to fall into that trap. Suddenly what could have been a terrific tool ends up being detrimental and builds resentment that eventually poisons the relationship. Typically, for client to agency surveys, attributes range from quality and service, to strategy, innovation, and delivery.

For agency to client surveys, attributes typically range from clarity of direction to transparency. The questions are likely to vary slightly by marketing communication discipline. Each question invites feedback on how any change in behavior, attitude, or engagement can significantly improve the quality of the work partnership, and ultimately, the quality and effectiveness of the work itself. These questions can be weighted based on their relative importance to the partnership. For example, innovation might turn out to be a particularly important attribute for a client in a highly saturated segment. The weighting can be assigned jointly. Or it can be computed by cross-referencing individual scores against overall satisfaction.

Client Viewpoint

"As a highly innovative and creative company, we value the exact same qualities in our agency partners."

JENNIFER BERGER, Director, Marketing & Advertising Services, Starbucks

Common Client Reflection Areas

Client side senior management is expected to play an important role in the formal evaluation process of key agency partnerships. At a minimum interval of once a year, client and agency senior management should meet to review the findings produced by their respective troops and share their own perspective:

- What impact are we jointly having on business objectives? What were the big wins this year?
- How has our contribution in key disciplines helped successfully position us vis á vis our competition?
- Are the agency people who are leading the business taking us where we need to go? Is there a firm commitment to play fair and an unalterable desire to do what it takes to win together?

- Do we have adequate access talent/expertise when needed?
- What have been the top strategic insights or innovations the Agency brought forward in the past six months?
- On what key areas would it be most valuable to have the agency's strategic insight and focus over the next six months?
- What two to three areas should we hold ourselves accountable for notable improvement in the next six months?
- Where are the hot spots right now? What's the root cause?

In addition, clients should also survey those in the trenches who directly interface with the client daily. For example:

- Does the agency understand our business and what we're trying to achieve overall?
- Do they apply their understanding of the target audience in ways that make their messaging more compelling?

There are a few topic areas that are important performance drivers: creativity and innovation, integration and digital, optimization, and globalization (if applicable).

Creativity and Innovation Agencies are expected to demonstrate their creative skills through innovative ideas or solutions to marketing problems. They are also expected to deliver innovative media solutions, finding the right delivery vehicle for their marketing messages. Innovation is at all intersection points of the client/agency engagement. Clients should encourage innovative, channel-agnostic ideas from all agencies, and joint ideation whenever possible. Typical questions can include:

Agency Viewpoint

"The most common pitfall is not to set specific goals in terms of sales, name recognition, etc. We once worked for a chain of restaurants that wanted to be sold. That was a good goal to have. You could work with that."

JEFF GOODBY
Co-Chairman and Creative Director, Goody, Silverstein & Partners

- In line with scope and funding, do the agency's creative ideas stand out and create impactful business?
- Does the agency innovate, coming up with fresh, compelling ideas that provide its client with alternative choices?
- Are innovation and new technologies the forefront of the agency's thinking and approach?

Integration and Digital Integration can take many shapes and forms. Media integration is a benefit that integrated agencies offer to clients. Non-biased media recommendations guarantee clients that the agency looks to their client's best interests rather than focusing on what the agency does best. As Abraham Maslow stated, "If the only tool you have is a hammer, you tend to see every problem as a nail." It's true for specialized agencies that will find that the answer to your marketing problem can only be found in the specific type of solution they provide.

Integration across audiences and segments ensures that marketing campaigns targeted at the same audience or the same segment will not overlap or, at the very least, not play against each other. For those clients with multiple agencies, integration can also take the form of cross-agency collaboration to make certain that the efforts of agencies who partner on the client's behalf are as synergistic as possible. Typical questions can include:

- Is the creative concept extensible enough and does it lend itself to execution in a variety of analog and digital formats?
- Are all messages consistent across touch-points, reinforcing each other across campaigns and media?
- Does the agency actively incorporate learning and results from other clients or past campaigns into its work?
- Does the agency demonstrate thought-leadership in digital interactive communication to achieve objectives?

Optimization Improving the efficiency of marketing campaigns and the process that supports it means that every effort is made to focus on business outcomes, the end goal of a particular campaign. That requires common metrics and measurement process to identify high and low performing campaigns in order to invest in the successful ones and de-invest in the unsuccessful ones, and thus fine-tune campaign performance. Focusing on progress versus motion, results versus activity, is the best way to have the agency focus on what matters most and to make the business successful.

Getting a marketing campaign out to market by a certain date does not guarantee that the marketing objectives of the campaign (generate 1,000 qualified leads, increase trials by 5,000, etc.) are met. Optimization also implies that testing and measurement are implemented, so that performance is improved consistently, generating insight that can be leveraged for other campaigns. Optimization can also be achieved by allowing high speed and low cost execution. Typical questions can include:

- Is campaign optimization and continual improvement a demonstrated competency of the agency?

Globalization (if applicable) For clients with an international presence, the agency must think globally but be relevant locally. The agency's ability to offer a global perspective during the creative development process is instrumental to make sure ideas have global appeal and can be easily adopted everywhere. Being able to repurpose creative assets helps reduce costs. It also implies that best practices are shared globally; saving time and helping clients avoid making the same mistakes again. Typical questions can include:

- Does the agency develop work that can be easily adapted in the local markets?
- Does the agency create messaging for local execution that is relevant, compelling, and consistent with the brand?
- Does the agency leverage ideas, assets, or resources from its network to create even greater value for the client?

Other common questions related to basic account management and customer service:

- Does the agency anticipate client needs, communicate effectively, listen well, and incorporate client input consistently into the work?
- Does the agency know how to effectively get things done within the client environment and culture?
- Does the agency proactively partner with its client to prioritize workload and manage resources?
- Is the agency responsive, following up in a timely manner, providing fast turnaround when needed?
- Does the agency act impartially, regardless of where the idea comes from?
- Is the agency staffing the account appropriately and retaining talent to successfully serve the business?
- Does the agency exhibit continued accountable stewardship of the client's budget as if it was their own?

Many of these questions touch on the notion of value, an assessment of the agency's overall contribution to the business relative to compensation and established expectations. Discipline-specific agencies may be asked questions relevant to their trade. For example, for media agencies, clients may ask, "Does the agency develop clear, insightful, effective, cost-efficient media strategies that meet client objectives?" When multiples agencies are expected to collaborate, clients may want to ask questions specific to the way they work together: "Does the agency work well with other agencies, partnering with them in the client's best interest?"

Common Agency Reflection Areas

Agency-side senior management at the agency is also expected to provide feedback to the client-side senior management about the health of the partnership. They may agree to a set of topics to be reviewed once a year or as needed:

- What one to two key areas would be most valuable to have the client focus on to help the agency develop and act upon the highest-value initiatives?
- Is there something either party should stop doing, in order to better focus on the things that will matter most?
- Has the client been bold enough to implement the agency's best ideas? Where have we missed the biggest opportunities?
- Are there any anticipated changes in the key positions at the agency in the next six months?
- What were the biggest wins with the client in the past six months?
- What two to three areas should we focus on together as partners in the next six months—holding ourselves accountable for notable improvement?

Client Viewpoint

"Successful relationships are based on trust, respect and accountability. As accountability grows in a partnership, so does trust and respect."

JAMES R. ZAMBITO, Global Marketing Group Controller, Johnson & Johnson

Other common questions:

- At the beginning of each project, is a detailed input brief provided to the agency as the central basis for developing its work? Does it provide actionable, insightful product and market information?
- Does the client provide a sound foundation for strategy development?
- Does the client provide a clear, measurable definition of success for each assignment?
- Is the client thoughtful about providing quality, relevant insight into the target audience, including customer and market research?
- Does the client share relevant competitive insight?
- Is the client inspiring and motivating the agency as part of its briefing process?
- Is the client open-minded, willing to think outside the box and let the agency come up with innovative ideas?
- Does the client provide an encouraging environment for the agency to consider new ideas and approaches?

- Does the client use the brief as the primary means of evaluating the agency's ideas?
- Does the client set aside personal, preferential perspectives when providing feedback to the agency?

Other Common Questions Related to Clients Interfacing with the Agency:

- Is there a clear understanding of who the decision makers are?
- Is the client responsive to agency inquiries and requests? Is the client open, honest and direct in its communications with the agency, addressing issues promptly?
- Does the client work with the agency in a way that makes the best use of the money it spends?
- Does the client set reasonable expectations for the agency?
- Is the client proactively alerting the agency to changes that may affect overall workload at the agency?
- Does the client enable the agency's best work by allowing time for creative thinking and idea development?
- Is the client willing to internally champion the agency's "big ideas" or new approaches?
- Does the client partner with the agency to use market data and campaign results to continually improve performance?
- Does the client involve the agency in a way that allows the agency to make meaningful contributions?
- Does the client invite, and work to implement, suggestions for improvement in its own processes and practices as well as in the ways it engages with the agency?
- Does the client demonstrate true accountability for its role in the success of the agency's work?
- Does the client give credit where credit is due, recognizing above-and-beyond efforts by the agency?

Key Design Points and Considerations

There are a number of important decisions that a client must make prior to implementing an evaluation program, including the type of questions asked, who should participate, how often it should be conducted.

Should the agency evaluation be one-way or bi-directional? A one-way evaluation means that it is limited to the client providing input to the agency on how it is performing. This is a common way for clients to deal with low-value commodity suppliers. One-way evaluations are therefore not adequate for value-add, interdependent partnerships that require mutual trust and contribution from both sides to be successful. Clients should implement 360-degree evaluations that give both parties the opportunity to share open, constructive feedback. From ballrooms to boardrooms, it always takes two to tango. Bi-directional feedback is not limited to both parties providing feedback to each other.

Self-assessments questions can also prove to be quite insightful. Whenever possible, the agency and the client should be asked to do a self-assessment. For example, if the agency consistently rates the client poorly on its ability to provide clear direction but the client rate itself high on that same attribute, it highlights potential gaps or a serious disconnect in the relationship. In self-assessments, participants tend to score themselves higher. Unusually high gaps indicate misalignments or misperceptions between clients and agencies that will most likely require intervention.

> **Client Viewpoint**
>
> *"At Campbell Soup, we understand the value of building strong, lasting partnerships with our creative agencies. We've been working with BBDO for over 47 years now. From a business perspective, It's always much better to work at fixing a relationship than to change it."*
>
> KEVIN PARHAM, Director
> Director, Global Advertising,
> Campbell Soup

> **Client Viewpoint**
>
> *"Perhaps the most important factor for successful client/agency relationships can be summarized in three words: communication, communication, communication."*
>
> TOM CHETRICK
> VP Advertising and Marketing
> Services, Bristol-Myers Squibb

How often should the evaluation be conducted? As often as deemed necessary is probably the best answer. Once a year is a minimum to keep a pulse on the relationship. Up to twice a year should suffice for most companies. Some may want to conduct a mid-year review, whether formal or not, so no one is blind-sided when the annual review unfolds. Adequate time should be set aside to take action and address some of the key take-away. The way clients interface with agencies has a dramatic impact on the relationship. Therefore, clients should consider ways to share and receive ongoing feedback during the course of the relationship. The French say that bad news is like bad wine. It never improves with time.

An open line of communication is most important to the partnership. No one wants to wait for six months to find out if the partnership is delivering to everyone's satisfaction. A continuous project-based 360-degree survey to provide on-going feedback can be a very powerful tool to inform post-mortems and ensure that more tactical requirements are met.

This type of project survey should be completely automated to minimize the time commitment, be conducted on a project above a particular budget threshold (that is, over minimum spend levels) to focus on major marketing activities, and be limited to a few, short questions focused on delivery and execution to avoid duplication and redundancy with the annual survey, which is intended to be less project specific and more relationship-based. This is about immediately-actionable tactical feedback.

This quantitative assessment at the end of each project provides continuous analysis of the client/agency performance relative to basic delivery and engagement. The focus is on ensuring that both parties are aware of what is required to plan and execute quality projects with consistency and mutual satisfaction. The same point scale as the annual or bi-annual assessment should be used. A target should be set.

Client Viewpoint

"Similar to anonymous employee surveys, agency surveys should allow agency staff to provide feedback to the client without the fear of being fired."

JULIE GIBBS, Director, Corporate Brand Marketing, Campaign Management, Adobe

Like any other survey mechanism, adequate adoption and coverage is needed to make this a worthwhile and representative exercise. This is intended not only to measure progress but more importantly, ensure actions, inspection and collaboration at all levels of engagement. Ultimately, it should be looked at and used as a leading indicator of future performance. The process of getting and providing input doesn't need to be extremely formal either. Clients and agencies should be comfortable having open, frank conversations regularly and informally, as often as needed. Those who do are probably the ones with strong partnerships.

Should the survey be anonymous? For most clients, this is a tough and unsettling question to answer. At the core of this question is whether or not the relationship has reached a certain level of trust. Another way to ask the question is: Can agencies and clients be candid in their feedback to clients? Some agree on principle but think that this type of survey should be anonymous, similar to employee surveys, encouraging more open feedback without having to fear potential retaliations or retribution. They do not believe it fosters trust and collaboration. Some argue that agencies would provide more direct, open feedback. There are certainly pros and cons to either scenario.

Others think it should be non-anonymous, to engender mutual accountability, making it easier to solve problems and look at each other in the face. Under this scenario, only comments can remain anonymous. If a client wants to establish a trusted relationship with its agency and avoid finger-pointing, can he or she be expected to build trust if participants do not have to be accountable for their words? It is debatable.

From my perspective, asking for anonymous feedback tends to skew results towards the negative as people take a chance to vent on issues that they would not otherwise bring up or prioritize for discussion. Conversely, both parties must be assured of their respective commitment to work on improving the partnership. They must trust that the information will be used constructively, with the interest of the relationship at center stage. Participants should be able to stand behind their ratings.

It also allows for richer discussions when it's time to take action on some of the improvement areas identified. If the feedback is anonymous, it's very difficult to know who should be involved in fixing open issues. There is no real relationship without trust. It is foundational and it is absolutely critical. How you gather input and how you use it will either reinforce it or weaken it.

Should the evaluation being handled externally or internally?
If the evaluation is not handled internally, should it be handled by the agency or by a third party consultant? A number of consulting firms or service providers have emerged in the past few years with specialty skills in agency evaluations. They offer professional expertise in this area, speeding up the process of selecting the attributes/questions and executing the survey, data collection, reporting, and analysis. This end-to-end service offering can be very appealing if you have limited resources to manage this process or are unsure how to get started. It can be more objective and therefore more appealing to both parties.

Third party agency performance assessment consultants offer an unbiased solution where feedback can be sent; this is appealing to those concerned about preserving anonymity and the confidentiality of their comments, and can be summarized to help fuel action plans. The client and agency may split the expense to ensure complete objectivity. In my experience, agencies are open to sharing this expense typically picked up by the client. These third party specialized firms provide consulting services as well as end-to-end technology solutions, advanced distribution, and reporting and analytical capabilities as alternatives to the manual, slow, laborious processes used by most companies. Using off-the-shelf survey tools or email might be sufficient for companies with a small number of participants and agencies.

Client Viewpoint

"Agencies not performing to our expectations are given a probation period to turn things around before they lose an AOR assignment. During that time, both the client and the agency review their progress monthly in a transparent manner. In the end, this is all about joint and individual accountability.

TOM CHETRICK
VP Advertising and Marketing Services, Bristol-Myers Squibb

Others operating with agencies on a larger scale should consider more robust, secure, scalable, and customizable solutions that allow them to spend more time on value-add activities such as analyzing results, diagnosing issues, identifying patterns, and consulting on action plans that up level both client and agency performance than on administrating the time-consuming data collection and reporting process.

Some third party vendors can also provide benchmarking data by client type, and industry type or attribute, providing even greater insight on where the relationship needs attention.

For example, one might find out that client briefing is an issue but that comparatively speaking, this particular client/agency relationship is doing a better job at it than other similar relationships, easing some of the pressure and helping with the stake-ranking of top issues.

What do high-performing evaluations have in common?

Agency/client performance evaluations have been around for a long time now. They have proven to be an effective feedback process that improves relationships and the quality of the engagement. Despite some common pitfalls, some companies are consistently getting the benefits from their evaluation efforts. They follow a common set of principles that are now best practices:

- Comprehensive: They must provide a holistic view of the relationship and the quality of the overall engagement.
- Effective: They must drive positive change in process, talent, or conduct to justify the time/resource investment.
- Sustainable: They must help identify trends over time, across geographies, or across agencies. To do so, survey questions and rankings must be somewhat consistent and predictable, building on past results.
- Affordable: They must be reasonable in cost (including the time commitment) and be as streamlined as possible. Think about them in terms of

representing a small percent of your agency spend each year, focused on improving the results of that marketing investment.

- Simple: They must be simple to understand, set up, and roll out, with well-considered training and communication.
- Participative: They must include a statistically representative sample of the client or agency population to be considered conclusive.
- Equitable: They must allow for feedback from clients and agencies alike, fostering collaboration and trust.
- Actionable: They must generate relevant insight that can translate into tangible improvements in process, behavior, procedures, timelines, skills, or personnel, and must be welcomed by both parties. The insight generated should help acknowledge joint successes or drive actionable improvement plans.

Evaluating employee performance is one of the most crucial roles played by management. It's about developing high-performing employees by providing both formal and informal performance feedback to those we care enough about to do so. The same principles followed by companies around the world about how to manage feedback to employees to get the most out of the evaluation also apply to agency/client performance evaluations. Everyone must play their part and produce valuable results. Some argue that only large scale, mature relationships benefit from a structured performance evaluation process.

Every relationship benefits from a constructive, honest feedback-loop process, even if the engagement is sporadic. Holding back feedback to either party is doing a disservice to the relationship. Coach Vince Lombardi summarized it best: "The achievements of an organization are the results of the combined effort of each individual." When clients and agencies take accountability for their shared responsibilities in an open, collaborative, transparent, respectful, and self-critical environment that strives for excellence, they create a shared vision and the partnership flourishes.

Client Viewpoint

"It all comes down to trust. If you trust your partner, you can talk frankly with one and another, you can get most value from the relationship. People who understand the agency business have better relationships with agencies. It's a collaboration of ideas, a sort of give and take, and a safe relationship where people can say things and not fear to be being penalized for it. My best agency relationships are those who tell me when I am being unreasonable."

SUSAN MARKOWICZ, Global Advertising Agency Manager, Ford Motor Company

{Taking Immediate Action}

TOP 5

BEST PRACTICES TO HARNESS THE MADNESS

❶ Accountability for the work relationship goes both ways. Conduct a 360-degree performance evaluation so the client and the agency both provide feedback to improve the work and the partnership.

❷ Formally review client/agency performance at least once or twice a year, but both parties should provide on-going feedback so that there are no surprises and issues can be addressed immediately.

❸ Clearly communicate externally and internally the importance of providing and receiving feedback and how to use this information to improve the partnership. Do not initiate this evaluation process unless you are 100% committed to doing something about the results.

❹ Encourage transparency and responsibility. As the client/agency relationship matures over time, consider making the feedback non-anonymous to foster even greater accountability.

❺ Consider hiring a consultant or an end-to-end performance evaluation solution, allowing you, the client, to focus all your efforts on improving those areas which will create the greatest impact.

10 GOTTMAN'S PAPER TOWEL TEST

Partnering towards mutual success

"Great things are done by a series of small things brought together."

—VINCENT VAN GOGH
Post-Impressionist painter

Success is said to be vastly contagious. Successful clients have relationships with successful agencies. This is a reality I've witnessed on both the client and agency side. Like the chicken and egg thing, one might wonder which came first. Senior agency executives may have the answer. They have long known that the secret of success and profitability for their agency is through the success of their clients, which is only possible through a successful client/agency relationship. A successful business relationship is defined by individuals coming together with a common interest in building an effective, sustainable relationship that yields results and produces concrete economic benefits to each other. It's the essence of a partnership.

Experts on either side extol the value of strong partnerships, in which individuals create professional bonds that are durable, authentic, prolific, and in the end, yield outstanding business performance. Clients consume any resources at their disposal: seminars, training, coaching, anything that might help them improve their odds of turning sub-optimal relationships into massively powerful competitive weapons of mass persuasion.

Agencies told us how wonderful their clients would be if only they were different. Clients told them the same. There has been a great deal of debate on how to build better relationships so clients can say: "I no longer have an agency. I now have a business partner." Sounds nice, doesn't it? The reality is that most clients don't get to say this too often. Although there are known principles that distinguish good from bad relationships, it remains a struggle for any client. Above all, it takes hard work.

Sadly enough, weak relationships take as much time and efforts as the strong ones. So why not do it right out of the gate? Strong partnerships are simply channeling these efforts in much more productive ways than weak ones. Strong partnerships don't mean agreeable ones, either. Strong partnerships seem to demonstrate a healthy dose of agreement, but also disagreement.

John M. Gottman, Ph.D., a professor of psychology at the University of Washington and author of a *New York Times* best-seller *The Seven Principles for Making Marriage Work*[53] has been studying what makes relationships stick at the Love Lab, formerly known as the Institute of Family Research Laboratory in Seattle. After years of scientific research and experiments, Gottman has come up with a way to determine with fair accuracy which relationships are most likely to succeed and those which are doomed to fail.[54] Gottman can actually tell 96% of the time whether a marital discussion will resolve a conflict after the first three minutes.

Among Gottman's many exercises, one of them is called the "paper tower" test where a couple is tasked to build a free-standing paper tower using scotch tape, a stapler, markers, newspaper, a ball of string, paper, and colored cellophane. The end result is less important than the way people interact during the exercise. The way a couple partners on accomplishing the task provides great insight into the health and strength of that relationship. Vulnerable couples might get lucky and complete their paper tower but at what cost?

Client Viewpoint

"At the core of building and sustaining a successful relationship with an agency is honesty, integrity, and relevancy. You need to keep things open and fresh. It is the same as in friendships, partnerships or even marriages."

BRETT COLBERT
Global Manager, Procurement Advertising, Anheuser Busch InBev

According to Gottman, successful relationships tend to follow a number of interaction styles that are producing positive outcomes and feelings. But those relationships are not conflict-free. It is true of any kind of business relationship as well. Client/agency relationships are no exception to that rule. So what are the prerequisites of strong client/agency relationships? What makes or break relationships? What's a true partnership? What's the recipe for success? What makes a good client? And reversely, what makes a good agency? What can we do about it? When things turn bad, how do you patch things up and recover? And how do you build on existing relationships to get most value from them? Companies have asked these questions for years before us, about any type of partnership. Many still struggle to come up with answers but one thing is certain: Asking the question is getting you one step closer to answering it.

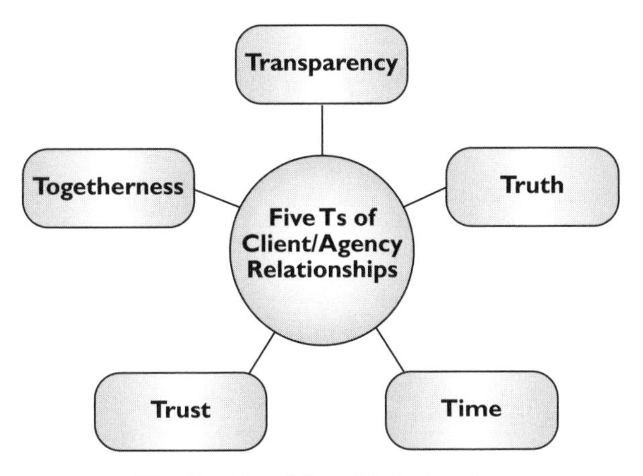

The Five Ts of Good Relationships

The DNA of Good Relationships, aka the Five Ts

There is a set of foundational principles that are at the core of any relationship, whether that relationship is personal or professional in nature. I refer to these principles as the Five Ts: Transparency, Truth, Time, Trust, and Togetherness. Mutual respect and trust is a vital part of any relationship and without it, any agency/client relationship is doomed to fail.

How does one establish trust? I've heard agency and marketing executives claim that trust must be established at the offset of the relationship, which is honorable but not realistic. Both parties must acknowledge to each other that this is their genuine intent and are committed to do what it takes, but a new relationship cannot truly establish the agency as a trusted advisor or the client as a trusted partner until they have been put to the test.

To get to this end point, both parties must be transparent about their objectives and expectations; they must be truthful about their relationship, soliciting and providing continual feedback about the work, the health of the relationship; and they must give each other time. They need time to get to know each other and have time to win each other's undivided trust. When trust has been earned and is a part of the way stakeholders from both sides are engaging with each other, a true sense of togetherness can develop. Unified by a common set of goals, the agency and the client feel that they are in this together, as companies and individuals.

Client Viewpoint

"At Starbucks, we believe that successful client/agency relationships are first and foremost about honesty and open communication, collaboration and partnership."

JENNIFER BERGER, Director, Marketing & Advertising Services, Starbucks

Personal relationships play a significant role in any business relationship. But personal chemistry in advertising and marketing services and relationship bonds are particularly critical in this category of services. It's no surprise. This is a people vs. capital intensive business that requires trust and commitments. Those elements are essential. Doubts, mistrust, and lack of commitment, in personal or professional settings, eventually shadow relationships and irrevocably condemn them to collapse.

Client Viewpoint

"Agencies establish relationships across the client sphere of influence, engaging at different levels. To be effective at building and sustaining a strong relationship, they have to understand and adapt to different perspectives, from the executive level, functional interactions to the procurement organization."

TIM WHITING, Senior Director Global Marketing, Motorola

At the heart of any partnership is the understanding of the need of the other party. What do clients and agencies need from each other? It's worth noting that the longevity of relationship, the nature of that relationship and the way the relationship is structured financially, for example, can have a profound impact on how individuals behave and interact together. For instance, long term relationships show signs of greater trust and partnership than newly appointed ones. Agencies with compensation systems that tie to client priorities are more likely to see their needs met than those who don't.

There have been a number of studies conducted over the years to shed some insight on this topic. These studies, often conducted by their respective trade associations, attempt to deepen that mutual understanding. Failure to have this understanding will make a relationship sour and will likely result in a change in the partnership. Not surprisingly, the list of key drivers that lead to a strong relationship and increased longevity doesn't change too much from one study to another. Motivated by their respective corporate agenda, the list combines hard and soft needs, from pure financially oriented needs and business metrics to psychological needs such as appreciation and self-actualization, equally important to a balanced and healthy partnership.

What Clients Need (or What Makes a Good Agency)

Ultimately, clients want to partner with agencies that can help them meet or exceed their business or marketing objectives, whether it is brand building, awareness, lead generation, or sales, and doing so efficiently and effectively. That implies a number of tactical needs but in reality, those are simply a means to an end. A client may say that he/she wants talented resources in the business, customer insight, and a strong account planning function from the agency, but what he/she really wants is to find ways to outrun the competition, strengthen the brand, increase customer satisfaction, and grow profitability and market share. They want value from the partnership, a mix of creativity and productivity that delivers real business results. It also means that both parties have a common understanding of how they want to work together, how to drive most value from the partnership. Here is what clients expect the most from their agencies:

Client Viewpoint

"Mutual accountability means that you succeed together or you fail together, as one. It's that simple. Client/agency relationships should be conducted more like joint ventures with business partners, with aligned goals and metrics, than as a transactional buyer and vendor relationships."

MICHAEL E. THYEN
Director, Marketing and Sales
Global Procurement, Eli Lilly and Company

"We want you to be accountable for driving business results." Clients want agencies that want to put themselves in their clients' shoes. Clients need agencies that first and foremost have a solid understanding of their client's business, are committed to solving business problems, and are laser-focused on driving impactful work and bottom-line results. All clients wish for fewer but more outcome-oriented, more valuable agency resources, for their business. Agencies must understand priorities and have the natural instinct to focus their energy and efforts toward most impactful activities. They can be trusted to prioritize their time and resources accordingly. That is the frame of reference for everything they do, always keeping their eyes on the end target and treating their client's budget as if it were their own. They are value-add contributors. As a result, they have ways to measure results and continually optimize.

Clients want to see agencies take more accountability for consumer-centric measurement that breaks media silos and provides an integrated 360 view of success metrics. Agencies promote a culture of accountability throughout their organization. They under-promise and over-deliver. Accountability for driving business results means that the agency is expected to be thinking about how to accomplish that goal through the lenses of advertising, marketing, and communication in the broadest sense possible. If that means coming up with ideas that might translate into new products, new services, new ways of serving clients, then be it. They are so accountable to their client's budget and success that when in doubt they always align with their client and do what's right for them, not for the agency.

The client wants to launch a campaign that could be quite profitable to the agency but doesn't seem to make good sense to the agency. Some in the agency will then push back against proceeding with the project in order to serve their client's best interest. Clients want agency people who share a common passion, live and breathe the brand every day, to the point where you can barely differentiate them from your own internal team. This is what I like to call the "We" moment. That time when folks from your agency start using "we" in meetings when talking about the company's challenges and opportunities, accentuating a deep sense of ownership and accountability of their client's success. There is no "us" or "them." "We" win or lose together.

Client Viewpoint

"Agencies are just people. The constant threat of being fired is not a motivator. This is not how to manage a partnership. Partnerships generate real value. It takes constant work however. The easy way out is to fire them and go somewhere else. But the reality is that it's not easy to switch agencies and make things work smoothly. I've put agencies in review but it rarely generates the outcome you expect. Don't give up on your agency too quickly. Like any marriage, you need to keep it fresh and exciting."

SUSAN MARKOWICZ, Global Advertising Agency Manager, Ford Motor Company

What they don't want: agencies who are more interested in producing work that wins awards than impactful work that drives tangible business results, whose intentions cannot be trusted, who add minimal value at high costs, or are more interested in ways to generate revenue for the agency than for the client.

"We want you to come up with and sustain brilliant creative that is based on actionable insight." Clients want strategic powerhouses that consistently generate brilliant ideas inspired by deep insight into the audience and business. They want agencies that grasp the company's direction. Top reasons for dissatisfaction in client/agency relationships are related to conflicts about the strategy, and disagreements about the creative work or lack of actionable insight. Clients want to work with agencies that listen well to their needs, leverage research and data they provide them, and bring them real business solutions to their challenges.

It's especially important, for example, in highly regulated industries with unique go-to-market requirements such as health care or telecommunications. They want agencies that come up with big ideas, foster a customer-driven approach and culture, promote fresh and compelling ideas from the ability to think outside of the box and across disciplines. Clients want agencies that provide unbiased, unique perspectives and relevant experience from rich audience and customer insight about when, where, and how customers are receptive to their brand.

They want agencies that are on the cutting edge of technology, culture, and various trends. Clients also expect a minimum level of monitoring of their competition (What is the competition's messaging and positioning, what is their media mix, what are they doing well in, what are their potential weaknesses we can leverage to our advantage?) so that this insight can be incorporated into the overall strategy.

What they don't want: Agencies that don't do their due diligence; have little to no insight about the audience or the competition; are out of touch; disregard any information provided by the client and shoot from the hip, hoping to get lucky, and miss the mark often; are often off strategy and have to go back to the drawing board over and over again; are followers, not leaders.

Client Viewpoint

"Agencies should proactively do more research, to better understand the audience rather than relying solely on third party market research. What to talk about, when to talk to them, how to talk to them all provide value insight to help build a dialog with customers."

MICHAEL FITZGERALD
Associate Director, Business Advertising, AT&T Inc.

"We want work that is fully integrated and provides cohesive customer experiences." Clients want end-to-end, fully integrated solutions from their agencies. This goes beyond the typical matching suitcases or simple cosmetic work. We are talking about leveraging all channels and messaging opportunities to deliver a cohesive message that is more than the sum of the parts. Clients do not hesitate to expand their agency roster when they feel that they must compromise discipline excellence for integration. They want agencies that break the silos and know how to partner well with other agencies to deliver on the client's desire to have one voice and deliver a cohesive customer experience.

Clients want their agencies to sit at the table and think together. When they do, ideas can be generated from any direction, not limiting agencies to their silo of most direct responsibility. The retail agency may contribute to an idea that would be executed in a digital environment, for example. The PR or the digital agency might be the one coming up with the idea that will be expanded across all other disciplines.

What they don't want: Agencies who don't have a broad perspective, are biased, work in silos and don't care to find ways to integrate the work themselves or in collaboration with other agencies.

"We want you to assign top talent to our business." Clients should demand the best people their money can buy on the account. It's all about getting and keeping the right talent working on your business: individuals with discipline expertise and know-how in creative, branding, media, digital, demand generation, PR, with breadth and depth of consumer knowledge and a wide range of service or technology capabilities to deliver them. Clients want top-notch talent, highly prized professionals with flawless résumés.

Client Viewpoint

"Agencies can make themselves more valuable to their clients by further investing in the professional development of their people. Agencies do not seem to train staff or are not as thoughtful about bringing them up to speed as much as they used to."

KEVIN PARHAM, Director Global Advertising, Campbell Soup

They want them to be highly qualified and deeply passionate about their business. It's not as simple as getting a top agency working on your business. Getting a top agency doesn't guarantee you to get top talent. Most likely, a client is getting a small group of individuals assigned to the account. If you are a large client, you are getting occasional access to the agency's leadership team who wants to "check in"—at no extra cost. Although talent rotation means leveraging the rich background of talent an agency has access to, ideally, clients do not want to see key folks on their business taken off the account or leaving the agency less than 36 months after they started. It takes time to learn the business, get in the "zone" and make a permanent mark.

Even among the best agencies in the world, quality is likely to be uneven between team A and team B. Clients want to see a qualified team of individuals who work well together and have the right skill set to do the job. They want to create an environment that attracts that talent. It is contagious. The rest usually follows. Soon everyone at the agency will want to work on that particular piece of business. Then the best talent in every functional role will want to be on the best account at the agency. Be the favorite client. It doesn't mean having the largest budget or the most creative work. It's about making them feel they are a highly valuable part of the team.

Client Viewpoint

"Agencies should always have somebody who is paid to apply a critical eye as to what the client is asking the agency to do and whether or not the work is delivering against the company objectives."

JULIE GIBBS, Director, Corporate Brand Marketing, Campaign Management, Adobe

Earn that right as a client. I strongly encourage clients to meet all the key people who work on their business, go out to dinner with them once in a while, and fully tap into that brain power. If clients wanted junior personnel on their business, something tells me that they would go and hire that talent themselves. But what clients need is the vast expertise and talent pool that only profitable and high growth agencies can provide. We can't discuss talent without emphasizing personal relationships.

Personal relationships play a significant role in any business relationship. But personal chemistry in advertising and marketing services and relationship bonds are particularly critical in this category of services. It's no surprise. This is a people vs. capital intensive business that require trust and commitments. Those elements are essential to a productive relationship. Doubts, mistrust, and lack of commitment shadows relationships.

What they don't want: Agencies with junior or second tier talent with a consistently high attrition rate and little continuity on the account, and arrogant, "know it all" creative resources who think clients don't get it.

"We want you to challenge conventional thinking and continuously innovate." Clients want thought-leadership and best practices combined with the agency's willingness to learn, innovate, and experiment. It means being gutsy enough at times to say "no" to their client. *No, we don't believe this is the right to approach this, it has been done before, etc. BUT we recommend another way to tackle this issue ...* It's not being difficult or having more of a "can do" attitude. It's being honest and transparent; it's about fulfilling the role of subject matter expert an agency is expected to play. Doing so with confidence, a luxury that only senior agency people can afford. Innovation doesn't take place only in digital and technology. There are plenty of opportunities for clients to leverage traditional media, retail, and other non-digital environments to be innovative.

It's especially important in tough economic times where agencies may be operating with smaller budgets and be less aggressive about bringing forward new, unsolicited ideas to their clients. Being proactive is therefore a requisite for sustained innovation, in the broad sense of the definition. Innovating might lead the agency to new ways of doing the same thing, not necessarily inventing or doing new things. Clients want agencies that genuinely embrace change as part of their DNA. Clients expect their agencies to proactively come up with new ways to look at things, new ideas and concepts that drive the business forward. Clients want them to take calculated risks that turn into a competitive edge.

What they don't want: agencies who don't to make waves, like to play it conservative, and don't have the guts or the skills to explore new grounds.

"We want you to move swiftly and execute flawlessly." Clients want fast, streamlined execution throughout the process from creative and content development, all the way to in-market deployment and measurement. Clients want agencies that are thoughtful, proactive but also responsive. They want agencies who share their passion and commitment to excellence, cost effectiveness, quality, speed, and flexibility. Clients want partners who are collaborative throughout the process. The growth of real-time digital marketing vehicles puts tremendous time pressure on agencies to significantly reduce typical go-to-market timelines. The agency must work faster, better, without impacting quality.

Client Viewpoint

"In my experience, it is imperative to build successful relationships with our agencies. We trust each other. We see them as strategic partners to our company. We continually encourage them to bring new, innovative ideas to the table."

MICHAEL FITZGERALD
Associate Director, Business Advertising, AT&T Inc.

It's not all about getting it done. It's about doing it right. A small typo, missing copy, or an ad placement on the wrong site can have disastrous effect on the company's reputation.

Quality must never be compromised, regardless of the time pressure or budget conditions. Once the agency accepts taking on the project, the client should not have to worry as to whether quality is at stake. Flawless execution is non-negotiable.

What they don't want: Agencies who have great ideas but can't bring them to life, who act carelessly, who don't have rigorous processes and adequate quality control, who cannot execute their ideas without messing up somewhere along the way.

"We want you to collaborate effectively with other agency partners." Clients want to work with agencies that are willing to collaborate with each other in the client's best interest. Easier said than done, it often requires time-consuming and sometimes wasteful interventions from the client to resolve potential agency disputes. They want agencies to operate in a non-silo, non-biased environment, where agencies have clear roles and responsibilities, but are willing to embrace ideas wherever they originate from. They want their agencies to overcome their instinctive fear of losing credibility or business to others agencies if they subject themselves to peer agency input/feedback. They want their agencies to overcome their desire to keep information to themselves to differentiate themselves or prove their worth to the client.

What they don't want: "Turf wars" among agencies in their roster. Agencies that are not communicative, or are not cooperative and act territorial. Agencies that dismiss ideas from others, do not share critical information in a timely manner, and that are not accessible or responsive to other agencies. Clients do not want to work with agencies that are more concerned about their own success than the success of the entire team.

As in any partnership, clients want to be heard and understood by their agencies. So agencies should listen carefully. Not only to clients but also to customers and partners. Agencies should send contact reports after every meeting, publish results and best practices, author whitepapers that set them apart from their competition, and demonstrate their commitment to excellence.

There is also a personal aspect to any partnership. Without chemistry or personal relationships, it might turn out to be an unpleasant ride. Every client may stake-rank what they deem most critical, based on the nature of their business, their corporate culture, or what they value most. Clients may expect all of this but are they willing to pay a higher premium for the one agency that can bring all of these benefits? It's ultimately the client's job to demand excellence in every aspect of the agency engagement. Once in a while, the agency should ask the clients how it can be a better partner to them.

Client Viewpoint

"My experience over the years has been that some agencies do not instinctively work well together. At Macy's, I want every agency on our business to know that they are a critical piece of the wheel but they must play their part in making us successful together. They must show their willingness to work with other partners. Every month, all our agencies sit together at the same table to partner and ultimately make us more successful."

MARTINE REARDON
VP of Marketing, Macy's

What Agencies Need (or What Makes a Good Client)

Some clients may wonder: "Why should I care about what the agency needs? After all, I am the one holding the budget. It's up to them to find ways to get what they need. There is always another agency around the corner waiting to jump in." This is clearly not the way to drive value from a partnership. To produce great work, agencies need great clients. A great client is an active, committed collaborator, looking for ways to enable their partners to do their very best work. This being said, there is an important distinction between what agencies "want" and what they may actually "need." Of course, all agencies want marquee clients, with iconic, high exposure brands. They want to work on the most engaging brands. They want accounts that win creative awards. They want to work with clients who are fun, reasonable and appreciative. They are not to blame. Wouldn't you? Understanding what agencies want enables clients to motivate them to deliver their very best work.

Client Viewpoint

"Ongoing communication is critical to successful relationships with agencies. Fierce conversation is what we call this here at Burger King Corp. Agencies must challenge, push back but they must do so with knowledge and insight."

CLAUDIA LEZCANO, Director of Advertising, Burger King Corp.

During my years on the client as well as on the agency side, I've learned that most agencies have reasonable expectations from their clients. Some of them arguably expect too little from their clients who will eventually throw the relationship off balance and impair the agency's ability or even willingness to retain and grow the relationship over time. I recall a vivid call to action in AdWeekMedia, a formal reply from the "outlaw culture" from Steve Simpson, a partner and creative director at Goodby, Silverstein & Partners San Francisco. Simpson refers to agencies as jailers "with a few rules of their own" and proposes a set of principles clients should follow. Although Simpson may not be speaking for the industry at large, explicitly stating what agencies need in order to do their very best work is something all clients should encourage and embrace. Let's look at agencies' most fundamental needs:

Agency Viewpoint

"Agencies need more time to think; today, they are getting much less. And procurement is choking off the lifeblood of creativity by evaluating the price of great thinking the same way they price a box of paper clips."

MARC A. BROWNSTEIN
President and CEO, Brownstein Group

"We want to be fairly compensated for our services." First and foremost, agencies need to run a profitable business to stay financially healthy and grow as any commercial enterprise. No agency wants to be in the business of giving away their precious time, resources, and ideas. Although agency executives may not put this at the top of their list at the risk of sounding pragmatically capitalistic, let's face it: There is a fundamental need for any for-profit organization to thrive and grow. Certainly agencies want high profile clients and world class brands on which they can unleash their creativity. But agencies need to be compensated fairly to provide quality services and valuable resources.

Although clients understand that basic vital requirement, they do not always agree on the definition of "fair" because of its subjective nature. Not all accounts are equally profitable of course, willingly (pro bono, volume discounts) or unwillingly (poor cost management, investments), but they strive for the most part to secure profitable accounts. If they share part of the risk, agencies want to share part of the rewards. A profitable agency can assemble better talent: the best talent wants to work for a profitable agency because profitable agencies can often compensate staff better and are also much more stable places to work. It's that simple, really.

A non-profitable agency spends a lot of time and effort figuring out how to be profitable, which can turn to be a major distraction for the agency and ultimately, the client. If multiple agencies are expected to work together, compensation must not get in the way of collaboration. It is critical to avoid territorial issues among agencies.

Clients must also set reasonable expectations for the partnership. If a client makes a mistake, then the client must take accountability for it. Same for the agency. Trust and credibility are established in these rare moments of truth. Although they may exceptionally ask the agency to clock insane hours, work on weekends and evenings, to deliver on an important and timely deliverable, they shouldn't expect the agency to do this frequently. It's not sustainable and would lead to unwanted and costly attrition on the agency side. It's easier to manage work expectations when both parties are similar cultures and work styles.

What they don't want: Clients who don't pay their bills, don't pay them on time, want the agency to share the risks but not the rewards, who don't understand why agencies should be profitable, don't care if they are, or think way too much of themselves as if working on their business was sufficient incentive for the agency.

"We want clear direction and easy, timely access to relevant information." Clients who provide well-articulated strategic direction are particularly valued by agencies because they provide them with the research and insight needed for agencies to give their best and deliver "on-strategy" work. According to an ANA survey (ANA Agency Relations Forum, Research conducted by Lightspeed Research, April 20, 2004) about maximizing the effectiveness in the client/agency relationship, the most important characteristic of a great client motivating agencies to beg them to allow them to work for their business is clear consistent direction (80% of agency responders). This is very consistent with the feedback I've heard over the years from agencies. Clear direction about what business outcome is expected is vital to a successful relationship. Educate your agencies about your business. Invite them to strategic planning discussions, way upstream of their usual engagement point, not only to get them embedded into the company's strategy early on, but to give them a voice to influence it.

Client Viewpoint

"Key account people from our agencies are in our offices nearly every week to meet with the marketing team. In my experience, face to face interactions yield stronger partnerships."

DELMAR WYATT
Director Advertising Operations, Qwest Communications

Agencies also need access to the wealth of information and knowledge available to learn about their client's business, its culture, people and industry. Unlike a brief situation where the client wants to provide succinct, relevant information, it is recommended that clients give wide access to the breadth and depth of their resources ***and*** let agencies navigate through them to decide what might be helpful to them. It might be wise for example to get the account and creative teams totally immersed into the products or services, experiencing them first hand as consumers would. They may want to be invited to the client's sales meeting, inbound call center or focus groups. In the process, they might discover something unique to be used in the messaging (what it takes to produce it, the care and attention to details, the quality control, the customer-friendly support, the environmentally-friendly procedures, and so on) that the client would never have thought about sharing with them.

Client Viewpoint

"We want agencies that get it, that get us as client, understand our culture and our customers. To bring great ideas and creative, agencies must intimately understand their client and their client's culture. That's what truly differentiates them and make relationships last."

CLAUDIA LEZCANO, Director of Advertising, Burger King Corp.

Clients should send them relevant announcements, research material, annual reports, studies and other reading material to help the agency business to gain a deep understanding of the client's business. Agencies need clients to do this, and they need clients to make themselves available to them. It also means setting up clear expectations for how the work should get done which has led clients to document those in Service Level Agreements (SLA).

I recommend that the SLA be added as an exhibit to the master contract to reinforce its importance to the parties concerned. As an exhibit to the contract, failure to meet SLA requirements seems to get people's attention. At least more so than a loose document trying to get its way to people's desks. Clarifying up front the nature of the working relationship, not just what they will do (as determined in the scope of work), but how they will interact, is a fundamental step.

I've witnessed numerous failed relationships over the years consistently resulting from breakdowns in trust and communication, from misunderstandings, missed expectations, and their inability to trouble shoot and solve problems in an equitable way to build long-term good will. Successful client/agency relationships depend on the ability and willingness of individuals on both sides to work together.

What they don't want: Clients who keep information to themselves, who are takers, not givers, make the agency find it on their own, don't trust the agency to have it, don't think the agency would understand it, value it or make good use of it. Lack of timely briefings that may result in downstream inefficiencies and wasted efforts. Agencies do not want side conversations with multiple decision makers with divergent opinions about the same assignment.

"We want adequate senior management engagement." Lack of clear ownership of the overall relationship can be particularly destabilizing to the agency. Senior leadership must be involved early on in the overall process and participate in agency briefings. Agencies need assignment briefs to be first approved by senior management to avoid fielding divergent input and potentially conflicting direction later on. Agencies also need to know who has final say over on matters related to the overall relationship including financial, staffing, and performance matters. They need to know who owns the client's brand and agency deliverable, and who has authority to make decisions that might impact the fate of the partnership or a particular assignment.

Client Viewpoint

"To build and sustain strong relationships with agencies, one must remember that this business is about relationships. We can't solely rely on processes, metrics and tools. Those can help make sure relationships stay healthy. But highly productive work partnerships are anchored into strong personal relationships that yield great results."

MOLLIE WESTON
Director Agency Management Operations, Best Buy

Senior management ownership of the relationship is a necessity for agencies that might be otherwise pulled into too many directions; receive mixed or even conflicting messages. It also ensures that the agency benefits from the wealth of knowledge and strengths the management team can provide. Too often, decisions are being revisited because senior management wasn't bought in to the strategy.

It's far more effective to argue back and forth on the strategy with senior management than wasting precious time and resources debating the creative execution or the copy. The agency must be clear on how to incorporate the feedback into the ideation process. But involvement from senior management must be carefully handled internally so that it doesn't go from a well orchestrated symphony to a cacophony that is more disruptive than it is helpful.

What they don't want: Clients who are too insecure to give access to their management for fear of losing control or credibility, who don't think senior management can add value, or think that senior management should only be involved at the end of the process.

"We want timely decisions that we stick to." Agencies want thoughtful, truly objective, informed input from their clients when reacting to the work. They want clients who come in open-minded, without a pre-set agenda or looking only for ways to pick holes at the work. Having a sound approval process that streamlines decision-making eliminates redundancies, endless approval loops, bureaucracy, wasteful and frustrating use of agency resources that cost more and slow everyone down. How often does an agency deliver work to a client, only to find out that the real "client approver" has yet to be introduced to the agency? Often times that same client has a diametrically opposed view and the agency must start all over or go through numerous and costly rounds of revisions.

How often does the agency have to defend its ideas to multiple organization layers without clarity as to who the final decision maker is? The process must be designed to accommodate a limited number of engaged clients with clear decision-making authority. Agencies want direct feedback: if you don't like it, say it loud and clear immediately. Articulate why you don't think the work will deliver on the project objectives. Refer to the brief. Don't zero down on details or duel on tactical points. Stay big picture, focused on the idea and the way the idea is supporting the overall objectives.

> **Agency Viewpoint**
>
> *"Treat your agency with respect, and you will get maximum performance out of them. 'Respect' means: access; fair compensation; regular, honest feedback (praise as well as constructive criticism); proper time to accomplish goals; post-mortems after big campaigns."*
>
> MARC A. BROWNSTEIN
> **President and CEO, Brownstein Group**

Offer the agency to preview work before important meetings, so you are not blindsided and the agency uses you as a sounding board. Insist that the people actively engaged in the project are the ones presenting. Compliment them when appropriate. Speak to strengths and weaknesses. Clarity of role is important as agencies may otherwise struggle to identify final decision makers because there are too many cooks in the kitchen, too many voices leading to excessive changes, delays and diluted deliverables. The client may decide to provide written feedback to the agency, first gathering input from internal stakeholders and then consolidating it to speak as one voice to the agency. No agency wants to work with a client who changes his/her mind frequently. Too many clients interfacing with too few account people may lead to role confusion, poor delivery, and performance issues.

Timely decision-making also means surfacing problems and issues as they arise. If there are occasional misunderstandings with the client, the agency should put down what has been agreed upon in writing to reduce the changes of confusion down the road. Agencies should do this for important decisions or key milestones only.

What they don't want: Clients who make random decisions, who don't explain them, who invite too many people to the process, who change their minds frequently, or at the last minute.

"We want a stable account and a predictable workflow." Clients must provide line of sight into flow of assignments, workload, and requirements. They want long-range plans and accurate and consistent timelines. The agency needs to know that there is continuity in the business. They can invest themselves fully into assignments if they don't have to worry about who's going to pick up the tab next month. Providing them a reasonable view into what's coming in the next six to twelve months will enable the agency to hire or dedicate resources they wouldn't otherwise.

They need to anticipate what resources and how many will be required to successfully service the account. Any significant variance in the scope of work can present some challenges for the agencies that might need to staff up, bring in freelancers at times during uptime, or load-balance resources across other clients during downtime. Lack of line of sight makes it impossible for the agency to guarantee proper staffing, timely and quality delivery.

What they don't want: Unexpected fire drills and last minute assignments as a rule, not an exception. Clients who can't commit to a body of work, who rush every assignment, change their minds frequently and cancel work already in progress, and who consistently threaten to take the account somewhere else.

Client Viewpoint

"Agencies don't know how to say no. Clients often take advantage of that. We ask agencies to do everything instead of focusing them on their core competency. It takes good clients to use them wisely."

SUSAN MARKOWICZ, Global Advertising Agency Manager, Ford Motor Company

"We want an open, direct dialog with you as well as continued feedback or praises about our work." Managers provide direct and continued feedback to employees. They also listen carefully. This is not different. Soliciting and providing ongoing and frequent feedback is critical to any partnership. Don't let issues build up over time to the point where they become unmanageable. Too often, the client won't take the time to provide feedback or won't listen to the agency. Or if they feel the agency is likely to be overly defensive, they won't bother. This is the sign of slowly dying relationship.

Clients must be transparent, provide clear, constructive, honest, direct feedback to agency staff, giving them the opportunity to course-correct if needed and learn from past mistakes. If you don't like something, by all means, tell the agency. Say it constructively but say it immediately. It's about working with the agency in a highly collaborative manner as a client would with any other internal teams. It's about trust, building an environment that welcomes feedback and makes it safe to do so. Agencies must encourage their clients to provide feedback. No feedback is actually worst than negative feedback.

Conversely, clients must be willing to listen to the agency, be self-critical at times, and take ownership of inefficiencies in the way they interface with the agency. Even in tough economic times, there is no substitute for constant communication and human interactions.

> **Client Viewpoint**
>
> *"Effective relationships are based on having open communications upfront. We speak to our agencies every two weeks to counsel them, give them insight on how to be more successful on our business. This is what partnership is all about."*
>
> A LARGE ADVERTISER

In addition to using collaboration and communication technologies, clients should maintain some travel budget for face to face meetings, even if that means being more thoughtful about how many are truly necessary and who truly needs to attend those. Acknowledging the great work the agency is doing and celebrating successes helps keep the agency highly motivated. The agency should receive full credit for its work. A simple mail from the CMO to the agency head stating how proud and satisfied they are about the work produced, or a celebration cocktail event, a dinner or any other social acknowledgment, will go a long way to build positive equity in the partnership as well as build confidence at the agency.

> **Client Viewpoint**
>
> *"Clients can get the most value from their agencies by understanding how they operate and what their main interests are and by making sure that transparency and honesty are always present in the relationship. Having an open communication and treating agencies as partners vs. vendors are the most effective ways to build successful relationships with agencies."*
>
> CARLA DODDS, Director, Multicultural Marketing and Marketing Vendor Management, Walmart U.S.

Giving out individual or team agency awards (quarterly or annually) is also a very effective way to emphasize areas of critical importance to the relationship or targeted improvement areas (Innovation, Cross-Agency Collaboration, thoughtleadership, etc.) by acknowledging outstanding performers within the agency roster. Allow the professional perspective and opinions of both parties to be acknowledged and respected. An open dialog culture, including regular face to face meetings with the client or at the agency, as well as inclusion in critical internal planning discussions, is vital to facilitate this ongoing exchange of information.

Clients should consider visiting the agency at least a few times a year, tour the agency, greet new agency hires to the team, get to know the people working on the account, and in the process, show the client's commitment to the agency.

What they don't want: Clients who don't say a word about the agency's work, whether good or bad, and when they do, go around the team directly to the agency leadership, blame the agency but don't offer anything constructive, never give a pat in the back, only provide feedback on the day they want to terminate the account, and who don't feel the need to get to know their agency.

"We want the opportunity to take risks and push the envelope."

With risk comes accountability. One without the other is the equivalent of bargain shopping with someone else's credit card. It might be fun but it's unlikely to turn out well. In my experience, successful agencies want a greater share of accountability and autonomy. They want to think proactively about their client's business. We, as clients, should cherish that. Agencies want to be empowered to do their best work. They need adequate time and room to do so. It doesn't mean that the client no longer has to take accountability (as if that was an option) or the agency no longer has to meet certain in-market campaign timing requirements. Agencies must have full accountability for how the work gets produced, unless there are specific client requirements that are justified.

As change agents, agencies need to be empowered by their clients. That implies giving the agency the necessary budget to do their job and sufficient time. That also implies giving them a seat at the table and allowing them to play a value-add role in the partnership. Agencies want to get input and feedback from clients about their problems, not solutions. Agencies do not want to work for clients who do not make a good use of their resources and skills. This being said, agencies must also be held accountable for business results, not for the activities they generate.

Client Viewpoint

"Agencies are often hesitant to push clients. Great agencies should have the confidence to be heard, to say "no" to status quo if they truly believe it's the right thing for their brand. They get their senior people to engage with a clients' senior management. They make concerted efforts to stop doing work that is little value-add to clients."

JAMES R. ZAMBITO, Global Marketing Group Controller, Johnson & Johnson

Agencies need clients willing to challenge themselves, occasionally getting out of their comfort zone, allowing agencies to think outside the box and produce breakthrough ideas. The inherent value of the advertising and marketing service industry is to challenge the status quo, and deliver compelling messages that stand out in the marketplace. Open-minded clients allow agencies to be change agents and draw the most value from the relationship. Creative awards are important to agencies because they provide them with a venue to be acknowledged by their peers and attract key talent to their agency. Who doesn't want to work with the agency that wins awards? Agencies need room to test ideas, challenge the client strategy, and bring up creative ways to give unconventional solutions for business issues.

Clients should allow their agencies to put on their thinking caps and think outside the client's box once in a while, giving the agency a chance to challenge itself and deliver breakthrough ideas in unexpected ways. The client must be ready to step up to the challenge and occasionally approve and pilot these less conservative concepts and ideas. That implies that they are allowed to fail at times as long as both parties continue to learn and improve as a result.

Risk-aversion is common nature but it must be fought against aggressively in the field of marketing communication. If the most innovative work doesn't occasionally hit a bump on the road, it may not be risky enough. Clients should stay away from overly comfortable, risk-free relationships that do not push clients to do their best work. The agency should be given the opportunity to take calculated risks that will occasionally pay big.

Agency Viewpoint

"Relationships built around campaigns don't yield long term customer value. It takes time to build brands. Products have longer lifecycle. Marcom is typically about short cycles. These days, too many companies are launching new brands like they are launching movies with a focus on quick hits, but not really long-term franchises."

DAVID KENNY
Managing Partner, Vivaki

What they don't want: Clients who want to play it safe at all times, confuse risk-taking with gambling, give them no time to think, who never follow their agency's recommendations, who systematically kill unconventional ideas, who don't like to test and learn, who don't like to be challenged, and only want order-takers, not thinkers.

Finally, agencies strive in a client environment in which people have fun, and are trusted and appreciated for their efforts. It is a business of people. Clients should take good care of their agencies: the stronger the ties and relationships, the more effective the partnership is and the better the work ends up being. Agencies want to be inspired to do their best work.

Once in a while, the client should ask the agency how it can be a better partner to them (you would hope the agency is doing the same periodically). It sends the right signal and you might be surprised by the outcome.

Making Relationships Work in a Digital World

The digital age has permanently changed the way marketing is done, and, therefore, how agencies and clients work together. Along with many of the great opportunities digital presents to marketers come many challenges of equal scale. Clients must identify the right agency model to address their expanding digital marketing needs. Inviting customers to dialog about brands in a digital environment means that marketers must develop sustained data and media-driven marketing activities rich in content, with a high refresh-rate instead of parachuting one-off campaigns.

Agencies must acquire the skills in experiential marketing, user experience, digital media planning and buying, data analytics and measurement, and content publishing, and redesign a channel-neutral strategic communication process to take those into consideration. The instantaneous nature of digital requires clients and agencies to move at great speed and with great agility. That means re-engineering the process of producing quality work in matter of days, not weeks. The complex, labor-intensive nature of producing, measuring, and optimizing digital campaigns means that the cost structure of marketing has changed as well.

Agency Viewpoint

"Agency internal processes are very linear today. But in reality, it's no longer a straight line. Deliverables must be continually reworked and optimized. Currently that's not the way most agencies think or produce. They must adjust the way they work to accommodate client workflows and production in real time."

TIM WILLIAMS, President, Ignition Consulting Group

Clients must rethink how they budget, and how much they budget. And agencies must find innovative ways to reduce cost out of the system and work much more efficiently than they ever had to before. To go to market, they must go out of their silo and learn to collaborate with a wider number of vendors (content aggregators, media agencies, publishers, solution providers, and other marcom disciplines such as PR, and events) across the entire marketing supply chain. Responsibilities between agencies and clients must also be redefined as clients hire senior digital talent and build internal competencies such as data and measurement that are less transactional but core to their business. Cross-agency collaboration becomes critically more important in a digital world that is moving from messaging to experiential marketing.

Fostering Cross-Agency Collaboration

As agency models involving multiple agencies continue to grow in popularity, clients need their agency partners to collaborate effectively with each other. They want agencies that can think and work together, especially on integrated campaigns that often require multiple agency partners. Agencies have always used a number of subcontracting vendors and specialty agencies, but these relationships were for the most past invisible to clients. Now clients are stepping up to declare who they want to work with, making that collaboration must more transparent.

Agency collaboration is a much more involved undertaking than simple coordination. Agency collaboration ranges from sharing ideas or timely business information, brainstorming together on challenges, exchanging client assets for co-developing or bringing diverse perspectives. Cross-agency collaboration can take many shapes and is determined by the client's strategy and roster of agencies.

Client Viewpoint

"The amount of cross-agency collaboration expected and required is in direct relationship with the task at hand. We don't like to over-engineer processes or meetings so collaboration is not a requisite for all agency assignments. We find it effective to have the best minds working on the most important projects, whether it's for planning and strategic development or for an integrated campaign. In these cases we expect a high level of collaboration from the senior members of our agency teams. We foster collaboration in different ways, both formally through annual evaluations and planning sessions and informally via briefings and status meetings."

Charlie Silvestro
Vice President, Global Agency Operations, MasterCard Worldwide

Clients with centralized agency models like Ford and P&G will look to the holding company, the network, or the lead agency to assign one or multiple individuals to steer collaboration among the various agencies under their responsibility and more often than not, under one single P&L. Clients with more decentralized agency models are more likely to play the central role of collaboration internally to connect the dots and align efforts and priorities.

The Red Lounge Coca-Cola virtual agency model during the Beijing Olympic Games illustrated that a few agencies could come and work together, collocated in one office space, under one team name, under unbiased team leadership, and yet pursue one agenda. Following common principles, operating under common goals, and one bonus team incentive, they showed that even clients with decentralized agency resources can realize the benefits of cross-agency collaboration. Post-Olympic campaign, Coca-Cola decided to continue its Red Lounge approach to boost innovation and integration for its brand efforts in China.[55]

As in any partnership, the key to strong cross-agency collaborative efforts is trust and shared accountability. Clients play an important role in enabling effective collaborative efforts among its agency roster and creating cohesive, integrated agency teams. To overcome agencies' natural reluctance to collaborate due to competing interests or occasional land-grabbing, clients must define and declare clear and distinct roles and responsibilities for each agency.

A client must also articulate clear rules of engagement and document those formally so that everyone is clear about expectations, operating principles, and agreed protocols for future agency to agency engagements. Clients can document these expectations into a service-level agreement or an agency to agency playbook. No matter how committed each agency is to cross-agency collaboration, it is likely a client will need to occasionally intervene when disagreements occur and provide a path for resolution and decision.

Clients can unify agency teams by rewarding team work and collective results instead of individual agencies using spot bonuses or by incorporating this into an existing pay for performance-based agreement. Clients should also consider ways to acknowledge team work at agency summits or regular meetings or by sending words of encouragement and appreciation to the various teams.

It doesn't mean that the individual contribution of an agency should not be acknowledged or taken into consideration. But the agencies must learn that they win or lose together on their client's behalf. Some accomplish this by establishing peer recognition rewards that encourage cross-agency nominations and highlights those teams or individuals most committed to team success. Some clients will gather their agencies once or several times a year to foster a collaborative approach to solving client issues and aligning their collective efforts against key company priorities. Clients benefit from agencies that share mutual trust and respect for each other, are working together productively, and interacting openly.

They also benefit from agencies that follow an unambiguous decision-making process which prioritizes the end product of the collaboration rather than the individual parts each agency is contributing to. Clients must encourage agency partners to come together as "Castellers of Catalonia" would. An 18th century tradition in the southern part of Catalonia, members of a team come together to form a human tower up to ten levels high and several hundred people.

It starts with a strong foundation of packed bodies, holding arms, and hands together. The base provides strength and stability to the structure. Then teammates climb on the shoulders of the ones below, one layer at a time, working together to build a unified, connected structure that is based on strength, coordination, trust and balance. Without it, the structure would fall and break apart.

Client Viewpoint

"To get most value from their agencies, companies must consider agencies as part of their own team."

BRETT COLBERT
Global Manager, Procurement Advertising, Anheuser Busch InBev

Putting to the Test the Culture of Partnership

Are all disagreements bad? Good client/agency relationships tend to gravitate toward positive professional experiences where both parties come to agreement on how to complete work assignments. However it doesn't mean that good relationships are free of conflicts. To the contrary. Conflicts are a healthy part of any relationship. It's not uncommon to see strong agencies and clients in prosperous partnerships embracing occasional feisty conflicts that bring out the best of the partnership.

Actually, a certain amount of tension is desired, as agencies respectfully question the client's strategy, seek to validate key research and business assumptions, ask challenging questions, or simply challenge the status quo because someone should. As a result, they often push them in new directions and unfamiliar territories. Can they disagree respectfully? They can do this in a constructive way, not for the sake of arguing, but to look at things from a multitude of angles. They can afford to challenge their clients because they've built enough equity in the "relationship" bank account that they can draw from when things occasionally go side-ways.

Thinking differently is an asset. This is an important part of the value realized by working with a third party like an agency that has no vested interest in getting the client to explore new approaches to existing challenges. Let's face it. There is no shortage of "Yes" people to support clients in their decisions. Agencies seek new perspectives that clients wouldn't consider unless challenged to do so. It takes a special client to welcome a healthy dose of tension in the relationship without getting to the point where it turns into a major distraction or an unpleasant, unproductive partnership.

There are good and bad conflicts. Good conflicts encourage clients and agencies to step outside of their comfort zone, requiring them to think constructively to deal with their differences of views and opinions. They usually influence the work to be more creative, more breakthrough in nature and less conventional or middle of the road. Bad conflicts are sources of strain in a partnership. Bad conflicts are those where no consensus or compromise can be reached and there is no win-win scenario allowing both parties to feel understood or simply appreciated.

There are a number of behaviors that clients should be on the lookout for that are the best predictors of a failed relationship. Gottman refers to the Four Horsemen of the Apocalypse. Although not all of them would apply to the business environment, a few seem to fit well with unhealthy client/agency relationships: criticism, defensiveness, contempt, and stonewalling. Who really wants to be in a relationship where one is misunderstood, criticized, unappreciated, feels excluded or is constantly worried?

Mutual Accountability in Asymmetric Relationships

There is no shortage of references to mutual client/agency accountability in speeches at industry events by agency leaders or their clients. In any partnership, alignment of objectives naturally implies a sense of accountability equally shared by both parties. Common interests and objectives keep partners aligned. The reality might be slightly different. After all, the client/agency relationships can be seen as asymmetrical for the most part. It doesn't mean joint accountability. Each party has a role to play to make the partnership successful. Most partnerships are built on mutual respect, trust, and integrity. Both should set high standards and demand each party to do what's needed to deliver according to their expectations.

Client Viewpoint

"I find mutual accountability a pretty hard concept to bring to life, especially given that someone is writing the check and someone else is cashing it."

JEFF DEVON, Director Global Marketing, HP

There are two primary school of thoughts among the client community on how to motivate agencies and foster a strong partnership: the carrot or the stick. The "stick" approach is based on the concept that there is a subordinate relationship between the client and the agency that is often the result of mistrust and lack of appreciation for what the agency can do. The agency is always on the defensive and constantly fears that it might lose the account. The relationship is not of equal weight and the client does not miss an opportunity to intimidate or pressure the agency. Whether it is by design or not, the work ultimately suffers and the relationship is doomed to fail in the long run.

The "carrot" approach is about treating agencies as trusted partners, motivating the agency to do well, by recognizing good work and rewarding exceptional performance. It is based on honesty, trust and respect. The result is better, stronger collaboration, healthier relationships, more innovation and greater performance. The agency doesn't have to play it safe. The agency is less restricted, can be more creative, argue more openly, be more transparent, and more entrepreneurial. The agency is motivated to give its very best to the client. The relationship is likely to prosper and last. Gottman says that people who stay married live four years longer than people who don't. Something tells me it might be true in business as well. But who really wants to find out?

Client Viewpoint

"We all have a part in making these relationships work as they do a great deal of the actual work on our behalf. Good relationships will yield desirable results. Relationships left unattended won't."

MIKE DELMAN, VP Global Marketing Xbox, Microsoft Corp.

{Taking Immediate Action}

TOP 5

BEST PRACTICES TO HARNESS THE MADNESS

❶ Make your agency accountable for driving measurable business results. Turn your relationship into a true strategic partnership by making your agency accountable for driving measureable results.

❷ Let your agency challenge conventional thinking, challenge status quo, challenge your ways of doing things, and take calculated risks. Reward people for doing this.

❸ Demand the best agency talent in your business. Compensate fairly for it. Apply these top resources wisely.

❹ Provide clear direction, give unrestricted access to critical information and senior management. Make decisions and stick to them.

❺ Listen to what your agency tell you it needs in order to be successful. Ask for contact reports to ensure everyone is on the same page. Foster a culture of open dialog and direct feedback. Be appreciative always, and celebrate successes.

11 A BRAVE NEW WORLD

A glimpse at the future and what it means to agency/ client relations

"One's destination is never a place . . . but rather a new way of looking at things."

—Henry Miller
American novelist and painter

If the world of marketing and the business of agencies are moving in such fast and frantic motion, where are they going? How is the marketing landscape changing the way we engage with customers? How is the advertiser-agency-media relationship evolving? How are disruptive technologies transforming the marketing value chain and agency offerings? How do we best leverage their competencies? As digital in everything becomes ubiquitous, how do agencies differentiate themselves? What should agencies do less or do more to make themselves more valuable to their clients? What do the client and the agency of the future look like? And how do we best prepare for it? So many questions, so little time. It seems as if everyone is running fast to take the lead, with divergent opinions as to where this is all going.

To illustrate that point, let's take a look at a company that knows quite a bit about running: Nike. But what is Nike to runners and people like you and me? Is that the company that sells me shoes and running gear? Or is it my one destination to manage my workouts and a trusted iconic brand that helps me manage an important part of my life? And which of these approaches has the best chance to build a lasting, loyal and profitable relationship with customers?

It starts with celebrating the unique YOU with NIKEiD. NIKEiD's site allows you to custom design your own sneakers and store your designs in myLOCKER, a personal storage space on the site. But Nike takes a step further and builds brand experiences that go beyond being just an athletic footwear, apparel, equipment, and accessories company. Nike+ helps you track your distance, pace, time, and burn calories while you run. After the workout, you can upload their stats to the Nike+ site where you can set goals, track your progress, access various tools such as Nike Coach that improve your runs and provide training schedules designed by professional coaches. You can discover new running tracks on a map, join challenges such as the Human Race10K and connect with friends, and the Nike community, the world's largest running club. This is what I call a brave new world, courtesy of Nike's main agency Wieden+Kennedy and digital shop R/GA (IPG).

"A brave new world" also happens to be the title of a book by Aldous Huxley published in the 1930s that speaks to new developments and technology that would eventually change society. In a way, the convergence of creativity and technology in marketing is changing society as well. The digital age has generously fed into a Western culture of togetherness, immediacy, and instant gratification, bringing more change in the past two decades than the ad industry has experienced in half a century. The digital age provides far more than a foundation for brand storytelling. The 24/7 availability of products and services at anyone's fingertips has accelerated customer realization that they are in control. Consumers have learned that they are stronger together and can influence the companies that serve them in dynamic two-way forums.

Client Viewpoint

"Digital is no longer about eyeballs, it is about customer engagement. Digital is becoming a major customer engagement platform. So Digital agencies are no longer running the show and the might see their role diminished overtime as clients step up their own leadership in this critical area of their business."

LYNNE SEID, Partner Global Marketing Officers Practice, Heidrick & Struggles

Advertising and marketing communication is not only adapting to the technology-empowered consumer culture; it's leading it in many ways. Companies are finding ways to give customers choice about how they communicate with them, how often and on what channels, over products and services customized to meet the unique needs of each customer. At the heart of the relationship between a brand and a customer is the opportunity for brands to become customer destinations that go beyond their original static identify to interactive experiences that brings life to a brand.

From Xbox's Halo "Believe" virtual experience, Adidas's Augmented Reality (AR)'s Originals Neighborhood,[56] Volkswagen's GTI Racing game, "In The Motherhood" online efforts, Burger King's Xbox trio branded videogame to Dove's "Evolution" viral sensation, great successes in marketing are clearly coming from the engaging, immersive, and viral nature of the brand experience.

Every phenomenon we are now experiencing, from the globalization of the marketplace to new social media, all result from rapid development in technology and the digitalization of everything in our personal and professional lives. In the brave new digital world, agencies now build brand digital experiences on their client's behalf that redefine the notion of the brand itself.

Although it is not done in isolation and is instead part of a broader effort, it changes the way customers interact with companies, dialog with them, transact with them, and build connections that transcend the limits of the traditional physical world as we knew it. These changes in the way we build more direct, value based connections between brands and consumers are impacted by markets and consumer trends and a number of complex developments to redefine how clients and agencies partner with each other.

Death at a Funeral

Consumers rely on the intricate web of signals that make up a brand to help them make a final buying decision they are comfortable with. The brand becomes the de facto decision criteria, assuming the price is perceived as reasonable. Consumers will continue to rely on brand perception to sort through vast amounts of information and misinformation to make, or more often justify, that purchasing decision they have mentally made. Unfortunately, consumers have learned to distrust advertising, the clutter, the irrelevance of messaging, and the constant interruptions it generates. They now proactively block advertisements, using technology such as DVRs and pop-up blockers, even paying premium services to avoid advertising. Building and nurturing brands, even in the face of an advertising-adverse audience is something that agencies do well by trade, and as a result, their unique perspective becomes increasingly more valuable to their clients.

They know what it takes to increase the relevancy of the brand to different customer segments and position it well against the competition. They know how to amplify the brand expression through a robust mix of marketing communications, so that their clients speak with one consistent voice in the marketplace. They know how to reach consumers in meaningful ways and make the brand an incredibly powerful asset on the balance sheet.

Agency Viewpoint

"As we go from brand-to-consumer messaging to consumer-to-consumer messaging, agencies must determine how they play in that world and add value to clients. Most agencies rarely go beyond the 'pre-purchase' phase in the customer lifecycle. Helping their clients with the actual brand experience in the 'purchase' and 'post-purchase' phases will not only provide much needed value to clients, but represents important new revenue stream opportunities for agencies."

TIM WILLIAMS, President, Ignition Consulting Group

The core principles of brand management are still vibrant and vital to the offering of an agency. The ability to embrace and energize brand principles and deliver solutions that bring the brand to life in every piece of communication has always been vital to an agency's success. But they are now facing new unprecedented challenges.

The traditional marketing model of mass production and analog marketing is obsolete. Advertisers can no longer rely solely on traditional media to move their business forward. Advertisers have been shifting their marketing spend to more effective disciplines. Marketing services have experienced tremendous growth in the past decade and the category is expected to continue to grow more rapidly than traditional advertising. Or at the expense of traditional advertising during a slower economy. Holding companies like WPP see their revenues generated from marketing services rapidly exceeding those previously dominated by advertising services. Advertising will continue to play an important role in the mix, now most frequently confined to driving awareness and buzz.

Client Viewpoint

"Digital agencies must learn to apply their skills to traditional advertising or direct marketing services. And traditional advertising and direct marketing agencies must continue to rapidly build digital skills. In the future, I believe pure digital agencies as defined today will cease to exist."

TOM CHETRICK
VP Advertising and Marketing Services, Bristol-Myers Squibb

Marketing services range from public relations, direct/database marketing, events marketing and sponsorship, brand consulting, design production, retail marketing, vertical industry-focused such as pharmaceutical, and a vast and rapidly growing category: digital/interactive marketing. These services can be best characterized by the fact that their strength doesn't come from scale as in traditional advertising, but from applied insight and discipline execution, not from artists, writers, or big idea tanks, but from various specialty consultants, programmers, data analysts, and optimization experts.

The growth of marketing services has been fueled mostly by marketers' continued interest in more targeted, measurable, accountable marketing vehicles and by agencies finding inspiration in delivering creative ideas on everything from the Internet to gaming devices and smartphones as consumer habits and interactions continues to shift.

Perhaps this trend is further accentuated by the higher cost of traditional media resulting from the increased fragmentation in broadcast media and a shift in media consumption habits (less time spent watching TV but more time playing games, using computers and Twittering), making marketing services attractive substitutes to advertising.

The years of the lavish TV production budget and standout 30-second spot placed on extravagant Super Bowl buys are now waning while advertisers desperately looking for new ways to bring meaning to their platforms. It appears as if traditional forms of media are slowing dying. Years ago, prime-time network television had such broad reach that advertisers were pretty certain to hit their target audience even with an inefficient buy. Now network television events of large scale—those in excess of 90 million viewers (such as the World Cup, the Olympics, and the Super Bowl) are in such limited supply that the cost has reached new heights: A 30-second spot reaching 90 million viewers like the Super Bowl will cost you over $2.5M in media alone. Network cost per thousand continues to rise faster than inflation.

Furthermore, the introduction of new consumer-empowering technologies such as DVR, giving audiences the ability to fast-forward or skip commercials altogether, is testing the viability of traditional advertising as we know it. It also forces brand advertisers to consider a variety of innovative sponsorship or programming opportunities to overcome these new challenges.

Agency Viewpoint

"The real impact of new technology is still based on story value and drama. Some new technology can really carry story and humanity—look at the iPod or streaming video. Lots of other stuff is merely a passing yo-yo that seems interesting for a few minutes and is gone."

JEFF GOODBY
Co-Chairman and Creative Director, Goody, Silverstein & Partners

Clients are shifting budgets to invest in podcasting, Webcasting, and videos sometimes intentionally shot on inexpensive digital video equipment to end up on YouTube. They are integrating these new tactics into their mainstream marketing plans. This is the world of Windows Media Center, TiVo and AppleTV. This is the rapid convergence of TV, the Web, and mobile. With the convergence of analog and digital, interactive displays, touch technology and digital signage appear both in stores and outdoors at malls and public places around the country, to communicate targeted and contextually relevant content to shoppers at the point of purchase. This connects consumers to fully immersive brand experiences.

Agencies must now look for new flavors of skills and talent in order to compete and thrive. Everyone at the agency must be fluent in the digital art form and science.

This phenomenon is also leading to the fragmentation of agency services. Under the traditional advertising service model, creative, and media disciplines allowed agencies to build scale and operational efficiencies. As agencies migrate to diverse marketing services, the number of

Client Viewpoint

"The world is changing. Traditional agencies have to shift their focus, have to think differently. The digital landscape is growing fast as clients like Ford invest more heavily in it. From an agency resource perspective, digital has a huge impact. After all, Digital is not an afterthought. It is no longer a linear process either."

SUSAN MARKOWICZ, Global Advertising Agency Manager, Ford Motor Company specialized offerings is likely to increase, making it challenging for them to replicate the scale and cost efficiencies they enjoyed from their traditional services. This loss in efficiency translates into higher cost for advertisers, who no longer benefit from the agencies' economies of scale.

By necessity, agencies will increasingly invest in specialized services that address the fragmentation of customer access points, differentiate them from their competition and begin to rebuild a profitable business. Higher profitability will enable them to invest in R&D and talent, and as a result, develop even more powerful offerings. To stand out, advertisers will embrace these new capabilities, even at higher cost. It will require advertisers to apply thoughtful consideration, relying heavily on a highly-tuned discipline of agency management to select, manage, and optimize these rapidly evolving relationships. They need to deal with a richer, larger set of agencies, operating with different business models and with unique and distinct engagements.

Digital Everywhere. For Everything.

Digital is not only a medium or a marketing discipline; it is a profound social and cultural force in today's society and economy. Digital is the reason behind the powerful and seamless blending of technology, branded entertainment, and media. The era of interrupting media is over. The post dot.com fallout didn't alter the ineluctable rise of advertising spend on the Web at the expense of other more traditional media. Digital media are pervasive and have revolutionized the way we talk to consumers, plan and execute campaigns, buy media and measure results. Digital enables "always on" marketing compared to the traditional "campaign drop"-based approach, changing the way clients and agencies must work together.

Client Viewpoint

"The marketing landscape is rapidly evolving. At the core of this rapid evolution is technology, technology, technology. It's impacting how we think and how we execute."

BRETT COLBERT
Global Manager, Procurement Advertising, Anheuser Busch InBev

The way information reaches audiences today is as equally impactful as the message itself. Media is considered by many to be the new "creative." Whether GPS-based messaging on smart phones, touch displays such as Microsoft Surface™ in retail, in-gaming or game console opportunities, advancements in SEO/SEA or set-top box functionality, digital media have forced us as advertisers and marketers to think differently about the timing, relevancy and contextual nature of the multitude of communication channels and social networks in which messages are distributed or conversations are held. Often the medium dictates the nature of the message, gaining life organically in active social webs. Advertisers can no longer rely on behavioral assumptions and inferences developed based on viewer demographics. They now have access to rich predictive behavioral data about actions of customers.

The radical and lasting transformation of the landscape propelled by the rapid growth of digital has not given traditional agencies much time for reflection. It has pushed them into reactive mode as they attempt to defend their endangered client territories against sparkly new capabilities sported by small digitally-savvy boutique shops. Countless analyst reports and articles in trade publications have thoroughly convinced clients and agencies alike that the trends are pointing to a bright and bold future for digital marketing.

The phenomenal growth and dynamic nature of digital media in all facets of our lives (the digital lifestyle as you might call it), societies, and economies has opened remarkable new opportunities for brand advertisers to engage and influence their audiences and provide consumers with an immersive convergent experience. In the era of Linedin and Flipcams, the new currency of the brand to consumer exchange is utility and value.

A new kind of agency is emerging addressing a more demanding consumer and evolved marketing department. Today, digital agencies are challenging traditional agencies in the way they approach clients. Large digital agencies and their holding companies have created R&D units or technology think tanks such as WPP Digital, IPG Emerging Media Lab, Publicis' Denuo and Vivaki Nerve Center, and OMG Digital, among many others, to push the development of new technologies in advertising and stir their future investments.[57]

They break the silos of marketing and technology, aligning priorities and erasing inefficiencies. They innovate constantly. They build prototypes and pilots to push the limit of what's possible. They leverage communities and crowd sourcing. They develop proprietary software solutions for desktop and mobile computing, interactive television and new form factors as those enter the marketplace. They build applications for iPhone, Windows Mobile and Android devices which become new sources of revenue and deeper branded customer experiences.

They hire technologists, data analysts, programmers, social media experts, and storytellers to build these online tools, applications, and communities, rather than using the Internet as another media channel to simply deliver punchy headlines, key words in search engines, microsites or fancy banner ads. Digital communications deliver unique addressability, immediacy, flexibility, and undeniable measurability.

Agency Viewpoint

"Fair compensation. Hiring the very best people—on their side and on ours— or the job at hand. The rest, as always, is about relationships that allow us to tell each other the truth."

JEFF GOODBY
Co-Chairman and Creative Director, Goody, Silverstein & Partners

While marketing budgets are no longer growing as fast as the GDP, they find themselves having to do more with less, spending their budget more effectively on higher return, higher-accountability marketing vehicles. If marketing budgets spent on digital media are proportionally smaller than the percent of consumer's overall time consuming digital media, it's not for long.

Budgets will follow consumer media preferences and will soon make up for the existing gap. Don't get me wrong: There are years ahead for traditional media. The only question unanswered is how far and how long the trend will continue until we reach a level of saturation of fragmented new media channels that make once again traditional media seem efficient and attractive, at least for a short while.

In light of this rapid growth in online media, there are growing concerns about the future of TV as we know it today, which remains for now the world's largest advertising vehicle. The area of the omnipotent TV commercial may no longer be but rest assured, TV will not go away. No doubt, consumers have assumed full control of their media consumption today. Consequently, TV will likely become increasingly digital and more interactively connected to other media to survive, completing the fusion of two powerful communication technologies.Regardless of the mix of new vs. traditional media, the multi-billion dollar advertising industry is expected to continue to grow to new levels, fueled by expanding Internet applications and companies wanting to establish a local or global footprint in a highly competitive landscape.

CFOs are asking CMOs to step up to greater fiscal accountability by investing into media outlets that allow them to test, scale, and optimize based on measurable marketing performance. These media outlets are allowing for more efficient targeting and are providing a new level of customer interaction, not only with products and brands but also among individuals, customers, partners, and brand advocates who are seeking venues to share experience and build their own personal brands. As a result, Google, Microsoft, and others are rushing to establish their lead position in the highly-measurable multi-billion plus global digital market, with revenues dominated by Website creation and selling advertising on search pages, key portals, and social sites.

The race for supremacy in the technology of advertising, deciding how we create, purchase, deliver, and analyze ads, is well under way and key contenders have shown up with their checkbooks wide open: Google spent $3.1 billion to acquire DoubleClick. WPP spent over $600 million to acquire 24/7 Real Media and Microsoft acquired aQuantive for over $6 billion to compete and stay in the game. These technologies serve a range of advertising objectives for advertisers, agencies, and publishers.

In this convoluted marketing and media ecosystem where there are increasingly blurry lines between software, media, and advertising, everyone seems to compete for marketing dollars and for IP. Are they friends or foes? Often referred as "frenemies,"[58] a term associated with Sir Martin Sorrell, CEO of WPP Group, companies like Google and holding companies like Publicis and WPP are partnering and competing at the same time, adding complexity for clients as to who does what or where to place bets. Advertising technology companies are building increasingly efficient ad delivery solutions, producing customer data and rich analytics, generating audience insights and automating virtually every step in the marketing funnel.

It's about delivering ROI and analytical tools to understand in real time how effective the various elements of the campaign are. It's also about automating the production and optimization of advertising. The automation goes as far as turning a single set of digital assets into hundreds, if not thousands, of unique ad combinations and permutations from audience profiles, and driven by actual results as in the case of Yahoo! SmartAds.[59]

Clients understand for the most part the value that agencies provide as trusted advisors and creative storytellers, but are less motivated to pay for the actual production and delivery of the multitude of variants on the laborious work itself. These auto-generated creative units are composed of various creatives and offer elements dynamically built based on pages searched and a myriad of profiling information available. Some of these tools offer a one-stop system to streamline client and agency workflows, the search and exchange of information, and the storage and distribution of marketing assets (creative units, videos, campaigns, etc.) It also improves the speed and quality of the transactional nature of relationships in the supply chain, removing the inefficiency and complexity that result from using separate tracking and billing systems with disparate data sources.

Agency Viewpoint

"Innovation in technology is changing the marketing game. Technology also allows agencies to move at the speed of business better, servicing clients the way they need to be serviced. The downside of technology is managing an expectation that technology enables agencies to create faster. That process should not be rushed, in my opinion. No one wins when ideas are half-baked."

MARC A. BROWNSTEIN
President and CEO, Brownstein Group

Agencies that use digital as a starting point to solve a marketing problem are better positioned to tap into the growth of digital media than agencies that look at it from a lens focused on which media the creative will appear in. It's about customer, not media centricity. As a result, media agencies and their "customer connection" planning departments have emerged as one of the most strategic assets to clients struggling to keep up and leverage an ever-complicated and rapidly changing media universe.

Digital-born agencies are more likely to succeed than agencies that are "transforming" themselves to be digitally-savvy. They understand how to bridge the gap between creative ideas and technical specs. Real success is not only gaining the technical acumen, it's about approaching the assignment from a different perspective, consistently innovating, experimenting, and remaining open to ideas that might sometimes spring from consumers themselves.

Agencies will continue to invest in their IT departments, ThinkTanks and R&D to incubate and experiment with new technologies. They will develop tools and applications on multiple platforms, identify M&A opportunities, depose patents, and secure strategic partnerships and alliances. Some of these agencies are turning into comprehensive software development entities, creating alternative sources of revenue.

It's about looking at digital media as opportunities to interact and engage audiences with experiences that augment the brand's relevancy to its customers and its impact, not as electronic billboards to blast messages to. It's about absolute media-neutrality.

Because digital is increasingly considered the entry point for the marketing idea, we will see more and more digital agencies take a lead, interdisciplinary role for clients that require both digital and traditional solution. This is evidenced by agencies like R/GA, Razorfish and AKQA handling both digital and other more traditional duties such as TV, direct mail, or print for some clients.

Consolidation will continue for years to come as agencies expand their offering to stay competitive. The content agencies create to engage audience has to be both informative and entertaining. So they must collaborate to provide richer integrated customer experiences, partnering with media outlets, content owners, entertainment companies and publishers. Not unlike the iPhone commercial "There's an App for That," there is an experience to be created for every audiences. Digital agencies will continue to grow in scale and importance in the years ahead, enjoying the benefits of being more agile than "old-school" agencies and therefore adapting to market changes more readily and ultimately, more successfully.

When everything is finally "digital," technical competencies will no longer be a relevant point of differentiation for agencies. It will be how agencies use data to improve customer brand experiences, optimize marketing campaigns and help clients make better decisions. Encouraged by clients, agencies will continue to invest in building or leveraging technologies such as phone apps, Amplified Reality, Online Couponing, community tools, and many others that enhance consumer brand experiences, but also streamline the flow and exchange of information within their agency as well between clients, content suppliers, and publishers.

The electrical appliance company Electrolux, for example, is using Adstream across the company's advertising supply chain to handle its print and broadcasting work in sixteen territories in Europe and to manage its campaigns and marketing resources worldwide. Agencies are implementing sophisticated collaboration solutions, resource management, and asset management systems as the agency's operations backbone. They are implementing semi- or fully-automated workflows to manage timelines and resources, to upload estimates, billings, briefs, concepts and creative approvals with the triple goal of improving time to market, reducing costs, and operating more effectively than their competitors. They are hiring Chief Content Officers and investing in vital content management and digital asset management systems.

Critical milestones and activities are tracked and reported real-time, providing a comprehensive and transparent view of every job. Information and assets can be easily shared and distributed. Agencies and clients alike are increasingly likely to source solutions from the large-scale, data consolidators and one-stop digital advertising operating vendors. The end result is greater insight, better targeting, greater efficiencies, and a much more dynamic, real-time exchange.

Client Viewpoint

"The marketing landscape is rapidly changing with more and more things being driven online and the acceleration of rich, paid or free, consumer-based online content and social media, to meet new demands. Agencies will help their clients navigate that landscape in the year ahead."

JULIE GIBBS, Director, Corporate Brand Marketing, Campaign Management, Adobe

The Power of ~~"YOU"~~ "US"

From customization to personalization, everything is done to ensure that consumers engage with products through having control, which they always had in a binary fashion, but without the explicit convenience and experience of customization that is now commonplace. On its December 2006 cover page, *Time Magazine* surprised everyone by introducing the Person of the Year: "You." "You control the Information Age. Welcome to your world." The balance of power has permanently shifted from advertiser to consumer in what some call the "democratization of marketing." Technology is opening up options to advertisers they never had before, turning the tables to talking less and listening more. Digital makes everything participatory and transactional.

As a result, customers engage more as well and companies are turning it into a competitive weapon. In the case of Doritos' annual ad contest, the brand's biggest fans get the opportunity to create and submit Doritos-themed commercials, then vote online to determine the few lucky ones that are to be aired during the Super Bowl. Advertisers want their customers to tell in their own words the brand's story.

Digital media are inherently social. OfficeMax's popular holiday viral sensation "Elf Yourself," powered by JibJab and created by Toy New York and EVB in 2006, is an excellent example of what clients can do to engage consumers and invite them to share their experience with others. Advertisers gain immediate audience insight. They have the opportunity to be responsive, and agile, adapting their messaging in real time and treating consumers with a greater level of attention, leading to higher customer satisfaction and brand advocacy. Today's knowledgeable consumers turn out to be willing programmers, media producers, publishers, and distributors all at once, using blogs, community forums, social networks and digital word of mouth vehicles to help brands tell their stories in authentic ways.

Agency Viewpoint

"The marketing landscape is changing at light speed. People's relation to media is changing. Media is part of their life and is getting more personal through social networks they trust. Social builds emotions, word of mouth, connections. You can build strong brands in social media. The connection to brands is increasingly more personal. So the marketing world must become more personal as well. And so should agencies."

DAVID KENNY
Managing Partner, Vivaki

What has been described as the age of interruption to describe methods used to grab attention to break through and stimulate unconscious desires in consumer's psyche, is long gone. Companies are now looking to actively, continuously, and deeply engage consumers with their brand, establishing a unique and compelling brand connection through personalized brand experiences.

This phenomenon doesn't come without challenges. The metaphor of a marketing funnel where the buying process happens in a very linear way is obsolete. This deliberate engagement is enabled through tools and vehicles that help advertisers generate value beyond transactions, based on their active involvement, interactions, and dialogs with the brand. The spread of broadband-connected PCs and mobile devices is accelerating the number of options for consumers and therefore for advertisers, transforming the dialog from a one-way monologue to a rich conversation with user-generated content and social networks of engaged customers weighing in.

We are learning about the complex consumer interactions taking place in new social environments or within a particular a social segment. It's permanently changing the way we think about the role of marketing. It's no longer a selling medium on which we sell products but a user-controlled vehicle by which we let consumers engage with, share and buy our products and services.

It's about marketing messaging as conversations. Social media are now considered "mainstream."

Advertisers are furiously scratching their heads as they wonder: At what cost and at what return? We are witnessing both a cultural and business phenomenon of magnitude. It's about customer enablement and empowerment, not intrusive, random, or unwanted push communications.

Participation becomes the currency of customer value and a critical way clients are measuring marketing performance. Advertisers are realizing that relevant messages through an online event or activity are more effective long term than 15 or 10-seconds spots as they draw a stronger level of engagement and deeper, richer dialogs. Social media are changing the conversation between the consumer and the advertiser, using communities to spread as ripples on water.

Agencies are encouraging advertisers to think of new ways to reach and retain customers. They are facilitating conversations, promoting the use of new technologies and media channels from Twitter, foursquare™ to iPhone, Android or Windows applications.

Agencies are tapping into the highly social and immersive nature of the digital world to create value-add, engaging experiences that supersede the traditional means of intrusive marketing techniques that turn off consumers. Agencies are generators of emotionally engaging, intellectually stimulating ideas and the digital world offers them a platform to express clients brand messages in creative new ways. As a result, advertisers now benefit from improved, innovative, more measurable technology solutions.

Client Viewpoint

"I would anticipate that the really smart agencies will make the digital agency concept obsolete by building the right degree of digital expertise into their core offerings."

AMY FULLER, Group Executive Worldwide Consumer Marketing, MasterCard Worldwide

What are the implications for agencies and advertisers moving forward? AKQA's Ajaz Ahmed superbly captured the essence of the rising dichotomy between two industries clashing out of simple necessity: "In many ways, the worlds of Madison Avenue and Silicon Valley are thousands of miles apart. In general, the advertising industry tends to be very conservative. The traditional advertising industry is reluctant to change while the technology industry is about relentless innovation."[60]

To adapt to this changing environment, traditional advertising agencies will need to change the way they approach client problems, experiment more aggressively, invest in research and tech labs to put consumer trends and technologies at the center of what they do.

This new breed of agencies will need to adapt their hiring strategy to attract talent that is culturally immersed into these trends and develop deep know-how on how to tap into them. They will continue to invest in knowledge-sharing and advanced collaboration and community-building tools, embracing internally new ways of working and adopting the rich tools and capabilities they are building for clients.

In return, advertisers must carefully evaluate their agencies for their ability to embrace, master and skillfully capitalize on these new participatory capabilities. This customer-centric, experience-driven way of thinking and going to market is not only changing how marketing is executed, it's also changing how advertisers must determine campaign objectives and campaign metrics.

The World Just Got Flatter

It's no longer enough for business executives to simply have a global mindset. It's about thinking and acting global. Arguably, every company on this planet is a global company thanks in part to widespread proliferation of Internet and the information age. The twenty-first century has participated in a global race for industrial and trade supremacy in all industries, with small to large companies entering international markets to offshore production, to find new distribution channels and new audiences. Global clients are looking to global agencies to support their marketing efforts in each of their subsidiaries, balancing global consistency with local responsiveness.

Client Viewpoint

"The marketing landscape is changing rapidly and is likely to change the agency industry as a result. New models are likely to emerge from it. From a communication standpoint, we are seeing the US market getting increasingly diverse and multicultural. Agencies are building competencies to be relevant to these many audiences."

CLAUDIA LEZCANO, Director of Advertising, Burger King Corp.

U.S. markets are increasingly more important to global companies as emerging markets outpace the growth of the U.S. and mature economies. Greater China is already a large and fast growing market for agency holding companies. By any measure, China and India's economic expansion is phenomenal. Thomas L. Friedman, without a doubt, said it best in his national bestseller about the history of the twenty-first century: *The World is Flat*, where he so eloquently points out the unstoppable globalization with compelling examples.

In his book entitled *The Clash of Civilizations and the Remaking of World Order*, Samuel Huntington reminds us that "It took the U.S. forty-seven years to double the per capita output, but Japan did it in thirty-three years, Indonesia in seventeen, South Korea in eleven and China in ten." If China is to become the world's largest economy, followed closely by India, and Asia is to have 70% of the ten largest economies in 2020, it is clear that the world of advertising as we know it now will look much different, especially given their unique cultural, social and economical DNA. Furthermore, globalization will not only come from Western cultures tapping into the incredible size of these populations but also from the growth of Asian-based multinationals, from Japan (Sony), South Korea (LG, Hyundai), China (Konka, Lenovo) and India (Infosys, Tata).

A predominant share of advertising investments is still coming from the United States, followed by Europe and Asia Pacific, Latin America, Middle East and Africa. So it's no surprise that some of the world's largest agencies and network holding companies (Omnicom and IPG) are headquartered in the United States since the world's largest brands—Coca-Cola, GE, Intel, and Disney—are U.S. based companies..

Although sources may vary, we can reasonably estimate these spends to be a growing part of the economy of any developed or mature country and to experience a disproportionately rapid growth in emerging markets such as Brazil, Russia, India, and China (BRIC). Outside of the U.S., U.K., France, Germany, and Japan are leading the pack in terms of advertising, marketing, and communication expenditures as one would expect as economic superpowers. U.K. and France are predominant markets, which explains why the other largest network holding companies (WPP, Publicis and Havas) are headquartered there.

Asia Pacific is showing tremendous growth potential and is expected to be a predominant market in years ahead, reducing the overall share of the U.S. and Europe. With over one third of the population living in China or India, there is no doubt that these emerging economic forces will witness incredible growth, perhaps to exceed the U.S. within a decade or two. Agencies will not only be expected to understand and talk to these new audiences as their existing clients attempt to seize market share in Asia Pacific countries, they will also need to service them as clients.

Agencies want to make themselves more appealing to global clients of partners with similarly ubiquitous international footprints. In a global marketplace, strong ideas can originate from anywhere. A new ad in the U.S. might originate today from a successful campaign originally created in China or in Italy. Agencies are exploring near-shoring and off-shoring solutions paired with innovative technology to provide clients with skilled yet inexpensive labor markets to reduce execution costs. They have realized that producing high speed, low-value deliverables within their existing agency infrastructure is not economically viable or sustainable. Taking work abroad to produce creative and digital assets (Websites, email, online display ads, and others) en mass and inexpensively is gaining interest from advertisers looking to reduce their costs and to maximize flexibility and efficiency.

Publicis' Digitas launched in 2007 a creative solution pairing innovation in technology and execution called Prodigious Worldwide, a company dedicated to offering Publicis, Saatchi & Saatchi, Digitas and Leo Burnet clients a global low cost digital alternative to traditional production with certified partners in China, Costa Rica, India, Czech Republic and many others. OgilvyOne Worldwide created Redworks, a high speed, low cost production capability to improve creative and production efficiencies with low cost hubs in exotic places like Kuala Lumpur, Bangalore, Dhaka or Bratislava to name a few.

Many agencies have built or are launching similar solutions with deliverables based pricing and low cost production capability. Network holding companies will continue to invest heavily outside of the United States to expand their global reach, especially in rapidly growing economies and emerging markets. Agencies also want to reap the revenue and profit-enhancing benefits of rapidly expanding markets, where advertising expenditures are mirroring and driving economic growth.

Historically, global advertisers only considered agencies with a global network to serve their offices around the world. Global advertisers who want to take their brand worldwide and want to speak as one voice must now either partner with an agency with local offices in each geography to take a common messaging framework and adapt it locally or with adequate advertising delivery technology to handle the translation, adaptation, and delivery worldwide. Some partner with companies like Tag Worldwide to streamline the process of getting assets to the right geography without the expense of a global agency. The end goal is for the work to resonate with local audiences around the world.

With the globalization of the marketplace and a workforce increasingly more diverse and specialized, agencies are building low cost offerings or centers of excellence in Latin America, Europe or Asia Pacific where operating costs and talent can be found.

This is a trend that is not likely to reverse anytime soon simply by looking at the way the economic and geo-political landscape is shaping. Today, even domestic advertisers with no current global ambitions should consider agencies with a global network to take advantage of the cost efficiencies and broad set of capabilities organized in centers of excellence that only these global agencies can offer. Although domestic agencies, creative boutiques and other local agencies are likely to maintain an important role in the agency ecosystem, advertisers are likely to complement these relationships with partners that can help them realize the benefits of this advantageous global marketplace.

Making Every Dollar Count

You can't finish a presentation or an all-hands meeting without someone asking about ROI. These three letters are the most powerful acronym in business and can make your CFO smile. It's about time. Marketing budgets have been on the rise but companies struggled to effectively measure ROI. In today's harsh economic climate, C level executives are asking questions about the accountability of every dollar spent. Return on marketing investment (ROMI), or the quantitative justification of marketing, is the new corporate buzzword on Wall Street and in every executive boardroom. The notion of accountability is now and more than ever a priority area for CMOs eager to keep their desk position a while longer.

Every marketing initiative is scrutinized and must be justified with a solid business case before getting funded. John Wanamaker, the 19th century department-store business man warned us: "Half the money I spend on advertising is wasted. The trouble is, I don't know which half." The digital era makes everything more measurable.

Client Viewpoint

"In the years ahead, we are likely to continue to see drastic changes in media consumption coupled with increasingly better performance indicators and measurement tools. The entire agency industry needs to reinvest itself from the ground up to deal with so many choices and the greater complexity."

KEVIN PARHAM, Director Global Advertising, Campbell Soup

However, the sea of tools, service providers, and data sources is making it harder to discern what's important from what's interesting. Thankfully, agencies are helping advertisers sort through and filter campaigns. At its core, the fusion of art and science gives birth to a new marketing life force that is highly traceable and measurable. At almost every industry conference, discussions turn to the evolution of the advertising as a dependable, measurable discipline. What you can measure, you can improve, and herein lays a world of opportunities to optimize marketing campaigns and ensure every dollar is spent wisely. The most common concerns are related to the changing media landscape which is uncertain and therefore a source of confusion.

Especially as it relates to accountability metrics, the flagship of Internet media is a big part of the momentum behind why marketing expenses are shifting to digital. It's far from being cheaper; this is a common misconception. However, many clients do cannot comprehend why a campaign that doesn't necessary call for large media budgets can be as expensive as one that does (hint: think of the number and pace of distinct individual executions vs. the single big tah-dah of a spot produced for television).

The concerns over the use of traditional media like TV are further accentuated by the fact that major TV shows have a high proportion of non-program content per hour, leaving audiences eager to skip forward past commercials. Therefore, agencies want to measure and negotiate not only for commercial time bought based on live ratings but also live plus a few days to include any time-shifted viewing on DVRs. The lack of measurement of consumer-controlled media such as time (DVRs) and place (portable devices) shifted viewing is affecting both advertisers and media companies eagerly waiting to see improvements in audience measurement.

Client Viewpoint

"Agencies must get more efficient in the years ahead to address some of the marketing challenges faced by their clients. Efficiency must be a priority."

MARIANN COLEMAN
Director, Global Media Relations and Performance, Intel

Accountability means different things in different media but increasing pressure is clearly being felt by traditional media. Deeply rooted in Internet media for which measurability is in the DNA, this level of accountability has clearly generated much interest in other areas of marketing communications less accustomed to such level of scrutiny.

Standard ROI measurement tools for traditional media are hard to find and pale in comparison with click-through measurements well-established in online advertising, promotional landing pages, email marketing, and search marketing. This explains how these have rapidly gained popularity among advertisers. Industry leaders such as Microsoft, Google, and Yahoo are challenging traditional media metrics and pushing agencies to adopt new measurement tools across the board. Nielsen struggles to keep up with ever more demanding agencies and clients, and media giants are combining resources with other agencies to respond to escalating client expectations.

Client Viewpoint

"We as marketers have to adapt and support these fundamental changes. We have to be evangelists. Business is more complex, customers are more demanding, budgets are constrained, agency talent is sporadic, traditional ways of doing business or compensating agencies are now obsolete. Everything has to be reevaluated with a higher focus on accountability."

JAMES R. ZAMBITO, Global Marketing Group Controller, Johnson & Johnson

This focus on marketing accountability has put many CMOs on the hot seat within their companies, with CEOs and CFOs demanding tangible proof that their marketing investments are paying off and that marketing dollars are ever-more efficiently spent. Because of this, the average CMO tenure is shorter than ever before. As a result, agencies are working hard to preserve existing client relationships, despite the revolving door of the CMO's office. With this amplified emphasis on marketing accountability and ROI, left-brained thinkers and their right-brained counterparts must come together to apply the right-brain creative process to the pursuit of measurable results. Agencies must provide reporting and analytical services that model and estimate in terms of dollars and cents or campaign performance, the potential of various campaign scenarios even before they are developed.

As the line between the various media channels continue to blur, clients are asking their agencies to address the intricacies of how one channel drives another so they can track which marketing investment triggers what actions. Agencies are hiring Ph.D.s in analytics, statisticians, and professionals in business intelligence (BI) as well as other quantitatively skilled staff with experience in building sophisticated and highly effective algorithms to up level not only their suite of services, but also their perceived value to meet client expectations.

Client Viewpoint

"Demand exceeds supply in digital talent. As most marketing becomes digital, digital talent is the company's leadership of tomorrow. The Chief Digital Officer is tomorrow's CMO. Clients have historically outsourced that competency to agencies but now realize that it is too critical to their business. There is a clear acceleration."

LYNNE SEID, Partner Global Marketing Officers Practice, Heidrick & Struggles

In the digital arena, agencies are licensing or making sizeable investments to build their own real-time BI and technology solutions. These solutions allow them to mine customer behavioral data, anticipate intent, improve the timing and accuracy of campaign reporting, and advance advertiser's use of new tools such as sentiment tracking, social mapping, and conversion attribution. These solutions also allow them to constantly test and optimize their work, and ultimately increase marketing ROI for the client.

Agencies are expected to structure their organization based on what's most important to clients. Agencies are hiring specialist procurement resources to assist with driving efficiencies into their business practices, including rigorous sub-vendor negotiations to reduce costs, and increase speed and quality. Agencies more than ever share the burden of efficacy with their clients, applying the same procurement rigor to pricing and contractual terms that clients are applying to them. Eric Samuelson of Jack Morton Worldwide calls this "Loving Your Shark."[61]

The relentless and almost irresistible drive towards measurability will require some degree of moderation and careful consideration, however, since measurement of ROI for certain types of marketing objectives may be an elusive goal. Poorly applied, it can end up favoring cost avoidance programs rather than high-impact campaign work and may not be a perfect panacea to measure results or decide where to invest marketing dollars. Highly-effective programs can result in long term, higher customer satisfaction and improved brand perception, but may be difficult to accurately and effectively tie to more tangible, short-term business results such as immediate increases in sales or leads generated.

Every dollar counts. As a result, agencies are pushed to experiment and innovate, looking for ways to do more with less. Agencies will continue to be expected to play a critical role in advising clients when to apply the rigor and science of ROI, and what mix of marketing programs will drive business performance. As a result, all agencies, without exceptions, will be compensated based on their ability to drive measurable business outcomes.

Scarcity of Talent

The advertising, marketing and communication business has always been labor intensive. The life-blood of the agency business is and will remain its people. No matter what technological advancements agencies are able to leverage to reduce labor dependencies and automate tasks, it's likely to remain a labor intensive business for years to come when key talent makes or breaks agencies. For the most part, agencies struggle to staff accounts with senior talent who have sufficient tenure and experience to lead vs. simply serve clients. Finding and retaining top talent is now one of the greatest challenges faced by agencies and a fundamentally limiting factor in their ability to grow. Especially when agencies have to compete with the 800-pound gorillas and digital talent grabbers like Google, Yahoo and Microsoft.

Thankfully, there is enough money at stake to motivate the entire industry to shake up and adjust. It has been a challenge. The talent hole, predominantly in digital but also in analytics, search, social media and other emerging competencies, is indicative of a generation gap in competencies and skills that will take time to close. Whether you are hiring experts in XHTML, Flash, Silverlight, .NET, Cold Fusion, Java or C#, or are looking for skills in 3D animations, digital video production, digital asset management and trafficking, data mining and architecture, ad serving, database management or business analytics, you are looking for a relatively small pool of talented resources.

The gap in these high-demand professionals is partially due to the fact that clients are hiring them faster than agencies are able to produce them. Clients have realized that they need highly capable and digitally-savvy employees with sufficient knowledge and work experiences to lead their organizations in the digital world.

Agencies also compete with their clients for the same talent. There is significantly more human capital required to service the growing number of digital channels and the associated number of tactics that support it. And when clients start challenging how much they pay their agencies, it's not helping agencies fill the gap. It is generally true across all disciplines but it appears to be having the greatest impact on media services.

The fee and margin pressure felt across the agency industry has resulted in some agencies reducing or, worse, cancelling training programs as well as reducing entry-level salaries. In some cases, the scarcity of talent has led to salary inflation in high-demand positions as agencies fight to attract and retain the best talent. The resulting pressure on the bottom line has required nimble agencies to look for more cost-effective ways to produce work for their clients. Off-shoring and near-shoring of production work can be attractive solutions for agencies wanting to reduce cost and retain their margin.

As clients' customers are increasingly drawn from around the globe, agencies are seeking geographic coverage and cultural diversity by hiring individuals with globe-spanning experience, a borderless, culturally-sensitive mind-set that lends itself to appreciate and understanding geographic nuances, a trait essential to effectively engaging a diverse range of audiences.

What are the implications for agencies and advertisers moving forward? As agencies staff for existing and future needs, they are hiring individuals from more varying professional backgrounds than they have historically, pursuing candidates who may not have considered advertising or marketing agencies a career choice until now. It means that agencies are tapping into recruiting firms with a broader coverage than traditional advertising or marketing services.

They are also tapping increasingly more in international resources, importing talent from other countries as needed. They are using some of their offices as hiring hubs with the intent to develop their own best talent and disperse it to other offices around the world. Domestic-only agencies will eventually suffer from not having access to similar benefits: access to larger pools of audience and technology-savvy resources, greater talent selection and training, and rotation of talent to develop skills and experience.

Client Viewpoint

"The agency business is challenged perhaps more than ever. Everyone seems to be competing for talent. In an environment where clients are cutting fees and squeezing agency profitability, it's increasingly more difficult for agencies to attract top talent. That's got to change. When agencies do well, the industry as a whole benefits with incredibly bright and clever people pursuing communications and advertising careers."

JAMES R. ZAMBITO, Global Marketing Group Controller, Johnson & Johnson

Advertisers face similar recruiting challenges as their agencies, so they understand well the challenges being faced. As clients hire top digital and analytical talent to handle what they consider to be increasingly more critical business functions, agencies will need to keep up with their client needs, or better, lead them into the digital future. The most savvy client/agency partnerships are experimenting with joint approaches to sourcing and managing talent. Ingenuity rarely comes from times of abundance but rather from scarcity.

Blurring the Lines Between Media, Content, Creative, and Digital

The agency industry has gone through tumultuous bundling and unbundling of services over the years, with the pendulum at times moving far in the direction of bundling, at times moving towards unbundling. It went through periods of blending of creative, media planning and buying, production and other agency services, switching à la carte and then remixing combined offerings many times as they attempted to find the ultimate model to best service clients.

Client Viewpoint

"To make themselves even more valuable to their clients, agencies must demonstrate breakthrough thinking, rich consumer insight, greater innovation, especially across digital channels, a willingness to bring new perspectives to the table without being afraid to challenge clients and lastly, an ability to perform and achieve outstanding results."

JENNIFER BERGER, Director, Marketing & Advertising Services, Starbucks

Attempts to combine services such as creative and media, consolidating planning and buying departments into free-standing companies, were intended to generate savings, allowing clients to generate much greater economies of scale. The growth of digital and earned media from social networks and the proliferation of digital agencies are pushing the limits of a world that deliberately unbundled creative and media at first but no longer can operate separately or autonomously to deliver well integrated communications.

In many ways, it has now reset the advertising and marketing assembly line, reordering how and when media, content and creative come together for more synergic results. The industry went through the blending of creative and media disciplines, followed by unbundling and then re-bundling to find the best model to meet client needs. The attempt to bundle services like creative, content, and media were intended to break down silos and bring media closer to the creative process. It also ensured media and digital were at the table from the start, not after-thought disciplines.

Digital became the starting point, rather than the "second treatment" behind traditional creative channels. Digitally-led ideas are now producing highly engaging consumer-centric experiences, even now blending digital and traditional media channels as evidenced by a number of agency changes over the years such as media planning and buying agency Carat USA's decision to merge with Carat-Fusion, an interactive agency, to become a "digitally-driven integrated marketing shop."[62]

On the media side, agencies have discovered that removing the artificial divide between media and creative while at the same time, offering it as a standalone service allows their media professionals to build deep expertise, providing focus and becoming a center of excellence that multiple creative agencies can tap into. Plus, they can represent more clients without as many client conflicts. Now, in a similar vein, clients are beginning to wonder whether or not the unbundling of production from creative presents economic benefits and are pushing agencies to consider cost-effective alternative models. Many clients are now directly engaging with production vendors on branded entertainment and long-form video projects such as documentaries, sometimes by-passing agencies.

In traditional media, the segregation of creative, production and media series is straightforward and easy to understand. Add media programming, Web development, content development, new platforms, and custom-developed applications, and suddenly the blender is on high. As a result, and in order to better manage their investments, clients are budgeting creative and content development and production and media separately, in silos, seeking best in class at the best price, in each of these disciplines. With the growth of digital, the blurring line is further diffused with innovative ideas and approaches that involve the fusion of creative development and delivery of custom content, direct to consumer, often based on earned media opportunities. Digital production often informs the creative process. Conversely, media is perhaps where the concept germinates, providing a fresh, multi-channel perspective on how to reach and speak to an audience.

Client Viewpoint

"Digital media and changes in consumer consumptions have changed the dialog between agencies and advertisers. There is a need for greater role clarity between creative and media. There is need for a better handle of the work. It's changing the work we work together."

Mollie Weston
Director Agency Management Operations, Best Buy

Digital media—a burgeoning part of the media mix—fundamentally changes the nature of the customer dialog. As a result, some agencies are re-bundling traditional and new media to better complement each other while others are re-bundling media planning with creative in response to the growing influence of audience insight, always-on marketing and digital media's ability to play a unique role in marketing strategy.

A majority of digital agencies have now moved to a bundled approach with creative agencies acquiring media agencies or building media capabilities from within, for example: Omnicom's Tribal DDB, or with specialized media agencies acquiring creative agencies. The point at which media is now integrated into the creative development process varies by agency as each looks for the optimal model to underscore the integrity of the creative product, while infusing media's expertise "how do we best bring great ideas to the customer" so breakthrough ideas that fuel the thinking of their colleagues can be generated from either camp.

Client Viewpoint

"If you are not decoupling production today, you probably missed the boat. Agencies should be more accountable to bring these solutions to forward and pass on the benefits to their clients."

BRETT COLBERT
Global Manager, Procurement Advertising, Anheuser Busch InBev

The integration of media into the sacred creative alchemy is changing the traditional, linear process that traditional advertisers and agencies were born with. The tension between distribution and content companies is being felt by clients, trying to make sense of the chaos. When a client uses multiple creative partners, a single media agency partner can serve as a hub that centrally connects to paid or unpaid content creators as well as media partners. Digital media offers levels of measurability and adaptability that require rapid creative evolution and media optimization.

Agency Viewpoint

"Many advertisers are not strategic enough about their media investment. I believe in coupling digital assets with media because in the end it's all about data and how clients use it to delight their customers on a personal and relevant level."

DAVID KENNY
Managing Partner, Vivaki

Today, rotation of creative units must be done in concert with media plan changes in ways that weren't possible or even desirable without instantaneous access to campaign results. Truly integrated marketing efforts that provide customers a unified experience across touch points—the Holy Grail for brand advertisers—tend to favor the needs of the whole over of each individual component produced in silo.

Advertisers need partners that have no particular bias for specific media channels and can deliver solutions across an infinite number of customer/prospect touch points in support of their marketing objectives. They also want their communication to ping-pong off each other so the end impact is greater than solely the sum of its parts. Advertisers want comprehensive, integrated communication services so that their agencies, not them, are on point to glue the various pieces together into a cohesive whole.

To address these needs, agencies are breaking out of the competitive box and partnering with each other, acquiring capabilities they didn't have, merging departments, and forging alliances in and out of their agency networks. They are forming integrated planning departments and specific agency roles to bring it all together in a unified offering from the start of the engagement.

Interestingly, few advertisers are staffing a role on the client side to enable and drive this all-new level of cross-agency collaboration. The role of integrated planning will be an increasingly critical new function that taps into customer-centric insights, rich media options and the creative synergies that can only be brought together like the exquisite ingredients of a gourmet meal. Analytical practices bring together marketing communications performance data that span the marketing mix.

As clients move away from single agency of record models to an increasingly popular multi-agency mix, the question as to where the center of gravity for cross-media 360 analytics should reside is still unresolved. Should it be like spokes around a central analysis hub at the client, fed by data from the entire agency roster? Or should agencies somehow come together to fulfill that data fusion and analytical role? While agencies must continue to make investments in technology and talent to keep up with client demands, clients probably won't relinquish these valuable corporate data and analytical assets unless they feel that agencies can drive incremental value if outsourced.

Client Viewpoint

"At MasterCard creative and media is decoupled and it works for us. There is a high degree of cooperation and collaboration among our creative and media agencies. Decoupling production isn't in our consideration set as we believe it would overly complicate the process and dilute the quality and effectiveness of our advertising. It may work for some, depending on the industry, the nature and complexity of creative product."

CHARLIE SILVESTRO
Vice President, Global Agency Operations, MasterCard Worldwide

Working with Agencies in Extraordinary Times

Through increasing governmental actions and regulation, domestic agencies such as the Federal Trade Commission (FTC) or Food & Drug Administration (FDA) in the U.S. as well as various consumer advocacy groups regularly affect the scope, content, and manner in which clients and their agencies can communicate with consumers. The marketing industry faces legislative and regulatory issues. Issues range from obesity and alcohol and pharmaceutical advertising, to direct-to-consumer drug advertising, political campaign constraints, censorship for indecency and obscenity, food-health claims, the environment, as well as blog rules and privacy and copyright protection in the digital world. Advertisers are facing huge pressure in the ever-changing advertising regulatory environment that brings its share of challenges.

Should there be limitations to the advertising of snack food and sweetened sodas to youth and in schools? How tightly regulated should the multi-billion direct-to-consumer pharmaceutical advertising industry in the U.S. be? Shall we allow college-newspapers and outdoor signage near college campuses to glamorize alcohol when it is known to be the substance most abused by youth? How about cigarettes? Credit cards for young people? Paycheck loans at exorbitant interest rates in low-income communities? The answers to these questions lie in the hands of elected officials, special interest groups and lobbyists paid to push their agenda on Madison Avenue.

Companies are proactively addressing these sensitive consumer issues. MasterFoods has decided not to market its Mars and Snickers candy bars to children under twelve, attempting to rally and self-regulate for fear of facing more draconian regulation. Soft drink companies are voluntarily withdrawing their products from school vending machines.

On the mirror side, the agency industry deals with a plethora regulatory and compliance issues, from Sarbanes-Oxley which aims at improving the quality and transparency in financial reporting, to local requirements such as the U.K. law to protect workers that requires agencies to hire employees from a client's previous agency when landing a new contract. The greater the role advertising plays in our society, the more scrutiny can be expected by influential groups and can be demanded by government officials tasked to protect the public from misleading or harmful use of corporate dollars invested in advertising. Advertisers and agencies will continue to be confronted with public interest and reform activists and regulations that require them to adapt their work or operations to new regulations.

Better yet, advertisers and agencies have the opportunity to proactively self-regulate to avoid constricting legal requirements that can compromise impact. Proactively addressing public concerns—for example, publicizing the company's sustainable environmental practices—are not only desirable for the good of society, but greatly beneficial to the advertising industry and advertisers. As change agents, agencies are blessed with the opportunity to positively impact the culture and society and drive powerful results for their clients.

Agencies must capitalize on a deep understanding of local and global legal requirements (not to mention a point of view on ethics, cultural sensitivities, and the greater good. The anvil of self-regulation is requiring agencies to take a more proactive role in understanding these cultural shifts, to regulative movements and stay ahead of the game for their clients while remaining intimately connected to consumer opinion. They must be plugged into consumer movements and debates of public interest to best counsel clients on how to deliver messages that are grounded into a sensible understanding of the issues. Agencies can no longer simply be observers of political, social, and economical factors but actively incorporate thought-leadership into their creative work in these arenas and use social media to engage them in a dialog.

Larger agencies can afford to send their senior staff to industry conferences, stay closely connected to pending legislation, and stay on top of the issues that may impact the quality and effectiveness of their messaging. Happily, the Web can help equalize the playing field for savvy upstarts. In return, advertisers want to be confident that their agency partner is sufficiently knowledgeable on these matters and has embraced ways to stay well informed of developments that can materially impact the planning and execution of responsible advertising and/or marketing messages. In highly regulated industries, working with knowledgeable agencies with proven experience will be even more vital to advertisers diligent about the perception and reality of their brand(s).

Agency Viewpoint

"Today's economic crisis is only reinforcing the critical need for agencies to rethink their business model, how they serve clients and how they make money in the process."

TIM WILLIAMS, President, Ignition Consulting Group

No company has been insulated from the effects of the most recent economic downturn. Companies are under intense scrutiny from all frontiers: investors, employees, customers, suppliers, partners, online forces, and community and consumer advocacy groups. Under such conditions, companies must rapidly gain control of both opinion and cost management. Addressing these imperatives requires astute management of every expense, including marketing, often one of the largest spending categories, scrutinizing every dollar spent by the company to ensure it provides a compelling return on investment.

Advertisers must design systems to apply increasing rigor and accountability in tracking and measuring marketing and business performance as it relates to investments and big bets, which in turns, gives C-level executives and corporate boards more confidence in the company's ability to win and curry favor in the marketplace. Companies are struggling to find new ways of doing things in these difficult times and are turning to their agencies to play an even stronger role in helping them weather economic uncertainties and business volatility.

To win share and grow, advertisers now require two simultaneous approaches to agency management: a more focused and disciplined use of agency resources and a more aggressive pursuit of models that motivate their agencies, encourage risk-taking, and link agency performance to business outcomes. It's no longer about what we say or how we say it, it's also about how get people to experience the advertiser's promise before a purchase is made, as an integral part of the brand experience.

As in any other industry, agencies are also largely influenced by economic drivers such as inflation, trade balance, fiscal deficits, consumer confidence, currency fluctuations, unemployment rate, and socio-demographic trends, including the aging of the population or the makeup of our ethnic and cultural diversity. Companies must make informed decisions about their capital expenditures based on these criteria. Discretionary expense categories such as advertising and marketing communication services are directly impacted by the moods of the world financial markets and the pressure experienced by CFOs looking to reduce operational expenses to stay competitive.

Agency Viewpoint

"As agencies, we must continue to explore ways for clients to do work that is both effective and cost-efficient. Agencies can help clients discover new and innovate ways to do more with less"

PATRICIA BERNS, EVP, Worldwide Account Director, Verizon, MRM Worldwide

In a booming economy spurred by growth and expanding markets, agency services can thrive or shrivel. Since marketing spend is mostly seen as a necessary investment to grow market share and revenue (after all, it was commonly said that "a product seen is a product sold"), it's no surprise that the agency business has enjoyed a successive number of years of overall expansion characterized by a highly competitive business sector, and fueled by new distribution channels and the growth of digital media.

Agency Viewpoint

"It seems as if clients are evolving much faster than agencies these days. Agencies have not been proactive enough and must now keep up with clients. Agencies have to retool their business to stay relevant to their clients."

TIM WILLIAMS, President, Ignition Consulting Group

The recession that followed has forced agencies to move more cautiously as marketing budgets evaporated. In the wake of economic turbulence, the agency industry is finding ways to overcome budget cuts and tough clients eager to control costs which in turn, are fuelling a drive for innovation and breakthrough thinking.

The trend toward faster, leaner and meaner is not going away. Companies will continually be faced with the financially-demanding task of managing their business to grow the customer base while meeting existing and future customer expectations. Outspending the competition is no longer the way to win. Clients are turning to their agency talent to help them navigate smartly and move decisively, with the conviction that comes from data, extraordinary insight and an understanding of what's working best.

In the end, world economies are cyclical, with ups and downs, with growth spurts and recessions. The agency industry must, by correlation, always experience an occasional boost during years of global or domestic political events such as presidential elections and major sport events like the Soccer World Cup or the Olympic Games, each of which occurs on a four year cycle (also known as the Quadrennial effect). These events of global importance have historically solicited huge advertising and promotional interest because of the broader viewership it generates. Whether advertisers will continue to invest in traditional advertising venues at times such as these, or shift a predominant part of their investment to the more measurable, viral and targeted world of digital, remains to be seen.

Client Viewpoint

"The agency industry should seize the opportunity to step up in the strategy area they were once known to master. Today, agencies are not simply expected to produce great creative but are helping clients solve fundamental business problems, especially in the pharmaceutical industry. Agencies should determine the strategic skill set they wish to offer, which will differ in scope from what is available from consulting companies."

Tom Chetrick
VP Advertising and Marketing Services, Bristol-Myers Squibb

Evolution or Revolution in Madison Avenue?

Agencies in marketing and communication services have evolved from a reputation of demonstrating strong creativity, ideas, and interpersonal skills to building upon a scientific body of knowledge and proven results. They have to, or face the risk of being devalued in the eyes of their clients. But there is still a fair amount of chaos in both agency business and client organizations today. This complex world of marketing and technology convergence is allowing agencies to deliver greater value to clients in desperate need of maps and playbooks.

The advertising industry of the future will be shaped based on the collective impact made by macro-level market business and social dynamics as well as new socio-demographic and technology-based advancements. Accordingly, we should see the predominance of large global agencies investing aggressively in emerging technologies, content and media opportunities as those veer towards the mainstream:

- They will proactively seek to self-regulate on major sensitive public issues.
- They will continue to adopt and evangelize more efficient and accountable communication channels.

- They will continue to place digital at the core of their strategic recommendations and become hubs of digital-content creation and distribution.
- They will drive personalized engagements that give customers ways to manage their relationship with their favorite brands.
- They will build, co-develop, or leverage existing ad technology to streamline the supply chain and improve marketing effectiveness.

Online ad networks will evolve as well, with the growth of highly efficient and more transparent Ad Exchanges (such as Microsoft's AdECN, DoubleClick and Right Media). Agencies will lead by driving greater relevancy and value in their offerings.

Today they are creating work styles that are more about partnership than vendor relationships. They are sharing office space with clients to be closer to the heartbeat and to reduce overhead. If not, they're using communication software and technology such as video conferencing and project management applications to narrow the space/time gap between their and the client's worlds. They are building virtual teams of top-notch subject matter experts by tapping into centers of excellence wherever they may be. They are creating, organizing, and assembling communities of like-minded individuals on their client's behalf, a role previously played by media companies now struggling with the increased audience and media fragmentation.

Agency Viewpoint

"I believe the agencies only way to positively influence the raging procurement debate is to develop and fully integrate procurement within their organizations. This will then elevate procurement from a theoretical debate to collaborative innovation between clients and agencies."

ERIC SAMUELSON, VP, Production Procurement, Jack Morton Worldwide

They are capitalizing on the growing sophistication and investment by clients to build customer insight and improve campaign per-formance. They are collecting rich customer data, embracing data management and analytics to enrich their targeting and optimization competencies. They are producing rich branded content vs. simple advertising. They are improving their senior to junior staff ratio by bringing in more experienced talent to the account to add value, not just push projects through the pipeline. They are building procurement-type functions within the agency to drive cost-efficiency with their own roster of outsourced suppliers.

They are fighting shrinking profit margins by staffing their agencies with compensation officers who can stand up to clients and have fact-based conversations. They are pushing back the notion that everything they produce should be owned by the client. They are finding creative ways to monetize the value they create by negotiating financial incentives tied to performance, preserving and licensing more intellectual property, especially software and digital tools developed as a by-product of a client assignment and by developing and distributing original creative content at a premium.

They are building innovative new services and delivery mechanisms. They are pursuing new revenue models from consulting services and software development to licensing new technologies and digital solutions in social media and mobile. In the end, the agency model of the future will be more like an ecosystem of interconnected competencies.

Agencies are waking up to their value, driven by a new accountability for success and they want a piece of the action. Advertisers are noticing a healthy change in agency attitudes and aspirations. Agencies understand that marketing strategy is first and foremost about business strategy. Their business models are now built on an understanding that marketing strategy must first and foremost be about business strategy.

They are eager to show off their ability to go beyond the communication layer to deliver on customer experiences, build brands, and even invent new products and new distribution channels to drive new business opportunities. They want to tap into their rich and unique customer insight and communities to influence business strategy, product development and product design, fulfillment and distribution, even customer service. They bring to their client solutions that demonstrate smart marketing is about enabling meaningful end-to-end conversations between brands and audiences.

It's an all new game. If they play it well, they can more effectively address what clients need from their agencies. If they don't, they risk permanently becoming commodities. Some pundits venture to say that the changes that Madison Avenue has experienced in the past decade are truly revolutionary and have profoundly, permanently, impacted its core nature. One cannot argue with the long-term economic and social impact of game-changing phenomenon like social media and technology-based digital lifestyles that touch the consumer 24x7x365, and how they are shaping the industry that feed from it.

Client Viewpoint

"The agency of the future is dramatically different from what it is now. Agencies have to reinvent themselves and gain an integrated approach for everything they do. The agency of the future will be leaner and much more mobile. They will constantly push the innovation button, sourcing talent from different sources of creativity, investing in customer based R&D to better anticipate vs. reacting to consumer and client needs."

JAMES R. ZAMBITO, Global Marketing Group Controller, Johnson & Johnson

"Madison Avenue" as a homogenous phenomenon is perhaps an old and outdated icon that holds it place in the annals of the advertising industry of the 21st century, and nothing more. But the agency world is fundamentally its own catalyst in revolutionizing the business of how clients establish, maintain, and grow relationships with their customers. The future of the agency-client-media troika is being played on a chessboard that looks more like a spinning, multi-dimensional globe than the flat map of Manhattan. Put your Nike sneakers on. This brave new world is a mad race.

12 ENTERING THE ERA OF "RELATIONSHIP CAPITAL"

Change or perish

"Coming together is a beginning; keeping together is progress; working together is success."

—Henry Ford
American inventor and automobile pioneer

Born in July 12, 1895 in Milton, twenty miles from Boston, a suburban community in Eastern Massachusetts that prides itself on a rich historical heritage, Buckminster Fuller had a reputation for coming up with ideas that were somewhat unorthodox and futuristic for his time. Ideas of this American architect ranged from flying cars to floating communities and geodesic domes. He invented words such as going "outstairs" and "instairs" (instead of "down stairs" and "upstairs") or "world-around" to acknowledge that movement is done in respect to the center of Earth. One of the most intriguing facts about Fuller, a frequent traveler, is that he was known to wear as many as three watches: one for the current time zone, one for the zone he came from, and one for the zone of his destination.

Today the agency industry and brand advertisers are at a critical inflection point. Like Fuller, we may need three watches on our wrist to keep us sane: one to remind of where we started, one for where we are today, and one for what the future might look like. However, many of us would disagree about the nature of the events in the time each of these watches signifies. Especially the one that tells of the future. It's partially due to the fact that the business world is profoundly changing. Seismic, tsunami-style waves in the advertising, marketing, and communication disciplines are fueled by continued drastic shifts in consumer psychographics and consumptions, rapid development and innovation in technology, in social networks and in the media landscape, the globalization of the marketplace, and a huge thirst for advanced data analytics, customer segmentation, and ROI. We might as well call this "client mania."

And the pace of change is far from slowing down. No one knows with certainty what's on the horizon. The scale and speed at which these changes are taking place is whiplashing both agencies and their clients. There is chaos in the advertising, marketing, and communication world today. Clients do not have the luxury to watch their agencies fail to think strategically about their business and to drive results. Clients cannot commit to agencies that are unable to anticipate their needs, and to build new services and competencies to address today the challenges of competitive pressures of tomorrow. Clients no longer want agencies that are exclusively paid by filling time sheets, without regard to business outcome or performance. Clients no longer have the patience to see agencies fight with each other over territorial issues when they need their entire marketing arsenal to work well together to compete effectively. In the end, consumers are too demanding, competition is too tough, business pressure is too great, marketing is too important, time and resources are too scarce, for clients to afford sub-optimal agency relationships.

Conversely, agencies don't have the means to jump from one account review to another in endless pitch situations. Agencies cannot afford to give away their valuable work or ideas. Agencies cannot build sustainable value when the CMO's office is a revolving door. They cannot act as banks for their clients. Agencies cannot realistically hire every possible top talent or specialized skill set to keep up with these changes. They cannot credibly be all things to all their clients. In a world of uncertainty, agencies don't always have the line of sight and commitment from their clients to make wise long-term investment decisions in people and technology. Agencies cannot afford clients who fail to understand that only reasonably profitable agencies translate into stronger partners that will contribute to their own success.

The clock is ticking. A fierce debate now rages about what the future looks like for client/agency partnerships. What becomes of clients that keep asking for more while expecting to pay less? What will get clients to be willing to take greater risks with their agencies? Will agencies risk more to earn more? What client commitment will get agencies to heavily invest in technology that dramatically improves the way they interact with clients and accelerates their time to market? Will clients similarly invest in up-leveling their competency in managing agency partnerships?

What are the characteristics of agencies destined to be commoditized? Under what circumstances will clients build more in-house agencies? What will it take to get clients to value external agencies as trusted advisors that multiply the impact of their human capital and aim their marketing firepower more effectively? Client/agency relationships are grossly sub-optimized and the opportunity is now to transform them into the powerful, fruitful competitive assets they were intended to be.

Only one thing is certain. Regardless of size or industry, savvy clients need the talent, creativity, perspective, know-how, and services/tools only expert agencies can provide. Agencies are unique contributors that generate actionable audience insight, innovate, break down consumer barriers, build engaging brands, and optimize the impactful use of marketing budgets. In the so-called "generation of conversation" where brands are also media channels, clients must partner with agencies as brand stewards, leading them in reconstructing and integrating the way they reach, converse, interact, and exchange with consumers. Agencies, still shaken by the massive force of a business in continued transformation, are adapting to these new conditions by reinventing themselves, not once, not twice, but as many times as needed to find the best way for them to deliver sustainable value.

Agencies are increasingly now competing to own data, content, and technology in addition to key talent. They are designing agile, responsive, nimble, results-oriented organizations. They can thrive in these new market conditions and have the ability to move quickly, change direction, take risks, adapt to ever changing client needs, and operate costs efficiently. They cannot do this alone and clients must play their role.

Clients must drive change internally in order to challenge the status quo in the tireless pursuit of excellence. Clients must empower marketing and procurement leaders and change-agents who will take full advantage of what their agencies can offer and turn those into valuable business partnerships that turbo-charge their business performance. Clients must take ownership of managing agencies and the client/agency engagement that result from it by setting up streamlined processes and relentless priorities. They must carefully examine their business drivers to determine their agency needs and come up with the right agency model to support their business objectives. They must apply rigor and discipline when searching for the right agency partners. They must set up contracts that are fair and equitable. They must rethink agency compensation to encourage the right behavior and generate the right business outcome. They must continually provide and also receive feedback to improve the partnership. They must brief agencies effectively. They must prepare and train their organization about how to work successfully with agencies.

Clients must encourage cross-agency collaboration. The opportunity to turn these relationships into partnerships, and these partnerships into competitive assets is considerable. Following years of economic progress driven by human, knowledge and intellectual capital, we are now entering an interconnected period of "relationship capital" where our greatest company assets are our business partnerships.

Clients and agencies of all sizes, from the boutique shop to the holding company, have heard the call. This is an opportunity to drive exponentially greater value from these relationships. This can only be done through mutual understanding, goal, and priority alignment, shared accountability, and thoughtful considerations about what makes strong partnerships deliver results over and over again.

How do we make the most of those partnerships in this new era? Over the years, we will see new partnership models and best practices emerge. Regardless of their flavor du jour, they are likely to have one important thing in common: They will be less about the client or the agency but more about winning the consumer. They will realize the transformational power of the multiplier effect that only strong partnerships can produce.

Agency Mania is nothing more than a genuine wakeup call to harness the madness rather than resist it or ignore it. An invitation to thrive in these challenging times and generate high impact business results requires a guide on how to successfully navigate the disorienting world of client/agency relationships. It suggests how agencies and clients can start this journey together, how to make the most of it and stay ahead of the competition.

Clients must manage their agency investment wisely and commit to driving greater business value from these partnerships. There is no better time to reset our watches. The client/agency relationship model of the past decade is now obsolete.

There is no business partnership more important to a company's success and longevity. Tick Tick Tick. Clients and agencies must change how they work together … or perish. Together, let's embrace this new era of "Relationship Capital" and harness the madness of client/agency relationships to deliver outstanding customer value and business results.

AFTERWORD by Skip Walter

"Perspective is worth 80 IQ points."

—ALAN KAY, *Xerox Dyanabook, Apple Mac, Disney Imagineer*

Where was *Agency Mania* thirty years ago when I first needed the deep expertise embedded in this book? As a young product development manager of a software product that became a $1 billion a year business for Digital Equipment Corporation, I first encountered our marketing department and the advertising industry at a boutique ad agency on Madison Avenue. I had no idea what to expect or ask for or any criteria for recognizing good or bad creative services.

Over the years as I progressed from a product development manager to a senior executive and to the CEO position of a range of enterprise software and consumer software businesses, I never was comfortable with the results I was getting from the large portion of my budget going to marketing and advertising. When it came to advertising, I never found a good surrogate for my lack of experience or inability to judge talent and their results (or lack thereof). With *Agency Mania*, I have the tools to work with marketing teams to set appropriate expectations for a given agency project and the ability to probe agency talent and their results early in a project to achieve desired results.

While *Agency Mania* is targeted at marketing professionals working at advertisers and agencies, it is just as valuable for any executive managing those marketing professionals and most especially for those executives managing product development. The first rule of good management is to "expect what you inspect." For those executives not trained in marketing, it is difficult to figure out what are the appropriate expectations of advertising let alone know how to inspect important projects. The first eleven chapters provide a wealth of "inspect" questions along with a "top five" best practices at the end of each chapter.

For non-marketing senior executives, the "Brave New World" chapter describes an exciting new world of digital marketing that screams all at once: Opportunity, Complexity, Challenge, High Risk, High Reward. As another important industry transforms to all "digital" everything changes, not just by a little, but by a lot.

At the center of the change is the transform of the Agency-Client-Media Troika to an ecosystem where the consumer is an equal player in the "conversation" and brand experience. As the author points out the conversation expands from a "brand to consumer" world to include a "consumer to consumer" world. All of a sudden the consumer becomes a producer not just of valuable content, but also of raw data, and in some cases software applications that surround the content and data. The consumer is no longer just a consumer but a producer or "prosumer."

The Nike example at the beginning of the "Brave New World" chapter is an excellent example of an ecosystem that began by putting a computer in a running shoe to instantaneously adjust the performance of the shoe to fit the demands of a particular workout and terrain. The minute the computer was a part of the physical shoe then it was a simple matter to communicate the data to an iPod to make it easy to then upload the information to a database where the prosumer can set goals and monitor performance. The availability of lots of actual data from millions of prosumers then lets Nike or the prosumer change and tailor the performance of a custom designed running shoe or custom tailor the performance tuning of the shoe. And if the system can go that far, why not change the music on the iPod to be in tune with where the prosumer is in the workout—calm music for warming up or warming down, changing to rock music as the pace of the workout increases. This virtuous cycle becomes rich fodder for the agency talent to mine to find a myriad of audience segments to further tune product offerings and brand experience offerings.

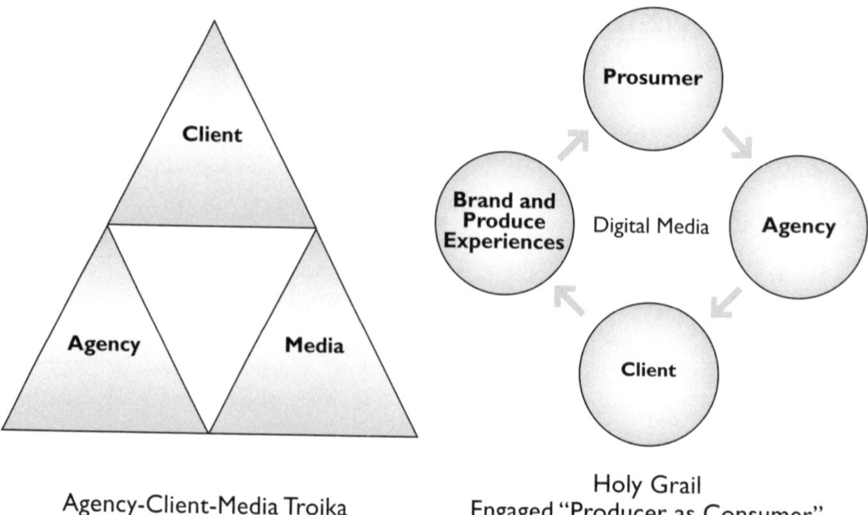

Agency-Client-Media Troika

Holy Grail
Engaged "Producer as Consumer"
Integrated Measurable System

Bruno Gralpois does an excellent job describing the inclusion of the engaged consumer as a first class citizen in the distribution of brand experiences and he hints at where this new digital world could really go—the inclusion of agency talent at the beginning of the product development cycle rather than at the end. Human-centered design professionals and user-experienced design professionals are dramatically changing the product development process by getting product teams to focus on the customer needs early and often in the process. Yet these professionals are not nearly as skilled as agency talent in capturing the consumers' emotions, creating engaging stories, and embracing and energizing brand principals and experiences. Executives should be asking "how do we make the best use of agency talent throughout the product development process" not "how do we cut costs?" It's about making sure that products are desirable from the very beginning of product development to ensure early emotional engagement on the part of the prosumer.

As traditional products become more "digital" the opportunities to include two-way communication in the product and new venues for "brand experiences" show up in the unlikeliest places. As home heating and air conditioning and electrical systems start including digital components, a new or remodeled house now has a plethora of LCD devices displaying rudimentary information to the consumer. Yet, these systems can have simple sensors connected to the Internet to identify problems long before a failure occurs. Currently these manufacturers are looking at these information sources as an opportunity to get a little more maintenance revenue, but what if they became a backbone for a whole thoughtful infrastructure like the Nike example. What if these display devices and systems became an outlet for "green advertising" and every day sustainability awareness and education.

In the midst of this insurmountable opportunity, lies a forest of risks and difficult issues at the heart of which is "who owns what?" As the creative work of the agency moves from the relatively simple world of copyrights and trademarks to the digital world of data and identity privacy and software patents, negotiating who owns what becomes extremely complex with lots of billable hours to expensive lawyers. Mr. Gralpois alludes to the challenges of contracting in the relatively simple world of traditional media which become much worse when trying to protect valuable intellectual property related to software (see the recent position paper from AAAA on "Software and Software Tools: Ownership and Use Contracting Considerations When Creating Digital, Online and Mobile Content"). The patent process is an expensive arena to participate at the cost level and in the learning required of the agency software development teams. Then as the prosumers enter this complex IP world simple user licenses may no longer apply as litigation risks of those who appropriate the user generated content and software and designs increase.

The challenge of just tracking what IP is being used at any one time can seem daunting.

While the complexity of the advertiser-agency relationship is challenging, adding the prosumer's rights into the mix is quite confusing. For the prosumer, the ability to design a new Nike shoe is a huge value-add, but what happens if Nike puts that design into mass production? Is the prosumer owed a royalty stream for their design? Who would be listed as the inventor for a patent on a new "collaborative" prosumer design? Many industries invest millions of dollars in "freedom to operate" searches to avoid future patent litigation. Will advertisers and agencies need to do the same kinds of expensive searches for high profile software based advertising? Will we see agencies banding together to invest in Intellectual Ventures types of patent holding consortiums to reduce the risks associated with technology development? Who owns the data that Nike shoes generate about the physical workouts and health of a consumer? Does this data need to be protected with the same care as medical records? The answers to these questions must be a part of the intellectual property strategy of the digital agency.

IP creation, protection, contracting, valuation, brokering, and management become new skills that both the advertiser and the agency must develop as part of the agency management process. These skills ultimately need a new breed of software due to the sheer volume of content and software applications that need to be tracked.

The pace of change in the relationship of the new tetrad of agency-client-digital media-prosumer is just beginning. The old proverb "may you always live in interesting times" is an apt description of the "brave new world" of agency management.

Throughout the book, I felt that Bruno Gralpois was my personal mentor guiding me through the labyrinth of how to manage the marketing department and agencies to achieve the business results I expect. I am very appreciative that Bruno Gralpois asked me to review his book as it has changed my view of marketing and advertising from something cloaked in creative mystery to something that can be managed.

Skip Walter
Founding CEO and CTO
Attenex Corporation

APPENDIX:
Best practices to harness the madness

Chapter 2: Golden Eggs
Understanding the mysterious world of Madison Avenue

❶ Don't be intimidated by the rapidly changing and often confusing world of advertising and marketing communications agencies. After reading this book, you are likely to be one of the most knowledgeable employees in your company. Ask your agency about their growth plans and how you fit in.

❷ Pay particularly close attention to the big network-holding companies as well as the top ten agencies in each of their respective marketing communications disciplines. By their sheer size, they influence and shape the entire agency community.

❸ Always keep an eye on dynamic, independent boutiques that challenge the status quo and come up with new, innovative approaches and business models.

❹ Use valuable industry resources such as trade magazines, and dedicate some time to stay abreast of new developments in the industry, such as mergers and acquisitions, agency awards (Cannes, Effie, Clio, etc.), client reviews, key account losses and wins in your industry, talent on the move, and more.

❺ Attend key industry events to network with peers and learn best practices and success stories that can then be applied to your own client/agency relationship(s).

Chapter 3: "The Buck Stops Here"
Mastering the discipline of agency management

❶ Build an agency management competency within your company, by assigning a seasoned individual or team to fulfill that role. Encourage everyone in the company—whether in marketing or procurement—to take accountability on how to realize most value from these investments and relationships. Ensure complete management support to make and enforce agency-related decisions.

❷ Define roles and responsibilities with key stakeholders. Partner with senior executive management, marketing, procurement, legal, IT and finance to understand their requirements and dependencies and to ensure a smooth integration with internal stakeholders groups.

❸ Set clear objectives and success metrics to ensure all parties are working toward the same goals, and effectively leveraging each other Review results and insights together and identify shared action plans to drive constant improvement.

❹ Take full accountability for the partnership. Serve as an internal advocate for the agency. Mediate or arbitrate as needed. Showcase the great work done by the agency and draw attention to the results generated from the partnership.

❺ Never compromise business performance, creativity, or staffing quality for arbitrary, short-term cost savings. Focus instead on driving up the value-add equation and turn agency relationships into powerful growth engines for your company.

Chapter 4: Marc, Catherine, and John

Building a sound agency strategy

---

❶ Carefully assess and rationalize your company's needs of its agency partner(s). Do not make decisions about your company's agency portfolio without seeking input from those directly impacted by it.

❷ Pick the best agency model to meet the needs and unique circumstances of your business. Determine the level of flexibility and agency choice desired and whether coordination between agencies be handled internally or externally. Secure adequate budget and resources to successfully bring the strategy to life.

❸ Partner with your agency to regularly showcase the work, campaign results and value generated from the partnership by using internal communication tools and company events. Regularly celebrate joint successes and recognize top agency performers and internal clients.

❹ Conduct regular business reviews with agency partners to foster a healthy, productive relationship. Discuss what's working and what's not, opportunities and potential roadblocks to success, and agree on joint action plans to drive immediate improvements and higher performance.

❺ Decide which operating principles should best support the company's approach to working optimally with agencies. Prepare for the unexpected by developing a contingency plan.

Chapter 5: Assortative Mating and the Sweaty T-Shirt Theory

Conducting a successful agency search

---

❶ Conducting an agency search is costly for everyone involved and doesn't always lead to a better partnership. So don't start a search unless you are absolutely certain that you need to, and have a clear idea of what you are looking for.

❷ Hire an agency search consultant if you don't have extensive experience in this area, if this is a large scale project, or if you simply want to accelerate the speed of the project without compromising the quality of its outcome.

❸ Set up a collaborative process with agency candidates that encourages open discussions, exchange of relevant information, as well as provides reasonable access to key stakeholders. Set a reasonable schedule.

❹ Be transparent about the selection criteria and the decision-making process. Determine upfront if you will compensate agencies for their participation in the review. If you are asking agencies to participate in the creative shootout, be clear about expectations as it relates to ownership of IP. Don't communicate your decision until you have negotiated competitive terms with the chosen agency.

❺ Look for compatible agency partners doesn't mean looking for a mirror image of your company. To the contrary. Look for partners that enrich, expand, stretch and strengthen internal skills and ultimately complement you as a client.

Chapter 6: Pacta Sunt Servanda

Setting up a rock-solid agency contract

---

❶ Use the contract to strengthen the relationship with your agency partner. Clients should invest the time to get the contract right with their agencies and enter negotiations with the explicit goal to establish fair, equitable, and mutually agreeable terms.

❷ Clients must include most common clauses in their agency contract, such as indemnification and compensation, but should pay close attention to critical clauses such as ownership and intellectual property (especially in the context of software and digital tools developed by the agency), as well as contract termination and competitive conflicts.

❸ Use addendums for the variable parts of the contract, such as fees, scope of work, and staffing, that must be updated periodically.

❹ Set up an audit schedule and hire skilled auditors with intimate knowledge of advertising, media, and marketing communication disciplines and common industry practices.

❺ Avoid conducting audits on a contingency basis. Clients shouldn't use audits with punitive intentions in mind but rather use audit to identify improvement areas in operational and financial transactions and processes.

Chapter 7: Just Six Numbers

Determining the right client/agency compensation

---

❶ Finalize compensation terms before making your agency selection. In year one of the relationship, do not overcomplicate. Pick a simple formula. Evolve compensation as the relationship matures.

❷ Prioritize compensation agreements that align your mutual interests and operating principles, and motivate the agency to act in ways that support your business priorities.

❸ Insist on rewarding agencies for outstanding business performance or value generated rather than based on activity, timesheets or efforts alone. Go beyond typical financial incentive arrangements and explore other creative ways to motivate agencies.

❹ Media discounts, credits, and float are potential sources of income and profit for agencies whose clients have not addressed those contractually. Make sure media discounts and credits are factored in your compensation agreement or, at the very least, consistently returned to the client.

❺ Don't ask your agency to act as a bank. Include equitable payment terms so cash flow does not become an unnecessary distraction in the relationship.

Chapter 8: Six Men of Indostan

Successfully scoping work & briefing agencies

❶ Institute a comprehensive scope of work planning process to set top line priorities and provide adequate line of sight to agencies about workload and staffing requirements.

❷ Invite agencies participate in upstream priority-setting discussions so they can advise senior management and strongly influence the company's strategy.

❸ Invest the time and efforts required to set clear, concise objectives in the brief before engaging an agency. Provide insightful, actionable data. Be transparent at all times.

❹ Set reasonable expectations. Define roles and responsibilities for everyone involved to avoid any confusion, duplication of efforts, and potential delays. Ensure client decisions are made decisively and in a timely manner.

❺ Tell the agencies what you need, not what to do or how to do it. Don't be too prescriptive or limiting. Empower agencies to do what they do best.

Chapter 9: The Lombardi Rules

Conducting productive agency/client performance evaluations

❶ Accountability for the work relationship goes both ways. Conduct a 360-degree performance evaluation so the client and the agency both provide feedback to improve the work and the partnership.

❷ Formally review client/agency performance at least once or twice a year, but both parties should provide on-going feedback so that there are no surprises and issues can be addressed immediately.

❸ Clearly communicate externally and internally the importance of providing and receiving feedback and how to use this information to improve the partnership. Do not initiate this evaluation process unless you are 100% committed to doing something about the results.

❹ Encourage transparency and responsibility. As the client/agency relationship matures over time, consider making the feedback non-anonymous to foster even greater accountability.

❺ Consider hiring a consultant or an end-to-end performance evaluation solution, allowing you, the client, to focus all your efforts on improving those areas which will create the greatest impact.

Chapter 10: Gottman's Paper Towel Test

Partnering towards mutual success

❶ Make your agency accountable for driving measurable business results. Turn your relationship into a true strategic partnership by making your agency accountable for driving measurable results.

❷ Let your agency challenge conventional thinking, challenge status quo, challenge your ways of doing things, and take calculated risks. Reward people for doing this.

❸ Demand the best agency talent in your business. Compensae fairly for it. Apply these top resources wisely.

❹ Provide clear direction, give unrestricted access to critical information and senior management. Make decisions and stick to them.

❺ Listen to what your agency tell you it needs in order to be successful. Ask for contact reports to ensure everyone is on the same page. Foster a culture of open dialog and direct feedback. Be appreciative always, and celebrate successes.

ENDNOTES

[1] Veronis Suhler Stevenson press release, VSS Releases 2009-2013 Forecast, August 3, 2009.

[2] Account Planning, http://en.wikipedia.org/wiki/Account_planning.

[3] Force Multiplication, http://en.wikipedia.org/wiki/Force_multiplication.

[4] Matthew Creamer, "Former Dentsu Creative Sues Over Trips to Brothel, Bathhouse, Sharapova Shoot," *Advertising Age*, October 31, 2007.

[5] *Advertising Week*, "Letter from Michael R. Bloomberg, Mayor of the City of New York," September 21, 2009.

[6] Advertising and Marketing Companies in the United States, Manta.com, accessed on April 18, 2010.

[7] Richard H. Levey, "Microsoft Splits CRM Duties Between MRM Partners and Young & Rubicam," Direct, February 12, 2004.

[8] Kunur Patel, "MasterCard Taps R/GA for Global Digital Advertising Duties," *Advertising Age*, October 12, 2009.

[9] Noreen O'Leary, "Changing the Nature of the Beast," *AdWeek*, February 28 2005.

[10] Jonah Bloom, "Publicis Builds a Re-bundled Full-Service Agency," *Advertising Age*, November 13, 2007.

[11] WPP Group's Corporate and Investor Relations Website,

[12] Rupal Parekh, "Enfatico CEO Answers Critics: We're Resetting' Agency Bar," *Advertising Age*, September 22, 2008.

[13] Omnicom Group's Corporate and Investor Relations Website, .

[14] Interpublic Group's Corporate and Investor Relations Website, .

[15] Publicis's Corporate and Investor Relations Website, .

[16] Brooke Capps, "Why United Tapped Tiny Startup," *Advertising Age*, April 9, 2007.

[17] Jeremy Mullman & Rupal Parekh, "Euro Named Agency of Record for Flagship Heineken Brands," *Advertising Age*, July 10, 2009.

[18] Sean Corcoran, Dave Frankland, Vidya L. Drego, "The Future of Agency Relationships," Forrester Research, March 29, 2010.

[19] Rupal Parekh, "Want More Out of Your Agencies? Write Better Briefs," *Advertising Age*, August 17, 2009.

[20] Harry S. Truman Library & Museum. "Truman: The Buck Stops Here," Available from Internet, accessed 4/2/2010.

[21] Jack Neff, "Package-goods Giants Lean on Agencies for Cuts," *Advertising Age*, July 13, 2009.

[22] David Berreby, "Studies Explore Love and the Sweaty T-Shirt", *The New York Times*, June 9, 1998.

[23] Rupal Parekh, "When an Incumbent Shop Should–and Shouldn't–Defend in a Review," *Advertising Age*, September 7, 2009.

[24] Trevor Jensen, "Agencies Abuzz Over P&G's Gillette Deal," *AdWeek*, January 31, 2005.

[25] Rupal Parekh, "Behind the Chevrolet Shift: Publicis Didn't Rate a Callback," *Advertising Age*, May 24, 2010

[26] David Beals and Stanley H. Beals, "Selecting an Advertising Agency," Association of National Advertisers, 2003.

[27] David Beals and Stanley H. Beals, "Selecting an Advertising Agency," Association of National Advertisers, 2003.

[28] Jeremy Mullman, "Heineken Wants Face Time with Its Manhattan Agency," *Advertising Age*, June 8, 2009

[29] Aaron Baar, "High Drama Defines Wal-Mart Re-Pitch," *AdWeek*, December 18, 2006.

[30] Natalie Zmuda, "Why Mtn Dew Let Skater Dudes Takes Control of Its Marketing," *Advertising Age*, February 22, 2010.

[31] Lawrence J. Flink, "Guidelines for Advertiser/Agency Contracts," Association of National Advertisers, 2001.

[32] "Please Be Ad-Vised: The Legal Reference Guide for the Advertising Executive," Association of National Advertisers, 1999.

[33] "Software and Software Tools": A Position Paper from the American Association of Advertising Agencies, March 1, 2010.

[34] "Conflict Policy Guidelines": A Position Paper from the American Association of Advertising Agencies, July 7, 2000.

[35] Martin Rees, *Just Six Numbers: The Deep Forces that Shape the Universe* (New York: Basic Books, 1999).

[36] Jean-Marie Dru, "Endless Pressure on Price Traps Agencies, Clients in Death Spiral," *Advertising Age*, January 25, 2010.

[37] Joe Burton, "A Marketer's Guide to Understanding the Economics of Digital Compared to Traditional Advertising and Media Services," American Association of Advertising Agencies, 2009.

[38] Jim Edwards, "Epic Drama Unfolds for Feds in Ogilvy, ONDCP Case," *AdWeek*, November 15, 2004.

[39] Stanley Beals & David Beals, "Agency Compensation: A Guidebook," Association of National Advertisers, 2001.

[40] David Beals, "Guidelines for Effective Advertiser/Agency Compensation Agreements," a Joint Position Paper from the American Association of Advertising Agencies and the Association of National Advertisers, October 2002.

[41] Andrew McMains, "P&G to Agencies: Use These Production Cos," *AdWeek*, July 6, 2009.

[42] Andrew McMains, "Unilever Set to Join Cost-Cutting Push," *AdWeek*, June 8, 2009.

[43] ANA-AAAA Compensation Guide: "Understanding Direct Labor, Overhead and the Components of Cost-Plus and Labor-based Arrangements," ANA-AAAA, May 2006.

[44] Andrew McMains and Noreen O'Leary, "Agencies in Catch-22 Over Client Finances," *Adweek*, May 18, 2009.

[45] Noreen O'Leary, "Your Big Idea, Their Next Great Thing," *AdWeek*, March 12, 2007.

[46] Jeremy Mullman, "Windy City agency sells Hogwash to Pepsi bottler," *Advertising Age*, October 12 2009.

[47] Baker, Ronald J., *2001 Professional's Guide to Value Pricing* (Harcourt Professional Publishing, December 15 2000).

[48] Baker, Ronald J., *Pricing on Purpose* (New York: John Wiley & Sons, 2006).

[49] Jeremy Mullman and Nathalie Zmuda, "Coke Pushes pay-for-performance model," *Advertising Age*, April 27, 2009.

[50] Rupal Parekh, "Agencies Go From Selling to Creating Products," *Advertising Age*, May 12, 2008.

[51] Michael Bush, "Omnicom Adds Procurement to Its Media-Buying Arm," *Advertising Age*, May 14, 2009.

[52] Rupal Parekh, "TBWA's Answer to Client Squeeze: Anoint a Chief Compensation Officer," *Advertising Age*, February 8, 2010.

[53] Gottman, John M., *The Seven Principles for Making Marriage Work*. (Three Rivers Press, 1999).

[54] John M. Gottman, "Making Relationships Work," Harvard Business Review, December 2007.

[55]Adaline Lau, "Coke Sticks with Red Lounge in China," Marketing-Interactive.com, January 13, 2009.

[56] Barbara Lippert, "Augmented Adidas," NEXT, February 15, 2010.

[57] Noreen O'Leary, "Holding Companies Tinkering with Tech," *Adweek*, May 5, 2008.

[58] Eric Pfanner, "Internet Companies and Ad Agencies Go from Old Enemies to New Friends," *The New York Times*, July 4 2009.

[59] Brian Morrissey, "I, Robot: When Creativity Meets the Machines," *AdWeek*, July 9 2007.

[60] Noreen O'Leary, "How Digital Shops Are Gaining Turf," *AdWeek*, July 30, 2007.

[61] Eric Samuelson, "Love Your Shark," Jack360, May 19, 2008.

[62] Dianna Dilworth, "Carat USA Merged with Carat Fusion to Form Carat," DM News, July 28, 2007.

RECOMMENDED READINGS AND RESOURCES

ANA White Paper "Marketing Procurement: Perceptions and Realities of the Function," December 2007.

Joanne Davis, "Optimizing Advertising/Agency Relations," Association of National Advertisers, 2004.

Melvin Prince, Ph.D. and Mark Davies, Ph.D., "Inside Advertiser and Agency Relationships," Association of National Advertisers, 2006.

"The Client Brief: A best Practice Guide to Briefing Communications Agencies," Institute of Communications and Advertising, Association of Canadian Advertisers, Association of Quebec Advertising Agencies, 2006.

"Client Compensation Practices Survey-Results," American Association of Advertising Agencies, June 2006.

David Beals, "Trends in Agency Compensation," Association of National Advertisers, 2007.

"Payment By Results, Advertising Agency Remuneration Best Practices," Institute of Canadian Advertising, 2001.

INDEX

B

ABOUT THE AUTHOR

Photo: Brant Photographers, Bellevue, WA

A seasoned and well-respected marketing professional with expertise in digital, relationship marketing, and agency relations, Bruno Gralpois has had extensive client and agency experience at fast-growing, innovative, and dynamic organizations. As Director of Global Agency Management at Microsoft Bruno developed a company-wide approach to working effectively and efficiently with advertising and marketing communication agencies. Bruno was instrumental in establishing Agency Management as a central global discipline within Microsoft. He received the 2004 Microsoft Marketing Excellence Award from Steve Ballmer, CEO, for his continued leadership in this area. As former General Manager at aQuantive Corporation, aka Avenue A/Razorfish (acquired by Microsoft) and formerly responsible for Worldwide Direct, Interactive & Database Marketing at Visio Corporation (also acquired by Microsoft), he played a critical role in building highly successful organizations and fast growing businesses. He also held positions as Director, Database Marketing and New Media Strategies at HMG/DDB Seattle, leading innovative data mining and interactive assignments for top brand advertisers.

A French native, Bruno grew up in Nantes where he graduated from business school. He held marketing positions in France before moving to the United States. He is a frequent author/speaker domestically as well as internationally. Bruno is an active member of associations and forums where he participates with other companies in influencing and improving client/agency relations and effective marketing communications around the world. He lives near Seattle, with his family.

Visit www.agencymania.com to contact Bruno, share your story, or get more information.